Order on the Edge of Chaos

Order and stability are tenuous and fragile. People have to work to create and sustain a semblance of stability and order in their lives and in their organizations and larger communities. *Order on the Edge of Chaos* compares different ideas about how we coordinate and cooperate. The ideas come from "micro-sociology" and offer new answers to the classic question of Thomas Hobbes: "How is social order possible?"

Edward J. Lawler is the Martin P. Catherwood Professor of Industrial and Labor Relations and Professor of Sociology at Cornell University. In 2001, he received the Cooley-Mead Award for career achievement from the Social Psychology Section of the American Sociological Association, and in 2003 his paper "An Affect Theory of Social Exchange" won the 2002 Theory Prize from the Theory Section. His recent book (coauthored with Shane Thye and Jeongkoo Yoon), *Social Commitments in a Depersonalized World* (2009), won the 2010 James Coleman Best Book Award from the Rationality and Society Section of the American Sociological Association.

Shane R. Thye is a professor of sociology at the University of South Carolina. He is the series coeditor (with Edward J. Lawler) of *Advances in Group Processes*. He recently completed *Social Commitments in a Depersonalized World* (2009) with Lawler and Yoon. He works primarily in the areas of group dynamics and experimental sociology. His work has appeared in outlets such as the *American Sociological Review*, the *American Journal of Sociology*, and *Social Forces*.

Jeongkoo Yoon is Professor in the School of Management at Ewha Womans University, South Korea. His research applies power and exchange theories to solve issues of contemporary organizations such as empowerment, leadership, and change. He coauthored the book *Social Commitments in a Depersonalized World* (2009) with Lawler and Thye. He also published two award-winning best-selling books in Korea, *Change Management for 100 Year Sustainable Companies* (2010) and *What Is Authenticity?* (2012). He served as editor of the *Korean Journal of Management* and chair of the Korean Association of Leadership. He is currently on the editorial board of the *British Journal of Management*.

Order on the Edge of Chaos

Social Psychology and the Problem of Social Order

Edited by

EDWARD J. LAWLER
Cornell University

SHANE R. THYE
University of South Carolina

JEONGKOO YOON
Ewha Womans University

CAMBRIDGE
UNIVERSITY PRESS

32 Avenue of the Americas, New York, NY 10013-2473, USA

Cambridge University Press is part of the University of Cambridge.

It furthers the University's mission by disseminating knowledge in the pursuit of education, learning, and research at the highest international levels of excellence.

www.cambridge.org
Information on this title: www.cambridge.org/9781107433977

© Cambridge University Press 2015

First published 2015

Printed in the United States of America by Sheridan Books, Inc.

A catalog record for this publication is available from the British Library.

Library of Congress Cataloging in Publication Data
Order on the edge of chaos : social psychology and the problem of social order / Edward J. Lawler, Shane R. Thye, Jeongkoo Yoon.
    pages   cm
Includes bibliographical references and index.
ISBN 978-1-107-07675-4 (hardback) – ISBN 978-1-107-43397-7 (pbk.)
1. Social structure. 2. Social interaction. 3. Social psychology. I. Lawler, Edward J., editor. II. Thye, Shane R., editor. III. Yoon, Jeongkoo, editor.
HM706.O73   2015
302–dc23   2015022166

ISBN 978-1-107-07675-4 Hardback
ISBN 978-1-107-43397-7 Paperback

Contents

List of Contributors

Matthew A. Andersson
Department of Sociology
Yale University
USA

Peter J. Burke
Department of Sociology
University of California, Riverside
USA

Karen S. Cook
Department of Sociology
Stanford University
USA

Daniel J. DellaPosta
Department of Sociology
Cornell University
USA

Hartmut Esser
Faculty for Social Sciences
Mannheim Center for European Social Research
University of Mannheim
Germany

Gary Alan Fine
Department of Sociology
Northwestern University
USA

David R. Heise
Department of Sociology
Indiana University
USA

Steven Hitlin
Department of Sociology
University of Iowa
USA

Theodore D. Kemper
Department of Sociology
St. John's University
USA

Clemens Kroneberg
Institute of Sociology and Social Psychology
University of Cologne
Germany

Edward J. Lawler
School of Industrial and Labor Relations
Department of Sociology
Cornell University
USA

Siegwart Lindenberg
Department of Sociology
University of Groningen
The Netherlands

Neil J. MacKinnon
Department of Sociology and Anthropology
University of Guelph
Canada

Michael W. Macy
Department of Sociology and Information Science
Cornell University
USA

Peter V. Marsden
Department of Sociology
Harvard University
USA

Anne Warfield Rawls
Department of Sociology
Bentley University
USA

Cecilia L. Ridgeway
Department of Sociology
Stanford University
USA

Wolfgang Scholl
Department of Sociology
Humboldt University
Germany

Jan E. Stets
Institute for Psychology
University of California, Riverside
USA

Shane R. Thye
Department of Sociology
University of South Carolina
USA

Jonathan H. Turner
Department of Sociology
University of California, Riverside
USA

Hannah Wohl
Department of Sociology
Northwestern University
USA

Jeongkoo Yoon
School of Business Administration
Ewha Womans University
South Korea

Morris Zelditch
Department of Sociology
Stanford University
USA

Preface

The classic question posed by the philosopher Thomas Hobbes, "How is social order possible?," is an enduring issue for the social sciences. Throughout the history of the social sciences, however, the prominence and salience of the issue waxes and wanes. A plausible hypothesis is that in times of great transformational change (e.g., the Industrial Revolution), the problem of social order tends to become front-and-center, whereas in times of great stability, it recedes into the background as social change takes precedence and becomes the dominant concern. This is a broad-sweeping and arguable hypothesis, but there are many reasons for viewing the early period of the twenty-first century as the dawn of another period of great transformational change, manifest, for example, in employment contracts, the technologies for communication, and global political and economic processes that blur nation-state boundaries. In this context, we address the larger problem of social order in a unique way, namely, by examining the micro-level foundations of social order.

By "micro-level" we mean social interactions and group processes within which people construct meanings, pursue individual goals, engage in group tasks, and generate collective goods available to them and perhaps a larger population. The social interactions are framed and shaped by macro structures and cultures, but it is in social interactions that larger structures and cultures are instantiated and essentially "come to life." The central premise of this volume is that macro-level social orders, in the form of organizations, institutions, nations, and societies, are necessarily grounded in the interactions of people within those larger orders. Macro orders exist and endure only if individuals in interaction with others enact, produce, or reproduce them. Thus, it is important to delve more deeply into how micro processes generate, sustain, or reproduce patterns of behavioral regularity that constitute social order.

This volume brings together in one place the major theories in sociology that concern micro-level social interactions. The intellectual traditions represented here are sometimes termed "micro-sociology" and sometimes termed "sociological social psychology." Whatever the value of these particular labels, the important point is that micro-sociologists have for many years developed theories of social interaction with implicit or explicit implications for social order. For this volume, we invited leading scholars from diverse theoretical traditions within sociological social psychology to develop the implications of their theories for the problem of social order, using Hobbesian framing as a foil. It is worth noting that eight of the authors in this volume have received the prestigious Cooley-Mead Award for career contributions from the Section on Social Psychology of the American Sociological Association.

We aim to produce an edited volume with greater coherence and unity than is typical of such volumes. The Hobbesian framing was one device for achieving this goal. We are especially indebted to the authors for taking this framing as a guide as they undertook to develop, recast, or reconceive their theories in these terms. They also worked to develop chapters that speak to the broader social science audience of graduate students and scholars. We greatly appreciate their efforts here and in other respects, such as in meeting deadlines and conforming to style guidelines. This was a great group of authors to work with. We also express our deep appreciation to Peter Marsden for providing us with a capstone chapter for the volume.

Finally, we would to thank Kathy Roberts for administrative assistance as we prepared the volume for submission, Robert Dreesen, Senior Editor at Cambridge University Press, for his guidance and support, and Brianda Reyes also of Cambridge University Press for her assistance with the production process. The National Science Foundation (NSF) has supported our related theory and research over many years; that NSF support enabled us to think about broader implications of our research on social exchange for social order at the micro and macro levels.

1

Social Psychology of Social Order

An Introduction

Edward J. Lawler, Shane R. Thye, and Jeongkoo Yoon

A person dropped into downtown Manhattan in the middle of the day for the first time would face an unpredictable, disorderly world: fast-walking people dodging around one another on sidewalks; pedestrians and cars contesting for street access at every corner; bicyclists running red lights; trucks double parking and blocking access to and from sidewalks; rampant herdlike jaywalking; horns honking; cabbies shouting; sirens of fire engines and ambulances blaring; and ever-present construction projects posing obstructions to most everybody. Yet, it would not take long for our visitor to sense a semblance of social order – in the form of repeated, predictable patterns of behavior. This patterned local world exists "on the edge of chaos," with order and predictability eroding and re-emerging moment-to-moment and situation-to-situation (see also Lawler 2013). Very soon this immediate, local social order would reveal both resilience and dynamism. This is a fundamental insight of sociological theories of social psychology on the emergence and maintenance of social orders (e.g., Rawls 2004; Turner 2007; Burke and Stets 2009; Lawler, Thye, and Yoon 2009; Fine 2012; Ridgeway 2011). Sociological social psychologists (micro-sociologists) construe patterns of regularity as social constructions that people create and sustain under conditions of uncertainty, instability, or tension.

The regularity, repetition, and predictability of everyday social lives are constitutive of social orders, at both macro and micro levels (see Collins 1981). However, without the "edge of chaos" or ever looming prospect of disorder, social order as such would draw little interest or have little meaning. Repetitive, predictable patterns of behavior are meaningful to people because of the contrast with disorder, real or hypothetical. Repetitive patterns that constitute order enable people with vastly different social backgrounds, conflicting cultural ideas or material interests, or diverse social affiliations to navigate close proximities, work around or take advantage of interdependencies, and produce joint goods of mutual value. To micro-sociologists, micro (local,

1

immediate) orders are taken for granted; they are subtle, obdurate, pervasive, and often invisible features of social life (Maynard 2003; Fine 2012). People do not consciously observe or ponder social order unless it is somehow disrupted or threatened. By contrast, disorder and conflict are generally salient, discomfiting, and often stressful or threatening. There is a fundamental asymmetry in the ontological status of social order and social disorder.

Modern treatments of the problem of social order are traced to Hobbes (1651). Hobbes starts from the premise that humans are prone to malfeasance, aggression, and force. People pursue passions (desires, ends) through rational means and do so without self-imposed limits, seeking to overwhelm, dominate, or destroy each other in pursuit of their own desires. Elements of human nature cannot be relied on to protect individuals from one another's avarice and power-seeking, because the social world is composed of individuals single-mindedly pursuing narrow, immediate individual ends in a context of interdependence and scarcity. The result for Hobbes is an inherent tendency to descend into "a war of all against all."

The Hobbesian solution to this fundamental problem of social order is straightforward: Individuals create and sustain order by consenting to some sort of social contract under the direction of a sovereign authority (i.e., the state). They accept limits on their freedom and discretion in exchange for security and safety. Thus, the human species is essentially saved "from itself" by human capacities for reason. For Hobbes the locus of the problem of order is the micro level, because this is where the "war of all against all" takes place, but the solution is at the macro level (e.g., a sovereign, government). A binding social contract regulates and enforces social order at both micro and macro levels but does so "from above." The implied consensual norms or rules are based on rational consent.[1] The emergence and pervasiveness of social order at the micro-sociological level, however, raises serious questions about the theoretical scope and adequacy of Hobbesian framing for the problem of order.

In modern parlance, the Hobbesian problem of order can be conceived in social-dilemma terms, that is, as an inherent tension between individually-rational action and collective or group interests (security). Individuals are motivated to rationally pursue their own individual desires or interests even when such actions generate collectively irrational results, and this underlies the hypothetical descent into the "war of all against all." In contrast, a convergent though generally implicit claim of disparate sociological theories of social psychology is that people have vast, almost unlimited, capacities to impose or find order in their social worlds and to resourcefully manage or resolve uncertainties and tensions. People take account of each other, not simply because they

[1] Parsons (1937) critiques the utilitarian basis for social order presumed by Hobbes, arguing that the ends (desires) and rationality (choice of means) are normative elements and embedded in a larger shared normative order. For Parsons, the problems of social order are to be found in the larger normative order (conflicting norms, anomie) as are the solutions.

have to, given structural interdependencies, but because they want to or are wired to do so (Condon and Sander 1974). Increasingly, theory and evidence affirms that people are naturally responsive to each other, empathic, and group or community oriented (e.g., Waal 2008; Goetz, Keltner, and Simon-Thomas 2010; Turner, this volume). One implication is that descent toward a Hobbesian "war of all against all" would likely be short-lived, because people reconstitute regularity and predictability rather quickly, especially when they are "on the edge of chaos." Even in the context of large scale disorder or conflict at the macro level, one often observes stable social orders emerging and being sustained at local, micro levels.

Contemporary analyses of the problem of social order are found especially in rational-choice theories (e.g., Hechter 1987; Coleman 1990; Fehr and Gintis 2007). The social dilemma is generally a defining element, and this clearly resonates with the classic Hobbesian statement of the problem, though the assumed malevolence of the human species is left behind in favor of individual self-interest (profit maximization). The crux of the problem is recast as self-interested or under-socialized individual actors, as reflected in free-riding, ineffective norm enforcement, or failures of socialization (i.e., internalization of norms). Virtually all variations on this social dilemma theme presume that people, if left to their own devices, will follow their own individual, self-interested, hedonistic, and often ill-informed ways (see Hechter 1987; Coleman 1990). That this framing has limits is well-known and recognized. People cooperate more than expected in prisoners dilemma settings; share more than expected in ultimatum games; process information in imperfect or biased ways, and often act pro-socially despite personal costs (Piliavin and Callero 1991; Batson 1991). The cumulative evidence on the limitations of the "self-interest" assumption suggests a dualistic concept of the human species, placing capacities for self-interest and for altruism on an equal plane. As a result, the key question becomes: Under what structural, cultural, or situational conditions are these dual capacities activated, in what proportions, and with what driving mechanisms? This is the theoretical juncture at which sociological approaches to social psychology (microsociology) have something important to say about the Hobbesian problem.

Sociological theories of social interaction and group processes contain a wide array of micro mechanisms of social order, that is, micro structures or processes that generate, sustain, or change social orders. This volume explicates and illuminates mechanisms for social order found in contemporary sociological theories. Some theories from sociological social psychology have not explicitly addressed the problem of order, whereas others have adopted social order as a central or overarching theme. This volume includes leading scholars from different theoretical traditions who develop and make more explicit the implications of their theories for the problem of social order, use Hobbesian framing as a backdrop. A central message is that micro structures and processes mediate macro level phenomena, as articulated in the now famous

"Coleman boat" (Coleman 1990), but the nature of these micro processes are more varied, more interactional, and more relational than the individual rationality mechanism assumed by Coleman. This volume is designed to explicate, amplify, and systematize "bottom-up" processes of social order, as well as reveal how "top down" processes are contingent on micro level structures and processes. Understanding the micro level dimensions of the problem of order in these terms seems especially vital in a highly complex and changing social world on the edge of chaos.

MICRO THEORIES OF SOCIAL ORDER

Microsociology (sociological social psychology) is marked by many well-developed theoretical traditions that address a wide variety of micro level processes. This volume represents a wide range of theories or theoretical traditions in sociology selected on the basis of several criteria: (*i*) how well-developed is the theory; (*ii*) the strength of its empirical foundation, and (*iii*) the creativity of its implicit or explicit message about the role of micro-level social processes in the construction and maintenance of social order. Specifically, we chose ten theories from sociology to address the following topics: evolutionary foundations, choice or rational choice, identity, social exchange, status and power, expectation states, trust, emotion, meaning, morality, and legitimacy. We will characterize in broad terms the implicit or explicit approach to social order for each theoretical tradition, and then explain briefly how one or more chapters elaborate the micro foundations of order for that theoretical tradition.

Evolutionary Theory

Evolutionary theories ask how humans developed the capacity to form groups and communities larger and more encompassing than local, kin-based groupings. There are cognitive and emotional interpretations of how this happened. The former is based on the "large brain" thesis that as homo sapiens evolved, their brains developed a larger and larger neo-cortex in response to selection pressures. A larger neo-cortex expanded cognitive capacities and enabled people to store more in memory, develop more intricate categorizations or abstract thoughts, and imagine further into the future and also into the past. As cognitive capacities grew, the ability to envision or conceive of collaborations and communities beyond kin groups also grew. An alternative explanation emphasizes the earlier growth of the brain's limbic system and associated human capacities to convey, interpret, and read a range of emotional states, states that signaled and allowed cooperative nonkin relations to form.

Two chapters examine the evolutionary origins of social order. The chapter by Jonathan Turner on "The Evolutionary Biology and Sociology of Social Order" makes a case for the role of the fine-grained emotional capacities in human evolution. The central argument is that emotions are the primary foundation for social order, and the human capacity to form larger, nonkin groupings can be traced to evolved capacities of the human limbic system. Natural selection produced an elaborate emotional repertoire that made it possible for humans to read others emotions and express emotions in detailed, fine grained forms. These evolved emotional capacities allowed them to develop forms of cooperation and affiliation in local but also larger communities especially as their cognitive capacities also grew.

The Lindenberg chapter on "Social Rationality and Weak Solidarity" argues it is the co-evolution of dual human capacities – for rationality and sociality – that made larger groups and communities possible. These capacities are rooted in humans "advanced brain power" in particular the cognitive and motivational conditions for the joint production of social order. Growing rationality was manifest in capacities for complex mental representations, for pursuit of both egoistic and collective goals and for self-regulation. Growing sociality was manifest in evolved capacities for empathy that are necessary for the collaborative production of joint goods. Turner and Lindenberg have somewhat different emphases but they each explain how the evolutionary foundations for mental and social capacities enabled humans to form ties beyond and larger than kin groupings. They also imply inherent limits on individual egoism or self-interest.

Choice Theory

"Choice theory" is not a standard label in sociology but it is useful to capture theorizing that takes human choice as central, yet departs from rational choice assumptions. This class of theories tends to assume that behavior is "choice," that options in choice sets are constrained by institutions, and that subjective inferences about consequences (gains, rewards) shape choice behavior. The individual-collective rationality problem frames choice theories. The problem of order therefore stems from the fact that peoples' choices affect each other due to structural interdependencies, and capacities to collaborate are limited by incentives for free riding. The solution typically is found in norms, informal or formal, and enforcement, also informal or formal.

This volume contains three chapters that analyze how and when choice processes generate social order. Lindenberg argues that "goal frames" are the key to understanding social order. Three goal frames shape perceptions and guide or orient behavior: (*i*) hedonic goals, oriented to fundamental human needs, (*ii*) normative goals, oriented to collective goods, and (*iii*) gain goals, oriented to individual resources. Situations activate goal frames; goal frames specify what goals are most important in the situation; and rational action occurs in the context of how these goal frames are weighted. Social order is problematic in part because, in evolutionary terms, hedonic goal frames are advantaged. The prominence and combination of normative and gain goal frames are most critical to social order. However, normative goal frames at the micro level generate high levels of ingroup solidarity and outgroup hostility, which tends to fragment the social orders. At the macro level, a dominant gain frame moderated by a normative frame promotes cross-cutting, expansive ties that hold together large, complex social orders. Lindenberg characterizes this as "weak solidarity;" he argues it is the strongest foundation for social order at the macro level. Overall, normative goal frames are crucial to social order, but they have different consequences at the micro and macro level.

The Esser and Kroneberg chapter presents a "frame selection" model for understanding the rational and nonrational foundations for social order. The model integrates elements of institutional and rational choice analyses of the norms and norm enforcement. The theory argues that dual process theory from cognitive psychology specifies different cognitive routes through which norms operate as taken for granted, unconditional imperatives or as conditional, deliberative, and incentive based. Situations activate automatic or deliberative information processing and this determines whether adherence or compliance to norms is spontaneous and taken for granted or deliberative and based on incentives attached to norm adherence. The general conclusion is that the strength of the cognitive frame is crucial. A strong frame (meaning the strongest weight is given to the automatic parts of cognitive or information processing) generates social order regardless of the incentives for norm adherence; whereas a weak frame (meaning the strongest weight is given to the deliberative parts of cognitive processing) generates variable degrees of social order contingent on the strength of the incentives for adhering to norms. Thus, this chapter suggests the role of norms in social order is conditional on situation-based cognitive framing.

DellaPosta and Macy approach the problem of order from a slightly different "choice" perspective. They look not at how deliberate and individual choices or frames impact preferences (akin to the Hobbesian problem of order) but, instead, on how strategically aligned preferences can motivate choices and how these choices, in turn, impact social order. They and others note that polarization – the tendency for preferences to become more extreme and aligned – is inherently threatening to social order. The typical response is to rely on "common ground" models of consensus or "split ground" models of pluralism. Yet, both solutions can be problematic. DellaPosta and Macy show how pluralistic opinion distributions, which are widely regarded to be stable and conducive to tolerance and order, can destabilize through homophily and social influence processes. Whereas consensus models focus on conformity around a common issue pluralists models allow for individuals to agree on one issue (e.g., abortion), while they disagree strongly on another (e.g., the death penalty), yielding a stable equilibrium. DellaPosta and Macy show that through homophily and social influence processes both cultural and political preferences can become aligned, and over time, these destabilize social order. This chapter traces the consequences of fundamental social processes for pluralism as a solution (or lack thereof) to the problem of social order.

Social Exchange Theory

In social exchange theory, social interactions entail an exchange of rewards or gains. The theory assumes self-interested actors who seek exchange partners in networks of three or more actors; in this context, relations form and are sustained to the degree that each individual actor receives valued rewards that are not readily available in alternative exchange relations. By implication, social orders are inherently instrumental but also relational because in *social* exchange, structures tend to generate repeated exchanges among the same actors (Emerson 1981). Understanding the relational dimension is key to the problem of order, and two interrelated questions are central: How do network structures promote repeated exchanges? And, in turn, how does repeated exchange generate ongoing relational ties? Two micro mechanisms are known to promote relational ties in repeated exchange: uncertainty reduction/risk (Kollock 1994; Molm 2003) and positive emotions (Thye, Yoon, and Lawler 2002; Lawler, Thye, and Yoon 2008). Repeated exchanges can reduce uncertainties but also arouse positive (or negative) emotions or feelings.

The chapter by Lawler, Thye, and Yoon explicates and critiques ideas about social order found in social exchange theory. They argue that the purely instrumental conception of actors and relational ties is an important weakness of social exchange theorizing, because with such a conception it is not possible to account for relational ties that become noninstrumental objects or take on intrinsic value. Their argument is that emotions are unintended byproducts of social exchange processes that lead actors to feel good (or bad) about their exchanges. If these feelings are attributed to local, micro or larger, macro social units (from relations and groups to organizations and communities), actors develop affective, noninstrumental ties to those social units and are more willing to make sacrifices for the collective welfare. The chapter elaborates structural and cognitive conditions under which affective social-unit ties are likely to develop and when they are directed at local, immediate social units (relations, groups) and/or larger more removed social units (organizations, communities).

Trust Theory

Trust theory is based on the idea that social interactions often entail substantial uncertainty and risk. Trust encourages people to cooperate and generate collective goods that involve risk of exploitation or malfeasance; it also promotes efforts to reach beyond existing affiliations and transact with new partners or form new social ties (Yamagishi and Yamagishi 1994; Fukuyama 1995). Trust is essentially an "expectation of cooperation by others" and one finds three forms of trust in the literature: (*i*) generalized beliefs about the trustworthiness of people in the abstract (Yamagishi and Yamagishi 1994), (*ii*) expectations based on knowledge of particular others, and (*iii*) relations of trust based on mutual perceptions by each actor that the other will take their interests into account, that is, trust as "encapsulated interests" (Cook, Hardin, and Levi 2005). Each form of trust is a potential source of social order because it strengthens the regularity and predictability of cooperation in transactional ties, making collective goods possible if not probable. Sweeping claims have been made about trust being the fundamental "glue" that holds together large, complex societies, but Cook in this chapter questions these claims.

The chapter by Karen Cook argues that trust generates or sustains social order at the micro level in ongoing interactions or relations, but it is not sufficient to generate order beyond the micro level (see also Cook, Hardin, and Levi 2005). The reason is that relational trust requires too much information about the other, more than is likely to be available in macro contexts characterized by "arms-length" social ties. Beyond the micro or relational level, alternative institutional or organization mechanisms are necessary to promote trusting behavior. Examples are the spread of reputations for malfeasance, informal sanctions, professional certifications, alignment of individual and organizational interests, and the like. Such institutional or organizational practices work only if they serve as "assurance mechanisms" that essentially substitute for trust as a mechanism for resolving uncertainties associated with cooperative social ties.

Identity Theory

Identity theory posits that social interactions produce or reproduce stable orders through consensual self-other definitions or identity meanings. People enact and seek to verify identities in social interaction. If self-other identity meanings do not converge, the result is some sort of disorder, and the behaviors enacting identities are adjusted to bring in line an actor's own definition of who they are in the situation with how others define them. Discrepancies are uncomfortable and stressful and people are motivated to resolve them. In sociology identity theory tends to focus on structural foundations. Social structures (interconnected roles or positions) frame or set broad standards for how to enact identities, as is clearly the case with identities attached to social or organizational roles (e.g., parent, neighbor, manager, coworker). The key point is that stable and predictable interactions with others are contingent on identities being sufficiently shared or consensual, as people seek to affirm or verify situational self-definitions.

Two chapters in the volume represent variants on this theme: identity control theory (Burke and Stets 2009) and affect control theory (Heise 2007). The Burke and Stets chapter, "Identity Verification and the Social Order," highlights the role of self-verification as a central motivational force in the construction and reconstruction of social orders. Social structures consist of roles that interweave identities, and resources that enable the enactment of behavior consistent with identity standards (expectations). Identity standards have both a local, micro dimension and a larger macro organizational or cultural dimension. Burke and Stets posit that when people verify their identities, they feel good and form stronger social bonds with each other or with larger units; where they fail to verify identities, the reverse occurs. The capacity to verify identities in organizations is contingent on the availability of resources. In sum, identity verification processes serve as the critical link between micro and macro orders. Cultural or organizational roles (macro structures) contain generic identity standards to which actors compare identity enactments; and these identity standards are fleshed out in more concrete terms at the micro level where actors also look to particular others to affirm or verify their situational (role-based) identities.

The chapter by Heise, Mackinnon, and Scholl emphasizes cultural sentiments attached to institutional roles and identities. The chapter identifies distinct ways that macro level cognitive and affective meanings together shape consensual role identities that underlie order and stability. Cognitive meanings incorporate "practical knowledge" about the enactment of identities, and affective meanings incorporate "cultural sentiments." At the macro level, cultural sentiments are intertwined with semantic systems that name or label identities. People strive for consistency between sentiments at the institutional level and behavior enactments at the micro, interactional level; inconsistencies ("deflections") cause adjustments. Overall, the paper argues and offers empirical data in support of the idea that identity meanings are consensual, because the semantics of those identity meanings (macro) are manifest in how individuals define their identities in local social interactions. In this sense, the institutional level filters downward to individual minds à la Durkheim.

Expectation States Theory

Expectation states theory addresses how status structures generate and sustain social orders. Status inequalities in the larger organizational units are activated at the micro level when two or more people interact around a collective task and once established, these status structures operate as self-fulfilling prophecies. This happens because people infer performance expectations and attribute competencies to others based on status characteristics, such as race, gender, class, education, and skills (Berger, Fisek, Norman, and Zelditch 1977). Those higher on a status dimension are given more opportunities to contribute in a collective task and their contributions are evaluated more highly. Once a status order develops in an ongoing group, the same status structure tends to reemerge time and again in concrete task interactions addressed by the same actors. For such reasons social order, based on differentially evaluated status characteristics, are highly resilient.

Cecilia Ridgeway develops the idea that the performance expectations underlying status orders are often grounded in "widely shared cultural beliefs" about the competencies or social worth of those in certain social categories (gender, age, education, etc.) (Ridgeway 1991, 2011) This idea creates an explicit connection between the macro cultural beliefs and the emergence of resilient status structures at the micro level. When local status orders comport with status ordering presumed in cultural beliefs, it creates a tighter connection between the cultural and the interactional level; among other things, this establishes the conditions for status orders to be generalized and interwoven across multiple institutional or organizational domains, from households to communities to jobs, workplaces, and organizations. The chapter by Ridgeway develops the argument that among status characteristics, gender is a wide-ranging and pervasive foundation for stable, convergent structures of inequality across institutional domains because gender beliefs operate as a "primary cultural framework" for organizing social interactions. The "gender frame" is highly adaptable; thus, it tends to survive social change by being "rewritten" into new social arrangements as they emerge, even though the changes may represent opportunities to leave behind gender status beliefs.

Emotions Theory

There are multiple theories of emotion in psychology and sociology. Sociologists tend to emphasize the structural (Kemper 1978) and interactional (Collins 2004; Turner 2007; Lawler, Thye, and Yoon 2009) foundations of emotions. One important idea is that people read, feel, and sometimes express emotions in social interaction, but the nature and expression of emotions are contingent on power and status positions. Positive emotions generally promote strong social ties and social order, negative emotions such as anger and shame undermine social order, but some forms such as guilt generate restorative behaviors that repair a damaged social order. Status and power positions shape the types of emotion experienced and the collective effects on social order.

The chapter by Theodore Kemper approaches the order inducing effects of emotion via the behavioral dimensions of power and status. His status-power and reference group theory suggests that individuals continually assess their own status and power standing in relation to others and to reference groups. The theory locates three forms of social order: order based on mutual conferral or status, order based on technical activity in which the parties abide by procedures for resolving task-related differences, and finally, order founded solely on power relations. Kemper sees emotions flowing from the interactions framed by these structural dimensions. The key insight is that emotional reactions stem from the power or status outcomes of social interaction. Kemper catalogues both the positive and negative emotional experiences that result from shifts in one's relative power or status. Importantly, the chapter traces mechanisms through which order may be restored when emotions create disorder. This chapter links well-understood dimensions of social structure (i.e., power and status) to emotional consequences and these consequences to the emergence, maintenance, or destruction of social order.

There are several other papers, already discussed, where emotions are important to social order. Jonathan Turner argues that positive emotions have their source at the micro level, specifically in social interactions that affirm or fulfill expectations; positive emotions spread upward to meso and macro entities especially if micro, meso, and macro levels are socially embedded or tightly interconnected. The most basic reason for this is that tighter connections across levels promote a "clarity of expectations" at the micro level, which in turn increases the probability of emotionally arousing or satisfying social interactions. In a related vein, Lawler, Thye, and Yoon suggest the emotions generated at the micro level can have effects on macro social order by creating affective ties to larger social units. This is especially likely when people repeatedly engage in joint tasks that foster a sense of shared responsibility, because under such conditions people attribute their emotions to social units at the micro and/or macro level. For Burke and Stets, the impact of identity verification on social order is due primarily to the positive emotions generated when identities are verified. Heise, Mackinnon and Scholl shift attention to macro-level cultural sentiments and meanings that spread downward to identity meanings of individuals. All in all, there is a growing consensus in sociological social psychology that emotions and feelings are an important dimension of social order.

Meaning Theory

Symbolic Interaction and ethnomethodology are distinct theoretical traditions with a common focus on the role of meanings. Symbolic interaction emphasizes the role-taking dynamics of social interaction – namely, that in social interactions people continually take the role (perspective) of the other, anticipate the other's interpretations and behavior, and act accordingly. Out of this process shared meanings emerge and make social coordination successful. Shared meanings mediate the link of social interactions at the micro level and cultures at a macro level (see Fine 2012). Ethnomethodology (and conversational analysis) analyzes meaning at an even more fundamental, subterranean level by revealing taken-for-granted (background) expectations that make it possible for people to take account of each other and generate an interaction order. What is necessary for order is not that meanings are shared but that people coordinate their meanings enough to "co-produce" joint or collaborate action. In symbolic interaction and ethnomethodology, the "edge of chaos" is always close at hand, although for somewhat different reasons.

Two chapters examine coordination and order, one each from these theoretical traditions. Rawls analyzes fundamentals of an "Interaction Order" framework by drawing on key elements from the theorizing of Garfinkel, Goffman, and Sachs. For Garfinkel, meaning and stability is based on expectations (rules) embedded in practices by which people "pull off" an instance of coordinated interaction; Goffman zeroes in on subtle processes and strategies in which actors produce or reproduce situational selves or meanings about self; Sachs suggests that coordinated interaction occurs in part because standard sequences are assumed, taken for granted, and enacted in interaction without thought. None of these processes require shared meanings but they do imply that people take account of each other's meanings as they enact an interaction order. For ethnomethodology orders emerge and are sustained by "bottom-up" processes, not "top-down" processes, which flips the Hobbesian problem on its head.

Wohl and Fine examine how people take the role of each other as they "act together" or successfully coordinate their actions. Social coordination requires, moment to moment, monitoring of self and other, mutual adaptations of verbal and nonverbal behaviors, and the capacity to improvise along the way. Three everyday examples of dyadic coordination serve as exemplars: walking together; loving together; and playing music together. These are distinct in many ways but Wohl and Fine reveal common processes that underlie each and that can be extended to other contexts of social coordination. The role of "collective intentionality" is a key point here, an idea from recent philosophical theory of groups.

Morality Theory

Theories of morality or moral behavior represent an important, emerging stream of theory and research (see Hitlin and Vaisey 2010, 2013). Few sociologists would question the notion that morality or moral norms are an important component of social order. The moral dimension of human societies was integral to classic sociological theories about the problem of social order (e.g., Durkheim, Weber) and as well as in Parsons (1937) critique of Hobbes. The normative order in Parsons, legitimacy in Weber, and collective conscience in Durkheim are all moral constructs. These notions imply that in any society some behaviors, interactions, and structures are conceived to be "right, proper, just," and therefore "good" in their own right. The "moral" in this sense extends beyond what is often termed the normative and institutional. Nevertheless, contemporary sociologists have generally left the moral component behind while focusing on the more tractable phenomena of rules and norms.[2] There are recent efforts to bring morality or moral behavior again to the forefront by reconceptualizing the moral dimension and laying a foundation for systematic theory and research. These efforts are in a germinating stage. This volume includes a paper from one of the leaders of emerging efforts toward a sociology of morality (see Hitlin and Vaisey 2013).

[2] Theory and research on justice and equity could be construed as an exception.

Hitlin and Anderson assert that dignity as a moral motivation should be at the cutting edge of micro-sociological theory and research on social order. Although it is sometimes viewed as a personal and highly private evaluation, they argue that dignity incorporates cultural evaluations and thus reflects larger macro-sociological structures. It taps the broader dimension of self-regulatory morality and, in this sense, bears on the problem of order. Dignity is defined as the achievement of social personhood. A key contribution of the paper is to recognize that dignity may exist in various states, including some that may seem paradoxical. Dignity can be ascribed or achieved, short-term and situational versus emergent over the life-course, or reflexive from a first-person perceptive or from the standpoint of a generalized other. Using this typology, the authors offer concrete strategies for conceptualizing and empirically measuring dignity alongside related social psychological constructs such as autonomy, self-esteem, and so forth. Whereas prior discussions of dignity are often mired in conceptual or philosophical issues, Hitlin and Anderson's approach offers a multifaceted conception of dignity with clear indications of how each may be empirically measured. The result is a more grounded understanding of dignity, which promises to inform and promote theoretical development pertaining to the self-regulatory facet of social order.

Legitimacy Theory

Legitimacy implies interconnected moral and normative justifications for an existing structure, social practice, or line of behavior. Legitimacy is a key process through which people come to enact existing social structures and practices, to consider them proper or right, and to support sanctioning systems that punish those who do not act in accord with the bases of legitimacy. Groups establish a micro order by cultivating a belief in the legitimacy of who they are, what they do, and why they exist. Legitimacy, in itself, does not create any particular ties, groups, or systems of social control but it shapes the micro processes through which the stability of an order emerges from them. Legitimacy is also a process through which substantial inequalities at the macro level can become acceptable or desirable to actors as they enact them at the micro level (Zelditch and Walker 1984).

The chapter by Zelditch examines the conditions and causes of legitimacy, its role in the mobilization of the necessary resources, and its effect on compliance. The legitimacy of a micro order is strengthened when the group shows a better fit with a pre-given framework of norms, values, beliefs, and procedures; when the group is conceived as attaining some valued end; when the group claims the resources of its members based on the principle of fairness; and when the interests of agents acting for the group are aligned with those of the group or its members. As the size of a group increases, the capacity of a group to maintain orders increasingly depends on its capacity to mobilize resources from members, and the legitimacy of the group plays the catalytic role in such resource mobilization. Zelditch asserts that members' acceptance of the legitimacy of its group's claims on their resources is determined by the additive effects of propriety (i.e., an individual belief) and validity (i.e., a collective belief) and how these effects of validity and propriety interact. Finally, the expected compliance of other members and their expected support of sanctions for noncompliance is crucial to overcome free riding and greed. The stability of a micro order therefore is contingent on the double-edged sword of coercion and consent.

CONCLUSION

Sociological traditions in social psychology offer a rich tapestry of theory and research on micro-level processes that produce or reproduce social order at micro and macro levels. The focus is on *how* and *when* social orders emerge and are sustained rather than *why*. Among the theories of this volume, several explain how and when *micro level processes activate macro level phenomena* and, as a result, produce local patterns or structures that reflect or translate macro cultural or structural phenomena. Examples are cultural status or power beliefs (Ridgeway, Kemper), identity standards (Burke and Stets), validity beliefs and legitimacy (Zelditch), and automatic versus deliberative cognitive processing of situational stimuli (Esser and Kroneberg). Micro-level situational activations are critical in each of these theories. Other theories specify *"top-down" institutional structures or patterns that are manifest in micro processes,* for example, echoing cultural sentiments (Heise, MacKinnon, and Scholl), or entailing organizational "assurance mechanisms" that promote resilient social orders in the absence of trust (Cook). Complementing these are theories that elaborate *"bottom-up" processes through which social interactions generate closely or loosely connected micro and macro orders.* Examples are normative goal frames that underlie "weak solidarity" (Lindenberg), social-unit attributions of emotions that generate noninstrumental group ties (Lawler, Thye, and Yoon), as well as the propensity of positive emotions to spread beyond micro to meso or macro levels (Turner). Finally, three papers *dig deeper at the micro level by specifying moment-to-moment behaviors* that underlie or enable social coordination or interaction orders (Wohl and Fine, Rawls), revealing the "moving sands" on which social orders rest, or theorizing the importance of "dignity" as a moral motivation in micro orders (Hitlin and Anderson). Overall, the theories in this volume capture different facets or dimensions of social order and suggest different theoretical ways to theorize and research interconnected orders at micro and macro levels.

It is important to highlight two orienting themes of this volume. The first theme is that the problem of social order is not inextricably based on or bound to the tension between individual and collective interests, as suggested by Hobbes and implied by contemporary social dilemma framing. A tension between individual and collective rationality is certainly a component of the problem, but this volume suggests that it is not a necessary component due to many other micro-sociological or social psychological processes well-documented at the micro level. A central message here is that social order is just as problematic when people have common interests or when they interact in a fully cooperative context, as when they face a social dilemma. Social orders are likely to be contingent on identity verification processes, normative goal frames that moderate gain goal frames, joint tasks that generate a sense of shared responsibility, the enactment of a constitutive interaction orders, and so forth. In this sense, the classical Hobbesian problem and contemporary social dilemma variants of this framing are misdirected and offer a more incomplete picture than normally presumed.

The second theme is that social orders are highly tenuous, fragile, and thus continually constructed or reconstructed. For this fundamental reason, micro processes are central to an understanding of the larger problem of social order. This is a common message of virtually all chapters in this volume. The conditions and processes of order differ across the papers but the convergent image of micro level processes is one of flux, instability, and movement, yet also of stability and repetitive patterns. This is not a new point in the abstract, but its theoretical meaning or import for the problem of social order have not been fully explicated. This volumes brings together in one place a wide variety of micro-sociological theories that reveal how and when people confront, mitigate, resolve, or fail to resolve these problems of social order while on the edge of chaos. A key implication is that Hobbesian problem needs to be reframed in order to focus more on micro foundations rather than macro solutions. Micro-level interactional and situational conditions are a necessary component of explanations of social order in the large, complex, geographically diverse human communities of the twenty-first century.

REFERENCES

Batson, Charles Daniel. 1991. *The Altruism Question: Toward a Social-Psychological Answer.* Hillsdale, NJ: Lawrence Erlbaum.
Berger, Joseph, M. Hamit Fisek, Robert Z. Norman, and Morris Zelditch Jr. 1977. *Status Characteristics and Social Interaction.* New York: Elsevier.
Burke, Peter J., and Jan E. Stets. 2009. *Identity Theory.* New York: Oxford University Press.
Coleman, James S. 1990. *Foundations of Social Theory.* Cambridge, MA: Harvard University Press.
Collins, Randall. 1981. "On the Microfoundations of Macrosociology." *American Journal of Sociology* 86: 984–1014.
  2004. *Interaction Ritual Chains.* Princeton, NJ: Princeton University Press.
Condon, William S., and Louis W. Sander. 1974. "Synchrony Demonstrated between Movements of the Neonate and Adult Speech." *Child Development* 45: 456–62.
Cook, Karen S., Russell Hardin, and Margaret Levi. 2005. *Cooperation without Trust?* New York: Russell Sage Foundation.

Emerson, Richard. 1981. "Social Exchange Theory." In *Social Psychology: Sociological Perspectives*, edited by Morris Rosenberg and Ralph H. Turner. New York: Basic Books.

Fehr, Ernst, and Herbert Gintis. 2007. "Human Emotion and Social Cooperation: Experimental and Analytical Foundations." *Annual Review of Sociology* 33: 43–64.

Fine, Gary Alan. 2012. *Tiny Publics: A Theory of Group Action and Culture.* New York: Russell Sage Foundation.

Fukuyama. Francis. 1995. *Trust: The Social Virtues and the Creation of Prosperity.* New York: Free Press.

Goetz, Jennifer L., Dacher Keltner, and Emiliana Simon-Thomas. 2010. "Compassion: An Evolutionary Analysis and Empirical Review." *Psychological Bulletin* 136: 351–74.

Hechter, Michael. 1987. *Principles of Group Solidarity.* Berkeley: University of California Press.

Heise, David R. 2007. *Expressive Order: Confirming Sentiments in Social Actions.* New York: Springer.

Hitlin, Steven, and Stephan Vaisey. 2010. *Handbook of the Sociology of Morality.* New York: Springer.

2013. "The New Sociology of Morality." *Annual Review of Sociology* 39: 51–68.

Hobbes, Thomas. [1651] 1985. *Leviathan.* New York: Penguin Books.

Kemper Theodore D. 1978. *A Social Interactional Theory of Emotion.* New York: Wiley.

Kollock, Peter. 1994. "The Emergence of Exchange Structures: An Experimental Study of Uncertainty, Commitment, and Trust." *American Journal of Sociology* 100: 313–45.

Lawler, Edward J., Shane R. Thye, and Jeongkoo Yoon. 2008. "Social Exchange and Micro Social Order." *American Sociological Review* 73: 519–42.

2009. *Social Commitments in a Depersonalized World.* New York: Russell Sage Foundation.

2013. "Being on the Edge of Chaos: Social Psychology and the Problem of Social Order." *Contemporary Sociology: A Journal of Reviews* 42: 340–49.

Maynard, Douglas W. 2003. *Bad News Good News: Conversational Order in Everyday Talk and Clinical Settings.* Chicago: University of Chicago Press.

Molm, Linda D. 2003. "Theoretical Comparisons of Forms of Exchange." *Sociological Theory.* 21: 1–17.

Parsons, Talcott. 1937. *The Structure of Social Action.* New York: Free Press.

Piliavin, Jane A., and Peter L. Callero. 1991. *Giving Blood: The Development of an Altruistic Identity.* Baltimore: Johns Hopkins University Press.

Rawls, Anne W. 2004. *Epistemology and Practice: Durkheim's The Elementary Forms of Religious Life.* Cambridge, UK: Cambridge University Press.

Ridgeway, Cecilia. 1991. "The Social Construction of Status Value: Gender and Other Nominal Characteristics." *Social Forces* 70: 367–86.

2011. *Framed by Gender.* New York: Oxford University Press.

Thye, Shane R., Jeongkoo Yoon, and Edward D. Lawler. 2002. "The Theory of Relational Cohesion: Review of a Research Program." *Advances in Group Processes* 19: 139–66.

Turner, Jonathan H. 2007. *Human Emotions: A Sociological Theory.* New York: Routledge.

Waal de, Frans B. M. 2008. "Putting Altruism Back Into Altruism: The Evolution of Empathy." *Annual Review of Psychology* 59: 279–300.

Yamagishi, Toshio, and Midori Yamagishi. 1994. "Trust and Commitment in the United States and Japan." *Motivation and Emotion.* 18: 129–66.

Zelditch, Morris, Jr., and Henry A. Walker. 1984. "Legitimacy and the Stability of Authority." In *Advances in Group Processes* 1: 1–25.

2

The Evolutionary Biology and Sociology of Social Order

Jonathan H. Turner

Abstract

By examining the evolutionary biology of hominins and then humans, it is possible to construct more robust explanations for how dynamics at the micro level of social organization affect the integration of the micro, meso, and macro realms that constitute social reality. In this chapter, the evolution of hominins and eventually humans is reviewed with an eye to understanding how the pre-adaptations and behavioral propensities of hominins could be selected upon to create a more emotional animal, Homo sapiens, that was not locked into the group and kin structures of most mammals, with the result that humans have been able to build up solidarities at the group level that do not lock Homo sapiens into the micro social universe. Rather, the same emotional dynamic that generate micro-level solidarities can, under specified conditions, cause integration of the micro with the macro social universe composed of institutional domains, stratification systems, and societies. Evolutionary sociology is not just an esoteric program of theory and research but, rather, an approach that can shed new light on old theoretical problems.

Sociology emerged as a discipline to explain the dramatic changes associated with industrialization and urbanization. These new social orders appeared to be on the edge of chaos for many of those living through the tumultuous transition from agrarian to industrial social formations. Indeed, the first generations of sociologists in the nineteenth century posited a wide variety of "pathologies" inhering in the structure and culture of modern societies. In analyzing these transformative transitions, most early theorists employed an evolutionary approach, outlining the forces that had driven societies from simple to ever-larger and more complex patterns of social organization; and all had implicit conceptions of how these formations violated the fundamental nature of humans, thereby generating personal pathologies from alienation through egoism to marginality. Indeed, these are still the central problematics of much critical sociology and sociology more generally, but now we can approach questions of human nature and the relation of this nature to patterns of social organization with more sophisticated analytical tools that reduce speculation and downplay the often highly evaluative overtones of much sociological analysis of the human condition and society.

Human nature can be conceptualized as the outcome of natural selection on primates and then humans' hominin ancestors as they adapted to niches in various habitats, whereas macro-level societies can be examined as outcomes of sociocultural evolution, driven by the dynamics outlined by the classical theorists and, over the last one hundred years, by contemporary macro-level theoretical sociology. But, in contrast to the past, sociology is now in a position to combine analysis of evolution at the level of societies with evolution of the human nature. By combining these two vantage points, we can better understand how humans as species have been able to create large and complex societies composed of millions, if not billions, of members (Machalek 1992) – something that no other mammal has ever done. The standard account of this accomplishment is that with language and culture, humans could create ever-larger and more differentiated societies; and although this is certainly true, it obscures the connection between (a) the evolved nature of humans as a species and (b) the evolved nature of the societal formations that humans as a unique species of primates have been able to construct. Humans' capacities and behavioral propensities should be part of any explanation of how societies have evolved and how they are sustained and tenuously integrated, at least for a time, in the face of powerful disintegrative forces.

Macro societies now seem on the edge of chaos not only because they are large and complex but also because they have been built by an evolved ape – humans – that has a unique evolutionary history. Complexity of any sort generates selection pressure for new mechanisms of integration, but this complexity would have not been possible without the capacities that humans' primate ancestors possessed. In fact, by examining those primates closest to humans, we can look back millions of years and still see the behavioral propensities of the ancestor that we once shared with extant great apes. Looking back in time allows us to appreciate the fact that humans at their genetic core are still a form of ape who, as startling as this may seem, is not as highly social or group oriented as almost all social thinkers presume. In fact, at our ape core, we are a low-sociality, weak-tied, and non-group-oriented animal when compared to most other mammals. Humans, as apes, are more oriented to larger communities more than to local groups; and, indeed, even after selection increased hominins' and then humans' sociality and capacities for interpersonal work in groups, actual face-to-face interaction still consumes a great deal of physical and emotional energy because groups are not "natural" social structures for great apes as they are for most other mammals. It is the dual capacity to recon community and, at the same time, to avoid the entrapment that comes with powerful bioprogrammers for local group ties that has enabled humans to construct macro societies that always seem chaotic, even as they endure for significant periods of time. Natural selection did indeed increase hominin and then human capacities for forging stronger interpersonal bonds and group solidarities, but we must remember that these new, evolved capacities do not wipe the older, low-sociality propensities programmed into all great apes. Humans are of two minds, as it were, one oriented to more meso- and macro-community formations and a more recent evolved mind capable of forging close social bonds and group formations, even as these consume energy and often cause emotional problems for humans.

As natural selection altered ape-like hominins to become capable of forming stronger ties and to live in more stable groups, it also provided the behavioral propensities that would allow for the integration of the complex societies that humans began to create about five thousand years ago. As I will outline, contemporary great apes and, hence, the last common ancestor of humans and extant great apes reveal many capacities and propensities for forming stronger social ties but, surprisingly, only humans among all of the apes that once existed have been able to do so and survive into the present. So, the chaotic world of societal formations in the contemporary age has only been possible by virtue of: (a) ape and hominin propensities to become oriented to larger-scale formations, adapt to weak social ties, and function in multiple groups that form and disband; and (b) evolved human capacities to form strong attachments and bonds that, under certain conditions, allow individuals to form not only stronger local solidarities but also commitments to macro structures. The world seems on the edge of chaos because it is built and sustained by two somewhat different behavioral dispositions of humans as evolved apes that, miraculously, can sometimes work in concert to sustain the huge and complex sociocultural formations of the modern world.

In this chapter, I will outline in more detail the points raised earlier. I will first present a general analytical model that can guide the discussion. Next, I will outline a strategy for understanding more precisely the biological nature of humans as an evolved ape. This analysis takes us back to selection pressures imposed by ecological niches of the forest habitats in which apes first evolved and, then, to the selection pressures of niches in the open-country terrestrial habitat of the African savannah in which humans' hominin ancestors were increasingly forced to adapt. I will then summarize the now rather well-developed literature on the behavioral abilities and tendencies of extant great apes – humans' closest living relatives in the primate order – and document how these can tell us about the distant ancestor of all present-day great apes, including humans as a unique type of evolved ape. With this greater understanding of human nature as it began to evolve in the forest and, later, in terrestrial habitats of Africa, I will finally turn to the evolution of societal complexity and the evolved traits of humans that allowed this complexity to emerge in the first place and, then, to be sustained – albeit often at the edge of chaos.

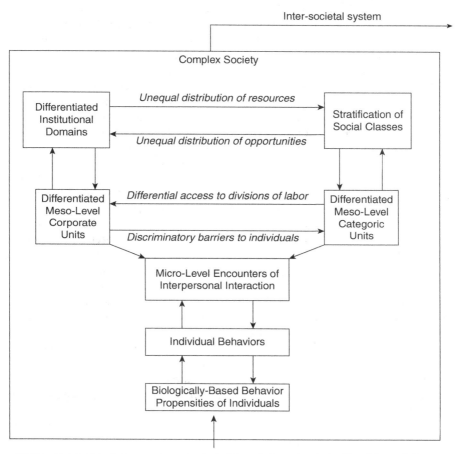

FIGURE 2.1. Elements of human societies.

AN ANALYTICAL MODEL FOR VISUALIZING HUMAN NATURE
AND THE EVOLUTION OF COMPLEX SOCIETIES

Figure 2.1 offers my views on the basic levels of social reality, beginning at the bottom of the figure with the biologically based behavioral proclivities of humans. As is emphasized by the arrow coming into the box enclosing a societal system, these behavioral tendencies are the result of natural selection as it worked on the primate family, especially apes and then hominins. All that occurs within the larger structural forms listed in the figure is ultimately made possible by the nature of humans as evolved apes. This nature affects how people behave, but for our purposes as sociologists, concern is with the micro realm of *interpersonal* behavior, or social interaction. Interaction in encounters is typically the most micro-level reality examined by sociologists, and, obviously, I encourage sociologists to move deeper into the evolved biology of humans because this biology has relevance for understanding how the complexity of sociocultural systems is built up and sustained.

Micro encounters are constrained, on the one side, by the behavioral tendencies of individuals, with these behaviors always having a biological and, hence, evolutionary component. On the other side, micro encounters are embedded in meso-level units created by humans. One generic type of meso-level sociocultural formation is the *corporate unit* composed of individuals organized into divisions of labor in pursuit of goals. Humans have created only three basic types of corporate units: *groups, organizations,* and *communities.* And these units tend to be embedded in each other, with groups as the basic building blocks of organizations, and with groups and organizations as the building materials for communities. Locations in corporate units – often defined as *status* locations in divisions of labor – carry with them normative expectations for individuals. The other generic type of meso-level sociocultural formation is what I term the *categoric unit,* which is created by the social distinctions that people make among members of a population, often termed *diffuse status characteristics* in social psychology. Examples of these distinctions include sex and gender, age, ethnicity, religious affiliation, and social class; and for my purposes, these "differences" can be conceptualized as *memberships* in categoric units that, in encounters, become diffuse status characteristics that define the moral worth of, and the behavioral expectations for, individuals in different categories.

Thus, it is from encounters that corporate and categoric units are ultimately created, but once formed, these meso-level units impose their culture as a series of constraints – status beliefs, expectations states, and norms – on individuals in encounters. And, as we will see, it is from this interplay among the forces operating in encounters that complex societies are ultimately created, via the building blocks of corporate and categoric units. Individuals in interaction respond to each other and the meso-level units of their own creation that now constrain them; and these responses can have large effects on macro-level social orders.

Corporate units are the building blocks of *institutional domains,* which can be conceptualized as congeries of corporate units addressing particular adaptive problems faced by a population. These congeries are integrated by various structural and cultural mechanisms and thereby provide one of the pillars on which societies and inter-societal systems are built and sustained (Turner 2010). Institutional domains, such as economy, polity, kinship, law, religions, education, science, art, sport, and potentially a few others, generate the resources that are ultimately distributed to members of a population, often unequally, and the evaluate belief systems, or *ideologies,* that provide moral evaluations for activities of individuals and corporate units in institutional domains.

Corporate units distribute valued resources unequally by limiting access of individuals to their divisions of labor or their movement up the hierarchies of divisions of labor. The result is the creation of a stratification system composed of categoric units – most importantly, social classes that are hierarchically ranked by their members, respective shares of resources and by their perceived moral worth as defined by the ideologies of each institutional domain and by the *meta-ideologies* combining the ideologies of the dominant institutional domains in a society. As part of the stratification system, there is almost always a certain amount of correlation between (a) diffuse characteristics, or *parameters* (Blau 1977, 1994), demarking memberships in categoric units and (b) social class locations of the larger stratification system. Depending on which categoric units correlate with higher- or lower-class memberships, individuals and families will be differentially evaluated by status beliefs derived from institutional ideologies and meta-ideologies. Perceived differences among of members in diverse categoric units and the moral evaluation of these differences by status beliefs (often prejudicial) have a large effect on individuals' access to resource-giving corporate units. Diffuse status characteristics become, in essence, markers that allow for discriminatory treatment of differentially evaluated social categories. The resulting stratification system becomes the second pillar of a society and, often, intersocietal systems; but, as is obvious, it can be a somewhat shaky pillar if the stratification system generates too much tension over inequality.

This simple model denotes the key structures and their cultures by which complex societies have been built up over the long term of societal evolution. For most of human history, societies were decidedly more micro, revolving around two basic group-level corporate units: (1) nuclear families in (2) bands of five or six families wondering delimited territories in search of food. Societal evolution would ultimately depend on building up more stable and larger communities, but even more important was the invention of organizations that could become to the foundations for new types of institutional domains that, among hunter-gatherers, are all compressed into kinship. With evolution of organizations and communities to house them, institutional domains and stratification systems would evolve, creating the chaos of complexity that stimulated the emergence of sociology. But, despite this complexity and its majestic character, societies must be sustained and reproduced by humans in face-to-face interaction; and humans, we must all remember, are evolved apes that have been altered by natural selection in ways that make reproduction of societal complexity possible.

HUMAN NATURE: WHY IT IS IMPORTANT AND HOW WE DISCOVER IT

The Evolution of Low-Sociality Apes

Some 64 million years ago, rodent-like mammals began to climb or claw their way into the forests of Africa (Maryanski and Turner 1992; Turner and

Maryanski 2005, 2008; Turner 2000). Over the next 30 million years, prosim-
ians (pre-monkeys), monkeys, and apes became differentiated, with promin-
ians being pushed to the island of Madagascar or to nocturnal niches in the
mainland African forests, and, most importantly, with apes eventually being
pushed to the terminal feeding areas high in the forest canopy where there was
not much food, structural support from branches, or room to accommodate
permanent groups. Monkeys had won out in the competition for the verdant
core of the forest habitat by 25 million years ago, even though apes were generally smarter and bigger than monkeys.

   Today, we still see among the great apes (i.e., orangutans, gorillas, and chimpanzees) the effects of the forced adaptation to the terminal feeding areas of
the forest habitat: (a) no permanent bonds between adult females and males
and (b) male and female promiscuity so that paternity is *never* known – hence,
destroying the possibilities for inter-generational groups save for mother-infant
bonds that are broken forever when adolescent females reach puberty and
leave their natal community forever, never to return. Such low-sociality and
non-groups formations are rare among mammals, underscoring the intense
selection pressures that apes were under as they adapted to the terminal feeding areas of the forest habitat.

   A network analysis (Maryanski 1986, 1987) of the three great apes reveals
that they have virtually *no strong ties*, although some moderate ties can exist
among chimpanzees. There are no permanent groups formed by these ties; and
an ape like the orangutan is virtually solitary, with males and females only joining up to mate and then disbanding and with females caring for her offspring
alone until both adolescent males and females depart the natal community
forever. Alexandra Maryanski's (1992, 1993, 1996) cladistic analysis of the
network structures of present-day apes – that is, orangutans, chimpanzees, and
gorillas – allows us to look back some 7 million years and see the social structure of the last common ancestor to apes and humans. In its organizational
features, this last common ancestor was most like the orangutan, even though
humans are genetically more closely related to common chimpanzees who are
more social than orangutans. Still, the common ancestor to the great ape and
hominin (human) line evidenced virtually no permanent social ties and group
structures; and at our ape core, this weak-tie and low-sociality is still part of
our biological programming, but is now overlaid with new, evolved capacities
to develop stronger ties and to form more stable groups.

   Many of the unique traits of all primates first evolved in the extremes of
the arboreal habitat. One of the most important traits is the shift in the sense
modalities of apes and monkeys, who became visually rather than olfactory
dominant (a shift that, as we will see, had huge neurological consequences for
human evolution). And, many of the unique traits of great apes are the result
of their adaptation to the marginal feeding areas of the forest canopy. For
example, apes are smarter than monkeys and have stronger and more dexter-
ous fingers, stronger wrist and shoulder joints allowing for brachiation (i.e.,

rotating their arms 360 degrees, something a monkey cannot do). And, most importantly, when compared to group-oriented monkeys, apes do not form permanent groups or even permanent ties with conspecifics.

Apes were, however, well adapted for millions of years to this high-wire act in the sparse niches of the forest habitat, but as the forests began to recede about 10 million years ago, many were forced down to the open-country savannah where they were doomed by their lack of strong ties and cohesive groups, their individualism and mobility, their high emotionality (over which they do not have high cortical control), their slow speed (they are built to swing around in trees, not run), their weak olfactory sense to locate predators, and their reliance of seeing predators in tall grasses and brush outcroppings. The result was carnage, with the last non-hominin apes trying to live on the savannah going extinct by 1.5 million years ago. For, to survive in open-country savannah conditions, where predators are prevalent, requires strong group ties for food collection and defense against predators – something that great apes did not have as they were forced to the African savannah.

Ape Nature and What It Means for Human Nature

How, then, did the hominin ancestors of the last common ancestors survive, given their lack of strong social ties and weak patterns of group organization, including a lack of kinship relations beyond mother-offspring ties that are forever broken at puberty? Let me answer this question by breaking down traits of our last common ancestor, as is revealed by a variety of literatures including: cladistic analysis, comparative neurology between humans and monkeys, experiments and training of apes in primate centers, and field studies on primate behavior (Turner and Maryanski 2012, 2015).

Pre-adaptations. Pre-adaptations – or, as Steven Jay Gould (2002) termed them, *spandrels* – are traits that evolved as a byproduct of selection for other traits. One of the most important examples of a pre-adaptation among apes is the rewiring of the ape brain for visual dominance, which, in turn, generated the basic wiring (in and around the inferior parietal lobe) for the language capacity that all great apes reveal (Geschwind 1965a, 1965b; Geschwind and Damasio 1984). The wiring for visual dominance was produced by simple chance, but it created the capacity for language among highly intelligent apes. This capacity was thus available for further selection *if* language facility became fitness enhancing.

A second important pre-adaptation among apes is their orientation to the larger regional community and territory rather than the local kin unit or group. Apes will form temporary patrol groups to defend their territory from incursions by males from other communities, but this temporary group is devoted to the servicing of the larger community order rather than for group solidarities, per se. The orientation of apes toward the regional community rather than to local groups, packs, troops, prides, pods, herds, and other grouping propensities of most other mammals was fitness-enhancing for the niches high in the trees where apes could still maintain a common community in the absence of the ability to support permanent group ties in the poorly-endowed niches of the arboreal habitat. Thus, natural selection *took away* bioprogrammers for close social ties and group formations under very intense selection pressures; and in their place, natural selection generated a propensity for weak ties, impermanent groups, individualism, mobility around a home range, and an orientation to the larger community rather than to kindred or to groups in general. These traits became the pre-adaptations that may have opened the door for the mass societies that humans now inhabit.

Behavioral Propensities. Even though apes reveal propensities for weak social ties and, at best, very temporary groups that assemble briefly and then disassemble, they nonetheless evidence many behavioral propensities that are the basis for the strong social ties and group solidarities among humans today. Indeed, the interesting question is why these behavioral propensities were not enough to allow apes to survive once they left the confines of the arboreal habitat and began to live on the African savannah where stronger ties and stable groups would be fitness-enhancing. It is not even clear that much selection on these traits would have even been necessary because apes often reveal them within the human measure. Cleary, something important was missing from this list of behavioral propensities, but let me first list these behavioral propensities before providing an answer to what was missing. All apes reveal the following behavioral propensities:

1. *Reading of Faces and Eyes of Conspecifics.* Apes are able to read gestures in the face and eyes of conspecifics for meanings (Osgood 1966; Menzel 1971; Mitani and Watts 2001). In fact, they will follow gaze and eye movements to determine what another is observing and thinking (Hare and Tomassello 2001; Hare et al. 2006; Povinelli 2000; Povinelli and Eddy 1997; Itakura 1996; Baizer et al. 2007; Tomasello, Hare, and Fogelman 2001; Okomot et al. 2002).
2. *Imitation of Facial Gestures Revealing Emotions.* The ability of both human and ape infants to imitate within two weeks of birth oral-facial movements of caretakers indicates that they are genetically programmed to learn visually based gestures carrying meanings at the very early age (Emde 1962; Ekman 1984; Sherwood et al. 2005; Tomonaga 1999; Subiaul 2007; Horowitz 2003; Gergory and Csibra 2006). Human infants are thus programmed to read emotions in face *years before* they can understand and use vocal gestures, indicating that this developmental sequence probably reflects an evolutionary sequence.
3. *Empathy and Role-Taking.* The great apes evidence the capacity for empathy by reading the gestures of conspecifics to determine their emotional states and, then, using this information to respond appropriately to others (deWaal 1996, 2009). Thus, the behavioral capacity for what

George Herbert Mead (1934) termed "role-taking" is evident among the great apes and, hence, was part of the behavioral repertoire of humans' hominin ancestors.

4. *Rhythmic Synchronization of Communication.* Apes evidence a propensity for the rhythmic synchronization of body and verbal sounds (Rizzolatti et al. 2002); and as with humans (Collins 2004), this synchronization aligns interaction and generates temporary solidarities.

5. *Collective Emotional Effervescence.* Field studies indicate that, on those occasions when chimpanzees assemble in propinquity to each other, the rhythmic synchronization can escalate into heightened emotional arousal that, in turn, leads to rather uninhibited acts typical of human festivals, such as Mardi Gras, just as Durkheim (1912 [1965]) emphasized in secondary reporting of Spencer's and Gillen's (1899) descriptions of the Arunta aborigines of Central Australia.

6. *Reciprocity.* Higher primates, including monkeys, possess a sense of reciprocity (Cosmides 1989; deWaal 1989, 1991, 1996; deWaal and Bronson 2006), as do higher mammals in general. Exchange reciprocity is one of the essential properties of strong social bonds in groups and the arousal of positive emotions to sustain these bonds; and even though apes do not form permanent groups, this capacity was available in our last common ancestor for strengthening group ties, once selection began to push in this direction during hominin evolution.

7. *Calculations of Justice.* Primates calculate justice and perceived fairness in exchange relations (Bronson et al. 2005, 2006; Bronson and deWaal 2003). Such calculations involve a comparison of the (reward) payoffs of an individual primate to the payoffs of others and their respective behaviors (costs) to get these rewards, which can be seen as not only a behavioral capacity that gives exchanges a moral character but also as a precursor to morality itself.

8. *Seeing Self as Object.* Apes along with other highly intelligent mammals (Gallup 1970, 1979, 1982), such as dolphins and elephants, can recognize themselves in a mirror. This neurological capacity suggests that they can see "themselves as objects in their environments," to use G. H. Mead's (1934) famous phrasing; and from this capacity it is a short step to having a sense of identity and evaluating this identity from the perspective of others and, if culture exists, from cultural standards or what Mead termed "the generalized other." Moreover, as Cooley (1902) emphasized in his notion of "the looking glass self," humans experience emotions about themselves in such evaluations of self. And, with the enhancement of hominins' emotional capacities, more robust and nuanced views of self could evolve.

9. *Weaker Hierarchies.* Monkeys tend to form linear hierarchies of dominance among males, and sometimes among females in matrilines. Such hierarchies impose a limit on the kinds of social structures that can exist

in monkey societies. Monkeys are locked into local groups and kin relations among females in these groups. In contrast, apes vary considerably on the strength and linearity of their hierarchies, with humans closest relative, chimpanzees, only developing moderate, mostly ad hoc, and situational hierarchies of dominance that arise and then recede. This weaker sense of hierarchy assures that apes will recognize status differences, but will not build the closed and rigid hierarchies of local groups that would pose an obstacle to building larger-scale social structures, if these became fitness enhancing.

By the logic of cladistic analysis in biology, these nine universal behavioral propensities of all the great apes were also present in the last common ancestor to extant apes and humans. In reading down this list behaviors, what immediately catches attention is that most of these would seem to enable apes to form groups because they are the *same* means by which humans do so! Yet, these traits alone were apparently not enough; otherwise, far more species of apes would have survived on the savannah by becoming more group-oriented.

Why were these behavioral propensities not enough, and especially so if the capacity for language was just "sitting there" ready to be selected on to provide one more hook to solidarity-generating communication? The answer to this question provides the key information solving the puzzle of how natural selection would create new bonding and group formation propensities among hominins, while at the same time *not* putting a roadblock to later abilities to break the hold of kinship and group solidarities so as to form and integrate macro societies of enormous size and complexity.

The Evolution of Emotions during Hominin Evolution. Natural selection appears to have hit upon a solution to the weak-tie and grouping problems among ape-like hominins: enhance emotions, first by increasing the number and range of *primary emotions* (happiness, fear, anger, and sadness), then by combining two primary emotions in *to first order elaborations* and, finally, by merging the three negative primary emotions (anger, fear, sadness) into *second-order elaborations* that generate the emotions of social control: shame and guilt (see Turner 2000; see also Plutchik 1980, Kemper 1987).

The evidence for this rewiring of the hominin brain can be found in comparative neuro anatomy comparing the relative size of modules in subcortical areas of ape and human brains. On average, the size of subcortical areas of the brain among humans, where emotions are generated, is twice that of the great apes (Stephan 1983; Stephan and Andy 1969, 1977; Turner 2000). Because humans shared a common ancestor with apes some seven million years ago, this change in relative size of key subcortical areas is the "smoking gun" for what selection was doing: increasing emotionality long before the growth of the neocortex increased hominin intelligence. These changes in the subcortical areas of the brain did not require mutations, which are generally harmful (Fisher 1930) and doubly so in complex neurostructures but, instead, the changes evolved by *directional selection*. Directional selection occurs when one side of the Bell curve arraying the distribution of traits enhances fitness more than the other side. As directional selection works on the favored side of the Bell curve, each new generation represents a new distribution of traits that is ever-more biased toward this favored side of the Bell curve. Over successive generations, traits on the favored side rapidly increase frequency in the genome of a species, while traits on the less favored side disappear because those members of a population evidencing these traits on this unfavored side of the distribution have lower rates of reproduction. Because the size of the hominin neocortex did not increase dramatically until very late with *Homo erectus* some 2.0–1.8 million years ago, selection was working elsewhere on the brain in the subcortical areas rather than on the neocortex. As the size of brain modules in the subcortex generating emotions grew, the capacity of hominins to forge stronger social bonds and group solidarities through emotions also increased. These changes would not be so obvious in measurements of the cranial size of hominins compared to other apes because they occur below the neocortex and hence to not push the cranium outward, as would growth of the neocortex. Still, this less visible growth of the subcortical areas of the hominin brain allowed the ancestors of humans to survive in the terrestrial habitats in Africa. This rewiring of the brain for more variety and intensity of emotions was, I believe, *the* key transformation to humans' hominin ancestors, beginning some seven million years ago.

By drawing upon the preadaptation for language that already existed among all great apes (Rumbaugh and Savage-Rumbaugh 1990; Savage-Rumbaugh and Lewin, 1994; Savage-Rumbaugh et al. 1993) and the last common ancestor to humans and present-day apes, natural selection created a "language of emotions" (Turner 2000). This language of emotions was *the first* language of hominins; and it evolved millions of years before spoken language was piggy-backed onto the neurology of this language of emotions. Supporting this conclusion is the fact that human infants possess the ability to imitate emotions almost right out of the womb, years before verbal babbling leads to articulated speech. Moreover, the language of emotions is not only more primal but also more primary in forging emotional bonds among humans today. Social bonds are more emotional than cognitive; and they rely more on what the body and face are "saying" than on what the mouth is articulating in speech.

What emotions apparently did was put some "teeth" into all of the nine behavioral capacities listed earlier. Without the enhanced, focused, and language-like qualities of this new emotionality, the behavioral traits already present in apes could not be effective in forming bonds of solidarity or sustaining group structures. For example, a reading of gestures in eyes and face is only useful for social bonding when emotions are being communicated; imitation of emotional gestures immediately generates attachments among infants and caretakers; empathy and role taking alone is only possible when emotions are in play. Furthermore, rhythmic synchronization is a visually-based emotional processes more than turn-taking process in speech can ever be, although auditory sounds (e.g., cries, beats from drums, and music) can heightened the power of rhythmic synchronization. Obviously, "emotional effervescence" – to use Durkheim's (1912 [1965]) term – is not possible without emotional arousal that can be used to forge and symbolize collective bonds. Reciprocity is an emotional response to giving back for what is given and for sanctioning those who do not reciprocate, and thus exchange depends on nuanced positive and negative emotions. Similarly, justice calculations are only effective when they arouse positive or negative emotions over the "fair" or "unfair" distribution of resources. Evaluating self and abiding by expectations only works to control behaviors if individuals experience positive emotions for affirmations of self and shame as well as guilt for failures to live up to expectations. And, hierarchies and differences in status are only effective if they are built around complex and nuanced positive and negative emotions.

Once we think about it, *none* of the behavioral propensities of apes and early hominins could meet the intense selection pressures for stronger social bonds and group solidarities *without first being imbued with a larger palate of positive and negative emotions*. Alone, the capacities listed earlier cannot generate solidarities, just as they fail to do so among great apes today (and, sadly, for virtually all other apes over the last ten million years that were forced to adapt to the African savannah). With dramatic emotional enhancements, however, the potential of the behavioral propensities listed above could *become an indirect route for replacing the long-vanished bioprogrammers* in evolving hominins that are evident in most mammals. This indirect route of using emotions to forge bonds of solidarity rather than genetically controlled bioprogrammers gave hominins and humans a tool for constructing solidarities in groups but solidarities that can be flexibly employed and modified under diverse circumstances. Hominins were not, therefore, locked into one type and form of group solidarity, as are most mammals. They could still see beyond local groups toward larger community formations; and this hard-wired propensity in all apes and, no doubt, all hominins became a preadaptation for human macrostructures.

Moreover, spoken language and cultural codes would have only instrumental and hence somewhat dry meanings without being tagged by a larger palate of emotions. Without emotions, speech does not forge strong bonds; with emotions in the intonations of speech, talk can build up solidarities. Even more importantly, the accompanying facial expressions and general body language allows speech to be turned into an even powerful bonding mechanisms, as inflections in speech coordinated with facial expressions and body countenance communicate a wide range of emotions. Similarly, a moral code has no morality without emotional tags of shame, guilt, approval, disapproval, and other moral emotions. Thus, it is not surprising that articulated speech and symbolic culture evolved only *after* enhancements in the range and nuance of emotions among hominins had evolved – an evolutionary sequence that is reflected in the developmental sequence of infants' capacity to imitate and learn emotions long before they can understand or use speech to communicate.

Evolution of the Nuclear Family. The micro societies of hunter-gatherers were not possible without kinship attachments, especially between males and females. The human septum – a subcortical area of the brain generating the pleasure of sex drives – is well over twice as large in humans as in very pro-miscuous chimpanzees, indicating that something beyond the sexual drive, per se, is involved in growing the septum to human proportions. So, selection may have first worked on the subcortical neurology of hominins' to increase male-female bonding and, thereby, make possible the formation of the nuclear family. Forming the nuclear family was a major evolutionary change for a ter-restrial ape, evolving millions of years before speech and other cultural sys-tems became possible with the expanded neo-cortex. The septum and other emotion centers generate, I believe, the "love" and "loyalty" of nuclear family members; and without the nuclear family, the viability of small bands would be in doubt. With the nuclear family, which is still a very unusual trait for a great ape, hominins could survive; and this was the central mode of adapta-tion among humans for well over 90 percent of their time on earth. But, we should not see it as "natural" in the same way as is evident in other mammals because it is not guided by bioprogrammers for mating and kinship but more indirectly through the arousal of a complex set of emotions revolving around "love." If families would become more unstable as societies grew, it is because the nuclear family has always been a somewhat jury-rigged construction held together by emotions.

Starting as far back at ten to twelve thousand years ago, however, settled hunting and gathering and eventually horticulture began to change the nature of human societies; and, in a very real sense, these changes represented the "big bang" behind the sudden expansion of the sociocultural universe (Turner 2010). But, unlike most other mammals, humans were not as constrained by a biology geared to group-based or even kin-based societies. Instead, they could live their lives out in multiple groups, with relatively low solidarity and little intra-group interpersonal "grooming" beyond verbally-expressed emotional pleasantries; indeed, at their ape core, humans are still oriented to the larger community more than the local group. In fact, as noted earlier, groups require a great deal of interpersonal and emotional work to be sustained, as do most human relationships compared to the relative ease with which humans iden-tify with their home towns, ethnicity, religion, and other meso-level sociocul-tural formations. Local group ties, I believe, are not nearly as "natural" as much sociology and social philosophy posits. But, this "weakness" of local group ties, coupled to a genetically driven orientation to the larger commu-nity, is what allowed humans to use secondary groups to build up ever-larger sociocultural formations, once selection pressures pushed for such formations.

THE EVOLUTION AND INTEGRATION OF COMPLEXITY

The scale of human societies has so dramatically increased over the last five-thousand years that the problem of linking micro-level interpersonal dynamics to the macro sociocultural realm became increasingly problematic – even for an evolved ape who was not trapped in local group solidarities. The development of the sociology of emotions now allows us to see that the very force – enhanced emotionality – that enabled stronger micro-level attachments to evolve among hominin is also the force most responsible for linking the micro, meso, and macro realms of the social universe together – much like gravity helps hold the physical universe together. Edward Lawler and his associates (Lawler, Thye, and Yoon 2009) have provided one of the best explanations of how individuals become emotionally committed to macro social structures from micro-level exchange processes; my approach is similar to this important theoretical research program but differs in some important respects. Let me briefly outline my theory – an approach that builds on Lawler and colleagues as well as my evolutionary approach to understanding human emotionality and sociality.

Looking back on Figure 2.1, I argue that any theory explaining the linkages among diverse levels of social reality must address (a) how embedding poses constraints on those structures lodged inside more inclusive structures and (b) how commitments of individuals to these structures and cultures emerge from micro-level encounters and, then, move up to meso and macro sociocultural formations.

Macro to Micro Constraints Imposed by Embedding

Societies evolve as they develop new types of differentiated institutional domains to address problems of adaptation (e.g., kinship, economy, polity, law, religion, education, science, etc.). Over the last five-thousand years, the combination of permanent settlements and population growth have caused the successive differentiation of distinctive institutional domains, with corporate units in these domains addressing diverse adaptive problems such as production, distribution, reproduction, regulation and control, and uncertainties and anxieties. As actors begin to address these adaptive problems in encounters within corporate units, their talk and discourse in an emerging institutional domain is increasingly conducted by what has been termed a *generalized media of exchange* unique to a domain (Parsons 1963a, 1963b; Luhmann 1982). An illustrative list of these media is summarized in Table 2.1. These generalized symbolic media develop some very important properties.

First, they became the moral terms of discourse that is eventually codified into an ideology constraining and, at the same time, legitimating the activities of individuals in corporate units, specifying what is right and proper activity. Second, and equally important, the generalized symbolic media often become

TABLE 2.1. *Generalized Symbolic Media of Institutional Domains*

Kinship	**Love/loyalty,** or the use of intense positive affective states to forge and mark commitments to others and groups of others
Economy	**Money,** or the denotation of exchange value for objects, actions, and services by the metrics inhering in money
Polity	**Power,** or the capacity to control the actions of other actors
Law	**Imperative coordination/justice,** or the capacity to adjudicate social relations and render judgments about justice, fairness, and appropriateness of actions
Religion	**Sacredness/Piety,** or the commitment to beliefs about forces and entities inhabiting a non-observable supernatural realm and the propensity to explain events and conditions by references to these sacred forces and beings
Education	**Learning,** or the commitment to acquiring and passing on knowledge
Science	**Knowledge,** or the invocation of standards for gaining verified knowledge about all dimensions of the social, biotic, and physical-chemical universes
Medicine	**Health,** or the concern about and commitment to sustaining the normal functioning of the human body
Sport	**Competitiveness,** or the definition of games that produce winners and losers by virtue of the respective efforts of players
Arts	**Aesthetics,** or the commitment to make and evaluate objects and performances by standards of beauty and pleasure that they give observers

Note: These and other generalized symbolic media are employed in discourse among actors, in articulating themes, and in developing ideologies about what should and ought to transpire in an institutional domain. They tend to circulate within a domain, but all of the symbolic media can circulate in other domains, although some media are more likely to do so than others.

the valued resource that is distributed unequally in a domain, leading to the evolution of stratification systems. Thus, *money* from the economy, *power/authority* from polity, imperative *coordination/justice* from law, *love/loyalty* from kinship, *learning* from education, *sacredness/piety* from religion, *competition* from sport, *aesthetics* from art, and so on are (a) the terms of discourse, (b) the symbolic and moral basis of ideologies with a domain, *and* (c) often the valued resource unequally distributed by a domain.

Third, with increasing differentiation of domains and their distinctive media, exchanges of one media for another occur among actors within and between institutional domains. As a result, generalized symbolic media began to circulate among actors in different institutional domains. For example, *power* and *authority* have increasingly been franchised by polity to corporate units within diverse institutional domains, thereby causing the circulation of power and authority across virtually all corporate units in all domains of complex societies. To take another example, *money* from the economy began to circulate in exchange in markets for resources from other domains such as *knowledge* and *learning* from domains like science and education. Another example of circulation is the *loyalty* of adult kin members to commit to work in the economy exchange for *money*.

Fourth, with circulation, many institutional domains began to distribute unequally several generalized symbolic media. For example, *money* is given by members of kin units as a sign of their *loyalty* in exchange for *sacredness/piety* from religion as an institutional domain. Or, *money* as salaries is given to teachers in exchange for their capacity to impart *learning* and knowledge. In contemporary economics, all exchanges of money for other generalized symbolic media are collapsed into a view of "The Economy," but as sociologists, it is important to remember that these circulating symbolic media have their *origins in distinctive institutional domains*. And, when we examine them as moving from their domain of origin to other domains, a very different picture of societal integration becomes evident than a purely economic analysis would reveal.

Fifth, much of this integration achieved through the circulation of generalized symbolic media is structural in that these media regularizes exchange interdependencies among diversely situated actors in a society. And exchanges of this nature, even when viewed from a macro perspective, provide one source of structural interdependencies so essential to integration of complex societies.

Sixth, because symbolic media are symbols and used to construct ideologies (while also being valued resources that are exchanged), they provide cultural integration by what I term *meta-ideologies* which are composites of ideologies from particular domains – say, the composite of the respective ideologies attached to capitalism, democratic use of power, learning in state-sponsored universal education, knowledge from science, and imperative coordination and justice by law becoming one of the prominent *meta-ideologies* in post-industrial societies. These ideologies commit individuals to multiple institutional domains and, hence, the more inclusive society as a whole.

Seventh, these meta-ideologies, I argue, are the moral basis for the formation of the *status beliefs* about actors in positional locations in corporate units within institutional domains or, equally important, beliefs about the *diffuse status characteristics* of actors in categoric units associated with the class-based stratification system. Thus, the evaluation of status locations in divisions of labor and diffuse status characteristics (i.e., what I term *categoric-unit memberships*) that are correlated with class inequality become powerful forces beyond the specific as expectation states in micro-level encounters embedded in corporate and categoric units.

Micro Reactions to Macro and Meso Constraints

In general, if people meet expectations and receive positive sanctions, they experience positive emotions (Turner 2007, 2010). The preadaptations and behavioral propensities summarized earlier offer some clues about what expectations are most important for humans as evolved apes and what arenas of social life are most important for meeting expectations and receiving positive sanctions. Some of these I have conceptualized in various places (e.g., Turner 2002, 2007, 2010) as *transactional needs* for (a) *verifying identities*, (b) *receiving profits*, reciprocity, justice and fairness in exchange payoffs, (c) feeling *trust* in others through empathy, role taking, and rhythmic synchronization, (d) feeling a sense of *efficacy* or control over one's actions and their outcomes, (e) experiencing a sense of *group inclusion* or being a part of the interpersonal flow, and (f) sensing *facticity* that self and others are experiencing the same external and internal states for the purposes of a given encounter.

Another set of important forces is successful formation and completion of interaction rituals around (a) rhythmic synchronization, (b) emotional entrainment, and (c) collective effervescence, and (d) symbolizaton of the solidarities generated by this collective effervescence (Collins 2004). These ritual processes are likely to emerge, per se, in most interactions but even more so when transactional needs are also being met.

Encounters always reveal expectations about appropriate behaviors for status locations within divisions of labor in corporate units and for diffuse status characteristics within categoric units. The propensities of apes and humans to recon status become important in connecting the culture of encounters to institutional and stratification systems. This micro culture composed of expectation states for status in the divisions of labor of corporate units and for diffuse status characteristics inhering in categoric unit memberships is derived from status beliefs that, in turn, are pulled from institutional ideologies and meta-ideologies legitimating institutional domains and the stratification system. As these levels of culture filter down to the encounter, they provide an important basis of cultural integration; and as individuals abide by expectation states in encounters, they behave in ways that sustain the more macro-level cultural tenets in a society.

Overcoming Blockages to the Flow of Positive Emotions

Lawler (2001) has posited an attribution dynamic in the arousal of positive and negative emotions in exchanges. For Lawler, positive emotions have a "proximal bias," whereas negative emotions reveal a "distal bias." As a consequence of these biases, positive emotions stay local and do not easily radiate outward as individuals make self-attributions for their positive emotional experiences and often express gratitude to immediate others in encounters. Conversely, negative emotions generate external attributions, often to social structure, and thus move outward and away from the encounter in order to protect self and to avoid expression negative emotions that would breach the encounter. This propensity to make causal attributions is, I believe, hard-wired in the human brain because, as early Gestalt theory suggested, it is universal in humans, as is the propensity among humans for contrast conceptions and cognitive consistency.

Moreover, I would also argue that attribution dynamics are more than a cognitive process; they are also one of the most important defense mechanisms protecting self from the pain of negative emotions. And, along with other defense mechanism, external attributions cause (a) intensify negative emotions, especially those about self and a person's success in exchanges with others (Turner 2002, 2007), (b) cause transmutations of powerful negative emotions, such as shame, into more acceptable emotional states like anger and alienation, and (c) push these negative emotions outward to safer targets at the meso and macro levels of social organization. Because there is often inequality in the resources of actors and their evaluations by status beliefs under conditions of inequality in divisions of labor and the broader stratification system, encounters among unequals always contain the potential for negative emotional arousal from a failure to meet expectations among some individuals and/or by their devaluation through stigmatizing status beliefs and the situational expectations states derived from these beliefs. Encounters are fragile enough without this possibility of negative emotional arousal, which may and may not breach the encounter, but the negative emotions aroused will nonetheless be likely to flow outward and de-legitimate meso and macro structures and their cultures, while reducing individual commitments to these macro-level sociocultural formations. The consequence of this distal bias – often intensified by repression and transmutation of repressed emotions like *shame* into *diffuse anger* (Turner 2007) – is to erode societal-level integration.

In contrast to negative emotions, there is no need for defense mechanisms when positive emotions arise from meeting expectations and verifying self and when encounters exhibit the dynamics that Collins (2004) outlines for interaction rituals. But the proximal bias increases the likelihood that these positive emotions circulate at the micro level of the encounter rather than move out to corporate units, institutional domains, or the broader society.

How, then, is this blockage to macro-level integration through the outward flow of positive emotions created by the dual operation of the proximal and distal biases to be overcome? My answer to this question follows from the evolved biology of humans. When people's transactional needs for self-verification, for just exchanges, for trust, for efficacy, for group inclusion, and for facticity are (a) *consistently* met in encounters across (b) a *wide range* of corporate units within (c) a wide range of *diverse institutional domains*, the positive emotions aroused will begin to migrate outward. And, the more these conditions under (a), (b), and (c) are realized, the more likely is the hold of the proximal bias to be broken, with positive emotions increasingly likely to target macro-level sociocultural formations. Furthermore, if people's expectations for status and diffuse status are realized in encounters, even if they are not highly evaluated, under conditions enumerated under (a), (b), and (c) earlier, positive emotions will also move outward. And, the more some encounters in some corporate units within at least some institutional domains (say, kinship and religion) allow people to hold more highly valued status (as parents and worshipers) and to see their diffuse status characteristics in a more positive light, the more intense will be the positive emotions and the further will these emotions travel along the conduits denoted in Figure 2.1 to macro-level sociocultural formations. And, even if individuals cannot hold high status, their interactions in encounters may still consistently fall into rhythmic synchronization and yield collective effervescence. The positive emotions aroused from this synchronization may also break the hold of the proximal bias and move outward toward corporate units and perhaps even institutional domains.

Disintegrative Pressures

Given the power of the distal bias and the fragility of micro encounters among evolved apes who can be highly emotional, there is always a high potential for delegitimation of macro-level structures and their cultures. This potential increases to the extent that discrimination has systematically denied people access to key resource-distributing corporate units in institutional domains and to the degree that the resulting stratification system reveals high levels of inequality in which status beliefs devalue members of particular categories and/or incumbents in low-level positions in corporate units. Positive emotions are difficult to sustain under these conditions, and the negative emotions aroused are likely to move rapidly outward, delegitimating corporate units, the unfairness of categoric distinctions, and the institutional domains and stratification systems from which all societies are built. And, in light of the evolutionary fact that humans are far more emotional than their great ape cousins and, moreover, that three of the four primary emotions and probably a majority of the combinations built from these primary emotions are also *negative*, this potential for disruption at the level of the encounter will exert considerable disintegrative pressure on a society. Humans are still apes at their core, but they are apes that have been supercharged by natural selection to be highly emotional. It should not be any wonder, then, that at all levels of social organization, social order and integration are always precariously achieved and chronically problematic, thereby making social order chaotic and tenuous.

CONCLUSION

The more general theory outlined in the last half of this chapter can be stated without reference to evolutionary biology and the evolution of primates, hominins, and humans. But, by knowing something about pre-adaptations and genetically driven behavioral propensities of great apes, we gain a much more robust explanation of the forces allowing for macro-based integration of societies as positive emotions break the proximal bias and flow outward toward ever-more macro structures. The ensuing commitment to, and legitimation of, these macro-level sociocultural formations is the principle reason that humans are able to construct macro societies. Insects are driven by genetics, even when they change roles when the distribution of genetically programmed roles becomes skewed (Machalek 1997). For humans, the route to macro societal integration is more indirect, working through the extra emotional charge given to the genetically driven behavior propensities inherited from our hominin ancestors.

As natural selection hit on the solution of using emotions to overcome the low sociality and weak grouping tendencies among apes, the problem of creating stronger bonds and group solidarities at the micro level of interaction was solved, thereby allowing hominins and then humans to survive open-country savannah conditions. But this enhancement of emotions also provided the solution of integrating the more complex societies. By supercharging the behavioral propensities in the ape line with emotions, these emotions will, under predictable conditions, move individuals in encounters to develop commitments to structures and their cultures at the meso and macro level of social organization. Furthermore, without the existing predisposition to form weak ties, to recon community over groups, and to use language, humans may have been trapped like almost all other mammals by their strong bioprogrammers for group and kin commitments. Such commitments would have made it very hard to build up large-scale societies because the natural social unit is the local group, whether a troop, herd, pod, pack, pride, or any other pattern of group formation. If humans had been locked into genetically driven bioprogrammers for group formations, as are monkeys and virtually all other mammals except great apes, population growth may have been fatal to the human line. Given that population growth among humans forced individuals to build up social structures by differentiating corporate units and eventually institutional domains, a group-oriented species of human (like almost all mammals) would not have had the capacity to build a sufficient "structural skeleton" to support the larger "social mass." Emotions thus gave humans more flexibility in adapting to the selection pressures generated by population growth that force humans to elaborate social structures and culture, or die. Human macro-level societies across the globe do indeed make the world a "planet of (the evolved) apes." Only because humans ancestors were apes rather than monkeys could such a large mammal like *Homo sapiens* construct macro societies that rival those among insects.

Alas, the emotions that generate commitments to macrostructures and their cultures are always a double-edged sword because there is a higher negative to positive ratio in their distribution at a neurological level and because their intensity can disrupt societies at the micro level of the encounter and, through collective mobilization of emotionally aroused subpopulations, at the meso and macro levels as well. Humans thus live in a precarious and often dangerous universe because of their biological legacy as an evolved ape that became more emotional and hence social, but also more dangerous. An evolutionary approach, then, allows us to see ourselves in a broader perspective; at the same time, it leads us to understand the interpersonal mechanisms by which both the micro and macro realms are created and sustained or, potentially, torn apart from emotion-driven conflict.

REFERENCES

Baizer, J. S., J. F. Baker, K. Haas, and R. Lima. 2007. "Neurochemical Organization of the Nucleus *Paramedinaus Dorsalis* in the Human." *Brain Research* 1176: 45–52.
Blau, P. M. 1977. *Inequality and Heterogeneity*. New York: Free Press.
　1994. *Structural Context of Opportunities*. Chicago: University of Chicago Press.
Boehm, C. 2012. *Moral Origins: The Evolution of Virtue, Altruism, and Shame*. New York: Basic Books.
Bronson, S. F., and F. B. M. de Waal. 2003. "Fair Refusal by Capuchin Monkeys." *Nature* 128–40.
Brosnan, Sarah F., Hillary C. Schiff, and Frans B. M. de Waal. 2005. "Tolerance for Inequity May Increase with Social Closeness in Chimpanzees." *Proceedings of the Royal Society of London* 272: 253–58.
Brosnan, Sarah F., Cassie Freeman, and Frans B. M. de Waal. 2006. "Capuchin Monkey's (*Cebus apella*) Reactions to Inequity in an Unrestricted Barpull Situation." *American Journal of Primatology* 68: 713–724.
Burghardt, Gordon M. 2005. *The Genesis of Animal Play: Testing the Limits*. Cambridge, MA: MIT Press.
Collins, Randall. 2004. *Interaction Ritual Chains*. Princeton, NJ: Princeton University Press.
Cooley, Charles Horton. 1902. *Human Nature and the Social Order*. New York: Scribners.
Cosmides, L. 1989. "The Logic of Social Exchange: Has Natural Selection Shaped How Humans Reason?" *Cognition* 31: 187–276.
deWaal, Frans B. M. 1989. "Food Sharing and Reciprocal Obligations among Chimpanzees." *Journal of Human Evolution* 18: 433–59.
　1991. "The Chimpanzee's Sense of Social Regularity and Its Relation to the Human Sense of Justice." *American Behavioral Scientist* 34: 335–49.
　1996. *Good Natured: The Origins of Right and Wrong in Humans and Other Animals*. Cambridge, MA: Harvard University Press.
　2009. *The Age of Empathy: Nature's Lessons for a Kinder Society*. New York: Three Rivers Press.
de Waal, Frans B. M., and Sarah F. Brosnon. 2006. "Simple and Complex Reciprocity in Primates." Pp. 85–106 in *Cooperation in Primates and Humans: Mechanisms and Evolution,* edited by P. Kappeler and C. P. van Schaik. Berlin: Springer-Verlag.
Evolution, edited by P. Kappeler and C. P. van Schaik. Berlin: Springer-Verlag.
Durkheim, Emile. 1912 [1965]. *The Elementary Forms of the Religious Life*. New York: The Free Press.
Ekman, P. 1984. "Expression and the Nature of Emotion." Pp. 319–343 in Approaches to Emotion, edited by K. Scherer and P. Ekman. Hillsdale, NJ: Lawrence Erlbaum.
Emde, Robert N. (1962). "Level of Meaning for Infant Emotions: A Biosocial View." Pp. 1–37 in *Development of Cognition, Affect and Social Relations,* edited by W. A. Collins. Hillsdale, NJ: Lawrence Erlbaum.

Fisher, R. A. 1930. *The Genetical Theory of Natural Selection*. Oxford, UK: Oxford University Press.

Gallup, G. G., Jr. 1970. "Chimpanzees: Self-Recognition." *Science* 167: 88–87.

1979. *Self-Recognition in Chimpanzees and Man: A Developmental and Comparative Perspective*. New York: Plenum Press.

1982. "Self-Awareness and the Emergence of Mind in Primates." *American Journal of Primatology* 2: 237–48.

Gergely, G. and G. Csibra. 2006. "Sylvia's Recipe: The Role of Imitation and Pedagogy." Pp. 229–55 in *The Transmission of Cultural Knowledge*, edited by N. J. Enfield and S. C. Levinson. Oxford, UK: Berg Press.

Geschwind, N. 1965a. "Disconnection Syndromes in Animals and Man, Part I." *Brain* 88: 237–94.

1965b. "Disconnection Syndromes in Animals and Man, Part II." *Brain* 88: 585–644.

Geschwind, Norman, and Antonio Damasio, 1984. "The Neural Basis of Language." *Annual Review of Neuroscience* 7: 127–47.

Goffman, Erving. 1961. *Encounters: Two Studies in the Sociology of Interaction*. Indianapolis, IN: Bobbs-Merrill.

Hare, B., J. Call, and M. Tomasello. 2001. "Do Chimpanzees Know What Conspecifics Know?" *Animal Behavior* 61: 139–59.

2006. "Chimpanzees Deceive a Human Competitor by Hiding." *Cognition* 101: 495–514.

Horowitz, A. C. 2003. "Do Chimps Ape? Or Apes Human? Imitation and Intension inn Humans (Homo sapiens) and Other Animals." *Journal of Comparative Psychology* 117: 325–36.

Itakura, S. 1996. "An Exploratory Study of Gaze-Monitoring in Non-Human Primates." *Japanese Psychological Research* 38: 174–80.

Kemper, Theodore D. 1987. "How Many Emotions Are There? Wedding the Social and the Autonomic Components." *American Journal of Sociology* 93: 263–89.

Lawler, Edward J. 2001. "An Affect Theory of Social Exchange." *American Journal of Sociology* 107: 321–52.

Lawler, Edward J., S. Thye, and J. Yoon. 2009. *Social Commitments in a Depersonalized World*. New York: Russell Sage.

Luhmann, Niklas. 1982. *The Differentiation of Society*. New York: Columbia University Press.

Machalek, R. 1992. "Why Are Large Societies Rare?" *Advances in Human Ecology* 1: 33–64.

Maryanski, Alexandra. 1986. "African Ape Social Structure: A Comparative Analysis." Ph.D. diss., University of California.

1987. "African Ape Social Structure: Is There Strength in Weak Ties?" *Social Networks* 9: 191–215.

1992. "The Last Ancestor: An Ecological-Network Model on the Origins of Human Sociality." *Advances in Human Ecology* 2: 1–32.

1993. "The Elementary Forms of the First Proto-Human Society: An Ecological/ Social Network Approach." *Advances in Human Evolution* 2: 215–41.

1996. "Was Speech an Evolutionary Afterthought?" In *Communicating Meaning: The Evolution and Development of Language*, edited by B. Velichikovsky and D. Rumbaugh. Mahwah, NJ: Erlbaum.

Maryanski, A. and J. H. Turner. 1992. *The Social Cage: Human Nature and The Evolution of Society*. Stanford, CA: Stanford University Press.

Mead, George Herbert. 1934. *Mind, Self, and Society*. Chicago: University of Chicago Press.

Menzel, E. W. 1971. "Communication about the Environment in a Group of Young Chimpanzees." *Folia Primatologica* 15: 220–32.

Mitani, John and David Watts. 2001. "Why Do Chimpanzees Hunt and Share Meet?" *Animal Behaviour* 61: 915–24.

Okamoto, S. M. Tomonaga, K. Ishii, N. Kawai, M. Tanaka, and T. Matsuzawa 2002. "An Infant Chimpanzee (Pan troglodytes) Follows Human Gaze." *Animal Cognition* 5: 107–14.

Osgood, Charles E. (1966). "Dimensionality of the Semantic Space for Communication via Facial Expressions." *Scandanavian Journal of Psychology*, 7, 1–30.

Parsons, T. 1963a. "On the Concept of Political Power." *Proceedings of the American Philosophical Society* 107: 232–262.

1963b. "On the Concept of Influence." *Public Opinion Quarterly* 27: 37–62.

Plutchik, Robert 1980. *Emotion: A Psychoevolutionary Synthesis*. New York: Harper and Row.

Povinelli, D. J. 2000. *Folk Physics for Apes: The Chimpanzee's Theory of How the World Works*. Oxford, UK: Oxford University Press.

Povinelli, D. J. and T. J. Eddy. 1997. "Specificity of Gaze-Following in Young Chimpanzees." *British Journal of Developmental Psychology* 15: 213–22.

Rizzolattti, G. L. Fadiga, L. Fogassi, and V. Gallese. 2002. "From Mirror Neurons to Imitation: Facts and Speculations." Pp. 247–66 in *The Imitative Mind: Devolopment, Evolution and Brain Bases*, edited by W. Prinz and A. N. Meltzoff. Cambridge, UK: Cambridge University Press.

Rumbaugh, Duane, and E. Sue Savage-Rumbaugh. 1990. "Chimpanzees: Competencies for Language and Numbers." In *Comparative Perception*, vol. 2, edited by William Stebbins and Mark Berkley. New York: Wiley and Sons.

Savage-Rumbaugh, Sue, and Roger Lewin. 1994. *Kanzi: The Ape at the Brink of the Human Mind*. New York: John Wiley and Sons, Inc.

Savage-Rumbaugh, S., J. Murphy, J. Seveik, K. Brakke, S. L. Williams, and D. Rumbaugh. 1993. "Language Comprehension in the Ape and Child." *Monographs of the Society for Research in Child Development*, 58. Chicago: University of Chicato Press.

Sherwood, Chet C., R. L. Holloway, K. Semendeferi, and P. R. Hoff. 2005. "Is Prefrontal White Matter Enlargement a Human Evolutionary Specialization?" *Nature Neuroscience* 8: 537–38.

Spencer, Baldwin, and Francis Gillen. 1899. *The Nature Tribes of Central Australia* (New York: Macmillan and Co.).

Stephan, H. 1983. "Evolutionary Trends in Limbic Structures." *Neuroscience and Biobehavioral Review* 7: 367–74.

Stephan, H., and O. J. Andy. 1969. "Quantitative Comparative Neuroanatomy of Primates: An Attempt at Phylogenetic Interpretation." *Annals of the New York Academy of Science* 167: 370–87.

1977. "Quantitative Comparison of the Amygdala in Insectivores and Primates." *Acta Antomica* 98: 130–53.

Subiaul, F. 2007. "The Imitation Faculty in Monkeys: Evaluating Its Features, Distribution, and Evolution." *Journal of Anthropological Science* 85: 35–62.

Tomasello, Michael, B. Hare, and T. Fogleman. 2001. "The Ontegeny of Gaze Folling in Chimpanzees, *Pan troglodytes*, and Rhesus Macaques, *Macaca mulatta*." *Animal Behavior* 61: 335–43.

Tomonaga, Michael. 1999. "Attending to the Others' Attention in Macaques' Joint Attention or Not?" *Primate Research* 15: 425.

Turner, Jonathan H. 2000. *On the Origins of Human Emotions: A Sociological Inquiry into the Evolution of Human Affect.* Stanford, CA: Stanford University Press.

2002. *Face to Face: Toward a Theory of Interpersonal Behavior.* Palo Alto, CA: Stanford University Press.

2007. *Human Emotions: A Sociological Theory.* Oxford, UK: Routledge.

2008. *Human Emotions: A Sociological Theory.* Oxford, UK: Routledge.

2010. *Theoretical Principles of Sociology*, Volume 2 on Microdynamics. New York: Springer.

Turner, Jonathan H. and Alexandra Maryanski. 2012. "The Biology and Neurology of Group Processes." *Advances in Group Processes* 29: 1–37.

2015. "Evolutionary Sociology: A Cross-species Strategy for Discovering Human Nature." Pp. 546–71 in *Handbook of Evolution and Society: Toward an Evolutionary Social Science*, edited by J. H. Turner, R. Machalek, and A. R. Maryanski. Boulder, CO: Paradigm Press.

Turner, Jonathan H., and Jan E. Stets. 2005. *The Sociology of Emotions.* Cambridge, UK: Cambridge University Press.

3

Social Rationality and Weak Solidarity

A Coevolutionary Approach to Social Order

Siegwart Lindenberg

Abstract

Social order is a phenomenon that is constantly produced and reproduced by processes that prominently include evolved capacities of human beings. This view sharply contrasts with a view in which social order is the result of a Leviathan or the result of shared values produced by the socialization of children. From the perspective suggested here, the central question of the microfoundations of social order concerns these evolved capacities, which may jointly be referred to as "social rationality". Part of social rationality and central to this approach is the dynamics of three overarching goals (mind-sets) in which cognitive and motivational processes are combined: hedonic, gain, and normative goals. An important part of the dynamics of these goals is that they are often in conflict with one another and that their salience changes with changing social circumstances. This also affects self-regulatory capacities. On the micro level, social order can be seen as being governed by the interaction of (macro and micro) social circumstances and the way they affect the changing salience of overarching goals.

The problem of order is traditionally connected with Hobbes and, in sociology, with the way Parsons criticized Hobbes's solution. These two authors also inspired this book. However, the traditional discussion of the problem of order in sociology as it is based on this Leviathan (Hobbes) versus normativity (Parsons) dichotomy is highly misleading because it confounds two problems of order: the microfoundational problem of order (what does the human nature look like that enables humans to produce and reproduce social order in their daily relating and behaving when the right conditions are present); and the institutional problem of order (what institutions are necessary to create a sustainable order in society). Of course, the two problems are linked, but neither Hobbes nor Parsons distinguished them. They failed to problematize the microfoundational problem of order by simply positing a human nature that was based on rationality (in the sense of purposefulness) and a set of preferences (either self-interested preferences or socialized norm-conformity preferences). Both Hobbes and Parsons treated the microfoundational problem of order as if we could leave that to God's creation: God had put humans on this earth as fully developed rational egoists or fully developed rational teachers and learners (socializers of newborn babies and socializees). For both authors one can say that their solutions to the institutional problem of order were more interesting and fruitful than their cavalier treatment of human nature, but these solutions were nonetheless hopelessly confined by these simple views of human nature. In this chapter, I will focus on the microfoundational problem.

If one does not opt for the idea that human beings were created fully developed as they appear today and then left to figure out how to solve their problem of order, the obvious alternative is to take an evolutionary approach. However, there too are various possibilities, some of which have not quite left the approaches to human nature of both Hobbes and Parsons behind: they assume that human beings are and have been rational creatures (somehow) and that evolution consists of the development of preferences, so that there are different types of human beings (egoists and social types) or that there are human beings who have both egoistic and social preferences (Gintis et al. 2003). Others are more strongly focused on the evolutionary development of cognitive and motivational abilities (e.g., Gigerenzer 2001). To me, a more useful approach is one that pays close attention to the complexity of human nature as it developed *together* with various forms of order. Among exponents of this latter approach are those that focus on an interplay between genes and culture pointing to processes of coevolution (Richerson and Boyd 2005). Coevolution is clearly highly relevant for the problem of order. However, because genes and culture are two ways in which important information is transmitted, attention in the literature has been strongly focused on transmission rather than on the micro processes that help create order.

Luckily, there are important evolutionary anthropologists who subscribe to some version of the coevolutionary view but also pay closer attention to the evolutionary development of cognitive and motivational abilities that are necessary for jointly realizing social order (Tomasello et al. 2012; Dunbar 2003). My own approach falls within this tradition but it differs in important ways due to its focus on what I call "social rationality" (see Lindenberg 2013). This approach is characterized by two basic propositions that are essential for the way social order is created and recreated at the micro-level: First, phylogenetically, human rationality in the sense of the capacity to have sophisticated representations, to pursue goals (egoistic goals as well as collective goals) and to self-regulate coevolved with human sociality (i.e., the ability to empathize, cooperate and jointly create collective goods with others). Second, ontogenetically, human rationality *and* sociality are heavily dependent on social conditions, both for their development and, importantly, also for their maintenance.

The important question is how this interweaving of rationality and sociality actually works, how it generates social order at the micro-level and what conditions facilitate or threaten this generative capacity.

THE SOCIAL BRAIN AND SOCIAL RATIONALITY

Maybe the most important insight from evolutionary anthropology (especially Dunbar 2003) with regard to the problem of order is that our most advanced brain power (made possible by relatively large frontal lobes) evolved in order to allow individuals to derive adaptive advantages (in terms of one's own survival and reproductions, as well as the reproduction of one's offspring) from living in groups in such a way that the group size could grow and still deliver advantages. In this sense, our brain is a social brain. This is the basis of a long-term development of social rationality.

A larger group can confer more individual adaptive advantages, given that individuals are able to jointly establish and maintain such a group. This ability to jointly form and maintain groups must be seen as having evolved step by step over a long period of time. In humans (together with some other species), social abilities for the very small social circle very likely evolved with pair-bonding (Immerman 2003; Dunbar and Shultz 2007) and what Hrdy (2009) called "cooperative breeding". Pair-bonding in which the fatherhood is acknowledged and the offspring stays in the vicinity (Chapais 2008) is the prototype of cooperation among humans. The origins of this relational development may be motivational (liking, caring for the partner, emotional empathy) but in humans they were over time linked to highly sophisticated cognitive abilities, especially increased working memory together with sophisticated abilities to produce cognitive representations (mental models) and to have shared representations with others; to read facial expressions; to discern trustworthiness of the partner; to regulate one's emotions; and to cognitively "mentalize," that is, understand others' thoughts, desires, beliefs, intentions, and knowledge (Blair 2005; Decety and Svetlova, 2014).

These abilities made it possible to share and help on the basis of discerned needs of others and to cooperate in the smaller group. They importantly include an evolved ability for the use of language and two coordinated adult-child linking mechanisms, both of which partially include language ability: (a) the child's ability to signal its needs and elicit empathic reactions and the corresponding responsiveness of adults to this elicitation (Hrdy 2009); (b) the ability to learn from adults not just by imitation and pattern recognition but also by being explicitly instructed, with the adult's corresponding ability to teach (Gopnik, Meltzoff, and Kuhl 1999; Tomasello 2008). The skills and abilities that are necessary for parent-child relations and longer-term parenting partner relationships are very likely the basis for skills and abilities that are necessary for entering and maintaining other kinds of relationships (Dunbar and Shultz 2007).

The Crucial Step: Group-Mindedness

The most important aspect of the development of these combined cognitive and motivational abilities is that it is the basis for the possibly most crucial step: the ability to bond emotionally and cognitively with the group as a whole, to be able to take the perspective of the group and act as a member of the group (Lindenberg and Foss 2011). The importance of this ability cannot easily be overestimated. There are group advantages that simply derive from numbers (such as schooling in fish), but, for humans, most advantages of living in larger groups derive from collective goods produced by the group. Without a mode in which humans are oriented toward group goals, these collective goods would only be produced sporadically, if at all. This mode is the basis for the human ability to function in groups of very different sizes and very different goals. Humans can act as members of small groups but also as members of large nations, and even feel embedded in a subgroup as part of a large group. For humans, this embedding of subgroups and flexible change of membership is seemingly much more developed than for any other species (Aureli et al. 2008). This group-mindedness is also the basis for most sociologically important collective phenomena, such as collective action, ingroup-outgroup dynamics, organizations, the ability of collectives to govern with or be governed by social norms and legitimate rules, and so on.

Group-orientation is thus also crucially important for the generation of social order at the micro-level, as we will discuss in more detail later on. The importance of this ability has long been recognized in sociology and social psychology. It is at the heart of role theory, minimal group and entativity theories, social identity theory, self-categorization theory, expectation state theory, and many theories of norm formation and norm conformity. Recently, its enormous evolutionary importance has been emphasized again by Tomasello et al. (2012). However, what is missing so far in all these notions of human group-mindedness is a theory that accounts for the fact that individuals flexibly move in and out of group-mindedness, that there are important mechanisms that make this flexibility possible. From an evolutionary point of view, the group is there mainly for the adaptive advantage of the individual, and not the other way around. If individuals were stuck in the mode of group-mindedness, they would not have much chance to get their genes into the gene pool. Other, less group-minded, individuals would likely displace the highly group-minded creatures. In other words, the evolution of group-mindedness must have gone along with the evolution of mechanisms that let individuals flexibility shift between self-directed and group-directed modes. How should we account for this? Saying that human nature is "double," that everybody is both selfish and group-minded, will not suffice because it does not tell us anything about the conditions under which the modes shift. A theory that aims at explaining the generative (i.e., micro-level) mechanisms of social order must be able to account for this shifting form of flexibility. In the following, I will discuss first the basics of a theory that can account for flexible shifts (goal-framing theory) and then apply it to our central question: the microfoundations of social order.

GOAL-FRAMING THEORY

The central thesis of this chapter is that at the heart of the microfoundations of social order lies the goal-based architecture of the human mind. Goals are mental constructs that combine motivational and cognitive processes that guide organisms to select and perform activities that are instrumental to obtaining them. This ability to have and pursue goals is not unique to humans. However, for humans, the combined motivational and cognitive processes that are involved in goal pursuit are so advanced that they can hardly be compared to that of any other species. These processes involve highly developed ways of mentally representing objects, symbols, relations, and desired states together with a large working memory capacity. Importantly, representations are differentially accessible and are only influential to the degree they are activated at a given moment (Förster, Liberman, and Higgins 2005). Built on these representational capacities (which are not necessarily conscious) humans have advanced goal-related capacities to monitor the degree to which a goal that is presently activated has been realized; to detect errors; and to react to this information in such a way that, when the goal is realized, one turns to another goal, or, when progress is not satisfying, to take action for improvement; to respond emotionally to success and failure in goal-pursuit and to quickly determine the direction of action (approach or avoidance); and to inhibit incompatible goals (see Carver and Scheier 1998).

This advanced human capacity to pursue goals is itself crucially enhanced by yet another advance: the development of overarching goals (or "mind-sets"). Overarching goals operate like goals but, in addition, they represent the contextual guidance for the selection and execution of concrete lower-level goals. In other words, concrete goals are embedded in overarching goals. For example, the concrete goal to help a fellow passenger in distress is embedded in the overarching goal "to act appropriately."

Overarching goals can "capture" the entire mind and its processes and they are supported by hormonal and emotional processes, but ultimately they are steered by the social environment. They can turn an individual into a norm-guided person at one moment and into a self-centered egoist at the next. For example, Liberman, Samuels, and Ross (2004) found that just labeling a social dilemma game as 'Community Game' (activating a normative orientation) versus labeling it as 'Wall Street Game' (activating a gain and competition-related orientation) made a big difference in the relative frequency of cooperative responses (66% versus 31%). These changing mind-sets create the situational flexibility of human beings which, in turn, is crucial for social order at the micro-level. Goal-framing theory (Lindenberg and Steg 2007; Lindenberg 2013) has elaborated the workings of overarching goals. In the following, I will present the basic outline of this theory.

Three Overarching Goals (Mind-Sets)

Overarching goals are chronically activated to varying degrees and in this sense human motivation is mostly "mixed." However, in most situations, one overarching goal (called the "goal-frame") is more strongly activated than the others, thereby inhibiting the other overarching goals to various degrees. It "frames" the entire situation, largely governing what we attend to; what information we are sensitive to; what we expect others to do; what we like and dislike; and what criteria we use for success of failure of goal achievement. There is a strong cognitive side to goal-frames as they also activate mental models about roles, relationships, and group situations, including chunks of causal knowledge concerning these situations. Conversely, goal-frames can also be activated by mental models. For example, the Wall Street versus Community game experiment just mentioned showed that by activating certain mental models (concerning competition or cooperation), the label itself also activated a different mind-set. Being combinations of motivational and cognitive processes, goal-frames also have a strong affective side. They are linked to characteristic emotions.

What we need to answer first of all for the microfoundations of social order is: What different overarching goals are there? How are they related to each other? What activates a particular goal-frame and what stabilizes or destabilizes it?

The Hedonic Goal. From an evolutionary point of view, it makes sense that the most basic overarching goal is related to the satisfaction of fundamental needs, both physical and social. Needs are distinguished from mere "wants" by the fact that for needs deprivation leads to pathological states (Baumeister and Leary 1995). For example, deprivation in physical needs (such as the need to eat) and in social needs (such as the need for social acceptance) lead to states that endanger one's functioning (Lindenberg 2013). Need deprivation makes itself known to the individual by negative feelings (e.g., feeling hungry) and need satisfaction does this by the positive feelings associated with satisfaction (such as enjoyment). Some of these feelings are emotions like joy and fear. In short, the most basic overarching goal is linked to focusing on improving/maintaining the way one feels and it is called *hedonic* goal. The more salient the hedonic goal, the less considerations of context (such as: decorum, or health, ownership, future consequences) play role. Because this goal is one step removed from needs themselves (because the focus is on the way one feels), the hedonic goal may be activated also in situations where needs are not directly involved but where feelings (say aroused by hearing somebody cry) or objects that are associated with feelings (such as a nice piece of cake) are made salient.

When the hedonic goal is the most salient overarching goal (i.e., when it is the goal-frame), one is highly sensitive to information in the environment about opportunities to improve the way one feels (say, easily detecting cues concerning possibilities for enjoyment) and about threats to the way one feels (say, easily detecting required effort levels for certain activities). Conversely, sensitivity regarding aspects of other overarching goals (such as costs or appropriateness) is diminished. The *social* situations that make people feel highly uncomfortable are quite specific to this overarching goal: situations in which people are uncertain about what would make them feel better and situations in which others lower the social need satisfaction (e.g., being unfriendly or disrespectful).

For social rationality, the most important development is that next to the hedonic goal, two other overarching goals evolved, very likely on the basis of the highly developed human ability to put oneself into the shoes of others: a *group-oriented* overarching goal (called a *normative* goals) and a *personal* gain-oriented overarching goal (called *gain* goal). Via these two "new" overarching goals and their dynamic interrelationships, the uniquely human combination of rationality and sociality became possible.

The Normative Goal. The individual adaptive advantages from living in larger groups (in terms of profiting from common gathering, hunting, defense, etc.) only materialize if the group can offer collective goods. In turn, the ability of groups to do that depends on the ability of group members to be in a state in which they are willing to contribute to these collective goods. The increased working memory that allows considerable tracking ability of who did what also allowed reputation and reciprocity effects of mutuality. This is likely to have contributed to the willingness not to free ride. However, keeping free riding at bay does not yet explain the human ability to jointly produce local order and collective goods. For example, in a hunting party, there is a complicated interplay of understanding the joint goal and the way the different abilities (in terms of tracking, shooting, carrying, etc.) mesh and contribute to the joint goal (see Liebenberg 1990). It requires a collective orientation and an understanding of what it takes to act as a member of a group. This capacity probably evolved on the basis of combining the empathic capacities with the advanced representational capacities that (a) allowed humans to cognitively represent the group as a social whole and (b) to see themselves as part of this group. The overarching goal that belongs to this state pertains to the realization of group goals, to do what is socially expected, what is appropriate. Because social norms and legitimate rules codify group goals, this overarching goal is called *normative* goal.

Even though the positive effects for the group of following a norm may lie in the future, the feeling of obligation created by a salient normative goal is "here and now," making future-related discounting effects unlikely. When the normative goal is the most salient overarching goal, one is highly sensitive to information about the expectation of others, about what the norms and legitimate rules are. Sensitivity to information that pertains to aspects of other overarching goals (such as costs or effort of a particular action) is diminished; the more so, the more strongly the normative goal is activated. In a normative goal-frame, people cooperate even if they do not consider the personal consequences of their prosocial action (Burton-Chellew and West 2013). The particular signature of the normative goal is enhanced by the fact that it is linked to social emotions, such as guilt, shame, and gratitude (Fessler and Haley 2003). The social situations that make people feel highly uncomfortable are quite specific to the normative goal: situations in which people are uncertain about what the norms are or which norms apply (such as uncertainty about one's relationship with one's interaction partner).

The Gain Goal. Ironically, it is very likely that the ability that led to the most social (the normative) goal is also the basis for the most egoistic goal: the *gain* goal that is focused on increasing/maintaining one's resources (today mainly money or social influence). It is made possible by the ability to put oneself into the shoes of one's own future self. In turn, this ability too evolved very likely by combining advanced representational capacities (including counterfactual thinking) with the ability to put oneself into the shoes of others. It is the basis for planning, investing, and quite generally for resource-oriented behavior. Its longer-term orientation makes people highly sensitive to changes in resources (such as possible losses, out of pocket costs, and opportunities for gain).

Cheating and exploiting others is also made possible on the basis of this sensitivity combined with the ability to take the perspective of the other (Epley, Caruso, and Bazerman, 2006). For this very reason, the social brain has also been called "the Machiavellian brain" (Barrett and Henzi 2005). Sensitivity to information that pertains to aspects of other overarching goals (such as information on how one's feelings or one's sense of obligation may be affected) is diminished; the more so, the more strongly the gain goal is activated. The particular signature of the gain goal is enhanced by the fact that it is linked to resource-related emotions, such as greed and envy. The social situations that make people feel highly uncomfortable are also quite specific to this overarching goal: situations in which they are truly uncertain about what the costs and benefits are.

OVERARCHING GOALS AND SOCIAL ORDER

Social order at the micro-level is solidly based on the dynamics of goal-frames. Situations contain certain affordances and constraints that could influence behavior. But in most situations, there are multiple affordances and constraints and in a given situation it depends to a large extent on the goal-frame (and the associated mental models that are activated in this situation) which affordances and constraints will actually become influential.

This power of goal-frames to influence what aspects of the situation are important and to guide behavior in a given situation is thus thoroughly intertwined with situational factors. Situations can activate certain goal-frames that, in turn, guide perceptions and behavior. Yet, these activation effects are far from random. Goal-frames are differentially linked to social relationships, to group membership and intergroup relations. Their activation is also highly dependent on cues in a given situation, and self-regulation consists to a large degree in anticipating these effects and choosing environments accordingly (Lindenberg 2013). In turn, this self-regulatory capacity varies among people, affecting the robustness and vulnerability of social order at the micro level. In the following, these linkages of goal-framing to social order will be looked at in some more detail.

The Dynamic Interdependence of Overarching Goals

For the understanding of overarching goals and their impact on social order, it is important to consider their interrelationships first. To begin with, the three overarching goals are a priorly not equally strong. From an evolutionary point of view, it is easy to see why this would be so. The hedonic goal caters to fundamental needs and is a priorly the strongest. Since the group is there for the individual and not the other way around, the normative goal, catering to the group, is a priorly the weakest. This means that the normative goal must have strong supports (mostly social and institutional), in order to trump the hedonic goal. The gain goal, catering to resources for the individual, is a priorly weaker than the hedonic goal but stronger than the normative goal. The relative strength of both the gain and the normative goal is thus strongly dependent on the social and institutional environment. For example for most economists, the gain goal is the "natural state" of individuals. However, as Weber (1961) has shown, it takes considerable institutional development to bring the gain goal to prominence in society.

Next, it is important that all three overarching goals are chronically activated to some degree, with one of them in the cognitive foreground (the goal-frame) and the other two in the cognitive background. In principle, the three goals are antagonistic in the sense that they vie for the foreground position and inhibit the other two if they succeed to be in that position. But total inhibition is highly unlikely. This means that the background goals will still exert some dynamic influence on behavior. For example, if (in a normative goal-frame) following norms (say helping) costs money, then these costs are much less decisive than in a gain goal, but they will have some kind of influence. The higher the costs, the stronger the gain goal in the background becomes and the more gain aspects (such as guarding expenses when helping others) will become prominent (Lindenberg and Frey 1993). Eventually, the costs can get so high that the gain goal displaces the normative goal, pushing it into the background. The same would happen with the hedonic goal if, for example, following the helping norm does not require monetary expenses but effort (such as helping a friend move book cases).

Finally, even though the three overarching goals are antagonistic, certain aspects of each goal in the background may actually serve to support the goal in the foreground. For example, when one is in a normative goal-frame, one may experience a warm glow (a hedonic aspects) in the background (Andreoni 1990). This good feeling about doing what is right (possibly enhanced by praise) then strengthens the normative goal and cushions the effect of antagonistic aspects in the background (such as sensitivity to resource loss or effort). A similar supportive effect could be achieved by increasing one's status or gaining other resources by following norms. Especially for the normative goal (which needs much support in order not to be displaced by one of the other two goals) this possibility of hedonic or gain support from the background is crucial.

A stable prominent position of the normative goal in a group without hedonic and/or gain supports is highly unlikely. But then, the calibration is essential: when people get a symbolic reward for following norms, it will support the normative goal-frame. But if the rewards cease to be symbolic (such as paying your child for mowing the lawn, see Lepper and Greene 1978) then the normative goal-frame may be "crowded out" by a gain goal-frame. The same holds for negative sanctions. If they are seen as supporting a common goal, they will support the normative goal-frame. If, however, they are seen as a "price" for deviating, they will weaken the normative goal-frame and strengthen the gain goal (Gneezy and Rusticini 2000).

In sum, goal-frames can be seen as dynamic constellations of overarching goals, one of which is dominant, with the other two being antagonistic to various degrees, and with certain aspects of these background goals being supportive to various degrees. This is especially relevant for the normative goal-frame because it is both crucial for the creation and maintenance of social order at the micro-level and a priorily the weakest (thus heavily in need of more or less constant support to retain its position in the foreground). Internalization of norms alone by no means guarantees such a position.

Relationships, Groups, and Overarching Goals

Social order at the micro-level is largely structured by social relationships. In turn, social relationships are structured by characteristic profiles of overarching goals. True to the evolutionary importance of "joint production," the most important generator of relationships are interdependencies, especially with regard to jointly realizing collective goals in groups or dyads (Lindenberg 1997). In this sense, social structure directly influences social order at the micro level.

There are relationships that are governed primarily by a hedonic goal-frame, with liking/disliking being the central hedonic aspect. Liking itself triggers a heightened tendency to consider the well-being of the liked other (Güroğlu et al. 2007; Lawler, Thye, and Yoon 2008). However, liking relationships are also affected to various degrees by one's normative and gain goals in the background (Dijkstra, Kretschmer, Lindenberg, and Veenstra 2014). There is a pragmatic side to liking. In general, one can say that we like others who are furthering our goal pursuits and dislike others who block our goal pursuits (Ferguson and Bargh 2004). Also, perspective taking itself, being so essential to group life, is not just an ability but also subject to motivational processes (Singer et al. 2006). Thus, liking and normative dynamics in relationships are often intertwined.

Relationships, in turn, are embedded in group contexts. In evolutionary terms, humans have evolved to function in so-called fusion/fission groups (Aureli et al. 2008). For example, at one moment one is member of a hunting party, at another moment one is in a larger group sharing food, and in yet another moment, one may take part in common rituals of a yet larger group, which, in turn, may later split up again into smaller groups for sleeping. Thus, relationships are embedded in groups and, in turn, smaller groups are embedded in more encompassing groups.

The importance of this fusion/fission inheritance is that the normative goal is flexibly adjusted to different (in)group contexts and relationship within these contexts. It covers a general and more or less universal set of social norms that pertain to relationships with all members of ingroups, and a set that is specific to a particular ingroup. Relations with the (members of) outgroups are generally not covered by the normative goal but by the hedonic goal (in the extreme: hate, derision, disdain) or the gain goal (in the extreme: exploitation, expropriation, elimination). This combination of a general and a specific set of norms allows humans not just to flexibly move in an out of embedded groups, but also to function in groups of various sizes without losing normative guidance. The set of general norms (also called "solidarity norms," Lindenberg 2014), pertain to the group's ability to produce collective goods and, together with the dynamics of liking, forms the basic foundation for generating social order at the micro level.

The General Set of Social Norms. The social brain has evolved bit by bit in such a way that this set of norms will emerge virtually in every group with common goals (see Lindenberg 2014 for additional detail). It is an open question, whether the norms themselves are hardwired or whether certain hardwired processes (such as liking and recognizing common goals, others' needs, and externalities) lead to spontaneous emergence of norms and sensitivity to learning by instruction.

The most basic norm in the general set pertains to *sharing* with others. This may have evolved step by step from tolerated theft to deliberate sharing. Sharing equalizes ingroup differences in ability and neediness and it is the basis for a division of labor with the group. Related to sharing is *helping* others in need which greatly enhances the group members' ability to provide collective goods. Children as young as eighteen months already recognize situations in which help is needed and are spontaneously willing to help (Warneken and

Tomasello 2009). The norms to *cooperate* in the joint realization of group goals by pulling one's weight and not free ride is an extension of the helping norm to the group level.

There are additional norms in the general set that are likely to have evolved later in response to the increased ability to put oneself into the shoes of others. As may be recalled, this ability also allowed for the development of the gain goal and the capacity to deceive others (Epley et al. 2006). This "dark side" of perspective taking, made *trustworthiness* (such as keeping one's promise) an important aspect of living in groups, codified in a social norm and coupled to the additional social norm to *understand and make oneself understood by others* (Gigerenzer 2001). Finally, as group life becomes more complex, positive and negative externalities are potentially increasing in number and intensity. Thus, *considerateness* (i.e., being mindful of externalities) grew in importance and was codified in a social norm that covers anticipating especially negative externalities and limiting doing harm to others. Prominently, it also covers apologizing when things inadvertently go wrong.

SOCIAL ORDER IN COMPLEX SOCIETIES: THE IMPORTANCE OF WEAK SOLIDARITY

Social order on the micro level is very much dependent on circumstances that activate the normative goal and particularly the set of general social norms. Strongly solidary groups are characterized by high normative activation, clear group boundaries, and more or less hostile intergroup relations. This facilitates social order but also highly restricts its range. Yet, the fact that we are always dealing with a particular constellation of foreground and background goals creates the flexibility for a social process the importance of which for social order cannot be overrated: weak solidarity (Lindenberg 1998). By bridging groups it stretches the range of the normative goal-frame, blurs the ingroup/outgroup divisions and allows sustainable exchange relationships (Lindenberg 2006).

Weak solidarity is brought about by a dynamic interdependence of the normative and the gain goal. In weak solidarity relationships, the gain goal is relatively strong but the normative goal limits its influence. Compared to strong solidarity, the social norms are adjusted with regard to gain related aspects: (a) the individual interests weigh more heavily; (b) the potential legitimate maximum sacrifice for conforming to social norms is relatively low; and (c) the sharing norm is equity rather than equality. When the pursuit of gain threatens conformity to the weak solidarity norms, the normative goal becomes relatively more salient, and when conforming to weak solidarity norms threatens to become too costly, the gain goal becomes relatively more salient.

Weak solidarity relations make it possible that social order is widely extended across groups. However, for this to happen, forces on the micro level that pull in the direction of strong solidarity must be relatively weak. For example, the pull of tribal or familial solidarity or the perceived threat to ingroup identities can be so strong that weak solidarity cannot be sustained. Thus, as Max Weber had also observed, where strong solidarity forces are at work, they have to be "tamed" before weak solidarity can be established (Weber 1961). For the weakening of strong solidarity claims, strong macro influences are necessary, most likely from the state or religious organizations, to credibly eliminate intergroup threats and create instruments of trust (in terms of loyalties, justice, media of exchange, etc.). Thus, even though weak solidarity is created and recreated at the micro level, it needs to be embedded in supportive macro structures to be maintained.

Normative Uncertainty and the Importance of Education

As Durkheim (1893/1964) had already observed, when social groups become larger and more complex and weak solidarity becomes more prevalent, norms become more abstract in order to cover more varied groups and circumstances. In addition, there will be more contexts in which the gain goal is relatively strong and the reach of normative behavior is not clearly established. This creates normative uncertainty. First, it becomes less clear (compared to less complex groups) when norms apply and when one is free to pursue one's hedonic or gain goals. For example, when one passes an injured person on the street, should one stop to help? Is he really needy and are there not other people or authorities that should help? Or how honest should I be with a business partner when negotiating a deal? Second, when norms and legitimate rules are more abstract, their exact meaning is often not clear. For example, if there is a (legitimate) rule that I should be on time for work, does that mean that I have to be there on the dot or is ten minutes late also okay? Third, many situations are not covered by norms and rules but by conventions and habits (what Cialdini calls "descriptive norms," see Cialdini et al. 1990) and people frequently encounter contexts for which they don't know what these conventions and habits are.

Given these developments that are due to increasing complexity, there are important changes in the way norms work. Because of the abstractness of norms, individual intelligent effort is needed to apply the norms in a given situation. Even the general social norms become less straightforward with increasing complexity of society. In many cases it is not at all clear what I have to do to be cooperative or considerate. In other words, people have to apply such norms using their head rather than simply follow them. This is why they have been called "smart norms" (Lindenberg 2008). The intelligent effort feeds on knowledge and savviness which makes norm conformity ever more dependent on education.

The uncertainty about norms and their range also increases the pressure for functional legitimacy. For example, why should I be at work on the dot? What does it matter if I am five minutes late? This increased pressure for functional legitimation has serious consequences for what is meant by authority

(Lindenberg 1993). Rules are no longer covered by the normative goal just because somebody "in authority" says so. Rules must make sense to elicit some feeling of obligation and this also holds for norms and for the auxiliary rules that govern the applicability of social norms. For example, why should I help somebody who was warned not to drive while drunk and did it anyway? For answering this question, would it matter what I knew about differences in self-regulatory ability? The need for functional legitimation also introduces an educational aspect into norm conformity. The better educated or savvy, the easier one can judge the functional significance of a rule or norm. The importance of education reinforces the need for macro embedding of weak solidarity in complex societies.

Cue Sensitivity and the Local Context

Uncertainty about norms and their range also boosts the importance of the local level by increasing the importance of social influence (especially imitation and cross-norm effects). The underlying mechanism is anchored in the fact that overarching goals need to be activated in order to influence behavior. As described earlier, this activation is sensitive to cues about the behavior of others; the more so, the less certain or clear the norms are. This opens the doors wide to social influence processes, including imitation (Cialdini et al. 1990).

But probably the most important cue effects for social order at the micro level are those that affect the relative strength of the overarching goals. They bring about so-called cross-norm effects: Observing cues of (dis)respect for norm A strengthens (or weakens) the normative goal in the observer and thereby also increases the likelihood that the observer will follow (or not follow) norm B. In recent times, we have gathered a considerable amount of evidence on such "cross-norm" effects. For example, observing graffiti (disrespect for norm A) increases the likelihood that people will steal (Keizer, Lindenberg, and Steg 2008). Conversely, observing a resident clean his sidewalk in front of his house (respect for norm A), increases the likelihood that the passerby will subsequently help somebody else (respect for norm B) (Keizer, Lindenberg, and Steg 2013).

Both imitation and cross-norm effects make local social contexts important for social order, even if one does not interact with the people who create the social context. Cross-norm effects are of particular importance because they make (dis)respect for norms spread through a social system (such as neighborhoods, organizations, and social groups).

Self-regulation

Context, both macro and local, have a big impact on behavior via their influence of the relative strength of overarching goals but this does not mean that humans passively undergo this influence. Humans are sophisticated self-regulators and the choice of contexts is an important instrument in the self-regulatory toolkit.

Self-regulation involves the conscious and unconscious pursuit of goal states (including comparison of present and desired states and error detection). It is not one particular capacity but a number of mechanisms with different degrees of voluntary control. To understand how this works, it is useful to distinguish roughly between lower and higher order self-regulatory mechanisms (see Lindenberg 2013 for more detail). The lower order consists of processes that have to do with bodily functions and fundamental needs, including regulation by hormones (such as oxytocin). The hedonic goal is closely (but not exclusively) tied to lower-order self-regulatory mechanisms. Higher order mechanism are concerned with the balance between lower order mechanisms, resource-oriented behavior and norm-oriented behavior. They are thus closely tied to the gain and the normative goals. For example inhibition of the hedonic goal ("temptation") by either the gain or normative goal is often called "self-control" (for example Inzlicht, Schmeichel, and Macrae 2014). Self-control thus necessitates that the supports of the gain or normative goals are strong enough to be able to inhibit the apriorily stronger hedonic goal. An important source of support for the normative goal are significant others who represent social norms, but not everybody has such significant others (Lindenberg 2013).

Self-regulation is not just self-control but includes also emotion regulation (in favor of situationally appropriate emotions) and, importantly, anticipation of the effect of contexts on the salience of a particular overarching goals. For example, one might (not) go to a party because one anticipates a strong hedonic shift once one is there. This ability to anticipate contextual influences on overarching goals is the basis for battling the automaticity of the context effects on the overarching goals. However, people are not equally able to anticipate context effects and also not equally able to choose their social context, even if they anticipate these effects. For example, in many places, inner city youths may be virtually unable to escape their social context, even if they would like to. Lower positions in organizations are also often highly restricted in the choice of contexts. Poverty (especially when accompanied with low education) is likely to have a similarly restricting effect. This restrictive effect on self-regulation may underlie the finding that a low sense of control reliably correlates with worse health (Marmot 2006).

Anticipation of context effects may also have a motivational component, such that whatever weakens the sense of self also weakens the motivation to anticipate future consequences. Interventions that strengthen the sense of self (say through self-affirmation) can thus also strengthen self-regulatory capacity (Lindenberg 2013, Cohen et al 2009).

Social factors that strengthen the ability to deal with smart norms (such as education) and self-regulatory capacity (such as significant others, context choice, and self-affirmation) make the production and maintenance of social order at the micro level more stable and less dependent on cue effects (such as observed (dis)respect for norms). They thus contribute importantly to the sustainability of social order at that level.

SUMMARY AND CONCLUSION

Human beings have not been dropped on this earth fully developed as they are today and left to figure out how they can create social order. The "social rationality" approach taken here proceeds from the proposition that human beings evolved together with the abilities to create and maintain social order (at any level). More specifically, human rationality in the sense of the capacity to pursue personal and collective goals and to self-regulate co-evolved with human sociality (i.e. the ability to empathize, cooperate and create collective goods). But ontogenetically, both human rationality and sociality are heavily dependent on social conditions both for their development and for their maintenance. The claim is thus that if we want to get a handle on the generation and maintenance of social order at the micro level, we have to know how this dependence of the abilities to create social order on social conditions works. This is what this chapter is about.

The central mechanism that governs both human rationality and sociality lies in the evolution of three overarching goals (mind-sets) and their dynamic interrelations. If it gets strong enough, an overarching goal can "frame" a situation, i.e. govern what we pay attention to and ignore, what information we are sensitive to, what we like and dislike, expect from others, and call success or failure. There are three such overarching goals: the hedonic goal (related to the satisfaction of fundamental needs, both physical and social and focused on improving the way one feels); the normative goal (related to the realization of group goals and focused on what is socially expected and appropriate); and the gain goal (related to farsighted goal pursuit, focused on the improvement of one's resources). The latter two overarching goals evolved on the basis of the ability to put oneself into the shoes of others, extended to the group as a whole, and to one's own future self, respectively.

At any given moment, all three overarching goals are activated to some degree, but, depending on which goal is presently the strongest (i.e. the goal-frame), one will behave quite differently. Apriorily, the hedonic goal is the strongest and the normative goal the weakest, with the gain goal in between. This means that both the normative and the gain goal need much social and institutional support in order to be situationally stronger than the hedonic goal. Social order at the micro level is dependent on both macro forces and local influences that affect the relative strength of the overarching goals. The big difference with Hobbes' approach is that Hobbes dealt with the gain goal as if it were fixed and the only overarching goal. The big difference with Parsons' approach is that he dealt with the normative goal as if socialization could make it permanently stronger than other overarching goals.

The normative goal, covering both general social norms ("solidarity norms") and group specific norms, is arguably the most important for social order, aided by aspects of the hedonic goal (liking), but it is highly precarious. Given the right support for the normative goal, the set of solidarity norms, and liking jointly form the basis for the creation of social order at the local level.

An important point of the argument is that in modern, complex societies, social order basically centers around the creation and maintenance of "weak solidarity." Tight groups create the strongest support for the normative goal and strong solidarity in groups is highly functional for local social order but it also creates hostile intergroup relations. In weak solidarity the gain goal and the normative goal keep each other in check. This allows productive intergroup relations but it also necessitates a strong macro influence that suppresses the forces that pull in the direction of strong solidarity (such as tribalism, familism, cronyism, sectarianism, chauvinism, etc.). In such societies local (weakly solidary) order could not exist without a strong institutional support. This is an ironic twist of both Hobbes's Leviathan and Parsons' normativity approach.

Next to the macro dependence of social order at the local level, there are developments that simultaneously increase the power of local contexts by the fact that greater complexity also implies greater normative uncertainty. In turn, the greater the normative uncertainty, the more norm conformity depends on intelligent effort (and thus education) and on the influence of local social cues. For example, cues that some people did not respect a particular norm (such the norm against graffiti), can weaken the relative strength of the normative goal and lead to other, possibly completely unrelated, kinds of deviance, including stealing.

Finally, human self-regulatory capacity helps in dealing with normative uncertainty and can make people being less influenced by social cues they happen to encounter. But this capacity is itself related to the relative strengths of overarching goals and thus depends itself on social factors (such as the link to norm-oriented significant others, the ability to change social contexts, and the degree of self-affirmation) which are luckily not necessarily the same as the conditions for weak solidarity.

In conclusion, understanding conditions that govern social order at the micro level necessitates an understanding of the evolved goal-related human capacities and proclivities concerning the production and maintenance of social order as well as the sensitivity of these capacities and proclivities to social and institutional influences.

REFERENCES

Andreoni, James 1990. "Impure Altruism and Donations to Public Goods: A Theory of Warm-Glow Giving." *The Economic Journal* 100: 464–477.
Aureli, Filippo et al. 2008. "Fission-Fusion Dynamics." *Current Anthropology* 49: 627–654.

Barrett, Louise, Peter Henzi and Robin Dunbar 2005. "The Social Nature of Primate Cognition." *Proceedings of the Royal Society Biological Sciences* 272: 1865–1875.

Baumeister, Roy. F. and Mark R. Leary 1995. "The Need to Belong: Desire for Interpersonal Attachments as a Fundamental Human Motivation." *Psychological Bulletin* 117: 497–529.

Blair, James 2005. "Responding to the Emotions of Others: Dissociating Forms of Empathy through the Study of Typical and Psychiatric Populations." *Consciousness and Cognition* 14: 698–718.

Burton-Chellew, Maxwell N. and Stuart A. West 2013. "Prosocial Preferences Do Not Explain Human Cooperation in Public-Goods Games." *PNAS* 110: 216–221.

Carver, Charles S. and Michael F. Scheier 1998. *On the Self-regulation of Behavior.* Cambridge: Cambridge University Press.

Chapais, Bernard 2008 *Primeval Kinship: How Pair Bonding Gave Birth to Human Society.* Harvard University Press, Cambridge, MA.

Cialdini, Robert B., Raymond R. Reno, and Carl A. Kallgren 1990. "A Focus Theory of Normative Conduct: Recycling the Concept of Norms to Reduce Littering in Public Places." *Journal of Personality and Social Psychology* 58: 1015–1026.

Cohen, Geoffrey L., Julio Garcia, Valerie Purdie-Vaughns, Nancy Apfel, Patricia Brzustoski 2009. "Recursive Processes in Self-Affirmation: Intervening to Close the Minority Achievement Gap." *Science* 324: 400–403.

Decety, Jean and Margarita Svetlova 2014. "Putting Together Phylogenetic and Onto-genetic Perspectives on Empathy." *Developmental Cognitive Neuroscience* 2: 1–24.

Dijkstra, Jan Kornelis, Tina Kretschmer, Siegwart Lindenberg, and Rene Veenstra 2014. "Hedonic, Instrumental, and Normative Motives: Differentiating Patterns for Popular, Accepted, and Rejected Adolescents." *The Journal of Early Adolescence* published online DOI:0.1177/0272431614535092

Dunbar, R.I.M. 2003. "The Social Brain: Mind, Language, and Society in Evolutionary Perspective." *Annual Review of Psychology* 32: 163–181.

Dunbar, R.I.M. and Susanne Shultz 2007. "Evolution in the Social Brain." *Science* 317: 1344–1347.

Durkheim, Emile 1964. *The Division of Labor in Society.* New York: Free Press originally 1893.

Epley, Nicholas, Eugene M. Caruso and Max H. Bazerman 2006. "When Perspective Taking Increases Taking: Reactive Egoism in Social Interaction." *Journal of Personality and Social Psychology* 915: 872–889.

Ferguson, Melissa J. and John A. Bargh 2004. "Liking Is for Doing: The Effects of Goal Pursuit on Automatic Evaluation." *Journal of Personality and Social Psychology* 8: 557–572.

Fessler, Daniel and Kevin Haley 2003. "The Strategy of Affect: Emotions in Human Cooperation." Pp. 7–36 in *Genetic and Cultural Evolution of Cooperation,* edited by P. Hammerstein, ed. Dahlem Workshop Report. Cambridge, MA: MIT Press.

Förster, Jens, Nira Liberman, and E. Tory Higgins 2005. "Accessibility from Active and Fulfilled Goals." *Journal of Experimental Social Psychology* 41: 220–239.

Frey, Bruno S. and Reto Jegen 2001. "Motivation Crowding Theory: A Survey of Empirical Evidence." *Journal of Economic Surveys* 15: 589–611.

Gigerenzer, Gerd 2001. "The adaptive toolbox." Pp. 31–50 in *Bounded Rationality. The Adaptive Toolbox,* edited by Gerd Gigerenzer and Reinhard Selten. Cambridge, MA: MIT Press.

Gintis, Herbert, Samuel Bowles, Robert Boyd, and Ernst Fehr 2003. "Explaining Altruistic Behavior in Humans." *Evolution and Human Behavior* 24: 153–172.

Gneezy, U., and A. Rustichini 2000. "A Fine Is a Price." *Journal of Legal Studies*, XXIX, 1–18.

Gopnik, Alison, Andrew N. Meltzoff and Patricia K. Kuhl. 1999. *The Scientist in the Crib: Minds, Brains, and How Children Learn.* New York: William Morrow and Company.

Güroğlu, Berna, Gerbert J.T. Haselager, Cornelis F.M. van Lieshout, Atsuko Takashima, Mark Rijpkema, and Guillén Fernández 2007. "Why Are Friends Special? Implementing a Social Interaction Simulation Task to Probe the Neural Correlates of Friendship." *NeuroImage* 39: 903–910.

Hrdy, Sarah Blaffer 2009. *Mothers and Others: The Evolutionary Origins of Mutual Understanding.* Cambridge, MA: Harvard University Press.

Immerman, Ronald S. 2003. "Perspectives on Human Attachment Pair Bonding: Eve's Unique Legacy of a Canine Analogue." *Evolutionary Psychology* 1: 138–154.

Inzlicht, Michael, Brandon J. Schmeichel, and C. Neil Macrae 2014. "Why Self-control Seems but May Not Be Limited." *Trends in Cognitive Sciences* 18: 27–133.

Keizer, Kees, Siegwart Lindenberg, and Linda Steg. 2008. "The Spreading of Disorder." *Science*, 322: 1681–1685.

　　2013. "The Importance of Demonstratively Restoring Order." *PLoS ONE* 86:e65137. doi:10.1371/journal.pone.0065137

Lawler, Edward J., Shane R. Thye, and Jeongkoo Yoon 2008. "Social Exchange and Micro Social Order." *American Sociological Review* 73: 519–542.

Lepper, Mark R. and David Greene eds. 1978. *The Hidden Cost of Reward: New Perspectives on the Psychology of Human Motivation.* New York: Wiley.

Liberman, V., Samuels, S. M., and Ross, L. 2004. "The Name of the Game: Predictive Power of Reputations versus Situational Labels in Determining Prisoner's Dilemma Game Moves." *Personality and Social Psychology Bulletin*, 30: 1175–1185.

Liebenberg, Louis 1990. *The Art of Tracking: The Origin of Science.* Cape Town: David Philip Publishers.

Lindenberg, Siegwart 1993. "Club Hierarchy, Social Metering and Context Instruction: Governance Structures in Response to Varying Self-command Capital." Pp. 195–220 in *Interdisciplinary Perspectives on Organization Studies*, edited by Siegwart Lindenberg and Hein Schreuder. Oxford: Pergamon Press.

　　1997. "Grounding Groups in Theory: Functional, Cognitive, and Structural Interdependencies." Pp. 281–331 in *Advances in Group Processes*, 14, edited by Edward Lawler and Barry Markovsky. Greenwich CT: JAI Press.

　　1998. "Solidarity: Its Microfoundations and Macro-dependence. A Framing Approach." Pp. 61–112 in *The Problem of Solidarity: Theories and Models*, edited by Patrick Doreian and Thomas Fararo. Amsterdam: Gordon and Breach.

　　2006. "What Sustains Market Societies as Open Access Societies?" Pp. 255–280 in *Institutions in Perspective*, edited by Ulrich Bindseil, Justus Haucap, und Christian Wey. Tübingen: Mohr Siebeck.

　　2008. "Social Norms: What Happens When They Become More Abstract?" Pp. 63–82 in *Rational Choice: Theoretische Analysen und empirische Resultate*, edited by Andreas Diekmann, Klaus Eichner, Peter Schmidt and Thomas Voss. Wiesbaden: VS Verlag.

2013. "Social Rationality, Self-Regulation and Well-being: The Regulatory Significance of Needs, Goals, and the Self." Pp. 72–112 in *Handbook of Rational Choice Social Research*, edited by Rafael Wittek, Tom Snijders, and Victor Nee. Stanford: Stanford University Press.

2014. "Solidarity: Unpacking the Social Brain." Pp. 30–54 in *Solidarity – Theory and Practice*, edited by Arto Laitinen and Anne Birgitta Pessi. Lanham: Lexington Books.

Lindenberg, Siegwart and Nicolai Foss 2011. "Managing Joint Production Motivation: The Role of Goal-Framing and Governance Mechanisms." *Academy of Management Review*, 36(3): 500–525.

Lindenberg, Siegwart and Bruno Frey 1993. "Alternatives, Frames, and Relative Prices: A Broader View of Rational Choice." *Acta Sociologica* 36: 191–205.

Lindenberg, Siegwart and Linda Steg 2007. "Normative, Gain and Hedonic Goal Frames Guiding Environmental Behavior." *Journal of Social Issues* 651: 117–137.

Marmot, Michael 2006. "The Status Syndrome. A Challenge to Medicine." *JAMA*, 295(11): 1304–1307.

Richerson, Peter and Robert Boyd 2005. *Not by Genes Alone: How Culture Transformed Human Evolution*. Chicago: University of Chicago Press.

Singer, Tania, Ben Seymour, John P. O'Doherty, Klaas E. Stephan, Raymond J. Dolan, and Chris D. Frith 2006. "Empathic Neural Responses Are Modulated by the Perceived Fairness of Others." *Nature* 439: 466–469.

Tomasello, Michael 2008. *Origins of Human Communication*. Cambridge, MA: MIT Press.

Tomasello, Michael, Alicia P. Melis, Claudio Tennie, Emily Wyman, and Esther Herrmann 2012. "Two Key Steps in the Evolution of Human Cooperation: The Interdependence Hypothesis." *Current Anthropology* 53: 673–692.

Warneken, Felix and Michael Tomasello 2009. "Varieties of Altruism in Children and Chimpanzees." *Trends in Cognitive Sciences* 13: 397–402.

Weber, Max 1961. *General Economic History*. New York: Collier Books.

4

An Integrative Theory of Action
The Model of Frame Selection

Hartmut Esser and Clemens Kroneberg

Abstract

The question of how norm adherence comes about against all temptations and fears of exploitation continues to loom large in the explanation of social order. It also divides major paradigms in the social sciences, most notably the normative paradigm that views norms as unconditional imperatives and the utilitarian paradigm that regards them as one conditional incentive among others. We introduce the model of frame selection (Esser 2009; Kroneberg 2014) as an integrative theory of action that reconciles these views and allows one to consider the interplay of interests, institutions, and ideas in the explanation of social order. Building on and formalizing insights gained in cognitive social psychology, this dual-process model pinpoints the conditions under which norms will be followed spontaneously rather than being subject to trade-offs. The model yields specific and testable hypotheses and has been applied in diverse fields of sociological research.

THE PROBLEM

The emergence of social order constitutes one of the fundamental problems in the social sciences. It involves the *reliable* regulation and stabilization of actions within social situations, even against conflicting interests and opportunities. This problem varies in character and severity, ranging from achieving coordination among actors with shared interests to ensuring mutual cooperation despite incentives to free ride in social dilemmas, to overcoming conflicts in which the gain of one actor involves the other's loss. These different problems call for different solutions. Coordination problems can be solved by simple agreements or conventions. Dilemma situations, however, already constitute a problem of "antagonistic cooperation": notwithstanding the potential gains of mutual cooperation, there is always the temptation to free ride on others' contributions as well as the fear that one's own contribution will be exploited. This particularly applies to the production of collective goods, which also includes the establishment of institutions that are capable of enforcing order in case of conflicts. Norms constitute an especially important (although not the only) solution to the problem of social order. However, the crucial question then becomes whether and how norm adherence comes about against all temptations and fears of exploitation.

This question actually breaks down into two questions: Where do norms come from? And, in particular: What accounts for their binding force once they exist? There is a general and largely uncontroversial answer to the first question: norms come into existence via learning and internalization based on the institutional and cultural evolution of supporting learning environments, as well as the psychobiological evolution of more deeply anchored motives of fairness and altruism. With regard to the second question, there are two answers, which are associated with fundamentally different views. One considers a norm as a combination of *particular* (social) preferences and expectations, which become relevant in *addition* to other (nonnormative) preferences and expectations. The other view perceives a norm as a complex combination of knowledge, affects, and associated behaviors, which is triggered within the respective situation as a *whole* and without further deliberation. The first view regards the adherence to norms as a "rational" decision and attributes its effects to actors' considerations of *future* expected consequences. Hence, the effects of norms will always depend on other incentives and opportunities and are therefore *not* unconditional but subject to trade-offs. The second view, in contrast, considers the effects of norms as a kind of direct response to *past* imprinting. This would lead to the *un*conditional adherence that solves the problem of antagonistic cooperation in the most reliable way: norms as *imperatives*.

These views have repeatedly given rise to debates that typically develop along the following lines: advocates of the first view emphasize that human actors are not "cultural dopes." Rather, they act reasonably and decide rationally, thereby evaluating norms alongside other incentives and opportunities. Critics of the first view reply that norms being understood as mere internal or external incentives lack the necessary binding force. According to the first view, this binding force can also be achieved via certain constellations of interests, as in the "evolution of cooperation" or game-theoretic equilibria more generally. However, it is argued that the "utilitarian dilemma" cannot be resolved this way, because in the absence of truly reliable commitments, social order would basically depend on the (in-)stability of the supporting environmental conditions (see Heiner 1983). Jon Elster concisely sums up the difference between the two views:

Rational action – be it economically or politically motivated – is concerned with *outcomes*. (Elster 1989a: 113; italics added)

TABLE 4.1. *The (Un-)Conditionality of Framing Effects in the Asian Disease Experiment by Tversky and Kahneman (according to Stocké 1996, table 6; all differences in votes between programs significant)*

	1 Survivors A vs B or C vs D	2 Difference Survivors	3 Frame "Save" % for A vs B	4 Frame "Die" % for C vs D	5 Difference %A vs %B
1	200/200	0	72	22	50
2	200/200	0	50	25	25
	201/200	1	53	32	21
	210/200	10	55	36	19
	250/200	50	61	40	21
	300/200	100	64	48	16

And:

I define social norms by the feature that they are *not* outcome-oriented.... The *imperatives* expressed in social norms ... are *un*conditional ... (Elster 1989b: 98; italics added; HE/CK)

The two views of norms refer to a basic controversy about the (micro-)foundations of the social sciences and of social order. In this chapter, we introduce an integrative theory of action that resolves this debate: the model of frame selection (Esser 2009; Kroneberg 2014). It is a formally specified dual-process model that pinpoints the conditions under which norms will be followed spontaneously rather than being subject to trade-offs. The theory thereby integrates both views of norms and allows one to consider interests, institutions, ideas, and their *interplay* in the explanation of social order.

AN EXAMPLE

Part of the reason why the controversy about the nature of norms as unconditional or subject to trade-offs continues is that there is empirical evidence for *both* views. As an exemplary illustration, Table 4.1 displays the results of a variation of the famous Asian disease experiment by Tversky and Kahneman (1981). As in the original experiment, subjects had to decide in favor of or against certain programs for fighting a deadly disease with six hundred casualties to be expected if nothing happens. In a first version of the experiment, 72 percent of the subjects voted for program A, which promised that two hundred of the six hundred people could be *saved* with *certainty,* and against program B, which expected a one-third *risk* that all would be *saved* and a two-thirds risk that nobody would be *saved.* However, in a second version of the experiment, 22 percent of the subjects voted for program C, which assured that four hundred of the six hundred people would *die* with *certainty,* and against program D, which would yield a *risk* of one-third that nobody would *die* and a risk of two-thirds that all six hundred people would *die*. Thus, the description of the programs was varied in two ways: certainty or risk and the labeling of the consequences as "save" or "die." The interesting point is that *objectively* the expected outcomes of all programs were identical: two hundred survivors in each case. But the linguistic representation of the decision between A and B with the label "save" and that of the decision between C and D with the label "die" produced a difference in the decisions of 50 percentage points (cf. row 1 of Table 4.1).

One could explain this "framing" effect as deriving from a simple norm that gets activated via the verbal cues "save" and "die": "One ought not to let someone die with certainty or expose someone to the risk of death who could be saved with certainty." However, a possible qualification is that such framing effects are limited to low-cost situations in which the opportunity costs of a wrong decision are small. To evaluate this possibility, the original experiment was extended to include a variation of the *objective* effectiveness of the programs (Stocké 1996: 53ff.). In the programs with certain outcomes (A and C), now 201, 210, 250, and even 300 people instead of 200 people survived. This implies a clear increase in the effectiveness of programs A and C as compared to programs B and D, starting from no difference (as in the original version by Tversky and Kahneman) up to a gain of one hundred additional survivors (cf. column 2 in Table 4.1). According to the view of norms as being conditional, one would expect that subjects consider these changes in objective incentives when reaching a decision and that the framing effect soon disappears in response to changing incentives. The results, however, were different: although approval for programs A and C clearly increased with rising incentives (cf. columns 3 and 4 for row 2 in Table 4.1), the differences in the votes for program A against B and C against D, which reflected the framing effects, remained nearly unchanged (column 5 for row 2 in Table 4.1).[1] A possible explanation for these results is that only some subjects reacted to the changing incentives, whereas a rather large number of others, were *in*sensitive toward these changes and adhered strictly to the earlier mentioned norm, activated by a verbal cue with a specific cultural meaning.

The experiment thus provides exemplary evidence for *both* views of understanding norms (see also the large body of research to which we point later in this chapter). Moreover, it illustrates a related but distinct third aspect: sometimes even very subtle *symbolic* cues activate *culturally* shaped beliefs, emotions, and the respective behavior. Rather than a "choice" or "decision" between well-defined options, this activation is a kind of immediate and

---

[1] The replication of the original experiment with two hundred survivors also yielded somewhat different results in this case: 50 percent for program A and 25 percent for program B (cf. the first line in row 2 of Table 4.1).

automatic response to the recognition of a specific pattern of objects in the respective situation.

THREE PARADIGMS

The two views of norms as conditional-rational or unconditional-imperative and the notion of a culturally and symbolically mediated activation of mental models correspond to the three major paradigms in sociology: the utilitarian, the normative, and the interpretative paradigm. *Interests* are at the heart of the *utilitarian* paradigm: opportunities, incentives, and rational expectations, the homo economicus, rational choice theory in its different variants, and the mechanism of deciding between options (whether consciously or not), considering future consequences. *Institutions* are at the focus of the *normative* paradigm: rules or norms of action, which claim obedience and may be reinforced by sanctions, the homo sociologicus, who unconditionally follows the demands of a normative orientation, normative theories of action (with classical role theory as a prototype), and the mechanism of a "definition of the situation" that activates behavior without further reflection based on the recognition of typical patterns in the situation, which are learned in the processes of socialization and internalization. Cultural *ideas* and the interpretation of associated symbols are at the heart of the *interpretative* paradigm: actors' internal models of typical situations and processes, which are represented and activated by significant symbols and are not mere triggers of a fixed "definition" of the situation (like the normative paradigm postulates), but rather the material for a reflective interpretation of what is going on, for strategic negotiation, for smart impression management, and for intelligently identifying a line of action that appears reasonable within a basically fragile world.

There are various ways in which the three paradigms overlap and are interconnected, and there are hardly cases in which only one of them seems relevant. *Interests* nearly always have an institutional and cultural background. *Institutional rules* define and give rise to certain interests, but interests also play an important role in their emergence and stability. Likewise, institutional rules are always based on certain ideas that legitimate them, provide them with emotions, and symbolically confirm and reinforce them through rituals. Finally, *cultural ideas* are often tied to tangible interests and normatively secured via institutions and sanctions.

The recognition that the three paradigms focus on essential and interrelated aspects of human behavior and social order has motivated projects on their theoretical integration (see, e.g., Alexander 1988; Emirbayer and Mische 1998). In the following sections, we introduce a formalized theory of action that pursues this aim in the spirit of an analytical or explanatory sociology. It thereby attempts to equip the social sciences with micro-foundations that allow one to consider interests, institutions, ideas, and their *interplay*.

THREE MECHANISMS

Three mechanisms constitute the conceptual basis of the model of frame selection (see Esser 2009; Kroneberg 2014). We will quickly summarize them as well as provide supporting evidence.

First: All actions are preceded by a *definition of the situation*, that is, a process in which actors make sense of the situations that they encounter (Young 2010). This meaning-making involves actors activating, applying, and constructing interpretations of their (social) world based on significant symbols. To incorporate this old sociological idea (e.g., Parsons 1937: 44; Thomas and Znaniecki 1927: 68–70; Goffman 1974) in an explanatory account, the model of frame selection uses the concept of schemas or mental models developed in cognitive social psychology and cultural anthropology (see Abelson 1981; DiMaggio, 1997; Kay et al. 2004; Haley and Fessler 2005). They can be defined as "a mental structure which contains general expectations and knowledge of the world. This may include general expectations about people, social roles, events, and about how to behave in certain situations" (Augoustinos and Walker 1995:32). Two kinds of mental models are especially relevant: *frames* are mental models of *typical situations*, whereas *scripts* are mental models of *typical sequences of action* (see Moskowitz 2005:162–3). Frames are activated by the recognition of objects within a situation. These objects therefore function as "significant symbols" for the internal ideas and "meaning" that define the frame. An important class of significant symbols are linguistic expressions, such as the labels "save" and "die" in the experiment by Tversky and Kahneman. Linguistic expressions activate frames and possibly related typical sequences of action, that is, scripts, which are then also prompted.

Recent empirical evidence that the definition of the situation matters comes in the form of a series of experiments and results in psychology and experimental game theory. For example, the mere labeling of a Prisoner's dilemma as "Wall Street Game" or "Community Game" has been shown to strongly influence cooperation rates, yielding much higher levels in the "Community Game" (Liberman, Samuels, and Ross 2004). Apparently, such labeling effects depend on the cultural meaning ascribed to the respective verbal cues and are therefore somewhat contingent. For example, the label "Community" does not have the same meaning everywhere and can thus give rise to different framings (cf., e.g., Dufwenberg, Gächter, and Hennig-Schmidt 2011; Ellingsen et al. 2012). Moreover, recent experiments show that even in the absence of such explicit labels, participants' behavior depends on how they define the seemingly "neutral" situation (Engel and Rand 2014; Eriksson and Strimling 2014).

Second: The interpretation of a situation, the selection of a script, and overt behavior itself can each be more or less thoughtful and deliberate. This idea of actors' *variable rationality* likewise has a long tradition in sociology. It underlies Weber's (1978) four types of social action as well as Schütz's (1970) theory of everyday behavior. The latter states that people are usually well equipped with mental models for typical situations, which they use routinely to define situations and act in them without any rational deliberation. This flow of habitualized behavior is only interrupted if some unexpected event seriously questions the applicability of the unconsciously used mental models, which leave them with the problem to rationalize what happens and what they could do to preserve some orientation and meaning of what is going on (Garfinkel 1967). Throughout the social sciences, the phenomenon of variable rationality has given rise to a number of influential theoretical distinctions (e.g., role-playing vs. role-making, conditional vs. unconditional trust) and theoretical divides (e.g., Allport's model of attitude-behavior consistency vs. Ajzen's and Fishbein's theory of planned behavior).

To capture this phenomenon, it is useful to distinguish two modes of information processing: an automatic-spontaneous mode (as) and a reflecting-calculating mode (rc). The as-mode stands for a spontaneous selection of one particular taken-for-granted alternative driven by experiences in the *past*. As it is based solely on the situational activation of mental models and their chronic accessibility, the as-mode frees actors from having to scrutinize competing alternatives (Fiske and Neuberg 1990). In contrast, the rc-mode represents a decision process in which actors deliberate on several alternatives and take into account the value and probabilities of possible consequences in the *future*. Selections in the as-mode are therefore closely tied to the demands of the immediate situation, including the activation of strong emotions or physiological reactions. In contrast, selections in the rc-mode are conditional and sensitive possibly even to relatively small changes in incentives and opportunities.

The breakthrough in theorizing and empirically demonstrating variable rationality comes from the so-called dual-process (or dual-systems) theories of social psychology (see Payne, Bettman, and Johnson 1988; Chaiken and Trope 1999; Smith and DeCoster 2000; Payne and Bettman 2002; Strack and Deutsch 2004; Lieberman 2007; Rilling and Sanfey 2011). According to Russell H. Fazio's (1990) pioneering MODE-model and supporting experiments, the activation of a (stereotypical) mental model is a consequence of symbolic stimuli within a situation. A more data-driven "rational" evaluation might only take place if there is a mismatch between situational stimuli and mental models (or a conflict with other stored models). In addition, the *motivation* and *opportunities* for such an elaboration must be present, and its *costs* (e.g., the mental effort required) must not be too high (cf. also Greifeneder et al. 2011; Rand, Greene and Nowak 2012). Neurophysiological brain research has confirmed these relationships: *only* if the situation contains *new* elements *and* if there are cues that *important* things are concerned, "awareness" and something like a "rational" calculation will occur. Moreover, this assessment of novelty and importance is itself a fully automatic process (cf., e.g., LeDoux 1999; Rolls 1999; Roth 2001).

Third: The mode selection is the starting point of any definition of the situation and is initially controlled by *categorization* processes: the recognition of perceived objects within a situation as a symbolic cue for a certain type of situation that the actor has encoded in the form of a mental model. In his later work, Herbert Simon (1983) argues that such processes are more fundamental in explaining human behavior than deliberate choices, which are only possible if a situation has already been framed in a meaningful way. The initial categorization process takes place *automatically* and thus *cannot* be deliberately controlled. If it results in a perfect *match* between the symbolic objects and a mental model, the relevant frames will be activated immediately and automatically (and a similar triggering can happen with respect to scripts and overt behavior). In the case that a disruption occurs, however, the level of attention increases (abruptly) and a search for memory contents and further cues to unravel the mystery begins. Again, a great deal of evidence has accumulated that demonstrates the effects of such categorization processes. In sociology, the seminal contributions of Harold Garfinkel (1967) document the immense impact of seemingly inconspicuous disruptions in the definition of the situation. Lab experiments on the impact of brands confirm the strength of categorization effects: if given a choice among no-name products (e.g., coffee, beer, or washing powder) for which the same objective information is available, the neocortex of the subjects is engaged in complicated cognitive activities that do not lead to a clear preference. But as soon as a well-known and emotionally anchored brand appears, the neocortex abruptly stops the intense calculation (see, e.g., Plassmann, Kenning, and Ahlert 2006; Hubert and Kennig 2008: 283ff.; on neurophysiological backgrounds, see also Bechara et al. 1997; Deppe et al. 2005; De Martino et al. 2006). Such effects depend on the accessibility of the brands (e.g., familiarity with the brand and presence of a well-known logo on the packaging), as well as on an easy and uninterrupted access to this information: the faster that categorizations take place, the more likely that they will follow anchored programs instead of "rational" considerations (Greifeneder et al. 2011; Rand et al. 2012; Costa et al. 2014). Finally, well-documented processes of symbolic priming of norms can be understood in a similar fashion: priming can make chronically anchored mental models temporarily accessible and thereby ensure that normative demands are more easily followed (Bargh, Chen, and Burrows 1996; Keizer, Lindenberg, and Steg 2013).

THE MODEL OF FRAME SELECTION

The model of frame selection (MFS) takes into account the definition of the situation, variable rationality, and categorization and specifies how these mechanisms interact.[2] With regard to the *definition of the situation*, the MFS

---

[2] For first formulations and versions of the MFS, see Esser (1993, 2001, 2009); for the integration, formalization, and an overview of empirical applications, see Kroneberg (2005, 2011, 2014).

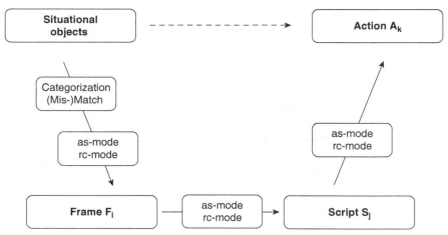

FIGURE 4.1. Frame, script and action selection in different modes of variable rationality.

distinguishes two types of mental models: *Frames* as mental models of *typical situations* and *scripts* as mental models of *typical sequences of action.* Frames answer the question, "What's going on here?", or "What kind of situation is this?" (Goffman 1974). Thus, actors define a situation in a certain respect by activating a particular frame. Scripts answer questions such as "How am I expected to behave?". In the MFS, the term script can refer to moral norms, conventions, routines, and emotional or cultural reaction schemes held by the actor. The processes of activating a particular frame and a script are, therefore, termed *frame selection* and *script selection.* Both precede the building of a behavioral intention, or *action selection,* by which an actor answers the question, "What am I going to do?" Thus, in contrast to theories that directly and exclusively focus on choices among action alternatives, like rational choice theory or behaviorism, the MFS allows researchers to consider the often large extent to which behavior is structured by mental models and cognitive processes of information processing.

Overview

Formally, F denotes the set of frames, S the set of scripts, and A the set of behavioral alternatives that are available to an actor in a situation. Figure 4.1 summarizes the internal cognitive processes that lead from the occurrence of certain external objects to the selection of a certain overt action A_k in a given situation, according to the MFS.

The starting point is a process of *categorization* as pattern recognition leads to a certain (mis-)*match* between the observable objects and a mental model of a typical situation. This process is *not* a matter of choice but takes place automatically. Depending on the strength of the match and additional conditions (see below), the actor uses this immediately accessible frame F_i to define the situation (and activates further, not necessarily observed features of this type of situation) or performs a frame selection in the rc-mode. Following this definition of the situation, a certain script S_j is selected. This selection likewise can take place either in the as- or in the rc-mode. In the same way the action A_k is finally selected.

As a theory of action the MFS thus allows zooming in on the internal action-generating mechanisms that govern how actors make sense of and deal with situations. This provides the basis for studying social processes. For example, the resulting action is often the object of other actors' definition of the situation, triggering a new sequence of script selections and actions. On a collective level, such *social framing* processes can reinforce or weaken the strength and accessibility of particular mental models, producing, for example, stable equilibria of shared mental models of moral order in social groups.

The Automatic-spontaneous (as-) Mode

The *as-mode* describes a process of *spreading* activation.[3] If uninterrupted, it can lead from a frame F_i, over a script S_j to a corresponding (observable) action A_k. This mode of selection allows the MFS to capture the *taken for granted* and sometimes *un*conditional manner in which norms get activated and guide behavior. In the as-mode the alternative with the highest *activation weight* (AW) is selected. The activation weights of a frame $F_i \in F$, a script $S_j \in S$ and an action alternative $A_k \in A$ for a selection in the as-mode are defined as follows:

$$AW(F_i) = m_i = o_i\, l_i\, a_i \tag{4.1}$$

$$AW(S_j|F_i) = AW(F_i)\, a_{j|i}\, a_j \tag{4.2}$$

$$AW(A_k|S_j) = AW(S_j|F_i)\, a_{k|j}, \tag{4.3}$$

with all parameters lying in the unit interval [0,1].

The activation of a *frame* F_i is determined solely by its *immediately* experienced match with the objective situation (see equation 4.1). This match is a function of three factors: the chronic accessibility of the frame (a_i), the presence of situational objects that are "significant" for the frame (o_i), and the associative or symbolic link between the frame and the situational objects (l_i). The chronic *accessibility* of the frame corresponds to an actor's general disposition to activate it and to interpret situations accordingly. It mostly reflects experience and learning and leads to relatively stable individual differences (e.g., cross-cultural differences due to differences in socialization). As a mental model of situations, each frame encompasses typical objects whose presence in the situation signals its applicability. Hence, the activation potential of frames

---

[3] The following description of the model follows Kroneberg (2014).

also depends on temporary situational influences (see Higgins 1996), including the ease with which the process of pattern recognition can proceed (see Rompf 2012; Costa et al. 2014). In particular, other actors' observable behavior serves as a source of significant cues, leading to the described behavioral cascades of social framing and other social processes.

When the *script* selection takes place in the as-mode, the activation of a script S_j will be greater the higher its chronic accessibility (a_j), the higher its temporary accessibility given the activated frame F_i and further situational cues ($a_{j|i}$), and the higher the match of the selected frame (see equation 4.2).[4] The chronic accessibility of the script represents how strongly it is mentally anchored, e.g., how strongly an actor has internalized a norm, has become accustomed to a routine, or is predisposed to show a particular emotional (e.g., aggressive) response. As scripts are more or less specific to certain situations, there is an internal spreading activation from the selected frame to the script, depending on the strength of their mental association. In addition, the temporary accessibility of scripts can increase directly due to situational cues that activate behavioral pre-dispositions and programs. Finally, the activation of a script also depends on how unequivocally the situation could be defined, i.e., the match of the selected frame. Uncertainty about the type of situation translates into uncertainty about the appropriateness of potential scripts.

Should the *action* selection occur in the as-mode, the actor follows the script-based course of action without consideration of other alternatives. The spontaneous impulse to follow a script will be weaker if an actor is unsure about the kind of situation he is facing or about the applicability of the script. So again the activation weight depends on the strength of previous activations. The only additional parameter is the degree to which the script S_j implies a certain action A_k ($a_{k|j}$). Scripts cannot regulate all potential behavioral choices within a situation in an encompassing and unambiguous way. If a script is incomplete with regard to a behavioral choice ($a_{k|j} = 0$), a spontaneous script-based action will be impossible.

The Reflecting-calculating (rc-) Mode

If the process of spreading activation in the as-mode becomes too weak at any point (see the next section on mode selections), the actor will start to reflect on the perceived alternatives. Given the interest in interpreting the situation correctly, the actor will choose the frame which seems most likely to be appropriate in the face of the available evidence. The same "logic of appropriateness" (March and Olsen 1989) governs the script selection. The *action* selection in

---

[4] The parameters are multiplicatively linked because in a defined situation, a script, which relates to a completely different type of situation and which is not activated by any cues (temporary accessibility $a_{j|i} = 0$), should by no means be selected, independent of how strongly it is mentally anchored in general (chronic accessibility a_j).

the rc-mode is, however, qualitatively different. As it results in overt behavior that might have several far-reaching consequences, an actor typically will engage in trade-offs by weighing different and rather specific consequences. Here, rational choice theories have their greatest explanatory power. While action selections in the rc-mode can often be modeled using expectancy-value theory, other forms of rational action are also possible. For example, if actors define a situation to be a strategic one, they will choose depending on the likely actions of others, who are anticipated to reason in the same strategic way. In such cases, actors may follow one of the rules of decision-making developed in game theory.

In the MFS, the rc-mode incorporates the forward-looking conceptions of rationality developed within rational choice theory as a special case of a more general theory of action, including narrow and wide versions of rational choice theories. Additionally, the MFS allows scholars to study the frame and script selection and to incorporate influences of the definition of the situation on rational action. Akin to more recent developments in economics (Akerlof and Kranton 2000; Bicchieri 2006; Dufwenberg et al. 2011; Fehr and Hoff 2011), one could specify how actors' perceived choice sets, preferences, and expectations vary depending on the selected frame and script. As has been stressed by sociologists (see Lindenberg 1989; Etzioni 1988:96–100), the definition of the situation also affects behavior in the rc-mode by activating knowledge structures, situational goals, values, and emotions. Moreover, once the situation has been defined, many objectively existing courses of action may lie beyond the horizon of meaningful action, leading to a first shrinkage of the set of alternatives.

Mode Selection

Many traditional sociological theories of action have stopped at contrasting a spontaneous and a deliberate mode of information processing. What has largely been missing is a specification of the conditions under which a specific mode governs a selection. In its answer to this question, the MFS relies on experimental and theoretical work in social psychology (Chaiken and Trope 1999; Smith and DeCoster 2000; Strack and Deutsch 2004). Most dual-process theories agree on four determinants of the mode of information processing: *opportunities*, *motivation*, *effort*, and *accessibility* (see especially the MODE-model proposed by Fazio 1990). With regard to the first two variables, a deliberating mode of information processing becomes more likely the less it is hampered by restrictions, e.g. in time or capabilities (opportunities), and the higher the costs of a wrong decision (motivation). Actors need this extra motivation to engage in a (subjectively) rational deliberation, because this more elaborated mode inevitably causes reflection costs in the form of foregone time and energy (effort). Finally, automatic-spontaneous selections depend on the accessibility of appropriate ready-to-use programs. As will become clear below, this fourth variable links actors' variable rationality to the spontaneous activation of mental models in a situation by the process of categorization.

While dual-process theories in social psychology have identified the factors influencing actors' mode of information processing (Strack and Deutsch 2004), they lack a formalized model that precisely specifies the interplay of these variables. The MFS offers such a specification using a decision-theoretical framework. The basic idea is that the employment of a certain mode of information processing can also be thought of as the outcome of a selection (cf. Heiner 1983). For each substantial selection – that of a frame, a script, and an action – there is one corresponding mode selection that determines whether it takes place in an automatic-spontaneous (as-) mode or in a reflecting-calculating (rc-) mode (see Figure 4.1). Using the formal apparatus of decision theory allows one to capture the so-called "sufficiency principle" (Chen and Chaiken 1999): The human brain seems to have evolved in ways that yield an adapted response to the trade-off between the potential gain in accuracy and the effort that is associated with a more data-driven mode of information processing. However, it is key to note that the mode selection is not a conscious calculation by the actor. Rather, it describes how the human brain reacts *automatically* to situational stimuli and how it is constrained by *objective* conditions when determining whether or not an actor assigns attention to an issue.

The mode selection depends on the opportunities for reflection, p ($\in [0,1]$); on the motivation for reflection, U (> 0); on reflection costs, C (> 0); and on the strength with which an alternative O_i (a frame, script, or course of action) is activated in a situation, $AW(O_i)$. This so-called activation weight can also be interpreted as the perceived probability that the alternative that can be spontaneously selected is valid. The derivation of the mode selection is given in Kroneberg et al. (2010: App. A1) or Kroneberg (2014). Here, as in empirical applications, it suffices to consider its main results. An actor will select the reflecting-calculating mode under the following condition:

$$p(1 - AW(O_i))U > C \tag{4.4}$$

Thus, an actor selects (in) the rc-mode if the additional utility of this mental activity will exceed its additional costs. The interpretation of the left side as an additional utility is as follows: If sufficient opportunities seem to exist (p), and if the spontaneously accessible alternative is estimated as not valid ($1 - AW(O_i)$), *only* the selection of the rc-mode will bring about the utility of a valid selection and avoid the costs of an invalid one (U). The parameter U represents what can be gained by selecting the rc-mode rather than the as-mode, and this corresponds exactly to the notions of "motivation," "perceived costliness of a judgmental mistake," or "fear of invalidity," as put forward by dual-process theories and confirmed in respective experiments (Fazio 1990: 92). The decision-theoretical formalization reproduces the insights of cognitive social psychology in other respects as well: Actors make use of a more elaborated, but also more strenuous mode of information processing when the stakes are higher, the situation is more ambiguous, the opportunities for reflection are more favorable, and its costs are lower.

If we conversely consider the condition for the as-mode, solving for the highest activation weight yields:

$$AW(O_i) \geq 1 - C/(pU). \tag{4.5}$$

Thus, the automatic-spontaneous mode gets selected if, and only if, the activation weight exceeds a certain threshold. The more strongly actors' frames and scripts get activated in a situation, the more likely it is that these will spontaneously govern their perception and behavior. The rationale is that strong activation signals to the actor that an alternative is highly relevant or applicable.

Replacing $AW(O_i)$ with the activation weights given in equations 4.1 to 4.3, one sees that the requirements for a spontaneous response increase from one step of the spreading activation process to the next (see again Figure 4.1). A frame selection in the as-mode requires that the situational objects signal *clearly* the validity of a certain frame (m_i). In order for the script selection to occur spontaneously, there must in addition be a strongly anchored script that is highly accessible in this situation $(a_j, a_{j|i})$. Finally, an action selection in the as-mode rests on the additional requirement that the script clearly implies the choice of a particular alternative $(a_{k|j})$.

Again, to properly understand the MFS, it is important to note that the mode selection represents a *spontaneous* process beyond the control of the actor. Consequently, the values of all parameters reflect *immediately* observed attributes of the situation, mentally encoded *accessible* experiences, and the *automatic* process of categorization. For example, the utility U_i associated with the frame i is based on the *earlier* emotional experiences an actor has made in this type of situation (see Strauss and Quinn 1997). Also based on actors' *past* experiences and *background* knowledge, certain situational objects signal the extent to which sufficient opportunities for reflection (p) exist, the magnitude to which reflection might be valuable (U_{rc}) or costly (C), and the degree to which a wrong selection can lead to costs (C_w). Hence, *no* forward-looking rationality is at work in the mode selection. The decision-theoretic representation of the process of mode selection should therefore not be interpreted as an exercise in "expected utility"-theory, to which processes like "categorization" or "(mis-)match" are basically unknown. The mode selection is *not* a "decision" on whether or not to decide and hence does not imply an infinite regress of deciding (not) to decide, as one might be tempted to object.

IMPLICATIONS AND EMPIRICAL EVIDENCE

A key implication of the MFS for explaining social order concerns the conditions under which actors *un*conditionally follow the demand of norms, leading to a *reliable* adherence, even in the face of opportunities and incentives to deviate and without external coercion. Two conditions in particular can be derived from equation (4.5) $AW(O_i) \geq 1 - C/(pU)$. First, as reflection always involves some degree of effort ($C > 0$), the actor will *never* leave the as-mode when the activation weight $AW(O_i)$ is 1. For example, an actor will define a situation as one in which norms of fidelity apply as long as there is a *perfect* match of this mental model (e.g., no "significant" signs of betrayal or untrustworthiness). Second, if opportunities to reflect are *completely absent* ($p = 0$), the activation weight $AW(O_i)$ will *never* pass the threshold for the transition to the rc-mode. For example, in an emergency situation that leaves no time to reflect, actors will behave spontaneously based on accessible frames and scripts even if their appropriateness is unclear.

The first result is particularly relevant for the controversy about the nature of social norms. The MFS implies that actors are more likely to follow a norm spontaneously, the more clearly the situation could be defined (m_i), the more unambiguous the norm applies in this type of situation ($a_{j|i}$), the more strongly the actor has internalized the norm (a_j), and the more strongly it regulates the respective behavioral choice ($a_{k|j}$). When these conditions are sufficiently met – a constellation to which we will refer briefly as "strong framing" –, an actor will be immune towards rational incentives. Hence, the MFS supports Elster's claim that strongly internalized norms can have a "grip on the mind" (Elster 1989a, b: 100) so that an actor's behavior becomes "unconditional" (at least with regard to the present situation).

However, norms can also be relevant in the rc-mode. Here, they operate as various kinds of incentives, e.g., as psychological costs or benefits, or as instrumental incentives tied to possible social sanctions. As such, social norms are no longer incommensurable or unconditional, but their value is exchanged against that of other non-normative incentives. In the MFS, norms can guide behavior *both* as autonomous incommensurable reasons and as calculated incentives, and the degree of their activation and internalization is itself one factor (among others) that determines which type of rule-following will prevail in a given situation. The MFS therefore allows us to resolve the longstanding debate over the status of normative action, arriving at a middle position that is close to the differentiated but informal accounts developed by Etzioni (1988) and Elster (1989).

On an empirical level, we gain a widely applicable hypothesis that allows one to uniformly explain various mixed-population phenomena. In the case of a strongly internalized and activated norm – which we call "strong framing" for the sake of brevity – actors will unconditionally follow the norm, whereas in the case of a weak framing actors will engage in reflecting-calculating choices, systematically considering other alternatives and incentives. This ceteris-paribus hypothesis implies a statistical *interaction* effect between the strength of the framing (measured by indicators of the activation weight) and the calculated incentives and opportunities: the higher the activation weight,

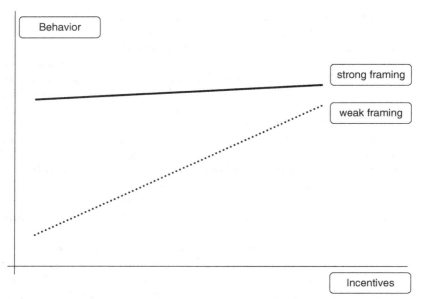

FIGURE 4.2. The effect of calculated incentives under the conditions of a strong and a weak framing.

the lower the impact of opportunities and incentives for breaking a norm; and in the extreme case of a very strong framing, other incentives are irrelevant. Figure 4.2 illustrates this expected interaction between framing and incentives.

The MFS therefore allows one to derive specific hypotheses that can be tested using survey data or experiments. Indeed, there has been a considerable and growing number of sociological applications of the model that demonstrate its heuristic value and provide indirect tests of its implications. These studies focus on a diverse set of phenomena including fertility, stability of partnerships and marriages, delinquency, donations to charitable organizations, participation in elections, environmental behavior, participation in high culture, trust and reciprocity, educational decisions, ethnic conflicts, and helping behavior under high risk (see the overview in Kroneberg 2014, Table 4.1). Most of these studies confirm the interaction effect illustrated in Figure 4.2: With *increasing* accessibility of the respective normative or cultural orientations and scripts, the impact of other incentives, risks, and costs *weakens* considerably – up to the complete *un*conditionality of norm adherence that has always been emphasized in the normative paradigm and is unknown to the utilitarian paradigm. Moreover, this result is not restricted to low-cost situations, such as cultural consumption, electoral participation, or occasional donations, but also holds for situations that entail high costs and risks, such as divorce, far-reaching educational decisions, or even the extremely risky support of Jews in Nazi Europe during World War II (Kroneberg, Yaish, and Stocké 2010).

At the same time, there is much room for further tests and applications. So far, the MFS has mostly been applied in non-experimental survey research focusing on parametric situations. Three lines of further research are therefore obvious (see already Kroneberg 2011, 2014). *First*, lab and field *experiments* could be used to conduct more direct tests of the model's implications. To be sure, the MFS is well in line with a great deal of experimental evidence, especially because main results of cognitive social psychology served as the very starting point for the model (see above). However, the model awaits a comprehensive and experimental test, which could be designed by combining experimental set-ups of dual-process theories with those of experimental economics.[5] *Second*, the MFS should be applied to situations of *interaction* and (strategic) *interdependence*. Of particular interest would be the modeling of strategic situations, in which players can switch between the rc-mode and the as-mode, for example, when adopting roles or organizational routines (as in Montgomery 1998). To this end, one would use systematically simplified versions of the model (on this feature of modularity, see Kroneberg 2014). Finally and *third*, the MFS could be used to study the *evolutionary development* of cultural milieus and institutional orders through *social framing* processes. Here, learning and socialization processes that affect the chronic accessibility of mental models as well as the processes of their situational activation play a key role. Agent-based modeling seems to be particularly suited to study such complex processes among heterogeneous actors.

SUMMARY AND CONCLUSION

The model of frame selection (MFS) is a theory of action that focuses on how actors interpret situations, which scripts of action they activate, and which actions they perform. In all these processes, actors can make deliberate reflected choices, but if strong emotions, normative beliefs, or unquestioned routines have been activated, actors may also ignore objectively existing alternatives or incentives. Building upon and formalizing insights gained in cognitive social psychology, the MFS explains under which conditions these different modes of behavior are to be expected.

As a formally specified dual-process model, the MFS also pinpoints the conditions under which norms will be followed spontaneously rather than being subject to trade-offs. The theory thereby helps to resolve the longstanding debate on the nature of social norms between the views of norms as conditional

---

[5] For precise decision-theoretic predictions, attempts to provide an (partial) axiomatization of the MFS would surely be helpful. Tutic (2015) shows that such an attempt can turn to substantially similar ideas and formal models in the economic field of procedural decision-making (e.g. Rubinstein and Zhou 1999; Salant and Rubinstein 2008; Sandroni 2011). These developments rebut one of the main objections against the MFS brought forward by advocates of a rather orthodox and narrow version of rational choice theory (see, e.g. Braun and Gautschi 2014): that due to its "complexity," an axiomatization of the MFS would be impossible.

incentives or as unconditional imperatives. This may well be regarded as its most significant contribution with respect to the problem of social order. The binding force of internalized norms against all temptations and fears of exploitation is a major piece of the puzzle. At the same time, the MFS stays clear of over-socialized conceptions of actors. In marked contrast to the behavior of "cultural dopes," the spontaneous adherence to norms has known scope conditions that are subject to considerable variation across situations and actors. The MFS can therefore be viewed as a "correcting" explanation and a kind of progressive problem shift (in the sense of Popper or Lakatos) that attempts to account for the limits and anomalies of rationalist, normative and interpretative approaches. As an *integrative* theory of action it specifies the conditions under which these approaches become applicable.

This is also true for the various solutions to the problem of social order developed in these and other approaches. In addition to spontaneous norm adherence, social order often emerges and gets stabilized due to (some) actors weighing their self-interest against their other-regarding preferences (like fairness or altruism). In the MFS, the important insights on social preferences gained in *behavioral economics* can be incorporated in the rc-mode. At the same time, its recognition of actors' variable rationality or the activation of reference points through categorizations and cues allows the MFS to account for recent experimental evidence that is difficult to explain in terms of beliefs, preferences, and constraints only (cf., e.g., Cookson 2000; Sandroni 2011; Engel and Rand 2014).

Another important (micro-)mechanism that underlies social order is captured by Boudon's (1996, 2003) concept of *cognitive rationality*, which refers to the adoption of cognitive beliefs or norms according to "good reasons." In this view, the emergence and stability of social order rests upon intersubjectively grounded beliefs about its legitimacy – which can be reduced neither to spontaneous rule-following nor to the right mix of incentives. In the MFS, such "good reasons" can be translated into reflected frame and script selections (see Esser 2001, 2009 for a comprehensive discussion). Such an acquisition of a belief or evaluation on the basis of their contextual "appropriateness" also captures the "logic of appropriateness" described by March and Olsen (1989). Again, theoretical integration of these ideas into the MFS is crucial for an adequate analysis of social order as neither Boudon nor March and Olson address how such reasoning interacts with incentives, automatic processes, and the like. And as interpretative sociology has long taught us, reflections on the appropriateness of alternative institutional rules or the competing demands of values require a stable background of much deeper, taken-for-granted assumptions about how the world operates – which might be seen as the most fundamental layer of social order and can be represented as a set of spontaneously activated frames and scripts.

As this selective and brief discussion already shows (for the relationship of the MFS to the ideas developed by Bourdieu, Habermas, and others, see Esser 2001, Kroneberg 2011), the MFS allows to integrate a variety of micro-mechanisms that underlie social order. Rather than advocating a partial theory at the expense of others, the MFS invites researchers to study the interplay of spontaneous norm-following, incentive-driven choices, the cognitive elaboration of good reasons or the taken-for-granted unarticulated assumptions about the functioning of the world, which might all contribute to the emergence, stability or decay of social order.

REFERENCES

Abelson, Robert P. 1981. "Psychological Status of the Script Concept." *American Psychologist* 36(7): 715–29.

Akerlof, George A. and Rachel E. Kranton. 2000. "Economics and Identity." *Quarterly Journal of Economics* 115(3): 715–53.

Alexander, Jeffrey C. 1988. *Action and Its Environments: Towards a New Synthesis.* New York: Columbia University Press.

Augoustinos, Martha and Iain Walker. 1995. *Social Cognition. An Integrated Introduction.* London: Sage.

Bargh, John A., Mark Chen, and Lara Burrows. 1996. "Automaticity of Social Behavior: Direct Effects of Trait Construct and Stereotype Activation on Action." *Journal of Personality and Social Psychology* 71(2): 230–44.

Bechara, Antoine, Hanna Damasio, Daniel Tranel, and Antonio R. Damasio. 1997. "Deciding Advantageously Before Knowing the Advantageous Strategy." *Science* 275(5304): 1293–95.

Bicchieri, Cristina. 2006. *The Grammar of Society: The Nature and Dynamics of Social Norms.* Cambridge: Cambridge University Press.

Boudon, Raymond. 1996. "The 'Cognitivist Model'. A Generalized 'Rational-Choice Model'." *Rationality and Society* 8(2): 123–50.

 2003. "Beyond Rational Choice Theory." *Annual Review of Sociology* 29: 1–21.

Braun, Norman und Thomas Gautschi. 2014. "'Zwei Seelen wohnen, ach! in meiner Brust': Ein Rational-Choice-Modell innerer Konflikte." *Zeitschrift für Soziologie* 43(1): 5–30.

Chaiken, Shelly and Yaacov Trope. 1999. *Dual-Process Theories in Social Psychology.* New York: The Guilford Press.

Chen, Serena and Shelly Chaiken. 1999. "The Heuristic-Systematic Model in Its Broader Context." Pp. 73–96 in *Dual-Process Theories in Social Psychology*, edited by S. Chaiken and Y. Trope. New York: The Guilford Press.

Cookson, Richard. 2000. "Framing Effects in Public Goods Experiments." *Experimental Economics* 3(1): 55–79.

Costa, Albert, Alice Foucart, Sayuri Hayakawa, Melina Aparici, Jose Apesteguia, Joy Heafner, and Boaz Keysar. 2014. "Your Morals Depend on Language." *PLoS ONE* 9(4). doi: 10.1371/journal.pone.0094842.

De Martino, Benedetto, Dharshan Kumaran, Ben Seymour, and Raymond J. Dolan. 2006. "Frames, Biases, and Rational Decision-Making in the Human Brain." *Science* 313(5787): 684–87.

Deppe, Michael, Wolfram Schwindt, Julia Krämer, Harald Kugel, Hilke Plassmann, Peter Kenning, and Erich Bernd Ringelstein. 2005. "Evidence for a Neural Correlate of a

Framing Effect: Bias-Specific Activity in the Ventromedial Prefrontal Cortex during Credibility Judgments." *Brain Research Bulletin* 67(5): 413–21.

DiMaggio, Paul. 1997. "Culture and Cognition." *Annual Review of Sociology* 23: 263–87.

Dufwenberg, Martin, Simon Gächter, and Heike Hennig-Schmidt. 2011. "The Framing of Games and the Psychology of Play." *Games and Economic Behavior* 73(2): 459–78.

Ellingsen, Tore, Magnus Johannesson, Johanna Mollerstrom, and Sara Munkhammar. 2012. "Social Framing Effects: Preferences or Beliefs?" *Games and Economic Behavior* 76(1): 117–30.

Elster, Jon. 1989a. *Nuts and Bolts for the Social Sciences*. Cambridge: Cambridge University Press.

 1989b. *The Cement of Society. A Study of Social Order*. Cambridge: Cambridge University Press.

Emirbayer, Mustafa and Ann Mische. 1998. "What is Agency?" *American Journal of Sociology* 103: 962–1023.

Engel, Christoph and David G. Rand. 2014. "What Does 'Clean' Really Mean? The Implicit Framing of Decontextualized Experiments." *Economics Letters* 122(3): 386–89.

Eriksson, Kimmo and Pontus Strimling. 2014. "Spontaneous Associations and Label Framing Have Similar Effects in the Public Goods Game." *Judgment and Decision Making* 9(5): 360–72.

Esser, Hartmut. 1993. "The Rationality of Everyday Behavior. A Rational Choice Reconstruction of the Theory of Action by Alfred Schütz." *Rationality and Society* 5(1): 7–31.

 2001. *Soziologie: Spezielle Grundlagen, Band 6: Sinn und Kultur*. Frankfurt/M., New York: Campus.

 2009. "Rationality and Commitment: The Model of Frame Selection and the Explanation of Normative Action." Pp. 207–30 in *Raymond Boudon: A Life in Sociology, Vol. 2, Part Two: Toward a General Theory of Rationality*, edited by M. Cherkaoui and P. Hamilton. Oxford: The Bardwell Press.

Etzioni, Amitai. 1988. *The Moral Dimension: Toward a New Economics*. New York: The Free Press.

Fazio, Russell H. 1990. "Multiple Processes by Which Attitudes Guide Behavior: The Mode Model as an Integrative Framework." Pp. 75–109 in *Advances in Experimental Social Psychology*, 23, edited by M. P. Zanna. San Diego: Academic Press.

Fehr, Ernst and Karla Hoff. 2011. "Introduction: Tastes, Castes and Culture: The Influence of Society on Preferences." *The Economic Journal* 121(556):F396–F412.

Fiske, Susan T. and Steven L. Neuberg. 1990. "A Continuum of Impression Formation, from Category-Based to Individuating Processes: Influences of Information and Motivation on Attention and Interpretation." Pp. 1–74 in *Advances in Experimental Social Psychology*, 23, edited by M. P. Zanna. San Diego: Academic Press.

Garfinkel, Harold. 1967. *Studies in Ethnomethodology*. Englewood Cliffs, NJ: Prentice-Hall.

Goffman, Erving. 1974. *Frame Analysis: An Essay on the Organization of Experience*. New York: Harper & Row.

Greifeneder, Rainer, Patrick Müller, Dagmar Stahlberg, Kees van den Bos, and Herbert Bless. 2011. "Guiding Trustful Behavior: The Role of Accessible Content and Accessibility Experiences." *Journal of Behavioral Decision Making* 24(5): 498–514.

Haley, Kevin J. and Daniel M.T. Fessler. 2005. "Nobody's Watching? Subtle Cues Affect Generosity in an Anonymous Economic Game." *Evolution and Human Behavior* 26(3): 245–56.

Heiner, Ronald A. 1983. "The Origin of Predictable Behavior." *The American Economic Review* 73(4): 560–95.

Higgins, E. Tory. 1996. "Knowledge Activation: Accessibility, Applicability, and Salience." Pp. 133–68 in *Social Psychology: Handbook of Basic Principles*, edited by E. T. Higgins and A. W. Kruglanski. New York: The Guilford Press.

Hubert, Mirja and Peter Kenning. 2008. "A Current Overview of Consumer Neuroscience." *Journal of Consumer Behaviour* 7: 272–92.

Kay, Aaron C., S. Christian Wheeler, John A. Bargh, and Lee Ross. 2004. "Material Priming: The Influence of Mundane Physical Objects on Situational Construal and Competitive Behavioral Choice." *Organizational Behavior and Human Decision Processes* 95: 83–96.

Keizer, Kees, Siegwart Lindenberg, and Linda Steg. 2013. "The Importance of Demonstratively Restoring Order." *PLoS ONE* 8(6). e65137. doi:10.1371/journal. pone.0065137.

Kroneberg, Clemens. 2005. "Die Definition der Situation und die variable Rationalität der Akteure. Ein allgemeines Modell des Handelns." *Zeitschrift für Soziologie* 34(5): 344–63.

2011. *Die Erklärung sozialen Handelns. Grundlagen und Anwendung einer integrativen Theorie.* Wiesbaden: VS Verlag für Sozialwissenschaften.

2014. "Frames, Scripts, and Variable Rationality: An Integrative Theory of Action." Pp. 97–123 in *Analytical Sociology. Actions and Networks*, edited by G. Manzo. Chichester: Wiley & Sons, Ltd.

Kroneberg, Clemens, Meir Yaish, and Volker Stocké. 2010. "Norms and Rationality in Electoral Participation and in the Rescue of Jews in WWII.: An Application of the Model of Frame Selection." *Rationality and Society* 22(1): 3–36.

LeDoux, Joseph. 1999. *The Emotional Brain. The Mysterious Underpinnings of Emotional Life.* London: Phoenix.

Lieberman, Matthew D. 2007. "Social Cognitive Neuroscience: A Review of Core Processes." *Annual Review of Psychology* 58: 259–89.

Liberman, Varda, Steven M. Samuels, and Lee Ross. 2004. "The Name of the Game: Predictive Power of Reputations Versus Situational Labels in Determining Prisoner's Dilemma Game Moves." *Personality and Social Psychology Bulletin* 30(9): 1175–85.

Lindenberg, Siegwart. 1989. "Choice and Culture: The Behavioral Basis of Cultural Impact on Transactions." Pp. 175–200 in *Social Structure and Culture*, edited by H. Haferkamp. Berlin: De Gruyter.

2008. "Social Rationality, Semi-Modularity and Goal-Framing: What Is It All About?". *Analyse & Kritik* 30: 669–87.

March, James G. and Johan P. Olsen. 1989. *Rediscovering Institutions. The Organizational Basis of Politics.* New York: The Free Press.

Montgomery, James D. 1998. "Toward a Role-Theoretic Conception of Embeddedness." *American Journal of Sociology* 104(1): 92–125.

Moskowitz, Gordon B. 2005. *Social Cognition. Understanding Self and Others.* New York: The Guilford Press.

Parsons, Talcott. 1937. *The Structure of Social Action. A Study in Social Theory with Special Reference to a Group of Recent European Writers.* New York: McGraw-Hill.

Payne, John W. and James R. Bettman. 2002. "Preferential Choice and Adaptive Strategy Use." Pp. 123–45 in *Bounded Rationality. The Adaptive Toolbox,* edited by G. Gigerenzer and R. Selten. Cambridge, MA & London: The MIT Press.

Payne, John W., James R. Bettman, and Eric J. Johnson. 1988. "Adaptive Strategy Selection in Decision Making.". *Journal of Experimental Psychology: Learning, Memory, and Cognition* 14(3): 534–52.

Plassmann, Hilke, Peter Kenning, and Dieter Ahlert. 2006. "The Fire of Desire: Neural Correlates of Brand Choice." *European Advances in Consumer Research* 7: 516–17.

Rand, David G., Joshua D. Greene, and Martin A. Nowak. 2012. "Spontaneous Giving and Calculated Greed." *Nature* 489(7416): 427–30.

Rilling, James K. and Alan G. Sanfey. 2011. "The Neuroscience of Social Decision-Making." *Annual Review of Psychology* 62: 23–48.

Rolls, Edmund T. 1999. *The Brain and Emotion.* Oxford: Oxford University Press.

Rompf, Stephan. 2012. "Trust and Adaptive Rationality. Towards a New Paradigm in Trust Research." Ph.D. dissertation, University of Mannheim. Retrieved from https://ub-madoc.bib.uni-mannheim.de/35963/.

Roth, Gerhard. 2001. *Fühlen, Denken, Handeln. Wie das Gehirn unser Verhalten steuert.* Frankfurt/M.: Suhrkamp.

Rubinstein, Ariel and Lin Zhou. 1999. "Choice Problems with a 'Reference' Point." *Mathematical Social Sciences* 37: 205–9.

Salant, Yuval and Ariel Rubinstein. 2008. "(A, f): Choice with Frames." *Review of Economic Studies* 75: 1287–96.

Sandroni, Alvaro. 2011. "Akrasia, Instincts, and Revealed Preferences." *Synthese* 181(1): 1–17.

Schütz, Alfred. 1970. *Reflections on the Problem of Relevance.* New Haven, CT: Yale University Press.

Simon, Herbert A. 1983. *Reason in Human Affairs.* Stanford, CA: Stanford University Press.

Smith, Eliot R. and Jamie DeCoster. 2000. "Dual-Process Models in Social and Cognitive Psychology: Conceptual Integration and Links to Underlying Memory Systems." *Personality and Social Psychology Review* 4(2): 108–31.

Stocké, Volker. 1996. Relative Knappheiten und die Definition der Situation. Die Bedeutung von Formulierungsunterschieden, Informationsmenge und Informationszugänglichkeit in Entscheidungssituationen: Ein Test der Framinghypothese der Prospect-Theory am Beispiel des 'asian disease problem'. *Research Report for the German National Science Foundation (DFG).* Mannheim: University of Mannheim.

Strack, Fritz and Roland Deutsch. 2004. "Reflective and Impulsive Determinants of Social Behavior." *Personality and Social Psychology Review* 8(3): 220–47.

Strauss, Claudia and Naomi Quinn. 1997. *A Cognitive Theory of Cultural Meaning.* Cambridge: Cambridge University Press.

Thomas, William I. and Florian Znaniecki. 1927. *The Polish Peasant in Europe and America.* New York: Alfred A. Knopf.

Tutic, Andreas. 2015. Revealed Norm Obedience. *Social Choice and Welfare* 44: 301–318.

Tversky, Amos and Daniel Kahneman. 1981. "The Framing of Decisions and the Psychology of Choice." *Science* 211(4481): 453–58.

Weber, Max. 1978. *Economy and Society*. Berkeley, CA: University of California Press.

Young, Alford A., Jr. 2010. "New Life for an Old Concept: Frame Analysis and the Reinvigoration of Studies in Culture and Poverty." *The ANNALS of the American Academy of Political and Social Science* 629(1): 53–74.

5

The Center Cannot Hold

Networks, Echo Chambers, and Polarization

Daniel J. DellaPosta and Michael W. Macy

Abstract

A longstanding literature in the social sciences – from James Madison to James Hunter and from Robert Dahl to John Rawls – regards opinion polarization as a threat to social order. Yet consensus may prove equally harmful due to the stifling effects of "monoculture." Contemporary social and political theorists have proposed a pluralist alternative in which cross-cutting divisions maintain diversity and tolerance. In this chapter, we examine polarization, consensus, and pluralism from a relational network perspective. We cite empirical evidence from studies of political polarization and cultural fragmentation suggesting that alignment across issue dimensions extends beyond hot button identity politics to include seemingly arbitrary lifestyle preferences. While pluralist theorists typically assume that cross-cutting divisions foster mutual tolerance and maintain diversity, we show that pluralism can also become unstable due to the self-reinforcing dynamics of homophily and social influence.

> Things fall apart; the centre cannot hold;
> Mere anarchy is loosed upon the world,
> The blood-dimmed tide is loosed, and everywhere
> The ceremony of innocence is drowned;
> The best lack all conviction, while the worst
> Are full of passionate intensity.
>
> William Butler Yeats, "The Second Coming," 1919

INTRODUCTION

Rational choice theorists attribute the "Hobbesian problem of order" to the tension between individual self-interest and the collective interest of all.

However there are empirical and theoretical limitations to this formulation of the problem. Empirically, some of history's most costly breakdowns of social order have involved "identity politics" whose practitioners are motivated by righteous indignation, religious zealotry, and ethnic prejudice, not by the maximization of individual payoffs. Theoretically, Van de Rijt and Macy (2009) used Heckathorn's (1991) "altruist's dilemma" (as when there are "too many cooks in the kitchen") to show that social dilemmas can arise even in a population whose members want nothing more than to do what is best for others, without any regard to self-interest.

Accordingly, in this chapter we argue that the problem of order goes much deeper than the tension between individual and collective interests. The more fundamental problem is what Van de Rijt and Macy characterize as the tension between individual autonomy and collective interdependence. Social life is a complex system, more like an improvisational jazz ensemble – whose members influence one another in response to the influences they receive – than a symphony orchestra whose members dutifully play their assigned parts. In a small jazz ensemble, the musicians have shared expectations about one another's likely behavior, but imagine an improvisational group with millions of members who only know about their immediate neighbors. How then do we not end up with "a nasty and brutish cacophony, a noisy war of all against all?" (Macy and Flache 2009).

This is the problem of order that we address: The vulnerability of improvisational social life to self-organizing dynamics that trap the population in undesirable emergent arrangements. We focus not on the "social dilemma" of strategic choices that maximize exogenous preferences but on the emergent alignments of preferences that motivate choices, including preferences that express emotionally charged identities and righteous zeal. More precisely, we focus on three problematic alignments: polarization, consensus, and pluralism, which we examine from a network analytic perspective.

An extensive literature in the social sciences regards opinion polarization as a threat to social order (see Baldassarri and Gelman [2008] for a recent example). Particularly worrisome is the formation of "echo chambers" in which members of a divided population only hear opinions with which they are in agreement. Polarized opinions tend not only to become extreme but also to become aligned, even when there is no substantive or logical basis for the correlation. A prominent example is abortion and capital punishment, with an inconsistent application of belief in the sanctity of life.

Theorists of social order propose two antidotes to polarization – consensus and pluralism – that differ in the analysis of the problem and the solutions that they identify. Consensus theories point to the dangers of divisive disagreement and the inability to reach compromise. The solution is the identification of a "common ground" to which each side can appeal. The common ground can be a common enemy or threat, or it can be fundamental values such as a belief in human rights. For example, liberal environmentalists have often found common ground with conservative Christians by framing ecological sustainability as a spiritual imperative: the preservation of "God's creation."

Critics counter that consensus and polarization share an underlying dynamic and differ only in the reduction in the number of camps from two to one. Theorists of "mass society" (Arendt 1968) warn that consensus is also vulnerable to "echo chambers" in which people interact mainly with those who already think similarly, thereby limiting social influence to the reinforcement of already-held beliefs. In the absence of contentious politics, echo chambers can impose a totalitarian grip on a population that loses the capacity for critical judgment.

In contrast, pluralist political theory points to solutions to the problem of order that dissolve the echo chamber altogether. Pluralism refers to a political philosophy based on the principle of countervailing power distributed across a multiplicity of groups, none of which are strong enough to dominate all the others. In place of universal agreement, pluralists propose cross-cutting divisions in which people who disagree on one dimension would ideally be no less likely to agree on another.[1] By a less stringent definition, two groups A and B may disagree on all issues without becoming mutually antagonistic as long as there is some third group C – agreeing sometimes with A and sometimes with B – capable of "bridging" the divide. Ideally, every group would act as a bridge between other groups on at least some issue, such that divisions can remain plural and cross-cutting even if some pairs of groups lack direct ideological overlap. The fear of polarization on one side and the tyranny of consensus on the other led Madison to advocate a pluralist "equilibrium in the interests & passions of the Society itself" as the "best provision for a stable and free Gov't" (1792: 158). The high-dimensionality that characterizes pluralistic opinion distributions is thought to produce social integration of diverse groups, tolerance of those with alternative political or cultural preferences, and a dynamic social order that is much healthier than a monoculture in which everyone agrees with everyone else (e.g., Dahl 1961; Truman 1951). Those cross-cutting divisions can provide a stable equilibrium that reconciles the tension between individual autonomy and collective interdependence so as to avoid the divisiveness of polarization on the one side and the stifling uniformity of consensus on the other.

We revisit the pluralist theory of cross-cutting divisions from a relational network perspective. We begin by briefly reviewing consensus and pluralism as alternative bases of social order. Consensus is often negatively associated with the stifling effects of "monoculture," whereas pluralism is regarded as both stable and conducive to tolerance of diversity, critical judgment, and culturally vibrant nonconformity. Contrary to the prevailing view, we point to empirical

---

[1] For example, groups that disagree on taxing the wealthy may nevertheless agree on a woman's right to legal abortion. Indeed, this particular alignment of fiscal conservatism and social liberalism has long been characteristic of New England Republicans.

and theoretical research that suggests the potential instability of pluralistic opinion distributions. Nationally representative surveys reveal a surprisingly high level of correlation across the vast majority of opinion items, including those that have no substantive connection (DellaPosta, Shi, and Macy 2015). Controlled laboratory experiments show how these correlations can be generated through the effects of social influence (Salganik, Dodds, and Watts 2006). Formal models show that when the effects of social influence are reinforced by homophily, pluralism becomes unstable and tends to devolve into polarization. Finally, we review a set of social and cognitive mechanisms that are thought to be strong candidates in producing this devolution, as well as some solutions that have been proposed in previous work.

IS CONSENSUS DESIRABLE?

The original argument for consensus as a basis of social order[2] emerged out of debates concerning the proper basis of political legitimacy, motivated by a simple puzzle: how can political action embody the will of the governed? The classic argument in political philosophy is most frequently traced to Rousseau's (1997) concept of the "general will," which – while often vaguely defined – corresponds loosely to a population-level consensus that could be determined from aggregate public opinion. When there is consensus in the underlying population, the puzzle of political legitimacy is solved because the aggregate view is shared by all of the individuals who are subject to governance. In contrast, widespread dissension introduces a crucial disjuncture between the aggregate and the individuals that comprise it. In a polarized population, the central tendency could represent a moderate position even though most individuals hold an extreme position, hence attributing the average view to any individual becomes ecologically fallacious.

Rousseau's formulation has since been substantially revised by contemporary consensus theorists. These revisions have mainly responded to the well-known difficulty of reaching a population-wide consensus on issues subject to political governance. A number of theorists in both political science and sociology have proposed that consensus across the range of specific issue dimensions is not necessary for political legitimacy as long as there is a "meta-consensus" on the basic institutions of the society and the fundamental values on which those institutions are based (Dryzek and Niemeyer 2006; Rawls 1993). Concluding that "nothing like a nationwide consensus is either possible or necessary," Bendix (1964: 21) argues that political authorities should instead take the "passive compliance" of population members as a sufficient indicator of legitimacy. When political action is out of step with the

---

[2] For interested readers, we recommend Dryzek and Niemeyer (2006) for a more in-depth discussion of the literature briefly summarized here.

"general will" on a particular issue, widespread deviance will render the disconnect obvious to those in charge.

A more vexing challenge has been posed by public choice theorists, who argue that expressions of the public will (i.e. voting) are ultimately sensitive to political actors' manipulation of the presented options. Given a "cycle" among three possible options – A beats B beats C beats A – the "consensus" revealed by voting is ambiguous (Dryzek and Niemeyer 2006; Riker 1982). Contrary to the implications of the principle of transitivity, A>B and B>C does not guarantee that A>C. Cyclic collective preferences of this type make up the Condorcet paradox of voting and leave no clear "general will" to be discerned.

Apart from the Condorcet paradox and related practical difficulties in achieving and detecting consensus, an equally important question concerns whether population-level consensus would even be desirable in the first place. In *The Division of Labor in Society*, Durkheim ([1893] 1997) famously contrasts mechanical and organic solidarity. Mechanical solidarity is predicated on consensus and similarity while organic solidarity – emerging from the modern division of labor – is based on interdependence among constituent parts in a complex social system. Despite the inherent difficulties in societal transitions away from a pre-modern reliance on mechanical solidarity, Durkheim ultimately concluded that difference-based organic solidarity would provide an even more powerful foundation of social cohesion. That is because organic solidarity can accommodate agreement without binding individuals to the views, attitudes, and practices held by the majority, as agreement on these dimensions is no longer the sole basis of solidarity. Indeed, critics of consensus are quick to point out that innovation, dissent, exploration, and individual freedom are often incompatible with a consensual "monoculture." The historical association between Rousseau's political philosophy and the violent excesses of the French Revolution have not helped to assuage these anxieties. Contemporary concerns for the rights of minorities have made the tyranny of a broadly consensual majority seem especially unpalatable. For example, countries with a high degree of internal agreement – for example on the criminalization of homosexuality, the dangers posed by immigrant minorities, and the desirability of laws restricting the rights of women – are generally derided for their intolerance rather than praised for their consensus-producing capabilities.

Critics of consensus also point to the mirage of universal agreement that can prop up "naked emperors." Even when each individual member of the population sees through the mirage, none may be willing to speak their mind for fear of inviting social disapproval. This false conformity becomes particularly insidious when it leads to false enforcement (Centola, Willer, and Macy 2005; Willer, Kuwabara, and Macy 2009). Poseurs who conform to earn social approval can use enforcement as a ready-made way to fake the "sincerity" of their compliance. In a remarkable recent study, Willer et al. (2013) found that heterosexual males engage in ostentatious displays of homophobia when their own conformity with norms of masculinity is called into question.

Vulnerability to naked emperors is a cornerstone of theories of "mass society" (Arendt 1968) in which critical judgment is eviscerated in a population that comes to be trapped in a single echo chamber. "The more people's standpoints I have present in my mind while I am pondering a given issue, and the better I can imagine how I would feel and think if I were in their place, the stronger will be my capacity for representative thinking and the more valid my final conclusions, my opinion" (Arendt 1968, p. 241; quoted in Mutz 2002). In short, rather than being an antidote to polarization, consensus turns out to be fundamentally similar. The key difference – that there is only one group instead of two – makes consensus even less appealing to those who worry about the stifling stability of a totalitarian "monoculture."

IS PLURALISM AN EQUILIBRIUM?

Rather than positing fundamental agreement as the basis of order, pluralists propose a counter-intuitive alternative to both consensus and polarization: order rests not on agreement but on division. The problem with both consensus and polarization is that in each case there are not enough divisions. A single-issue division is just as totalizing as consensus in that agreement on one issue implies agreement on all others. The key to the avoidance of echo chambers and the preservation of diversity, tolerance, and critical judgment is the multiplicity of division through cross-cutting social cleavages (Dahl 1961; Mutz 2002; Truman 1951). In pluralistic societies, one may agree with a neighbor on a hot-button social issue and still disagree on another issue that is equally charged with moral righteousness. Multiple and cross-cutting divisions are thought to be conducive to social order because agreement on some issues makes one less likely to dismiss or vilify a neighbor who expresses dissenting views on other issues, thereby preventing all-encompassing conflict between opposed camps.

Instead of one or two internally homogenous "camps," a pluralist society has a multiplicity of mini-camps, with a healthy mix of agreement and disagreement on orthogonal issue dimensions that promotes diversity, tolerance, and critical judgment. The more axes of division, the more stable the society because no single group is likely to become dominant and no single eigenvector is likely to account for more than a small fraction of the variance in the socio-matrix. Each individual's simultaneous involvement in multiple cross-cutting lines of disagreement prevents any single identity from becoming all-encompassing (Baldassarri and Gelman 2008). Paradoxically, divisions *sustain* – rather than weaken – social order so long as divisions are *plural*. Because one's opponent in one conflict is one's ally in another, no one allows disagreement to evolve into intergroup rivalry. For this same reason, cross-cutting divisions discourage identity politics in favor of the "strange bedfellows" options that are possible with interest-based politics.

It is unsurprising that pluralist theorists reached their apex of influence in both sociology and political science during the early years of the Cold War. Pluralists framed the bickering and skirmishes typical of American politics as indications of a healthy "civil society" in contrast to the rigid and forced consensus attributed to the Communist "second world." Dahl, Truman, and others linked the cross-cutting nature of American cleavages to the robustness of the political system as a whole, while Stouffer (1955) and Nunn, Crockett, and Williams (1978) famously argued that exposure to dissenting viewpoints explains the individual link between education and tolerance for nonconformity.

The celebration of pluralism was dampened by the outbreak of polarizing divisions in the 1960's, beginning with civil rights which then became overlayed with opposition to the escalating war in Indochina, the flowering of the counter-culture, and the emergence of the women's movement. It was not just that these four movements incited extreme passions for and against, but more importantly, all four movements were closely aligned. By 1968, one could predict a stranger's political views on civil rights, Vietnam, and reproductive rights by the choice of fashion ensemble (e.g., shirtless overalls, a red bandana headband, and Frye boots) or exclamatory expression ("dynamite" and "right-on" instead of "wow").

Although the collapse of pluralism might be attributed to an historical peculiarity – the simultaneous emergence of multiple social movements (Gitlin 1987) – we propose a more troubling diagnosis. Following Madison, pluralists argue that the multiplicity of division is an equilibrium in which the small size of internally homogenous groups motivates members to "agree to disagree," such that no group becomes dominant and no division becomes fundamental. But is pluralism an equilibrium?

According to recent scholarship on political polarization and cultural fragmentation in the United States, it may not be. Baldassarri and Gelman (2008) take an innovative approach to tracking baseline changes in political polarization. First, they select forty-seven items that have been asked in multiple editions of the American National Election Study (NES). They then estimate pairwise correlations between each of these items and two measures of political partisanship (liberal/conservative ideology and Democrat/Republican party identification) for every year in which the item appeared in the NES. Using the resulting "sample" of correlations, the authors estimate multilevel mixed-effects models to capture baseline issue partisanship (the extent to which one's opinion on an issue is correlated with one's political ideology or party identification), item-specific and overall time trends in partisanship, and variation across issue domains. Using this procedure, they find evidence of significantly greater alignment between issues and partisan affiliations in recent years. In 1980, a typical item was correlated with political ideology at $r = .22$; this correlation increased by about .04 with each subsequent decade. This pattern suggests that political parties have become increasingly ideologically coherent and all-encompassing political identities. When the authors adapt their procedure to capture pairwise correlations between pairs of specific political issues, they again find evidence of extensive opinion alignment. However, increases over time in the extent of alignment are mainly concentrated among what they characterize as "moral" issues rather than questions of economics or civil rights. The observation of increasing partisan alignment without accompanying dramatic changes in issue alignment led the authors to conclude that political parties have become more polarized in recent decades while the public at large generally has not.[3]

While Baldassarri and Gelman provide a compelling analysis of political alignments, they may have given insufficient attention to the possibility that polarization is primarily cultural rather than political. The increasing alignment on moral issues fits a broader pattern in which partisans have taken increasingly polar positions in the "culture wars" surrounding abortion, gay rights, and sexual mores (Baldassarri and Gelman 2008; Evans 2003). Less intuitive is the fragmenting of the American public along lines that seem only tangentially related to politics and ideology, particularly with regard to patterns of consumption and lifestyle. In *The Big Sort*, Bishop (2008) suggests that the divide between "red" and "blue" states extends beyond politics to cultural divisions. For example, the liberal politics of Portland, Oregon are not merely incidental to the culture of "books, beer, bikes, and birkenstocks." To this end, DellaPosta, Shi, and Macy (2015) have extended Baldassarri and Gelman's analysis to include not just explicitly political issues, but also a range of seemingly apolitical issues such as musical preferences, consumer tastes, and even affinities for New Age spirituality. While belief in astrology does not correlate as strongly with political ideology as do attitudes toward abortion or firearm regulation, the authors nonetheless find evidence that "lifestyle" is widely correlated with politics, often at the .001 level of significance and even after controlling for a host of standard demographic measures. Using the cumulative file of the General Social Survey, they found that about 67 percent of all possible pairwise correlations between lifestyle and ideology were statistically significant ($p < .05$). Furthermore, these correlations reveal ideological differences across a highly eclectic set of lifestyle preferences, from belief in the power of dead ancestors to gun ownership to blues music.

This alignment of political and cultural dimensions is problematic for pluralistic theory precisely because it implies encompassing rather than cross-cutting divisions – one's position on issue A also predicts positions on issues B, C, and D. These encompassing divisions increase the social distance between groups, which undermines tolerance of differences and opens the door to conflict. Individuals who agree on some issues and disagree on others can choose to

---

[3] This does not completely assuage the potential negative implications for social order, particularly from the perspective of pluralism. Because public opinion often takes cues from party-affiliated opinion leaders, rather than vice versa, there remains the potential for polarized divisions among political elites to "trickle down" to the broader populace.

focus their conversations on their common ground and avoid discussion of issues on which they disagree. This is not possible when individuals differ on all observable dimensions.

Explanations for these potentially contentious political-cultural alignments have often been broadly grounded in individual experiences and material interests (Bourdieu 1984) or in underlying "moral principles" (Haidt 2012). The problem with these explanations is that they tend to be post hoc, requiring considerable theoretical imagination to account for the thousands of specific pairwise correlations. For example, why do liberals have greater faith in both science and astrology? Perhaps it is because both science and astrology can be regarded as inconsistent or even incompatible with religion. Then why do conservatives prefer hunting? Presumably it is not because hunting is compatible with religion, in which case one must look for yet another theoretical epicycle to account for each perturbation of ideological orbits.

We investigate a much simpler and more parsimonious explanation for the alignment of culture and politics, based on two empirical patterns that come as close as any to the status of a "lawful regularity" in social life: homophily and social influence. We review two sets of formal models of the self-reinforcing dynamics of homophily and influence, focusing on the vulnerability of pluralism first to the relentless creep of monoculture and then to the collapse into polarization.

PLURALISM AND MONOCULTURE IN FORMAL MODELS OF SOCIAL INFLUENCE

In 1964, Abelson used a formal model to pose a conundrum that continued to intrigue social theorists for the next half century. Building on earlier work by Harary (1959), Abelson demonstrated that convergence on "monoculture," a population-wide opinion consensus, is inevitable in a connected population whose members continuously update their views by moving toward the weighted average of their neighbors' opinions. The unique equilibrium is an outcome in which the entire population holds identical views. The theoretical inevitability of monoculture is poorly supported by empirical observation, which led Abelson to wonder, with puzzled consternation, "what on earth one must assume in order to generate the bimodal outcome of community cleavage studies" (1964: 153).

Later models by Friedkin and Johnsen (1990, 1999) responded by assuming that individuals might cling steadfastly to their most dearly held views even while adjusting others in response to social influence. While this assumption preserves diversity that is exogenous to the model, it does not allow for diversity or disagreement to increase over time (Flache and Macy 2011a).

Axelrod (1997) proposed a resolution to the "Abelson problem" by introducing two intuitively simple assumptions. First, while most previous models, including Abelson's, had followed Harary's assumption that opinions were continuous, Axelrod instead proposed a nominal distribution. This innovation allowed Axelrod's model to accommodate key "all-or-nothing" lines of cultural differentiation, such as religion and language.

Second, whereas most previous models of social influence assumed a fixed network (in which the likelihood of interaction between two agents depended only on the existence of a network tie between them), Axelrod assumed that interaction could also depend on the level of similarity between the two neighboring agents. This widely documented homophily principle (McPherson, Smith-Lovin, and Cook 2001) creates a self-reinforcing dynamic in which the likelihood of interaction between two neighboring agents increases with similarity, and similarity increases with interaction. Models that couple social influence with homophily formalize the problem of "echo chambers." Agents who are already similar on a few issues at time t are more likely to interact and further increase the number of shared opinions at $t+1$, thereby making it even *more* likely for them to interact again given the opportunity.

Rather than monoculture, Axelrod's model showed that homophilous interaction between agents preserved global diversity. Local clusters of agents would eventually converge on shared opinions. As long as different clusters converged on different local opinion profiles, the absence of social influence between sufficiently dissimilar clusters prevents the emergence of global consensus. The dazzling paradox was that local consensus emerged as the key to maintaining global diversity. Agents were sheltered from homogenizing tendencies precisely because of the homogeneity generated within their own distinctive local subcultures.

Unfortunately, the generality of Axelrod's results turns out to be highly sensitive to the deterministic assumption in Axelrod's model of nominal dimensions. As Flache and Macy (2011a: 988) point out, "With nominal features, people are either identical or different, there are no shades of gray." In fact, one can argue that even seemingly nominal dimensions such as religion can be reasonably envisioned as a continuum. In American religion, for example, Christian denominations could be placed along a continuum according to their espoused beliefs on key social and political issues. If opinions are "shades of gray," even those at opposite ends of a continuum might retain a small positive probability to interact, in which case we find ourselves right back in Abelson's puzzle. Diversity inevitably collapses into monoculture. Flache, Macy, and Takacs (2006) found that Axelrod's model inevitably implies monoculture rather than global diversity if just a single opinion dimension is continuous rather than nominal.

Other studies (Deffuant et al. 2000; Hegselmann and Krause 2002) restored global diversity by imposing "bounded confidence" on continuous opinions. Beyond some threshold of disagreement, the probability of interaction is zero. However, Klemm et al. (2003a, 2003b) showed that monoculture obtains even with nominal opinions if the agents inhabit a nondeterministic world like our own, in which there is some amount of noise such that agents with different

opinions on every dimension nevertheless retain a positive probability to interact. When there is even a vanishingly small possibility for agents to randomly
permute their traits in response to idiosyncratic influences (such as through
the spontaneous invention of new knowledge, as assumed by Mark [1998b]),
previously dissimilar agents can find sufficient common ground to open the
door to social influence. Once the hermetic seal between dissimilar agents is
broken, the cultural diversity produced by Axelrod's model inevitably collapses
into monoculture.

Flache and Macy (2011a) discovered a seemingly innocent assumption in
Axelrod's model which, when relaxed, restores the robustness of his original finding. The assumption is that social influence is dyadic rather than
social. Whereas earlier models in the Abelson tradition assumed that individuals adjust their views by simultaneously considering those of all neighbors, Axelrod instead assumed that individuals are only influenced by a single
neighbor at a time. When Flache and Macy (2011a) replaced dyadic influence with a social influence function similar to the "weighted average" used
in most other models, they discovered that global diversity became much
less vulnerable to random perturbation. They concluded that the "power of
the group" (Festinger, Schachter, and Back 1950) is key to the stability of
global diversity. Whereas the combination of idiosyncratic noise and pairwise
dyadic influence allows a single permutated neighbor to convert his or her
neighbors one at a time, listwise social influence causes the permutated neighbor to be regarded as deviant and to be pressured back into conformity with
the dominant views in the group as a whole. Nevertheless, they caution that
cultural diversity remains vulnerable to the shrinking of global networks in
a connected age.

In addition to continuous opinions and random perturbations there is yet
another cause of the collapse of diversity in Axelrod's model: population size.
Contrary to the empirical findings in anthropological studies of small societies
(Redfield 1941), Axelrod's model predicts greater diversity in a remote tribal
society than in a large post-industrial country like the United States. However,
when Flache and Macy replaced pairwise with listwise social influence, collapse into monoculture was not only less likely overall but the effect of population size on diversity also reversed: monoculture was more likely the smaller
the population.

PLURALISM AND POLARIZATION

The third corner of Abelson's puzzle is "the bimodal outcome of community
cleavage studies," which he contrasts with diversity on the one side and monoculture on the other. While much of the initial response to Abelson focused on
the collapse into monoculture, more recent empirical and theoretical attention
has targeted the emergence of polarization. Global polarization first occurred
in The Great War, captured in 1919 by Yeats in *The Second Coming*: "The best

lack all conviction, while the worst are full of passionate intensity." When the center cannot hold, social order falls apart.

A century later, conflicts over abortion laws, gay rights, school prayer, and other "hot button" social issues have led commentators to warn of an impending "culture war" (Hunter 1991). For example, in *The Restructuring of American Religion* (1988), Robert Wuthnow sees "a deep hostility and misgiving" between "two opposing camps" in American society, with "'fundamentalists,' 'evangelicals,' and 'religious conservatives' in one and ... 'religious liberals,' 'humanists,' and 'secularists' in the other" (4:371).

The "culture war" hypothesis has been challenged by DiMaggio, Evans, and Bryson (1996) and by Mouw and Sobel (2001), who analyzed survey responses over a twenty-year period using National Election Studies and the General Social Survey. Across a wide range of social and political issues, these studies found little evidence that views have become more extreme. However, this finding does not address the prediction that positions on one item are increasingly correlated with positions on others. Here, the critics seemed to implicitly accept Hunter's basic thesis, that the formation of ideological "camps" is grounded in an underlying intransigence characterized by hard-line attitudes and narrow identification with a highly salient symbolic issue. Both sides in the debate seem to assume that polarization at the level of the group (attenuation of cross-cutting cleavages) reflects polarization at the level of the individual – reluctance to set aside predispositions, explore other viewpoints, or think about issues in other domains. The critics argue that there is little evidence of ideological hardening, which they assume contradicts the "culture war" hypothesis of polarization at the macro level.

Yet it is polarization at the macro level that erases the "cross-cutting" divisions that undergird pluralism, leading instead to homogeneous "echo chambers" that stifle innovation, dissent, critical judgment, and tolerance for nonconformity – identical to monoculture. Unlike monoculture, polarization poses the risk of conflict between warring factions. In its most extreme form – where every member of the population holds one of only two possible opinion profiles – polarization replaces multiple overlapping social and political commitments (e.g., being pro-choice but anti-gun control) with all-encompassing sociopolitical identities – if my neighbor agrees with me on issue A, then she must also agree with me on issues X, Y, and Z – identical to the issue alignment in monoculture but with two groups instead of one.

Ironically, the same formal models that were used to investigate the seemingly ineluctable march to monoculture can also generate polarization by relaxing a key assumption – that influence is positive. Although influence is intuitively understood to refer to a process that increases similarity, the opposite tendency to differentiate is also a form of influence, only the effect is negative. When "ties of enmity" are introduced into models of homophily and influence (along with "ties of amity"), the outcome is polarization instead of consensus (Kitts 2006; Flache and Macy 2011b; Macy et al. 2003). For example, Flache and

Macy (2011b) show how the same social influence mechanism that produces global convergence in a "small-world" network (Watts 1999) leads instead to global polarization when influence can be negative as well as positive. When agents share similar views, positive social influence reinforces this similarity. When agents disagree, however, negative social influence leads them to further differentiate themselves from the perceived out-group.

Despite these important theoretical findings, laboratory experiments have found that negative influence tends to be much weaker than positive influence (Flache and Takacs 2013; see also Brewer 1999; Mummendey et al. 1982; Struch and Schwartz 1989). In other words, the tendency to emulate those who are similar is stronger than the tendency to distinguish oneself from dissimilar others. However, more recent theoretical research has found that the relative strength of negative influence may have only limited consequences for population-level polarization. Using an "urn model" where agents update their views by drawing at random from an urn holding the weighted views of their network alters, DellaPosta, Shi, and Macy (2015) show that negative influence is essential for producing polarization but it need not be as strong as positive influence. In fact, almost any non-zero negative influence is sufficient.

The core of DellaPosta, Shi, and Macy's (2015) model lies in the incorporation of another complementary mechanism derived from McPherson's (1983, 2004) theory of the ecology of affiliation: homophily on fixed as well as fluid dimensions. When observing a correlation between two issue dimensions in surveys based on random samples, the predominant explanatory strategy would be to attribute both inputs in the correlation to a common causal prior (Davis 1985), usually originating in socio-demographic traits that are either static (e.g., race) or "sticky" (e.g., religion). However, McPherson (2004) makes the provocative argument that opinions, attitudes, and behaviors can instead become concentrated in socio-demographic "Blau space" simply due to homophily and influence. Even when sampling independently from the population, such processes operating beneath the surface can produce alignment across issue dimensions – such as those between lifestyle and politics documented by DellaPosta, Shi, and Macy (2015) – as a consequence of social influence among individuals who interact predominantly with those within the same demographic "niche."

This combination of homophily and influence produces *network autocorrelation*: the tendency to resemble one's network neighbors with regard to opinions, attitudes, and behavior (Dow, Burton, and White 1982). In addition to explaining correlations between static demographic dimensions and dynamic opinion dimensions, the coordinating effect of demographic similarity also explains alignment across seemingly unrelated opinion dimensions (DellaPosta, Shi, and Macy 2015). This coordinating effect of demographics is similar to the "tipping" dynamic in Schelling's (1978) model of residential segregation, in which weak co-ethnic preferences can carve out deep and lasting patterns of residential segregation. Just as Schelling showed that sharp residential segregation need not reflect deep-seated ethnic intolerance, so too the model of network autocorrelation shows that strong demographic correlations with opinion need not reflect equally strong demographic effects. Even a weak demographic signal is sufficient to channel social influence toward the creation of "echo chambers."

In other recent work, Mäs and Flache (2013) show that polarization could emerge even in the absence of negative influence if positive social influence causes agents to take increasingly extreme positions on continuous issue dimensions. The key polarizing mechanism is the exchange of supporting arguments that favor one's current position. Interactions between two agents with similar views can strengthen their convictions if the interaction gives them access to new supporting arguments. Awareness of different reasons for holding a particular view enhances confidence in the validity of the position.

Dandekar, Goel, and Lee (2013) suggest biased assimilation as a similar alternative to negative social influence. When social interaction presents agents with mixed or inconclusive evidence on a particular issue, they may respond not by moderating their views but rather by drawing unwarranted support for their original views. In other words, the agent's perception of the available evidence and arguments is biased by his or her currently held opinions, thereby lessening his or her susceptibility to change and strengthening existing divisions in the population.

Baldassarri and Bearman (2007) take a different approach to modeling political polarization. Their analysis begins with the observation that individuals often perceive polarization as being stronger and more extensive than survey evidence would warrant. The reason, they propose, is that people are more likely to discuss issues on which public opinion is polarized. As an issue becomes more polarized, it becomes a hotter topic for conversation. As the issue becomes increasingly discussed, in turn, those discussions become increasingly animated and polarized. As a result of this feedback loop, some topics become hot-button "takeoff" issues that dominate the public conversation while others remain relatively low-profile and do not contribute to polarization.

SUMMARY AND CONCLUSION

From a pluralist perspective, consensus and polarization are ultimately two sides of the same coin, with similar consequences for social order. Both embed individuals in homophilous echo chambers. In contrast to consensus, pluralism allows for dissent, innovation, and nonconformity. In contrast to polarization, pluralism entails cross-cutting divisions that discourage identity politics and encourage tolerance of other groups. If I disagree with my neighbor on issues X and Y, we will at least agree on some other issue Z. To return to an analogy from the introduction, the optimal arrangement for improvisational social life is to strive for dissonance, not synchrony, an outcome that is not necessarily unfamiliar in some avant garde expressions of "free jazz."

The cross-cutting divisions that make pluralism desirable are also typically thought to make it a stable equilibrium, with diverse opinion distributions held in place by each individual's access to a variety of discordant views. In this chapter, we have reviewed suggestive empirical and theoretical evidence to the contrary. First, nationally representative surveys show substantial correlation across pairs of opinion items and between opinion items and measures of political ideology. Recent work shows that these correlations are not limited to hot-button political and moral issues, but also include seemingly arbitrary lifestyle choices, including consumer tastes, aesthetic preferences, and personal morality.

Finally, we have reviewed an extensive history of formal models that show how pluralistic alignments can devolve into either consensual monoculture or divisive polarization. Monoculture is thought to result from a combination of homophily and positive social influence. When social influence can also be negative – entailing ties of enmity in addition to amity – the result is polarization, even if negative influence is weaker than positive by orders of magnitude. In addition to negative influence, formal models show that polarization can result from biased assimilation when faced with new information, opinion reinforcement from interaction with like-minded neighbors, and selective attention to hot-button "takeoff" issues.

This range of polarizing mechanisms further highlights the potential instability of a pluralistic equilibrium based on cross-cutting divisions. Political scientists and sociologists have addressed this vulnerability by emphasizing the importance of civil society, based on the hope that formal organizations can foster interaction across the social divides generated by homophilous in-group preferences.

Unfortunately, the widely lamented decline in civic participation captured most famously in Robert Putnam's *Bowling Alone* (2000) has negative implications for the possibility of civic integration across fundamental axes of social division. Furthermore, while Baldassarri (2011) finds little evidence of changes over time in patterns of group affiliation among Democrats and Republicans, she also finds that those who belong to multiple civic organizations have become increasingly radical rather than moderate in recent years. Again complicating the pluralist narrative of cross-cutting allegiances fostered by interaction with dissimilar alters, polarization is apparently deepest among those who engage most regularly with politics: members of civic organizations (Baldassarri 2011) and political elites (Baldassarri and Gelman 2008). As political parties and other opinion leaders become increasingly polarized in their political views, it becomes easier for this polarization to "trickle down" to less engaged members of the populace who take their cues from these elites (DellaPosta, Shi, and Macy 2015; Hetherington 2001; Lazarsfeld, Berelson, and Gaudet 1944; Watts and Dodds 2007). Even in civil society, it seems, the center cannot hold.

REFERENCES

Abelson, Robert P. 1964. "Mathematical Models of the Distribution of Attitudes under Controversy." Pp. 142–60 in *Contributions to Mathematical Psychology*, edited by Norman Frederiksen and Harold Gulliksen. New York: Holt, Rinehart, and Winston.

Arendt, Hannah. 1968. "Truth and Politics." Pp. 227–64 in *Between Past and Future: Eight Exercises in Political Thought*, edited by Hannah Arendt. New York: Viking Press.

Axelrod, Robert. 1997. "The Dissemination of Culture: A Model with Local Convergence and Global Polarization." *The Journal of Conflict Resolution* 41: 203–26.

Baldassarri, Delia. 2011. "Partisan Joiners: Associational Membership and Political Polarization in the United States (1974–2004)." *Social Science Quarterly* 92: 631–55.

Baldassarri, Delia, and Andrew Gelman. 2008. "Partisans without Constraint: Political Polarization and Trends in American Public Opinion." *American Journal of Sociology* 114: 408–46.

Baldassarri, Delia, and Peter Bearman. 2007. "Dynamics of Political Polarization." *American Sociological Review* 72: 784–811.

Bendix, Reinhard. 1964. *Nation-Building and Citizenship: Studies of Our Changing Social Order*. New York: John Wiley & Sons.

Bishop, Bill. 2008. *The Big Sort: Why the Clustering of Like-Minded America Is Tearing us Apart*. Boston: Houghton-Mifflin.

Bourdieu, Pierre. 1984. *Distinction: A Social Critique of the Judgment of Taste*. Cambridge, MA: Harvard University Press.

Brewer, Marilynn B. 1999. "The Psychology of Prejudice: Ingroup Love and Outgroup Hate." *Journal of Social Issues* 55: 429–44.

Centola, Damon, Robb Willer, and Michael Macy. 2005. "The Emperor's Dilemma: A Computational Model of Self-Enforcing Norms." *American Journal of Sociology* 110: 1009–40.

Dahl, Robert. 1961. *Who Governs? Democracy and Power in an American City*. New Haven, CT: Yale University Press.

Dandekar, Pranav, Ashish Goel, and David T. Lee. 2013. "Biased Assimilation, Homophily, and the Dynamics of Polarization." *Proceedings of the National Academy of Sciences* 110: 5791–96.

Davis, James A. 1985. *The Logic of Causal Order*. Beverly Hills, CA: Sage Publications.

Deffuant, Guillaume, David Neau, Frederic Amblard, and Gerard Weisbuch. 2000. "Mixing Beliefs among Interacting Agents." *Advances in Complex Systems* 3: 87–98.

DellaPosta, Daniel, Yongren Shi, and Michael Macy. 2015. "Why Do Liberals Drink Lattes?" *American Journal of Sociology* 120: 1473–511.

DiMaggio, Paul, John Evans, and Bethany Bryson. 1996. "Have Americans' Social Attitudes Become More Polarized?" *American Journal of Sociology* 102: 690–755.

Dow, Malcolm W., Michael L. Burton, and Douglas R. White. 1982. "Network Autocorrelation: A Simulation Study of a Foundational Problem in Regression and Survey Research." *Social Networks* 4: 169–200.

Dryzek, John S., and Simon Niemeyer. 2006. "Reconciling Pluralism and Consensus as Political Ideals." *American Journal of Political Science* 50: 634–49.

Durkheim, Emile. 1997 [1893]. *The Division of Labor in Society.* New York: Free Press.

Evans, John H. 2003. "Have Americans' Attitudes Become More Polarized? – An Update." *Social Science Quarterly* 84: 71–90.

Festinger, Leon, Stanley Schachter, and Kurt Back. 1950. *Social Pressures in Informal Groups: A Study of Human Factors in Housing.* New York: Harper.

Flache, Andreas, and Michael W. Macy. 2011a. "Local Convergence and Global Diversity: From Interpersonal to Social Influence." *Journal of Conflict Resolution* 55: 970–95.

2011b. "Small Worlds and Cultural Polarization." *Journal of Mathematical Sociology* 35: 146–76.

Flache, Andreas, Michael W. Macy, and Karoly Takacs. 2006. "What Sustains Stable Cultural Diversity and What Undermines It? Axelrod and Beyond." *Proceedings of the First World Congress on Social Simulation* (pp. 9–16), Kyoto, Japan, Vol. 2.

Flache, Andreas, and Karoly Takacs. 2013. "Is There Negative Influence? Disentangling Effects of Dissimilarity and Disliking on Opinion Change." Unpublished manuscript.

Friedkin, Noah E., and Eugene C. Johnsen. 1990. "Social Influence and Opinions." *Journal of Mathematical Sociology* 15: 193–205.

1999. "Social Influence Networks and Opinion Change." *Advances in Group Processes* 16: 1–29.

Gitlin, Todd. 1987. *The Sixties.* Toronto: Bantam.

Haidt, Jonathan. 2012. *The Righteous Mind.* New York: Pantheon.

Harary, Frank. 1959. "A Criterion for Unanimity in French's Theory of Social Power." Pp. 168–82 in *Studies in Social Power*, edited by Dorwin Cartwright. Ann Arbor: Institute of Social Research, University of Michigan.

Heckathorn, Douglas D. 1991. "Extensions of the Prisoner's Dilemma Paradigm: The Altruist's Dilemma and Group Solidarity." *Sociological Theory* 9: 34–52.

Hegselmann, Rainer, and Ulrich Krause. 2002. "Opinion Dynamics and Bounded Confidence Models, Analysis, and Simulation." *Journal of Artificial Societies and Social Simulation* 5. http://jasss.soc.surrey.ac.uk/5/3/2.html. Accessed May 16, 2014.

Hetherington, Marc J. 2001. "Resurgent Mass Partisanship: The Role of Elite Polarization." *American Political Science Review* 95: 619–31.

Hunter, James Davison. 1991. *Culture Wars: The Struggle to Define America.* New York: Basic Books.

Kitts, James A. 2006. "Social Influence and the Emergence of Norms Amid Ties of Amity and Enmity." *Simulation Modelling Practice and Theory* 14: 407–22.

Klemm, Konstantin, Victor M. Eguiluz, Raul Toral, and Maxi San Miguel. 2003a. "Global Culture: A Noise Inducted Transition in Finite Systems." *Physical Review E* 67.

2003b. "Non-Equilibrium Transitions in Complex Networks: A Model of Social Interaction." *Physical Review E* 67: 026120 (R).

Lazarsfeld, Paul F., Bernard Berelson, and Hazel Gaudet. 1944. *The People's Choice: How the Voter Makes Up His Mind in a Presidential Campaign.* New York: Duell, Sloan, and Pearce.

Macy, Michael W., and Andreas Flache. 2009. "Social Dynamics from the Bottom Up: Agent-Based Models of Social Interaction." Pp. 245–68 in *The Oxford*

Handbook of Analytical Sociology, edited by Peter Hedstrom and Peter Bearman. Oxford: Oxford University Press.

Macy, Michael W., James A. Kitts, Andreas Flache, and Steve Benard. 2003. "Polarization in Dynamic Networks: A Hopfield Model of Emergent Structure." Pp. 162–73 in *Dynamic Social Network Modelling and Analysis: Workshop Summary and Papers*, edited by Ronald L. Breiger, Kathleen M. Carley, and Philippa Pattison. Washington, DC: The National Academies Press.

Madison, James. 1792. "Notes for the *National Gazette* Essays." Pp. 157–169 in *The Papers of James Madison, Volume 14 (6 April 1791-16 March 1793)*, edited by Robert A. Rutland, Thomas A. Mason, Robert J. Brugger, Jeanne K. Sisson, and Fredrika J. Teute. Charlottesville: University Press of Virginia.

Mark, Noah. 1998a. "Birds of a Feather Sing Together." *Social Forces* 77: 453–85.

1998b. "Beyond Individual Differences: Social Differentiation from First Principles." *American Sociological Review* 63: 309–30.

Mäs, Michael, and Andreas Flache. 2013. "Differentiation without Distancing: Explaining Bi-Polarization of Opinions without Negative Influence." *PLoS One* 8.

McPherson, Miller. 1983. "An Ecology of Affiliation." *American Sociological Review* 48: 519–32.

2004. "A Blau Space Primer: Prolegomenon to an Ecology of Affiliation." *Industrial and Corporate Change* 13: 263–80.

McPherson, Miller, Lynn Smith-Lovin, and James M. Cook. 2001. "Birds of a Feather: Homophily in Social Networks." *Annual Review of Sociology* 27: 415–44.

Mouw, Ted, and Michael E. Sobel. 2001. "Culture Wars and Opinion Polarization: The Case of Abortion." *American Journal of Sociology* 106: 913–43.

Mummendey, Amelie, Bernd Simon, Carsten Dietze, Melanie Grunert, Gabi Haeger, Sabine Kessler, Stephan Lettgen, and Stefanie Schaferhoff. 1982. "Categorization Is Not Enough: Intergroup Discrimination in Negative Outcome Allocation." *Journal of Experimental Social Psychology* 28: 125–44.

Mutz, Diana C. 2002. "Cross-cutting Social Networks: Testing Democratic Theory in Practice." *American Political Science Review* 96: 111–26.

Nunn, Clyde Z., Harry J. Crockett, and J. Allen Williams. 1978. *Tolerance for Nonconformity*. San Francisco: Jossey-Bass.

Putnam, Robert D. 2000. *Bowling Alone: The Collapse and Revival of American Community*. New York: Simon & Schuster.

Rawls, John. 1993. *Political Liberalism*. New York: Columbia University Press.

Redfield, Robert. 1941. *The Folk Culture of Yucatan*. Chicago: University of Chicago Press.

Riker, William H. 1982. *Liberalism against Populism: A Confrontation between the Theory of Democracy and the Theory of Social Choice*. San Francisco: Freeman.

Rousseau, Jean-Jacques. 1997. *The Social Contract and Other Later Political Writings*. Cambridge, UK: Cambridge University Press.

Salganik, Matthew J., Peter Sheridan Dodds, and Duncan J. Watts. 2006. "Experimental Study of Inequality and Unpredictability in an Artificial Cultural Market." *Science* 311: 854–856.

Schelling, Thomas C. 1978. Micromotives and Macrobehavior. New York: Norton.

Stouffer, Samuel. 1955. *Communism, Conformity, and Civil Liberties*. New York: Doubleday.

Struch, Naomi, and Shalom H. Schwartz. 1989. "Intergroup Aggression: Its Predictors and Distinctness from In-Group Bias." *Journal of Personality and Social Psychology* 56: 364–73.

Truman, David. 1951. *The Governmental Process*. New York: Knopf.

van de Rijt, Arnout, and Michael W. Macy. 2009. "The Problem of Order: Egoism or Autonomy?" *Advances in Group Processes* 26: 25–51.

Watts, Duncan J. 1999. *Small Worlds: The Dynamics of Networks between Order and Randomness*. Princeton, NJ: Princeton University Press.

Watts, Duncan J. and Peter D. Dodds. 2007. "Influentials, Networks, and Public Opinion Formation." *Journal of Consumer Research* 34: 441–58.

Willer, Robb, Ko Kuwabara, and Michael W. Macy. 2009. "The False Enforcement of Unpopular Norms." *American Journal of Sociology* 115: 451–90.

Willer, Robb, Christabel L. Rogalin, Bridget Conlon, and Michael T. Wojnowicz. 2013. "Overdoing Gender: A Test of the Masculine Overcompensation Thesis." *American Journal of Sociology* 118: 980–1022.

Wuthnow, Robert. 1988. *The Restructuring of American Religion: Society and Faith Since World War II*. Princeton, NJ: Princeton University Press.

6

Social Exchange and Social Order
An Affect Theory Approach

Edward J. Lawler, Shane R. Thye, and Jeongkoo Yoon

Abstract

We theorize how social exchanges at the micro level generate social order at higher or macro levels of analysis. There are two themes in the argument. The first extrapolates an implicit theory of social order found in exchange theorizing, highlighting both its strengths and limitations. A key strength is that it is a relational theory. A key limitation is that it adopts a purely instrumental conception of people and their relations. The second theme is that this strength can be built upon and the limitation mitigated if one considers the emotional byproducts of social exchange. Social exchanges generate emotions; and when people attribute their feelings to social units, they have an impact on their affective sentiments about group ties. Such social unit attributions link social exchange at the micro level to social ties at the macro level. Exchange-based interpersonal ties are transformed into affective person-to-group ties that promote group-oriented behaviors and sacrifices for the collective welfare.

The Hobbesian problem of social order can be recast in terms of two fundamental social ties: *person-to-person* and *person-to-group*. The Hobbesian framing posits that problems with forming and sustaining productive *person-to-person* ties – humans' avarice and aggression toward one another – make necessary strong *person-to-group* social ties, designed to control an inherent tendency of person-to-person social interactions to descend into a "war of all against all." To understand modern manifestations of this Hobbesian problem, both dimensions clearly are important.

The relational ties of people to each other (*person-to-person*) and their ties to social units (*person-to-group*) represent distinct types of social bonds (see

Authorship is alphabetical. This chapter is based on a larger program of theory and research supported by five grants from the National Science Foundation.

Prentice, Miller, and Lightdale 1994 for evidence). Person-to-person ties entail micro level social interactions in which people develop bonds with other people; whereas person-to-group ties entail a direct link between people and an encompassing social unit, which could be a small local unit or large more distant organization, community, or even nation state (see Lawler, Thye, and Yoon 2009, 2014). This paper reviews theory and research that specifies how and when person-to-group ties emerge from person-to-person ties, and in particular, the implications this has for the Hobbesian problem of social order.

The distinction between person-to-person ties and person-to-group ties is generally conflated in contemporary sociological theorizing of the problem of social order. This relegates to a subsidiary role questions about how such ties are interconnected, which are central to our work over the past two decades. For example, in network theorizing, network structures organize or configure social ties and generate collective results or outcomes, but networks are not generally conceived as distinct objects of attachment or commitment for actors (cf. Lawler et al. 2009; Willer 1999). Analogously, institutional structures impose normative frames and generate enforcement mechanisms that address collective problems of coordination and order, but there is little analysis of the nature of actors' ties to the social unit or how these relate to social interactions among actors. It has long been presumed that people form ties of varying strength to larger social entities of which they are members and that these ties have an important bearing on group-oriented behavior (e.g., Durkheim 1915; Mead 1934; Parsons 1950).[1] Yet, for some reason these phenomena are not an explicit component of contemporary theories regarding the problem of social order.

A related distinction is that between instrumental social ties based solely on individual rationality or cost/benefit calculations, and expressive social ties based on affective sentiments about the group (see Durkheim 1915; Parsons 1950). Our orienting theoretical claim is that purely instrumental person-to-person ties, as represented by exchange relations, can and often do generate affective ties to group entities – local, immediate or larger, more removed groups (see Lawler et al. 2009). In other words, instrumental ties are sometimes transformed over time into expressive ties, making a group or organizational affiliation a salient object of attachment in and of itself. By implication, affective person-to-group ties promote greater institutional capacity to mobilize and capture the benefits of collective goods and greater propensity of individual actors to orient their behavior to collective interests. As it relates to the problem of order this implies that individuals are willing to sacrifice their individual interests for the group. In this way, person-to-group ties have the potential

---

[1] There is a noteworthy convergence on this point in writings as diverse as Talcott Parsons (1950) who explicitly distinguished person-to-person and person-to-group dimensions, George Herbert Mead who contrasted specific and the generalized others, and Tajfel's (1982) argument that group ties have effects on people in the absence of interpersonal ties.

to solve free-rider problems that threaten or undermine social order (Hechter 1987); and, there is some evidence in support of this claim (e.g., Willer, Flynn, and Zak 2012). An important reason for this is that affective person-to-group ties promote the fusion of group identities and personal or self-identities. This fusion in turn strengthens the "moral force" of the communal unit and dampens forces centered on self-interest.

This chapter reviews a program of theory and research that explicitly connects person-to-person ties to person-to-group ties. Two orienting ideas shape this work. First, we assume that social ties (whether person-to-person or person-to-group) start as purely or solely instrumental. That is to say, social ties have a rational-choice foundation. People form ties to others or align themselves with groups or organizations because it serves their individual interests, that is, they receive benefits, rewards, payoffs as a result. In some theoretical traditions within sociology (Hechter 1987; Coleman 1990) this claim is axiomatic and non-controversial; in others it is hotly contested if not altogether rejected (e.g., see Collins 2004; Fine 2012; DiMaggio 1988). Our goal is not to engage this debate here. Instead, we accept that rational choice foundations underlie many if not most social interactions and we theorize how these give rise to emotional or affective bases.[2] Second, we argue that, while rational or instrumental conditions may account for the initial formation of social ties, these conditions cannot adequately account for the enduring ties necessary to uphold or maintain social order more broadly. The reason is straightforward. As instrumental incentives shift and erode over time so does the fabric and strength of social ties and by implication social order. As such, instrumental conditions provide an inadequate explanation for the problem of social order.

In contrast, our position can be stated as follows: *Social structures generate repetition of behaviors and experiences in social interactions; and repetition is a major precursor to order and stability because it has social byproducts that cannot be fully explained by rational choice principles* (see Lawler et al. 2009; Chapter 10 for more discussion of these byproducts). The particular byproduct of concern to us is emotion. Emotions are the linchpin between person-to-person ties and person-to-group ties. Social interactions generate emotions or feelings and, under certain social conditions, these individually-felt emotions shape sentiments about person-to-group ties. In a nutshell, we theorize that repeated person-to-person interactions generate affective person-to-group ties when (*i*) the person-to-person interactions produce positive emotions (e.g., pleasure, excitement), and (*ii*) actors attribute these individual feelings to a group entity (see Lawler et al. 2009).

---

[2] Extant instrumental ties can be construed as a scope condition of our theoretical analysis. We surmise that an instrumental starting point is vastly more common in the contemporary social world, but argue that, because of micro-level emotional mechanisms, noninstrumental ties are overlaid or intertwined with instrumental foundations.

Our program of work conceptualizes social interactions and social structures in social exchange terms. Social exchange is useful framework for us because it adopts and formalizes purely instrumentalist assumptions about actors and relations and it is the only developed micro-sociological theory that does so. Moreover, social exchange is a theory about how relations are formed and sustained in social networks (Emerson 1972; Markovsky, Willer and Patton 1988; Willer 1999) based on payoffs or rewards to individuals. The problem of social order is an implicit backdrop for social exchange theorizing, and we bring that backdrop into the foreground.

There are three main sections in the pages to follow. The first extrapolates and makes explicit the general approach to social order in social exchange theory. The second shows how the emotional/affective byproducts of social exchange can transform the instrumental foundations of an exchange-based order into a more resilient affective and expressive social order. Emergent person-to-group affective ties are central to this transformational process. The third and final section is an initial effort to theorize how such person-to-group ties strengthen the "moral force of the community."

SOCIAL EXCHANGE AND SOCIAL ORDER

Social exchange theory offers a decidedly individualist and instrumentalist approach to social order. It presumes actors who are pursuing individual benefits in the context of structural constraints. There is a rational choice, Hobbesian core at the base of social exchange theory. However, unlike the individualist assumptions of rational choice theory, in social exchange theory profit maximizing is not necessarily assumed, only that individuals seek gains and avoid costs. In other words, actors are assumed to pursue an increase of payoffs from their current levels (Molm and Cook 1995; Willer 1999) rather than maximize *per se*.

While individualist, social exchange also is a relational theory in which structural interdependencies lead actors to exchange items of individual value. Three orienting ideas of social exchange theory help to flesh out the relational aspects of the problem of order. First, broader social structures (opportunities and constraints on interaction) promote repeated exchanges of benefit between actors in a network. Second, these repeated transactions generate and sustain a set of ongoing relational ties, precisely because of their instrumental value. Finally, patterns of instrumentally-based relational ties "overlap" or are contingent on one another to form social networks. The fact that social exchange theory interweaves structural, interactional, and relational dimensions helps to distinguish it from economic approaches (Emerson 1972). The core theoretical propositions about social order are captured abstractly in Figure 6.1.

The social and structural dimensions of this process speak to the problem of order. What makes exchange *social* is that people transact (interact) with the same others across time forming exchange relations (Emerson 1972, 1976).

FIGURE 6.1. Core social order propositions of social exchange theory.

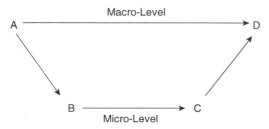

FIGURE 6.2. The Coleman boat conception of role of micro level.

The relational ties are an immediate, recognized object to which actors orient instrumental activity. In contrast, the network is a removed and often unrecognized overarching entity. What makes exchange *structural* is that such relational ties are interconnected by interdependencies in networks. In social exchange theory, relational, person-to-person ties are the fundamental units of activity and social order; networks interconnect and organize relational activities and ties. Individual preferences, benefits, and incentives shape what relations form and endure, and thus, underlie the composition and configuration of the overarching network. This implies a multi-level framework that speaks to the maintenance of social order.

Coleman (1990) analyzes the explanatory role of micro processes in macro explanations in a framework known as the "Coleman Boat." Figure 6.2 shows an abstract representation of the Coleman boat. The point of the framework is to assert that explaining how a macro antecedent (A) generates a macro consequent (D) requires an analysis of the underlying micro process. In Figure 6.2, this entails understanding how actors with preferences (B) produce patterns of behavior (C). For example, in a reinterpretation of Weber's famous thesis, Coleman argues that the Protestant Ethic (A) generates values at the individual level (B) that in turn produce patterns of economic behavior (C) that, in the aggregate, are the basis for capitalism (D) (see Coleman 1990: 8). This simple, artful construction is designed to specify how rational choice processes can explain macro level patterns or results, and it has become a paradigmatic method for conceptualizing macro-micro interconnections. For our purposes it offers a useful way to frame a social exchange approach to the micro-foundations of social order.

In social exchange terms, the macro antecedents are institutional and organizational structures that render actors interdependent, that is, create a social context in which they cannot achieve certain individual gains without exchanging with others. Structural interdependencies (i.e., the macro antecedent) set the stage for patterns of frequent or repeated exchange to develop among select actors (i.e., B, the micro antecedent). Repeated exchanges generate exchange relations (i.e., C, the micro consequent) in which profitable exchanges produce relational ties that are recognized by actors themselves. These ties induce them to continue exchange with the same others rather than face the uncertainties associated with new exchange partners (Kollock 1994). Finally, the macro consequent (D) is a social network with a configuration of ties that reflect the relational underpinnings. It is the realized or operative network within which flows of benefits are accessible to actors. The network is a purely instrumental entity, as are the exchange relations within. A social order based solely on this instrumental foundation is likely to be tenuous and unstable, because it is dependent on what is presumed to be a fixed network structure and stable underlying incentives.

To summarize, the primary sources of social order in exchange theory are structural dependencies or interdependencies that shape the incentives of actors to exchange goods of value with others (Emerson 1972; Cook et al. 1983; Markovsky et al. 1988). Actors choose among potential exchange partners, but the "availability" of prospective partners varies based on the structure of dependence, interdependence, and power in the network. Those with more power accrue more benefits because they can extract more benefits from exchange partners. Therefore, over time, a micro level, rational choice process (B → C in the Coleman boat) generates stable network level allocations of profit, that is, stratification and inequality (Willer 1999). This micro process, however, tends to be assumed and exchange theorists then look for effects that, in Coleman-boat terms, are A → D. The underlying mechanisms of order and stability are secondary to the structural effects. We argue that repeated exchange and relational commitments are central to implicit ideas about social order in exchange theory. These create and sustain stable orders even in the context of changing structures and associated incentives, due to unintended byproducts of social exchange.

A classic study that speaks to such a process was conducted by Kollock (1994). Kollock tested the idea that under high uncertainty people involved in exchange are more likely to form relational commitments than under conditions of low uncertainty. Uncertainty refers to whether actors know or can predict the value of goods from exchange. Commitments imply a propensity to keep exchanging with the same others despite opportunity costs or foregone benefits. To test this idea, Kollock created a laboratory setting that compared two product markets repeatedly across time. In one, product quality was standardized and, thus, a buyer did not face uncertainty about the value of the product; in the other, product quality was variable and unpredictable. The buyer could not know the quality of the product until after the exchange was consummated. The results revealed that actors were more likely to form commitments – that is, enduring exchange relations – under conditions of high uncertainty.

The role of repetition as a precursor to order is echoed in Emerson's (1972) definition of social exchange and central to Homans (1950) classic work. Those outside of exchange theory agree. Wrong (1995) theorizes that repeated interaction generates the habits or regular patterns that transform descriptive norms (i.e., the capacity to predict others' behavior) into prescriptive norms (i.e., expectations of behavior shared by others) that guide and control behavior. Berger and Luckmann (1966) portray repetition as leading to incipient institutions, that is, practices and patterns that become "taken for granted" and increasingly enacted without thought or reflection. Collins (2004) arrives at a similar conclusion based on his theory of interaction ritual chains. Here, the common focus and shared moods that accompany social interactions create group ties of solidarity through the emotional energy (uplift, confidence) produced in social interaction. Collins (2004) explicitly argues that recurrent interactions are the micro-foundation for macro social orders. In sum, scholars of various academic stripes concur that mere repetition of behavior in interaction sets the stage for more stable relations and groups (see Lawler et al. 2009: 168).

In the social exchange tradition, there are two distinct mechanisms for the impact of repeated exchange on relational commitments: trust and affect. The trust explanation claims that stable, cohesive relational ties emerge in response to high uncertainty (Kollock 1994) or to the risk of non-reciprocity (Molm, Collett, and Schaefer 2007). Finding a partner who is predictable and trustworthy is especially valuable in a highly uncertain or risky context. Mutual trust is a plausible bonding agent at the relational level (Fukuyama 1995). The affect mechanism indicates that stable, cohesive relational ties emerge when exchanges produce positive emotions (pleasure/satisfaction, interest/excitement) that actors attribute to their relation or a larger social unit within which it is embedded (Lawler and Yoon 1996; Lawler et al. 2009). There is some evidence that trust and affect are "dual processes" and that they operate in a complementary way to generate stable, cohesive exchange relations (see Lawler, Thye, and Yoon 2000, 2014; Yoon and Thye 2000, 2002). The remainder of this chapter explicates the affect-based explanation for how social exchange generates social order.

THE AFFECT MECHANISM

The central idea is that emotions or feelings mediate and explain the impact of repeated interaction on the emergence of relational ties between two actors. Homans (1950) originated this idea in his activities/interaction/sentiments framework. He proposed that interaction frequencies actualize a set of opportunities available in the social context; and more frequent interaction fosters relations that constitute a group. The bonding agent or mechanism is positive sentiments about specific interaction partners (Homan 1950). More frequent interaction is posited to produce more positive sentiments. Relational

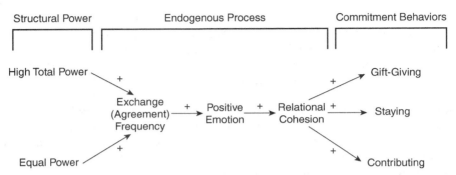

FIGURE 6.3. The Theory of relational cohesion (adapted from Lawler and Yoon 1996). Reproduced with permission from Lawler and Yoon (1996).

Cohesion theory (Lawler and Yoon 1996) extends the interaction-to-emotion link by theorizing how this process leads actors to see the relation itself as a cohesive object of affective or intrinsic value. Following Emerson (1972), this process is grounded in structures of power and dependence.

Emerson's (1972) structural approach to social exchange was based partly on the assumption that dyads are nested in networks and, therefore, should be studied in this context. Isolated dyads are rare empirically and of little socio-logical interest. For Emerson and others in the 1980s and 1990s (see Cook et al. 1983), structural power and allocations of payoffs within and across dyads in networks were the main research problem. Exchange frequencies were assumed and given little theoretical attention (see Skvoretz and Lovaglia 1995 for exceptions). Relational cohesion theory shifts the emphasis to exchange frequency in an effort to explain how social exchange generates relational ties that take on intrinsic value, and to which actors orient their behavior (Lawler and Yoon 1996). Emotions represent the proximal cause of relational cohesion, and relational cohesion represents the proximal cause of commitment to the relation as a social unit.

Relational cohesion theory has direct implications for the problem of social order. It stipulates that when people engage in repeated exchanges over time, expressive elements tend to be introduced into an instrumental exchange rela-tion. The theory explains how and when this transformation from instru-mental to expressive ties is most likely to occur by specifying a causal chain through which structural conditions generate this sort of non-instrumental tie. Figure 6.3 presents the theory in model form.

The structure, following social exchange theorizing, is conceived in power-dependence terms. The dependence of A on B (and vice versa) is deter-mined by the value of the rewards or costs at stake and the availability of alternative sources of those valued rewards. The causal chain starts with the proposition that equal dependence relations are more likely to gener-ate expressive ties than unequal dependence relations, and the same goes for greater mutual dependence (interdependence or "total power" in the relation). Importantly, these structurally-based effects are indirect, that is, they operate only through the endogenous process specified by the theory, that is, through the *frequency-to-emotion-to-cohesion* link. Relational cohesion, defined as a perception of the exchange relation as a "unifying" force, is the proximal cause of relational commitments (see Lawler and Yoon 1996). Note that both instrumental (stay behavior) and expressive (unilateral gift giving) behaviors stem from relational cohesion. This affect mechanism is a counterpoint to uncertainty reduction explanations for commitment. Relational cohesion theory predicts that emotions generated by exchange will strengthen both the instrumental and expressive foundations of the exchange relation.[3] Expressive ties make the relation an object valued in itself. To the extent that the relation is a valued object the relation should be more stable and orderly.

Research has tested the predictions of relational cohesion theory for three basic forms of commitment behavior: (*i*) the propensity to stay in the relation which is the standard indicator of instrumental commitment, (*ii*) the giving of token unilateral gifts, an indicator of expressive commitment, and (*iii*) investing in a new joint venture that involves risk (i.e., cooperating in a social dilemma), which likely stems from both instrumental and expressive elements. Applied to the social-order problem, these forms of commitment imply together that social orders are likely to be more resilient if the benefits provided by a group tie are sufficient to motivate members to stay with group, if members exude generosity by giving each other items of value without exchange contingencies, and finally if members are prepared to collaborate in new joint efforts that carry a risk of exploitation or malfeasance by others.[4]

Empirical tests consistently support the endogenous process predicted by relational cohesion theory (for reviews, see Thye, Yoon, and Lawler 2002; Thye, Vincent, Lawler, and Yoon 2014). Repeated exchanges generate positive feelings that, in turn, produce greater relational cohesion; the result is commitment behaviors along all three dimensions. The broader implication is that structural equality and structural interdependence foster more resilient social orders, and do so because of the positive emotions and cohesion that stem from repeated exchanges among the same actors. Relational cohesion theory also can pinpoint where "pockets of cohesion" or small micro orders will develop within networks (Lawler and Yoon 1998), and when networks as a whole take

---

[3] This theory proposes that while uncertainty reduction helps to explain the instrumental tie of the exchange relation, the affect mechanism helps account for both the expressive and instrumental elements of the relational tie.

[4] Relational cohesion theory assumes five general (scope) conditions. (*i*) Three or more actors in a network are pursuing individual gain; (*ii*) a social (network) structure creates incentives for select exchanges to be consummated; (*iii*) actors exchange with partners who are available and from whom they expect the greatest individual gain or profit; (*iv*) exchanges occur in an emerging or extant social unit; and (*v*) local units (relations, groups) are nested within larger social units (organizations, communities, nations) (Thye, Vincent, Lawler, and Yoon 2014).

on subtle group properties that transform the network into an operative group order (Lawler, Thye, and Yoon 2008; Thye, Lawler, and Yoon 2011). In sum, the affect mechanism is well-documented by research on relational cohesion theory. It seems clear that person-to-person instrumental ties have the capacity to generate person-to-group bonds under the conditions assumed.

There is, nevertheless, an important gap or omission. It is not clear (a) exactly how individual emotion from social exchange becomes associated with or attached to relations or group units, or (b) whether local (proximal) or more removed (distal) groups are prime objects of emergent emotional ties. The question of how individually-felt emotions become affective group ties or sentiments was initially taken up by the "affect theory of social exchange" (Lawler 2001). Subsequently, it was abstracted beyond social exchange in a general "theory of social commitments" (Lawler, Thye, and Yoon 2009), and it is this theory that explicitly addresses the second question about ties to proximal or distal groups. The next section addresses these issues.

INTERACTION AND SOCIAL COMMITMENTS

Social exchange is a quintessential joint task because, by definition, it involves an accomplishment that can only be achieved with one or more others. The "theory of social commitments" (Lawler et al. 2009) picks up on this point and proposes that joint tasks are an important structural foundation for social (noninstrumental) commitments to social units, for example, including relations, small groups, organizations, communities, or even nation states. The main idea is that if social interactions involve a joint task, they are likely to generate stronger or weaker social commitments. Three forms of commitment are commonly found in related literature: instrumental, normative, and affective (Kanter 1968; Meyer and Allen 1997). We define social commitments as affective commitments or affectively-based normative commitments; these are noninstrumental ties that exert influence beyond what is produced by instrumental or instrumentally-based normative commitments. A distinctive feature of *social* commitments is that they have an affective component and make the group affiliation an object of intrinsic value and an "end it itself" (see Lawler et al. 2009: 23–28 for more discussion).

Social commitments theory interweaves three foundational ideas. First, when people interact with others, they are likely to feel good if they successfully accomplish an interaction task and feel bad if they do not. Any interaction can be construed as entailing an implicit or explicit task that varies in jointness. Second, if people repeatedly experience these feelings within the same social context, they are inclined to interpret their emotions as due partly to shared or common aspects of the social context. Their individual emotions or feelings are perceived or interpreted in group or social unit terms. Third, given both a joint task and a propensity to interpret emotions in relational unit terms, it is reasonable to suspect that individuals attribute their emotions to enduring and salient social units in the context. Repeated interactions and the resulting person-to-person ties, therefore, lead to affective sentiments about groups that make the person-to-person interactions possible or necessary in the first place (see Lawler et al. 2009). The affective sentiments may be directed at proximal, local groups or more distant and removed organizations. The theoretical question is: Under what structural conditions do people attribute individual feelings (positive or negative) to a social unit – local or larger. These cognitions are termed "social unit attributions" (Lawler 2001; Lawler et al. 2009).[5]

Social Unit Attributions

Social commitment theory identifies two conditions for social unit attributions to generate affective group ties. First, the interaction tasks or activities are high in jointness. Second, from these joint tasks, actors develop a sense of shared responsibility for the results of their task activity. Task jointness has a structural foundation but also an interpretive dimension. Interaction tasks guide instrumental behaviors by defining or activating objectives and a set of practices or procedures for reaching those objectives. The objectives and practices may be tacit and informal or explicit and formal. The emphasis is on the interdependence of behaviors that make up the task, rather than the interdependence of the task outcomes. *Task jointness* refers to the degree that the task behaviors are blended or interwoven, such that it is difficult to tell how much each member contributed to the collective result, in other words, individual behaviors and contributions are indistinguishable.[6] Task jointness is important because it shapes the sense of *shared responsibility* actors have for the results of their task activity. A greater sense of shared responsibility makes it more likely that individuals make social unit attributions of their emotions and feelings from the task activity.

The central predictions, therefore, are that social interactions are most likely to generate social unit attributions of emotion when (*i*) those interactions produce positive individual feelings, (*ii*) the task is high in jointness so people cannot tell who contributed what or how much to the task, and (*iii*) people perceive a high degree of shared responsibility for the results of their task activity. Given the repeated experience of these conditions, members develop stronger affective and non-instrumental ties to the group. Williamson (1985) implies a similar point when he suggests that workers develop a strong sense of solidarity or "being in this together" if work structures make it difficult to distinguish each worker's contribution to collective (task) results, that

---

[5] These attributions are about the causes of one's own emotions, not the attribution of qualities to self or other which is the focus of attribution theory in psychology.

[6] We posit that these are process effects of task jointness that apply to both fully cooperative group settings and mixed-motive settings in which actors face a social dilemma. The scope of this theory is broader than social exchange.

is, task behaviors are "non-separable." We introduce the idea that an underlying affective process transforms those solidary group ties to include an expressive component. The sense of shared responsibility is a key contingency, that is, a moderating condition for social unit attributions of emotion and affective person-to-group ties.[7]

Several studies provide support for the prediction that joint tasks generate stronger affective group ties and suggest that these effects are due to the fact that perceptions of shared responsibility promote social unit attributions. A study of exchange structures found that productive forms of social exchange produce stronger affective ties to the group than negotiated, reciprocal, or generalized exchange (Lawler et al. 2008). Productive forms of exchange involve person-to-group investments or contributions from which actors can receive their maximum payoffs (Emerson 1976; Lawler et al. 2000). Beyond the impact on affective person-to-group ties, productive exchange structures generated more frequent exchange, more positive emotions from that exchange, and stronger perceptions of shared responsibility (Lawler et al. 2008). These effects support the underlying logic of the theory.[8]

A study outside of the laboratory by Taylor and Pillemer (2009) examined the effects of joint task and shared responsibility on staff turnover in nursing homes. They conceive of "care giving" as a joint task in which the contributions of individual staff are blended and difficult to distinguish or separate. The data were from a longitudinal survey with two measures, six months apart, in twenty randomly chosen nursing homes in New York State. The main findings are that perceived success at the joint task (caregiving) reduced actual turnover within the six month period studied, but this effect was indirect. Success at the joint task produced stronger person-to-group affective ties (sentiments) which, in turn, reduced staff turnover in the nursing home. These results are consistent with our affect mediation hypothesis.

Three other studies support select components of the theory. Research by Kuwubara (2011) affirms the importance of joint tasks. He specifically compared the emergence of cohesive (group) ties in an integrative versus distributive negotiation (study 1) and also in a one-way versus two-way (bilateral) trust games. In both studies, the more joint the task (integrative negotiation, bilateral trust), the greater the cohesion of the relational or group tie (Kuwubara 2011). A study by Willer, Flynn, and Zak (2012) found that the strength of group identification mediated the impact of generalized exchange on group-oriented

---

[7] The sense of shared responsibility mitigates the strength of self-serving attributions for success or failure, that is, the propensity to take credit for positive results and blame others for task failure. In other words joint tasks that promote a sense of shared responsibility are a plausible antidote to self-serving attributions of group success/failure.

[8] Molm and colleagues develop an alternative analysis of generalized exchange in which the expressive value of unilateral giving and absence of a competitive structure enhances the solidarity or cohesion effects of generalized exchange but they do not compare productive and generalized exchange (see Molm, Collett, and Schaefer 2007).

behaviors in part because group identification entailed greater jointness. Finally, Thye, Lawler, and Yoon (2014) apply the theory to a fully cooperative group context, directly testing and finding support for the moderating effects of shared responsibility; that is, the combination of positive feelings from the task activity and perceptions of shared responsibility generated stronger affective ties to the group and a greater willingness to act pro-socially toward other group members. In sum, there is growing evidence that joint tasks and a sense of shared responsibility play an important role in group ties and, by implication, social order. These effects operate through emotional processes.

Proximal and Distal Social Commitments

Local, immediate social units (i.e., work groups) tend to be nested within larger social units (i.e., organizations). The "fact" of nested groups raises a question about what group units are the object or target of social unit attributions. On the one hand, if the local enactment of joint tasks promotes ties to the proximal local unit, but not the larger unit, one would expect to observe a fragmented larger unit in which it is difficult to foster collaboration at that larger unit level. The larger unit probably would remain a solely instrumental object while the proximal unit becomes affectively-imbued and expressive. On the other hand, if the larger unit is the primary object of commitment, that unit will have greater capacity to mobilize and sustain collaborative actions across units at the local level and to do so with lower surveillance and enforcement costs. This is termed "the nested commitment problem" of social order (see Lawler et al. 2009: chapters 6 and 7). We suggest that this common problem, faced especially by decentralized, federated, or loosely coupled organizations, has an important emotional dimension.

An earlier formulation of nested commitments theory proposed that people tend to attribute positive emotions to proximal (local) groups and negative emotions to distal (larger and removed) groups (Lawler 1992). The rationale is as follows: Proximal groups are the immediate locus of repeated social interactions, and the place where "pleasurable" task activity is experienced in collaboration with others. Proximal groups are more salient than an overarching, removed unit, especially when people are engaged in task activity and they respond to their perceptions of control or discretion. Proximal social units are perceived as having more control over and being more responsible for positive events and emotions, whereas distal social units tend to be perceived as more responsible for negative events and emotions. Thus, local units receive more credit for pleasant events than the larger organization, whereas the larger unit receives more blame for unpleasant events than the local unit.[9]

---

[9] Turner (2007; this volume) develops a related argument in which he argues that positive emotions originate at the micro level, and the resilience of macro social orders depend on the spread of these positive emotions from micro to meso and macro levels.

Social commitments theory draws particular attention to whether and where people are likely to perceive *shared* responsibility. The nested commitment problem is tied to not only individuals' control or discretion but also to where they are most likely to engage in joint tasks that generate a sense of shared responsibility. If joint tasks in an organization are designed and controlled in local units (e.g., local departments, work groups, chapters, retail outlets), then those joint tasks are likely to foster stronger affective ties to the local than to the larger unit. If joint tasks are designed and controlled by the larger unit, stronger affective ties to the larger unit may result. Yet, these are socially based definitions of control and responsibility that are malleable and shaped heavily by social interactions in the local unit.[10] Definitions of responsibility, credit for positive events, and blame for negative events tend to favor the local, proximal group rather than the distal more removed or encompassing organization. The core prediction is that positive feelings from task activity build stronger ties to the local group than to the larger organization, and negative feelings from task activity weaken ties to the larger organization more than to the local one. These effects are likely to be contingent on perceptions of whether the locus of control is proximal or distal but also whether the locus of shared responsibility is proximal or distal.

A study by Mueller and Lawler (1999) tested the idea that proximal units generate stronger ties than distal units, by comparing the strength of commitments in a decentralized (schools within a school district) and a centralized organization (medical centers within the air force). The hypothesis was that work conditions have different effects on local and larger unit commitments, contingent on whether work conditions are controlled locally or centrally. Surveys included an affect measure of job satisfaction and measures of commitments to local or larger units. The findings indicate that when work conditions are controlled by the local or proximal unit (schools in a school district), they have an impact on commitments to that local unit; yet, when work conditions are controlled in the larger unit (the air force for the medical center), they affect commitment to that larger organization. The locus of control and responsibility determine the primary object of commitment, proximal or distal group. Moreover, affective responses to the job (satisfaction) partially mediate these effects, consistent with the theory of social commitments. There also is evidence of greater commitment at the proximal, local level in the decentralized than at the distal level in centralized organization. Overall, this study supports the plausibility of the nested-commitment propositions of social commitments theory (Lawler et al. 2009).

THE MORAL FORCE OF PERSON-TO-GROUP TIES

An undeveloped implication of social commitments theory concerns the relationship between affective ties to a group and the moral force of that group.

[10] Commitments to the local and larger units are not necessarily inversely related. However, the advantages of the local group remain and the theory would predict stronger commitment effects at the local than at the larger unit level.

Examining the moral force is one way to elaborate the implications of expressive group ties. We know that ties to a group and ties to other persons are different in fundamental ways. Among those differences, it is noteworthy that group ties have an imagined, supra-individual quality not present in person-to-person ties. Groups, large and small, represent "imagined communities" in Anderson's (2006) terms, "generalized others" in Mead's (1934) terms, and "collective consciousness" in Durkheim's (1895) terms. Groups are cognitive, abstractly constructed entities that frame and give larger meaning to social interactions or exchanges. These larger meanings are likely to have a moral dimension. A moral dimension is present to the degree that group members' ideas or beliefs about the "good," the "right," and "the proper" are developed and shaped within them (see Turner 2010). Judgments of goodness or rightness are known to be highly ambiguous and subjective, and this makes micro-level social interactions especially crucial to the shaping and enactment of moral beliefs. Below we outline some ideas about how affective group ties bear on the moral force of a group.

In recent years, the sociology of morality has re-emerged as a central concern of sociology (e.g., see Hitlin and Vaisey 2010, 2013). The concepts of morality vary widely as do the nature of the questions addressed and the approaches to answering the questions chosen. For our purposes, the "good," "right" and "proper" represent a useful conception consistent with much of available literature.[11] Moral judgments can be found at all levels of analysis, from the individual to societal, and moral consensus is clearly a problematic notion. Nevertheless, it is reasonable to presume that in group settings some moral beliefs are widely shared among members or at least perceived to be. This should apply whether the group is small or large, local or remote, organized or unorganized, hierarchical or communal. Widely shared moral beliefs can be construed as theoretically analogous to "widely shared status beliefs" specified by status construction theory (Ridgeway 2011). They are abstract, generalized ideas that may or may not be used or enacted in social situations. Personal moral beliefs need not correspond to widely shared beliefs but actors must perceive the widely shared beliefs as reasonably consensual for them to be enacted.

Using the simple definition of moral above, such beliefs conceive in general terms what constitutes a good behavior, a good person, or a good group. Our conjecture is that widely shared moral beliefs are more readily activated and enacted as people become affectively committed to a group. This is partly due to the salience of the group as an important social object but also due to the pleasant emotions or feelings experienced as a group member. To feel a tie to a group is not only to believe the group is present and real, but also to feel like it is part of you as you are part of it. Group attributes or qualities become a part of how members define their own personal qualities.[12] The expressive value or

---

[11] These are common elements of most definitions of morality, moral judgment, or moral action (see Hitlin and Vaisey 2010).

[12] This should apply to both "good" and "bad" qualities, although here we are mainly considering "good" qualities.

meaning of the group spreads to moral beliefs that are perceived as associated with the group and regularly enacted by its members.

There are two underlying processes that may help to understand how and why affective group ties promote the enactment of widely shared moral beliefs of the group. First, stronger affective ties are likely to enhance the salience and centrality of a group identity, leading actors to more heavily use the relevant identity standards to guide their behavior and interactions with others (Stryker 1980; Burke and Stets 2009). We assume that group-based identity standards are partly moral. Second, the group-based moral beliefs that legitimate and give larger meaning to those identity standards are internalized to the degree that the group entity is a positive affective object. Extending social commitments theory, we offer two propositions.

(1) The salience and centrality of a group identity increases in groups where individuals frequently engage in joint tasks, experience positive feelings, and perceive shared responsibility for collective results.

(2) As a group identity grows in salience and centrality, members are more likely to internalize moral beliefs associated with that group identity.

In these terms, the identity effects of affective person-to-group ties are a precursor to the internalization of the group's moral beliefs and standards. Person to group ties promote internalization of prevailing moral beliefs indirectly through the identity effects of those ties.

The summary implication is that a group identity becomes stronger when core principles of social commitments theory apply. As people become more affectively committed to a group, the salience and centrality of that group identity also grows. This may occur without subsequent internalization of identity standards associated with the group identity, but the identity effects establish a necessary condition for members to internalize widely shared moral beliefs of the group, that is, to adopt those moral beliefs their own. Future theory and research should analyze the structural and interactional conditions under which these processes occur.

CONCLUSION

Theories that address the problem of order tend to focus on (*i*) tensions between individual and collective interests (Hechter 1987), (*ii*) taken-for-granted cultural beliefs and institutional structures (DiMaggio 1988), or (*iii*) emergent shared meanings (Berger and Luckmann 1966; Fine 2012). These approaches are not mutually-exclusive but there is an important omission in all them – namely, lack of focused attention to emotional/affective processes. Jon Turner's work (2007; this volume) is an important exception, as is our own work over the last twenty years or so. Beyond the early work of Ekeh (1974), until recently social exchange theorizing has not had much to say explicitly about how orders come about or are sustained. In this paper, we first extrapolate the elements of the implicit social exchange approach to social order and then modify that approach, arguing for the centrality of an affect mechanism. The modification involves two ideas – social exchange generates everyday emotions and feelings and, under some conditions, these feelings strengthen (or weaken) affective ties to groups. These simple points suggest a significant shift in exchange theorizing, by moving from a concept of actors as instrumental, information-processors to actors as emoting, expressive beings.

To summarize, the theory of social order outlined in this chapter combines five abstract principles to analyze how and when social exchanges generate and sustain micro and macro orders. The first principle is: *Joint tasks, around which social interaction occurs, is a foundation for the emergence and reproduction of a social order.* Tasks are a neglected component of social structures but also an integral feature of many contexts where people interact with others. Social exchange is by definition a joint task and, thus, an important context in which to examine jointness that varies across tasks. The second principle is that *social exchanges produce emotions (positive or negative) and repeated exchanges raise awareness of these feelings and motivate actors to seek positive and avoid negative feelings.* The third principle connects the first two: *If repeated joint tasks generate a sense of shared responsibility for the task, people attribute their emotions from exchange to social units that they also share.*

Perceptions of shared responsibility are the key contingency for social unit attributions of emotion, and these perceptions are tied to the tasks implicit or explicit in the social structure. The fourth principle stems from the idea that social unit attributions may be directed primarily at proximal, immediate groups or distal, more removed ones, and this depends on whether the emotions are positive or negative: *Positive emotions are likely to be attributed to proximal, immediate groups whereas negative emotions are attributed to distal more removed groups.* This helps to explain why social order is easier to maintain at local (micro) than at larger (macro) levels. However, we add a fifth principle here, suggesting that the target of positive emotions is contingent on the locus of control and responsibility: *If perceived control and responsibility for joint tasks is proximal, positive emotions from exchange strengthen those local group ties, but if control and responsibility is distal, the larger unit is the target of social unit attributions.* Thus, larger, more removed organizations may "solve" the social order problems manifest in the fourth principle by assuming, claiming, or asserting control over and responsibility for the joint tasks that actors interact to accomplish at the local level. In closing, *joint tasks* grounded in social structure, perceptions of *share responsibility*, which constitute a subjective interpretation of those tasks, and *social unit attributions* which forge an affective link between micro-level interactions and macro level affiliations are the central explanatory ideas of the theory of order proposed here. Together these suggest how person-to person, instrumental exchanges bear on affective ties to macro entities, and specify fundamental conditions under which individuals make sacrifices for the collective welfare.

REFERENCES

Anderson, Benedict. 2006. *Imagined communities: Reflections on the Origin and Spread of Nationalism.* New York: Verso.

Berger, Peter, and Thomas Luckmann. 1966. *Social Construction of Reality.* New York: Anchor Book.

Burke, Peter J., and Jan E. Stets. 2009. *Identity Theory.* New York: Oxford University Press.

Coleman, James S. 1990. *Foundations of Social Theory.* Cambridge, MA: Harvard University Press.

Collins, Randall. 2004. *Interaction Ritual Chains.* Princeton, NJ: Princeton University Press.

Cook, Karen S., Richard M. Emerson, Mary R. Gillmore, and Toshio Yamagishi. 1983. "The Distribution of Power in Exchange Networks: Theory and Experimental Results." *American Journal of Sociology* 89: 275–305.

DiMaggio, P. J. 1988. "Interest and Agency in Institutional Theory." Pp. 3–22 in *Institutional Patterns and Organizations: Culture and Environment,* edited by L.G. Zucker. Cambridge, MA: Ballinger.

Durkheim, Emile. 1895. *The Rules of the Sociological Method.* New York: Free Press.

  1915. *The Elementary Forms of Religious Life.* New York: Free Press.

Ekeh, Peter. 1974. *Social Exchange Theory.* Cambridge, MA: Harvard University Press.

Emerson, Richard M. 1972. "Exchange Theory Part II: Exchange Relations and Networks." Pp. 58–87 in *Sociological Theories in Progress,* edited by J. Berger, M. Zelditch Jr., and B. Anderson. Boston: Houghton-Mifflin.

  1976. "Social Exchange Theory." *Annual Review of Sociology* 2: 335–362.

Fine, Gary A. 2012. *Tiny Publics: A Theory of Group Action and Culture.* New York: Russell Sage Foundation Publications.

Fukuyama, Francis. 1995. *Trust: The Social Virtues and the Creation of Prosperity.* New York: Free Press.

Hechter, Michael. 1987. *Principles of Group Solidarity.* Berkeley: University of California Press.

Hitlin, Steven, and Stephen Vaisey. 2010. "Back to the Future." Pp. 3–16 in *Handbook of the Sociology of Morality,* edited by Hitlin and S. Vaisey. New York: Springer.

  2013. "The New Sociology of Morality." *Annual Review of Sociology* 39: 51–68.

Homans, George Caspar. 1950. *The Human Group.* New Brunswick, NJ: Transaction Publishers.

Kanter, Rosabeth M. 1968. "Commitment and Social Organization: A Study of Commitment Mechanisms in Utopian Communities." *American Sociological Review* 33: 499–517.

Kollock, Peter. 1994. "The Emergence of Exchange Structures: An Experimental Study of Uncertainty, Commitment, and Trust." *American Journal of Sociology* 100: 315–45.

Kuwabara, Ko. 2011. "Cohesion, Cooperation, and the Value of Doing Things Together How Economic Exchange Creates Relational Bonds." *American Sociological Review* 76: 560–80.

Lawler, Edward J. 1992. "Affective Attachments to Nested Groups: A Choice-Process Theory." *American Sociological Review* 57: 327–36.

2001. "An Affect Theory of Social Exchange." *American Journal of Sociology* 107: 321–352.

Lawler, Edward J., and Jeongkoo Yoon. 1996. "Commitment in Exchange Relations: Test of a Theory of Relational Cohesion." *American Sociological Review* 61: 89–108.

1998. "Network Structure and Emotion in Exchange Relations." *American Sociological Review* 58: 465–81.

Lawler, Edward J., Shane R. Thye, and Jeongkoo Yoon. 2000. "Emotion and Group Cohesion in Productive Exchange." *American Journal of Sociology* 106: 616–57.

2008. "Social Exchange and Micro Social Order." *American Sociological Review* 73: 519–42.

2009. *Social Commitments in a Depersonalized World.* New York: The Russell Sage Foundation.

2014. "Emotions and Group Ties in Social Exchange." In *Handbook of the Sociology of Emotions II*, edited J. Stets and J. Turner. New York: Springer.

Mead, George Herbert. 1934. *Mind, Self, and Society.* Chicago: University of Chicago Press.

Markovsky, Barry, David Willer, and Travis Patton. 1988. "Power Relations in Exchange Networks." *American Sociological Review* 53: 220–36.

Mead, George Herbert. 1934. *Mind, Self and Society.* Chicago: University of Chicago.

Meyer, John W., and Natalie J. Allen. 1997. *Commitment in the Workplace: Theory, Research and Application.* Thousand Oaks, CA: Sage.

Molm, Linda D., and Karen S. Cook. 1995. "Social Exchange and Exchange Networks." Pp. 209–35 in *Sociological Perspectives on Social Psychology*, edited by K. S. Cook, G. A. Fine, and J. S. House. Boston, MA: Allyn and Bacon.

Molm, Linda D., Jessica L. Collett, and David R. Schaefer. 2007. "Building Solidarity through Generalized Exchange: A Theory of Reciprocity." *American Journal of Sociology* 113: 205–42.

Mueller, Charles W., and Edward J. Lawler. 1999. "Commitment to Nested Organizational Units: Some Basic Principles and Preliminary Findings." *Social Psychology Quarterly* 62: 325–46.

Parsons, T. 1950. *The Social System.* New York: Free Press.

Prentice, Deborah A., Dale T. Miller, and Jenifer R. Lightdale. 1994. "Asymmetries in Attachments to Groups and to Their Members: Distinguishing Between Common-Identity and Common-Bond Groups." *Personality and Social Psychology Bulletin* 20: 484–93.

Ridgeway, Cecilia L. 2011. *Framed by Gender: How Gender Inequality Persists in the Modern World.* Oxford: Oxford University Press.

Skvoretz, John and Michael J. Lovaglia. 1995. "Who Exchanges with Whom: Structural Determinants of Exchange Frequency in Negotiated Exchange Networks." *Social Psychology Quarterly* 58: 163–77.

Stryker, Sheldon. 1980. *Symbolic Interactionism: A Social Structural Version.* Menlo Park, CA: Benjamin/Cummings Publishers.

Tajfel, Henry. 1982. "Social Psychology of Intergroup Relations." *Annual Review of Psychology* 33: 1–39.

Taylor, Catherine, and Karl Pillemer. 2009. "Using Affect to Understand Employee Turnover: A Context-Specific Application of a Theory of Social Exchange." *Sociological Perspectives* 52: 481–504.

Thye, Shane R., Edward J. Lawler, and Jeongkoo Yoon. 2011. "The Emergence of Embedded Relations and Group Formation in Networks of Competition." *Social Psychology Quarterly* 74: 387–413.

2014. "Affective Bases of Order in Task Groups: Testing a New Theory of Social Commitments." Unpublished Manuscript.

Thye, Shane R., Aaron Vincent, Edward J Lawler, and Jeongkoo Yoon. 2014. "Relational Cohesion, Social Commitments and Person to Group Ties: Twenty Five Years of a Theoretical Research Program." Pp. 99–138 in *Advances in Group Processes* 31, edited by Shane R. Thye and Edward J. Lawler. London: Emerald Press.

Thye, Shane R., Jeongkoo Yoon, and Edward J. Lawler. 2002. "The Theory of Relational Cohesion: Review of a Research Program." Pp. 89–102 in *Advances in Group Process*, Vol. 19, edited by S. R. Thye and E. J. Lawler. Oxford, UK: Elsevier.

Turner, Jonathan. 2007. *Human Emotions: A Sociological Theory*. New York: Routedge.

2010. "The Stratification of Emotions: Some Preliminary Generalizations." *Sociological Inquiry* 80: 168–99.

Willer, David. 1999. *Network Exchange Theory*. Westport, CT: Praeger Publisher.

Willer, Robb, Francis J. Flynn, and Sonya Zak. 2012. "Structure, Identity, and Solidarity: A Comparative Field Study of Generalized and Direct Exchange." *Administrative Science Quarterly* 57: 119–55.

Williamson Oliver, E. 1985. *The Economic Institutions of Capitalism*. New York: Free Press.

Wrong, Dennis. 1995. *Power: Its forms, Bases, and Uses*. New York: Harper and Row.

Yoon, Jeongkoo, and Shane R. Thye. 2000. "Supervisor Support in the Work Place: Legitimacy and Positive Affectivity." *Journal of Social Psychology* 140: 295–316.

2002. "A Dual Process Model of Organizational Commitment." *Work and Occupations* 29: 97–124.

7

Institutions, Trust, and Social Order

Karen S. Cook

Abstract

Trust theories suggest that the human capacity to trust and to be trustworthy is an important element in the production of micro social order. Trust can take the form of generalized beliefs (attitudes) about the trustworthiness of people in the abstract or be based on information about behaviors indicative of the trustworthiness of specific others in particular situations. In either case, trust involves an expectation that one or more others will cooperate or collaborate, despite the opportunity to exploit or act out of pure self-interest. We explore the general role of trust in the production of collective efforts and its limits as the basis for large-scale cooperation and macro-social order.

INTRODUCTION

Trust is important not only because it increases the regularity and predictability of social interaction, but also because it leads people to collaborate and generate joint goods that otherwise would not be produced (Yamagishi and Yamagishi 1994; Fukuyama 1995; Yamagishi, Cook, and Watabe, 1998; Zak and Knack 2001; Knack and Zak 2003; Cook, Hardin, and Levi 2005). It also extends the reach of social control mechanisms especially when monitoring and sanctioning are not possible. In addition, in many circumstances it reduces transaction costs since if the parties to an exchange are generally trustworthy with respect to one another and have some interest in maintaining the relationship and/or their reputations as trustworthy actors they will behave in a reliable manner, making for more beneficial transactions.

Despite the generally recognized benefits of trust, Cook, Hardin, and Levi (2005) argue that while trust may generate order at the micro level it is typically ineffective as a source of macro-level social order. Information requirements are simply too great to know whom to trust in a large complex organization or community and the risks involved are often too substantial to leave to the vagaries of individual behavior. In this chapter I explore the conditions under which trust does operate to produce micro social order and the conditions under which we rely on institutional mechanisms instead to undergird and create the conditions for macro social order.

Alternatives to reliance on trust include elements of organizational structure that support reliability and the reduction of exploitation such as monitoring and certain types of management compensation schemes that reward such behavior (or make exploitation costly). Other mechanisms include the self-regulation schemes central to professional associations, reputational mechanisms that make violations of trust costly, and institutionalized enforcement strategies that limit the vulnerability of the parties to a bilateral exchange or multi-party collective effort. We explore the implications of the use of these various mechanisms for securing trustworthiness in the production of social order.

How social order is produced and maintained in society has been a central concern of philosophers, political scientists, and sociologists, among others, for centuries. Without cooperative social relations social order is fragile at best. Theories about the production of social order range from arguments that sovereign authorities that demand and even coerce cooperation are needed to theories that base cooperation on shared values and norms that constrain freeriding and compel cooperation. Prominent social scientists, from Luhmann (1980), Arrow (1974) and Fukuyama (1995) to Putnam (1995) have argued that trust is "at the heart of social order." It makes cooperative social relations possible and provides the backdrop for cooperation even when distrust is widespread in the broader society.

However, as Cook, Hardin, and Levi (2005: 1) argue: "Trust is important in many interpersonal contexts, but it cannot carry the weight of making complex societies function productively and effectively." It is most important in the domain of interpersonal relations, where it affords continuing interaction that is beneficial for the parties involved in part because they can be more accurately assessed as trustworthy and reliable over time. But, we often rely on and cooperate with others not because we have come to trust them but because we acknowledge the existence of incentives that operate to make cooperation safe and productive. The presence of organizations, institutions and networks in which we are embedded constrains exploitation, allowing us to take risks on one another even if we are strangers and have no information about past interactions. Before exploring the ways in which informal communities, organizations and institutions facilitate cooperation *without trust* let us consider definitions of trust and how we assess the trustworthiness of others in our daily lives. Our main argument is that the effectiveness of trust as the basis for cooperation and social order is limited thus we more often rely on other devices to ensure cooperation and a stable social order.

TRUST

Trust has been defined in a number of ways in the social sciences, to some extent along disciplinary lines. In psychology, for example, the definitions of trust that have emerged tend to focus on *trust as a disposition*, a component of one's psychological makeup. People are said to be more or less trusting based on early life experiences and socialization practices that imbue children at an early age with a disposition to trust others. From this perspective it may be hard for those who are harmed early in life by those close to them to learn to trust others in any setting. In contrast, children raised in benign environments who experience little in the way of betrayal of trust are more likely to develop generally trusting attitudes toward others (Hardin 1993). As Yamagishi (2001) has argued this kind of optimism or, more generally social intelligence about others often leads people to take risks and thus to be able to learn whom to trust and whom not to trust. Those who are more cautious (typically for good reason) may never take such risks and thus may fail to develop a sense of who is and who is not trustworthy in their environments, which requires risk-taking at least initially. This factor becomes important in contexts such as business in which judicious risk taking can lead to better outcomes.

Julian Rotter (1967, 1971), one of the first psychologists to conceive of trust in dispositional terms, defined trust as a "generalized expectancy held by an individual that the word, promise, oral or written statement of another individual or group can be relied on." Rotter views trust as something that is learned and not innate. Rotter finds in the surveys he conducted that there is a moderate correlation between trusting and being trustworthy such that those who are high trusters tend to be more trustworthy than those who are low trusters. Moreover he finds that high trusters are not simply gullible (Rotter 1980). Instead, they are more discriminating concerning whom to trust. It is this capacity that gives them grounds for engaging in more cooperative relations and extends their networks in ways that are beneficial.

Psychologists who study organizational behavior also tend to adopt a dispositional orientation when defining trust. A common definition used frequently in this literature is that *trust is the willingness of one party to accept vulnerability*, such as "the willingness of a party to be vulnerable to the actions of another party based on the expectation that the other will perform a particular action important to the party" (Mayer et al. 1995, see also Rousseau et al. 1998). It is this acceptance of vulnerability in a situation of interdependence that signals trust. The definition of trust as based on a willingness to be vulnerable is psychological at its root, but it acknowledges that the object of trust is another party in whom one is placing trust. This definition, common in the organizational behavior literature, thus tends to be both dispositional, focusing on the attitude of the person who is trusting (or not) and relational, focusing on the object of trust who is either worthy of trust (or not).

Sociologists and some political scientists have developed more explicitly *relational definitions of trust*, arguing that trust is a characteristic of a relationship more so than an individual even though it is acknowledged that some people are clearly more "generally" trusting than others or "optimistic" in dealing with them. Relational trust is at the center of Hardin's (2002, Cook Hardin, and Levi 2005) "encapsulated interest" conception of trust. It views *trust as a characteristic of the relationship between two parties A and B with respect to some domain of activity, represented as "A trusts B with respect to X,"* which is said to occur when *A has reason to believe that his or her interests are encapsulated in the interests of B or that A has grounds for believing that B will act in his or her best interest.* This can occur because A knows from past experience that B will do so, or because A assumes that B will do so, because B wants to maintain a relationship with A and values it. It may also be the case that B is invested in his or her reputation and thus has an interest in behaving in a trustworthy fashion toward A in order to preserve the reputation of being a trustworthy partner. In each case Hardin argues that the individuals involved have incentive to trust one another enough to cooperate or to provide for the collective welfare of the dyad (or the group, if extended beyond the dyad).

The application of this conception of trust to a wide range of settings is developed more fully in Hardin (2002) and Cook, Hardin, and Levi (2005). What makes this approach compelling is that it focuses attention on the grounds for trust, clarifies the conditions under which these grounds are unlikely to be present, and places the emphasis on the specific domains of activity and social contexts in which trust relationships occur. Too many arguments about trust are decontextualized and too generic to represent the real complexities of trust relationships. On this conception of trust, trust relations are specific, often deeply embedded in social contexts (social and cultural), and have high information requirements. Trust relations are only a small subset of the cooperative relationships in which we typically engage. In many situations and cultures cooperation is obtained *without* reliance on trust.

The two main approaches[1] to defining trust are psychological, treating trust as a disposition, or sociological, treating trust as a characteristic of a relationship between two or more parties. For our purposes the relational approach is most useful since it focuses attention not on the internal cognitive processes of individuals or their early childhood development, but on the features of the social relations involved and the context in which these relations are embedded as significant determinants of the capacity for trust-based cooperation and the

---

[1] A third approach is often delineated which involves treating trust as an aspect of morality. On this view trust is a dimension of one's moral character. That is, it is argued that it is good to be a "trusting person." While this may be the case, this perspective moves too far beyond social science to be useful in empirical analyses of the actual role of trust in the production of social order. In addition, as some philosophers have pointed out, it makes more sense to speak of trustworthiness in moral terms, rather than trust. It can't be moral to trust when it is not warranted, yet it might be considered moral to be a trustworthy person.

production of micro social order. It also reveals when the specific requirements for trust are not likely to be met and why therefore we rely on other organizational and institutional devices to secure cooperation and macro social order more generally.

MICRO-SOCIAL ORDER: TRUSTING OTHERS TO COOPERATE

Cooperation is clearly central to the production of micro social order on a daily basis (Lawler, Thye, and Yoon 2008). Interaction between individuals in their day to day worlds requires that each actor play his or her roles and that there be some kind of common cultural understanding regarding the expected behaviors of those enacting these roles or what psychologists refer to as "scripts." There are a number of features of social interaction that provide micro-social order in day-to-day activities, as indicated by the chapters in this volume. One such feature is the level of relational trust that arises between actors in their personal and work lives.

Although trust may not characterize the bulk of our interactions, as we have argued, it is characteristic of some of the most important relationships in which we engage. Trusting co-workers, for example, can increase cooperative activities within organizations and even reduce the cost of managing such activities, when co-workers prove to be trustworthy with respect to one another. Trust is important since it allows for the extension of social control whether built into the organizational hierarchy or a result of peer-based accountability in less hierarchical (or team-oriented) organizations. It is also often the basis for what are called organizational citizenship behaviors (OCBs), those that clearly indicate that the members of the organization are committed and loyal frequently working overtime and engaging in activities that generate greater productivity and help to build communal ties within the organization (McAllister 1995; Dirks and Ferrin 2002).

A key issue in such settings is the how we go about assessing whether or not a co-worker or partner is trustworthy? I contend that we use cognitive judgments (sometimes flawed) based on relevant information obtained from characteristics of the individuals involved, our own past interactions with them or similar others, and reputational knowledge we obtain from third party sources. We also examine the nature of the incentives that constrain the actions of our co-workers or partners and make them more or less likely to be trustworthy in their relationship with us. This process allows us to judge who is and who is not trustworthy and fosters cooperation based on trust in our interpersonal relations.

Securing Trust-Based Cooperation

In the absence of specific information that allows us to know who can be counted on to be trustworthy we rely on various devices to assure ourselves that we can cooperate or engage in larger scale collective efforts even in the face of uncertainty and the risk of being exploited. It would be impossible to get through the week without having to trust someone with whom we interact over a range of outcomes from those with little risk and low value to those of high value and increased risk. Just getting through the day requires coordination and cooperation with others. For much of our activity coordinated expectations and behaviors work to facilitate cooperation and make us productive, as indicated by theories articulated elsewhere in this volume (see chapters on identity theory, expectations states theory, etc.). But, for some activities and in some contexts we simply have to rely on the trust we place in others. For this category of action we need some sense of how judgments of trustworthiness are made and in what ways we can be wrong. Often this category of action includes activities that are personal, that lie outside the domain of organizations and institutions and may involve significant risk and uncertainty. In other situations trust enhances cooperation but is not the basis for it.

Assessing Trustworthiness

Given the "encapsulated interest" model of trust, both parties to a trust relation assess their partner's trustworthiness. They can do so on the basis of information they have received from third parties (who can be trusted to provide accurate advice) or from past experience. Without these sources of information the best they can do is to guess about the likely trustworthiness of those with similar characteristics or to extrapolate from their own experience engaging with similar others. These assessments are based not only on characteristics of the person(s) being judged but also on features of the context or setting, the nature of the relationship, and the level of risk involved (i.e., what is at stake). Assessments of trustworthiness are the core of our trust judgments about those with whom we interact, especially when the activities are important to us. But such judgments are not easy to make and may lead to exploitation when inaccurate.

Context can offer information that is essential to making accurate assessments of trustworthiness. There is adequate evidence that cultures vary in the extent of generalized trust, or the degree to which individuals in that culture are likely to believe that "most people can be trusted" and that "you do not need to be as cautious in dealing with others" (e.g., the well-known General Social Survey measure of general trust). For example, generalized trust is quite high in the Scandinavian countries and much lower in the countries in the former Soviet Union and parts of South America (where nations vary a great deal in level of general trust). Research indicates that general trust is associated with lower income inequality and more democratic institutions (Bjornskov 2012). Independent of our judgments of specific others then it is likely that in some cultures distrust is the norm. Such contextual factors matter for our assessments of the trustworthiness of a specific person with whom we might wish to interact since our "default" estimate of the likely trustworthiness of others would be different in different places in the world and in different contexts within countries. Thus, our sense of the potential for others to be trustworthy in general varies by context and culture such that we are wise to be more cautious and less trusting in some settings. Context clearly provides clues as to whether or not we can cooperate without fear of exploitation.

Judgments of the trustworthiness of individuals are often based on assessments of both competence and motivation. In the absence of good information we often have to rely on reputation or professional certification, provided by third parties. As Bacharach and Gambetta (2001) note, however, we must be wary of those who can mimic traits and appearances in order to appear to be competent and trustworthy. For example, physicians have been known to practice without a license and various professionals have attempted to fake degrees. Because con artists exist we cannot always rely on our own independent assessments of trustworthiness, even in interpersonal relationships in which information sources are more often reliable. Thus we design various mechanisms to ensure the reliability of the people with whom we interact and these mechanisms facilitate cooperation where it might not otherwise occur.

Reputational Mechanisms for Securing Cooperation

In the current era many online interactions and transaction-based businesses, including the world of social media, have learned to invest heavily in making their reputation systems foolproof and to create the security that people have come to expect when their transactions are mediated and their lives recorded and stored as information to which others have access. These efforts sometimes fail, as we know from well-known cases in the Internet world in which there has been a breach of security often leading to the demise of the platform or company involved and in lesser cases a reduction in profit due to a shift in consumers' product allegiance as they lose faith in the security of their credit card information. Even high-profile cases such as that of the National Security Administration (NSA) in the United States and fugitive Mr. Snowden who leaked information to the world about the private profiling of its own citizens and world leaders alike raise doubts about the integrity of the organization and the legitimacy of its activities with certain reputational consequences.

Reputation thus matters not only for individuals and government organizations, but it is also critical in the world of online transactions (Kollock 1999) and mediated interactions that often involve risks (either personal or financial). Yamagishi et al. (2003) investigate the effectiveness of different types of reputational systems and argue that positive reputation systems work best in open, unbounded networks in which there is no closure. In contrast, negative reputation systems seem to work well in closed networks, but are less helpful in open networks because the users can alter their identities fairly easily and continue to exploit those with whom they transact often with impunity.

Internet companies thus invest heavily in these reputation systems since any breach of security can lead to organizational failure. In such cases micro-social order is based on mediated interpersonal interactions that are secured by organizational actions that attempt to mitigate the potential effects of any failed transactions or outright fraudulent activity by those who use the system and sometimes abuse it.

Incentive-Based Trustworthiness

In general, a solution to the problem of the lack of trust or pervasive distrust is to create incentives that get people to engage in the expected behavior perhaps only appearing to be trustworthy in the beginning. Such incentives are built into most of the devices that get people to cooperate in the absence of interpersonal trust whether in organizations, communities or larger social institutions. These incentives often create the conditions under which cooperation can occur sometimes under difficult circumstances. In some cases military or police action is what is required to restore macro social order and create the grounds for limited, if not extensive micro-level cooperation. At least such action can restore enough order to enable initial cooperation and efforts to rebuild the grounds for positive collective action. Of course such action may also seed further conflict and lack of cooperation if it is not perceived as legitimate or if it fuels the conflict instead of reducing it. In less extreme environments the existence of laws and legal remedies for failed trust offer the background typically needed to reduce risk and encourage cooperative endeavors.

Next we discuss some of these devices for motivating cooperation in the absence of trust or where it is not possible simply to rely on the relational trust between those involved at the more micro level either because too much is at stake and the risk of failed trust too high or because it is impossible to determine the extent to which those we interact with are in fact trustworthy. Trust may exist between individuals in such settings, but it is frequently hard won, and even then not the basis of the majority of our cooperative relations. We also explore the ways in which relational trust, when it does exist, can extend the reach of these organizational and institutional devices in securing cooperation. Before delineating more formal devices that facilitate cooperation, we begin with a discussion of the informal mechanisms for inducing and sustaining cooperative social relations that may result in trust but do not rely on it.

INFORMAL SOCIAL ARRANGEMENTS AND COOPERATION

It is unlikely that we trust most of those with whom we come into contact, whether in person or "online," and in many circumstances law cannot regulate the cooperative relations in which we engage. They exist outside the legal apparatus. Even when this apparatus is used the costs of appealing to it may often outweigh the benefits, as many have learned by engaging in legal action in efforts to obtain recompense for exploitive or harmful interactions and even simple contractual failures. Some forms of cooperation also occur outside the reach of organizations and institutions, in the communities in which we live. And, in some settings the organizations are too specialized and the institutions are too weak and limited in the extent of their reach, so we must rely on the informal social devices that are common to small communities and villages instead, especially in less developed economies.

Informal contractual dealings are common in less developed economies as well as in more developed economies due to the fact that contracts can never fully specify the terms of agreement. This means that other mechanisms for securing cooperation beyond the contractual elements come into existence to fill the void, especially when legal remedies are weak or non-existent (cf. McMillan and Woodruff 2000). A number of studies reveal how important transactions are "secured" with a handshake between individuals that have reason to believe they have incentive to fulfill the trust placed in them, often because they are invested in a continuing relationship with the party involved or because they clearly care about their reputation with respect to that party. The encapsulated interest view of trust highlights these grounds for reliability. Examples include the well-known case of diamond dealers discussed by Coleman (1988) and the Magribi traders analyzed by Grief (1989, 1993). Extensions of these informal arrangements are also discussed by Hart (1988) and by Ensminger (2001) who identifies "fictive" kinship as one such arrangement used by Kenyan cattle owners to secure the trustworthiness of the nomadic keepers of their herds.

In other domains such as in the world of professionals, more formal associations may arise to regulate the practice of the professionals involved when other forms of regulation are ineffective or too costly. In medicine, for example, in the United States, reliance on control by professional associations and informal peer monitoring was the norm until the health care system became so complex that external regulation by states and the federal government became necessary to protect consumers (primarily patients) from the worst abuses of shoddy medical practice. Legal remedies subsequently also became much more available for malpractice in the United States, which fueled massive growth in the health insurance industry. Just a few violations of trust in domains in which there is much at stake (e.g., health, life and safety) can thus lead to the move from reliance on more informal norms of professional behavior and licensure to a regulatory regime that clearly requires greater investment in monitoring and sanctioning. Studies of the growth of the insurance industry in general document this trend.

Many of the informal devices we use to secure cooperation in the absence of legal constraints rely on *reputational mechanisms*. If we know that you care about your reputation and want to maintain it as a trustworthy person we can assume that you will have incentive to cooperate simply to maintain your reputation, which is of value in a larger number of interactions. Or, you may value or need our continued cooperation with you so much that you engage in trustworthy behavior with respect to us to maintain the relationship or group membership. Reputations work to support cooperation in a number of settings at the micro-level as well as at the organizational level since organizations invest heavily in protecting their reputations in order to maintain legitimacy, as we have noted.

We typically rely on *norms* to enforce cooperation at the communal level, but such norms of cooperation are most effective in small groups and relatively closed communities in which exit is low and individuals have reason to interact (Cook and Hardin 2001). They know about one another either directly or indirectly through those they are connected to and they usually care about their reputations with respect to one another. Putnam (2000) developed the concept, *social capital*, to refer to the norms, networks and trust that sustain cooperation and a civic culture (see also, Coleman 1990). Norms serve to enforce compliance even in the absence of legal and regulatory systems and they help govern relationships in such a way as to enforce cooperative arrangements (Ostrom 1990). Closed networks may also emerge to reinforce existing informal norms of cooperation.

Norms of Cooperation

In small towns and communities it is clear that communal norms often provide the basis for cooperation. Social networks in such communities are small, well connected, multiplex or "thick" and more stable than in urban settings in which networks are thin, more sparsely connected and the relationships involved much more specialized (i.e., less multiplex). Norms of exclusion may also arise in small communities to foster compliance with the norms of cooperation (Cook and Hardin 2001). This fact is represented in the frequently noted downside of small towns or exclusive communities that deviants are treated as pariah, and excluded from community engagement (Lofland 1995).

Social capital in the form of network connections that provide access to resources of value also serves to foster cooperation. These connections provide trustworthy sources of resources given that those in the network often have close or strong ties, which provide relevant information either through past experience or network reputation of the reliability of those to whom one is connected. Even networks in which the ties are weak tend to generate resources, sometimes in the form of information about opportunities for additional contacts and even jobs (Granovetter 1973). A very large literature now exists concerning the role of networks and the nature of ties in the provision of resources to those in the network (see the work of Granovetter 1973; Putnam 2000; and Lin 2001, among many others). Such networks facilitate dyadic exchange and even the formation of small subgroups or cliques that arise to support various types of collective action. An example is the type of network formed by those who contribute funds to create loans for small enterprises in settings in which bank loans would rarely be proffered.

Communal norms support what are called "rotating credit associations" that do not involve a third party, but are sustained by the contributions of those who belong to the group. In such cases, the amounts contributed by each person are often quite small, but each person in the network is committed to repaying the loan in order to make funds available to others in the group when needed in the future. Despite the fact that default can occur as well as betrayal of the group norm of contributions over time, many such associations have come into existence in the Third World with notable success, most often mainly involving women. They rely on the informal enforcement of norms among group members. The Grameen Bank is another example of norm enforcement among small groups of friends who gain loans at various times to start up business enterprises (Yunnus 1998, 1999). Others in the group can obtain loans for their activities once the initial loan recipients have begun to repay their loans. This mechanism incentivizes the group to monitor the repayment behavior of the members of their network in order to preserve their own right to obtain funding when needed.

Although such norms may work in small groups or closed networks, as the groups or networks get larger and the people involved engage in greater mobility communal norms become much less effective in regulating behavior and defaults would likely be more common. Norms work to constrain behavior in most social and organizational settings, but they are not the most common form of social control for large organizations or institutions that must coordinate the activities of many people and incentivize the behaviors that result in success at achieving the organization's primary purpose. This is true in the world of non-governmental organizations as well as government.

ORGANIZATIONS

A range of social and organizational devices serves to manage conflict and improve workplace productivity. And these devices do not assume that communal norms or trust are the primary basis for cooperation. When trust exists it facilitates cooperation, but it is not required and thus operates as a complement to the structured flow of activities. Trust can extend the reach of organizational authority or social control, but it does not suffice as a substitute for it. It adds to the arrangements that make cooperation possible and incentivize behavior that aligns with the goals of the organization allowing workers to be more productive and organizations more successful. It can even increase the range of cooperative activity and reduce management costs, especially if it decreases the need for monitoring and sanctioning, as we noted earlier. But trust between individuals requires the kind of personal knowledge that allows those who work together to accurately assess trustworthiness or at least know about the reputations of those they work with concerning their reliability and integrity and this is not always possible in many large-scale and increasingly decentralized and often distributed organizations (Currall and Epstein 2003).

Within organizations and institutions it is also the case that power differences between employees or between employees and their employers or managers often hinder the formation of trust relations (Cook, Hardin, and Levi 2005, chapter 3) because it is not clear under what conditions those who are at a power disadvantage can ever fully trust those who exercise power over them. It is certainly much less likely that mutual trust will emerge in such hierarchical relations than in horizontal or peer relations within organizations. Hierarchy is frequently relied on in organizations in which there is little tolerance for deviation from prescribed roles and duties and when coordination of effort requires tighter control.

When power inequalities exist and trust is desired it is important for those in power to exercise their influence in a transparent way and to make their commitments not to exploit others credible. To some extent they do this by abiding by fairness principles based on both procedural and distributive justice. When these principles are not followed and the exercise of power is viewed as exploitive distrust often arises reducing cooperation, thwarting collective efforts and potentially sowing the seeds of discontent and ultimately disorder or exit. These same principles apply to government and to broader institutions in society.

Organizational and institutional design is mainly about setting up arrangements that constrain behavior in ways that contribute to the primary goals of the organization. Bradach and Eccles (1989) make the point that authority relations (involving power differences often embedded in hierarchy) are only one such mechanism. Incentive systems are most frequently used to induce people to be reliable and to enforce the performance of relevant duties. These are realized in wage and employment contracts, which as we have noted can never function to completely specify performance details. Such contracts can be either explicit or implicit, but in either case contracts are imperfect devices (Malhotra and Murnighan 2002). Furthermore, if incentives actually worked perfectly to align individual interests and organizational interests there would be little need for monitoring and sanctioning or even much oversight at all (Frey 1993). However, they are not perfect. People do shirk their duties and have conflicting interests that draw them in different directions sometimes incongruent with the goals of the organization. It is clear in the organizational literature that treating organizational members, especially employees, as if they are trustworthy, granting them some discretion, can lead to trustworthy behavior (Braithwaite 1998), but it is not sufficient to guarantee it.

One somewhat ironic outcome of too much oversight and regulation is that workers can become less trustworthy over time. A focus on the external control of behavior can undermine internal incentives to perform well as evidenced in the social psychological literature on the effects of using extrinsic versus intrinsic rewards (cf. Lepper, Greene, and Nisbett 1973). In the management literature this conundrum is also referred to as the "paradox of control" or the "paradox of sanctioning" (Mulder et al. 2006). Too much emphasis on

sanctioning and social control can backfire; undermining incentives to perform well and to engage in organizational citizenship behaviors, which empirical research indicates are mediated by levels of trust (Dirks and Ferrin 2002).
Resentment and distrust of supervisors may also emerge under tight monitoring and sanctioning regimes undermining reliability and performance (Brehm
and Gates 1997). Failure to share information, "working to rule" – performing
as required rather than performing as necessary for task success – and even acts
of sabotage may result.

One might argue that it could be good if we had both trust relations and
contractual or other mechanisms for enforcement that might have legal standing (Sitkin 1993). Although perhaps preferable, it is likely somewhat rare,
especially in large organizations. It is clear, however, that having enforcement
mechanisms to block the worst abuses of trust enables us to take risks and to
trust others in our day-to-day social and business relationships where trust
does facilitate interactions (Dyer and Chu 2003). A number of institutions and
practices, as we have noted, exist to make cooperation possible in the absence
of trust or in settings in which distrust is pervasive. In fact, these institutional
practices might be necessary to create the possibility of trust as a basis for
cooperation to emerge and create or sustain micro social order (Misztal 1996).
In this way macro social order and micro social order are often entwined.

INSTITUTIONS

At the macro-level institutions can serve to ensure reliability thus making cooperation possible, sustaining complex markets and making for governments
that can be held accountable. Often we design institutions to create incentive
compatibility between the individuals involved and the organization or institutions in which they are embedded. These incentives work to ensure appropriate
behavior and reduce opportunism. But incentives, as I have argued, often do
not serve to create perfect alignment of individual and collective goals or to
eliminate any conflicts of interest that might exist. Thus institutional design
includes practices that ensure some form of monitoring, even if only occasional, and sanctions for failure to perform or produce.

But such elements of institutional design, however rational, do not always
work. In some organizations and some governmental institutions corruption
may occur undermining confidence in government and fueling citizen distrust.

Once distrust of government is widespread it is unlikely that it will ever
serve the purpose of providing the context for reliable and trustworthy governance. Citizens are then left to their own devices in securing reliable and trustworthy exchange partners and locating those with whom they can cooperate to
produce collective goods outside the reach of government. When governmental
authorities exercise autocratic control over the society there is even less room
for institutionally induced cooperative efforts among the citizenry beyond the
realm of close knit communities of families and friends where trustworthiness

is based on a long history of commitment and cooperative interaction (Cook, Rice, and Gerbasi 2004).

The uncertainty that comes with the lack of legitimate institutions at the macro-level clearly limits exchange at the micro-level, as we know from the case of Russia in the post-Communist era. As Radaev (2004a, 2004b) suggests in his research on Russia, the fact that the primary institutions of government were weakened and primarily corrupt meant that people tended to engage in exchanges only with those they knew or with those whose reputations were known to them thus limiting the reach of economic activity. Enforcement of contracts devolved to third parties, hired to monitor and sanction those who reneged on their deals or engaged in fraudulent activity. Without the security of the rule of law and the institutions that support it, corruption prevails and distrust persists. In such settings macro-social order is precarious and citizens must work to create vestiges of micro-social order from the ground up depending on those they know enough about to collaborate with and sometimes trust.

Distrust and Institutional Design

We typically require that institutions in society make it possible for us to interact and exchange with those we do *not* know and to help guard against exploitation or failed transactions. In this way macro social order can provide the context for micro social order. In a world now much smaller given the capacity to transact and interact with people in far away places through computer-mediated connections distrust is a pervasive concern. Many forms of interaction cross borders and cannot be managed by any single government. Even proper legal recourse is difficult to produce for interactions that extend across the globe. The threat of terrorist groups has also fueled distrust and in many societies has sparked intense focus on security. In the United States, the growth of gated communities is only one such sign, as is the massive investment in "homeland security". It is hard to imagine what international institutions could even provide the background for macro social order on a global scale.

But to argue that distrust is generally bad and to be avoided – a common perception – is to ignore the role of a healthy level of distrust in focusing on alternative mechanisms for securing transactions against default and bad actors, even providing protection for those who may not know how to protect themselves (or even have the capacity to do so). It can also lead to improved institutions when distrust is used to create proper mechanisms for dealing with conflicts of interest and a balance of power as in most democratic institutions. In this sense it can actually facilitate cooperation and even limit exploitation putting the right kinds of checks and balances in place. If so, legitimacy of the institution may increase even if widespread distrust motivated the move to proper treatment of conflicts of interest and abuses of power. In the face of large risks, however, many would argue for the benefit of having a powerful enough state at least in the background to ensure that social order is maintained.

Government

In civil society and in the market place government most often operates to facilitate exchange and to support cooperation allowing for collective action that does not hinge on the capacity of the individuals involved to trust one another (Uslaner 2003). The role the state plays is to foster trustworthiness of its citizens and to build confidence in the government in order to enforce contracts, to provide significant services needed by the citizenry (i.e., protection and welfare) and to guarantee the presence of macro social order in the larger society. Without a more or less legitimate state disorder and conflict is likely to be the norm leading to rampant distrust among the citizens often fueling intergroup conflict and civil wars. Police, the military, and even everyday bureaucrats who make up a large part of government organizations produce social order on a daily basis. This is true primarily of stable governments especially those which are democratic. Autocratic regimes maintain order but more typically through control of the military and a heavy hand.

Democratic states, like other institutions, rely on the legitimacy they are granted by those they serve. For governments citizens often grant legitimacy when they are provided with reliable public services and protection, not to mention stable regimes that engender the confidence required for prosperity and economic growth (Levi 1998). Such states also often have to deal with factors that generate distrust among citizens or among those who want control over state bureaucracies or even the military arm. Maintaining democracy is a delicate balance of managing expectations for the reliable delivery of services and maintaining distance from those who would confiscate the means of control for their own ends. Constant vigilance against such efforts to undermine governmental control, as well as the many forms of corruption that can occur is required to maintain legitimacy.

When citizens view their government as reliable and legitimate they are much more likely to comply with its demands, rules, and regulations as Levi (1988) argues in her book on contingent consent and as Tyler (1990, 1998) has also argued. In her conclusion, Levi (1997) contends that it is the states that treat their citizens fairly and can reliably and competently deliver on their promises to serve the public interest that are viewed as worthy of consent and compliance. Social welfare states and democracies are the best examples.

It is clear that governmental institutions are central to the production of macro social order, but the interaction between macro social order and micro social order is complex. In the best of circumstances both exist. In the absence of macro social order, however, people do their best to create pockets of social order relying on micro-level processes to generate the order that is required to manage life on a daily basis. In the worst of circumstances even this is impossible due to the massive breakdown of the state and government run institutions or the imposition of military rule, which restores order in the midst of chaos, but produces a form of order that is fragile.

CONCLUSION

Although many authors claim that trust is indeed at the heart of social order as did Luhmann (1980) it is hard to find enough social science evidence to support this claim. Some even make the argument that a breakdown of trust is one of the most important problems facing contemporary society, or at a minimum they argue lack of trust is at the core of the problems we confront. On the face of it this claim is certainly grandiose. What we do know is that trust is a significant dimension of social life and that it is clearly important in the realm of interpersonal relationships, whether they are highly personal as is the case with friends and family or less personal as in business and workplace relationships, or even quite casual, relatively brief encounters that make up many of our interactions from day to day. Trust within the domain of interpersonal relationships can also foster harmony, reduce conflict, and provide the grounds for beneficial group-level collective action, including citizenship behaviors at work and in the community. It can also make many productive activities more efficient and increase the extent of trade between parties to an exchange. It can even make important negotiations, sometimes involving major conflicts, run more smoothly. What it can't do is carry the weight of creating macro-social order. Along with my collaborators (see Cook, Hardin, and Levi 2005), I have argued that the role of trust is limited and that we need to look elsewhere to locate the devices we use to fully secure the grounds for cooperation and sustain social order at the societal level.

The broad class of devices we use to generate collective effort and the cooperation necessary for productive activity include informal social arrangements and community norms as well as professional associations and other certifying entities that provide assurance of trustworthiness. More formal mechanisms include organizational strategies and systems for aligning the incentives of workers and their employers to generate coordinated action and organizational success. Beyond incentive systems, control mechanisms include strategies for monitoring and sanctioning that work to induce appropriate effort and commitment on the part of the employees. A downside of too much reliance on monitoring and sanctioning, however, is the potential for a reduction in trustworthiness, loyalty and citizenship behaviors. A delicate balance is required to avoid the "paradox of sanctioning." These strategies work to support cooperation and productive activity within nongovernmental as well as governmental organizations. But these strategies work best when backed by institutions that support contractual arrangements and corporate authority. Clearly legal institutions and the rule of law provide this assurance, when they exist and are not corrupt. Without this background assurance organizational strategies are less effective, because there is no binding recourse to failed transactions and fraud.

Beyond the rule of law typically essential to the production of macro social order, stable governments can provide the backdrop for concerted collective action and cooperation within the society, especially in the context of democratic regimes. Autocratic regimes more often rely on the strong arm of the military to support a more precarious macro social order and may run the risk of disorder and intergroup conflict at the micro-level when the seeds of discontent and group-level competition for resources exist. In the absence of macro social order cooperation at all levels in society is at risk as currently evident in parts of the Middle East and in some of the former Soviet countries, among other "hotspots" in the world. In this global context, a continuing dilemma is to understand how to secure cooperation and maintain macro social order in an age of increasing distrust and threats of state-less violence. Understanding how to produce social order when institutions are weak or corrupt and the grounds for interpersonal trust and other sources of micro social order do not exist remains a conundrum. This volume should provide a window into the relevant social science, highlighting the many mechanisms beyond trust that facilitate micro social order under varying conditions.

REFERENCES

Arrow, Kenneth J. 1974. *The Limits of Organization.* New York: Norton.
Bacharach, Michael, and Diego Gambetta. 2001. "Trust in Signs." Pp. 146–84 in *Trust in Society*, edited by Karen S. Cook. New York: Russell Sage Foundation.
Bjornskov, C. (2012). "How Does Social Trust Affect Economic Growth?" *Southern Economic Journal* 78(4): 1346–68.
Bradach, Jeffrey L., and Robert G. Eccles. 1989. "Price, Authority and Trust: From Ideal Types to Plural Forms." *Annual Review of Sociology* 15: 97–118.
Braithwaite, John. 1998. "Institutionalizing Distrust, Enculturating Trust." In *Trust and Governance*, edited by Valerie Braithwaite and Margaret Levi. New York: Russell Sage Foundation.
Brehm, John, and Scott Gates. 1997. *Working, Shirking and Sabotage: Bureaucratic Response to a Democratic Public.* Ann Arbor: University of Michigan Press.
Coleman, James S. 1988. "Social Capital in the Creation of Human Capital." *American Journal of Sociology* 94: 250–73.
   1990 *Foundations of Social Theory.* Cambridge, MA. Harvard University Press.
Cook, Karen, and Russell Hardin. 2001. "Norms of Cooperativeness and Networks of Trust." Pp. 327–47 in *Social Norms*, edited by Michael Hechter and Karl-Dieter Opp. New York: Russell Sage Foundation.
Cook, Karen S., Russell Hardin, and Margaret Levi. 2005. *Cooperation without Trust?* New York City, New York: Russell Sage Foundation.
Cook, Karen S., Eric R. W. Rice, and Alexandra Gerbasi. 2004. "The Emergence of Trust Networks Under Uncertainty: The Case of Transitional Economies." In *Building a Trustworthy State in Post-Socialist Transition*, edited by Janos Kornai and Susan Rose-Ackerman. New York: Palgrave Macmillan.

Currall, Steven C., and Marc J. Epstein. 2003. "The Fragility of Organizational Trust: Lessons from the Rise and Fall of Enron." *Organizational Dynamics* 32: 193–206.

Dirks, Kurt, and Don Ferrin. 2002. "Trust in Leadership: Meta-Analytic Findings and Implications for Research and Practice." *Journal of Applied Psychology* 87(4): 611–28.

Dyer, Jeffrey H., and Wujin Chu. 2003. "The Role of Trustworthiness in Reducing Transaction Costs and Improving Performance: Empirical Evidence from the United States, Japan, and Korea." *Organization Science Special Issue: Trust in an Organizational Context* 14: 57–68.

Ensminger, Jean. 2001. "Reputations, Trust, and the Principal Agent Problem." Pp. 185–201 in *Trust in Society*, edited by Karen S. Cook. New York: Russell Sage Foundation.

Frey, Bruno S. 1993. "Does Monitoring Increase Work Effort – the Rivalry with Trust and Loyalty." *Economic Inquiry* 31(4): 663–70.

Fukuyama, Francis. 1995. *Trust: The Social Virtues and the Creation of Prosperity*. New York: Simon and Schuster, Free Press Paperbacks.

Granovetter, Mark. 1973. "The Strength of Weak Ties." *American Journal of Sociology* 78(6): 1360–80.

Greif, Avner. 1989. "Reputation and Coalitions in Medieval Trade: Evidence on the Maghribi Traders." *Journal of Economic History* XLIX(4): 857–82.

——— 1993. "Contract Enforceability and Economic Institutions in Early Trade: The Maghribi Traders' Coalition." *American Economic Review* 83: 525–48.

Hardin, Russell. 1993. "The Street-Level Epistemology of Trust." *Politics and Society* 21(4): 505–29.

——— 2002. *Trust and Trustworthiness*. New York: Russell Sage Foundation.

Hart, Keith. 1988. "Kinship, Contract, and Trust: The Economic Organization of Migrants in an African City Slum." Pp. 176–93 in *Trust: Making and Breaking Cooperative Relations*, edited by Diego Gambetta. New York: Basil Blackwell.

Knack, Stephen, and Paul Zak. 2003. "Building Trust: Public Policy, Interpersonal Trust, and Economic Development." *Supreme Court Economic Review* 10.

Kollock, Peter. 1999. "The Production of Trust in Online Markets." Pp. 99–123 in *Advances in Group Processes*, edited by Edward J. Lawler. Greenwich, CT: JAI Press.

Lawler, Edward J., Shane Thye, and Jeongkoo Yoon. 2008. "Social Exchange and Micro-Social Order." *American Sociological Review* 73: 519–42.

Lepper, Mark R., D. Greene and R.E. Nisbett. 1973. "Undermining Children's Intrinsic Interest with Extrinsic Reward: A Test of the 'Overjustification' Hypothesis." *Journal of Personality and Social Psychology* 28: 129–37.

Levi, Margaret. 1988. *Of Rule and Revenue*. Berkeley: University of California Press.

——— 1997. *Consent, Dissent, and Patriotism*. Cambridge, UK: Cambridge University Press.

——— 1998. "A State of Trust." In *Trust and Governance*, edited by Valerie Braithwaite and Margaret Levi. New York: Russell Sage Foundation.

Lin, Nan. 2001. *Social Capital: A Theory of Social Structure and Action*. Cambridge, UK: Cambridge University Press.

Lofland, Lynn 1995. "Social Interaction: Continuities and Complexities in the Study of Non-intimate Sociality." Pp. 176–201 in *Sociological Perspectives on Social Psychology* edited by Karen S. Cook, Gary A. Fine, and James House. Boston, MA: Allyn and Bacon.

Luhmann, Niklas. 1980. "Trust: A Mechanism for the Reduction of Social Complexity." In *Trust and Power*, edited by Niklas Luhmann. New York: Wiley.

McAllister, D.J. 1995. "Affect and Cognition-Based Trust as Foundations for Interpersonal Cooperation in Organizations." *Academy of Management Journal* 38: 24–59.

McMillan, John, and Christopher Woodruff. 2000. "Private Order under Dysfunctional Public Order." *Michigan Law Review* 98(8): 2421–58.

Malhotra, Deepak, and J. Keith Murnighan. 2002. "The Effects of Contracts on Interpersonal Trust." *Administrative Science Quarterly* 47: 534–59.

Mayer, R.C., J.H. Davis, and F.D. Schoorman. 1995. "An Integrative Model of Organizational Trust." *Academy of Management Review* 20(3): 709–34.

Misztal, Barbara A. 1996. *Trust in Modern Societies: The Search for the Bases of Social Order*. Cambridge, UK: Polity Press.

Mulder, Letitia B., E. Van Dijk, D. De Cremer, and H.A.M. Wilke. 2006. "Undermining Trust and Cooperation: The Paradox of Sanctioning Systems in Social Dilemmas." *Journal of Experimental Social Psychology* 42: 147–62.

Ostrom, Elinor. 1990. *Governing the Commons: The Evolution of Institutions for Collective Action*. New York: Cambridge University Press.

Putnam, Robert. 1995. "Tuning In, Tuning Out: The Strange Disappearance of Social Capital in America." *PS: Political Science and Politics* 28(4): 664–83.

2000. *Bowling Alone: The Collapse and Revival of American Community*. New York: Simon and Schuster.

Radaev, Vadim. 2004a. "Coping with Distrust in the Emerging Russian Markets." In *Distrust*, edited by Russell Hardin. New York: Russell Sage Foundation.

2004b. "How Trust Is Established in Economic Relationships When Institutions and Individuals Are Not Trustworthy: The Case of Russia." In *Building a Trustworthy State in Post-Socialist Transitions*, edited by Janos Kornai and Susan Rose-Ackerman. New York: Palgrave Macmillan.

Rotter, Julian B. 1967. "A New Scale for the Measurement of Interpersonal Trust." *Journal of Personality* 35(4): 1–7.

1971. "Generalized Expectancies for Interpersonal Trust." *American Psychologist* 26(5): 443–50.

1980. "Interpersonal Trust, Trustworthiness, and Gullibility." *American Psychologist* 35(1): 1–7.

Rousseau, Denise M., S. B. Sitkin, R.S. Burt, and C. Camerer. 1998. "Not So Different After All: A Cross-Discipline View of Trust." *Academy of Management Review* 23: 393–404.

Sitkin, Sim B., and N. L. Roth. 1993. "Explaining the Limited Effectiveness of Legalistic 'Remedies' for Trust/Distrust." *Organization Science*. 4(3): 367–92.

Tyler, Tom. 1990. *Why People Obey the Law*. New Haven, CT: Yale University Press.

1998. "Trust and Democratic Government." In *Trust and Governance*, edited by Valerie Braithwaite and Margaret Levi. New York: Russell Sage Foundation.

Uslaner, Eric. 2003. "Trust, Democracy, and Governance: Can Government Policies Influence Generalized Trust?" In *Generating Social Capital: The Role of Voluntary Associations, Institutions and Government Policy*, edited by D. Stolle. New York: Palgrave Macmillan.

Yamagishi, Toshio. 2001. "Trust as a Form of Social Intelligence." Pp. 121–74 in *Trust in Society*, edited by Karen S. Cook. New York: Russell Sage Foundation.

Yamagishi, Cook, and Watabe, 1998. "Uncertainty, Trust and Commitment Formation in the United States and Japan." *American Journal of Sociology* 104(1): 165–94.

Yamagishi, Toshio, Masafumi Matsuda, Noriaki Yoshikai, Hiroyuki Takahashi, and Yukihiro Usui. 2003. "Solving Lemons Problem with Reputation: An Experimental Study of Online Trading." In *Working Paper, CEFOM/21, Hokkaido University.* Sapporo, Japan.

Yamagishi, Toshio, and Midori Yamagishi. 1994. "Trust and Commitment in the United States and Japan," *Motivation and Emotion* 18(1994): 129–66.

Yunus, Muhammad. 1998. "Alleviating Poverty through Technology." *Science* 16 October: 409–10.

   1999. *Banker to the Poor: Micro-Lending and the Battle against World Poverty.* New York: Public Affairs.

Zak, Paul, and Stephen Knack. 2001. "Trust and Growth." *Economic Journal* III: 295–321.

8

Identity Verification and the Social Order

Peter J. Burke and Jan E. Stets

Abstract

We outline how identity verification has consequences for the construction and reconstruction of the social order. Identity verification occurs when individuals *perceive self-relevant meanings in the situation* that match who they are in that situation (their identity). Verification of an identity feels good. This generates solidarity (when facilitated by others) and adherence to norms. Identities are verified by individuals controlling the flow of *resources* in interaction, and it is this flow that maintains the social structure. Resources either can be ready to be consumed (*active* resources) such as food for nourishment, or they can have some future use (*potential* resources) such as education for adaptation. We discuss how identity verification is accomplished by using *symbols* and *signs* attached to potential and actual resources in situations. The control of resources helps verify not only one's own identity but also others' identities. Since the process of identity verification produces positive feelings and stronger social bonds, this should facilitate maintenance of the social order. Identity nonverification will have the reverse effect on the social order, generating negative emotions, conflict, and chaos.

In identity theory, identity verification means changing the world (as we perceive it) to be the way it is supposed to be (according to our identity standards). Our perceptions are the meanings that we control to accomplish this. Perceptually, meanings are conveyed through signs and symbols emanating from the situation. Much of the research and theory within the identity theory framework has focused on symbols, whose arbitrary meanings, learned from the common culture, are shared with others. In this chapter, we emphasize this but also bring more attention to the other source of meaning noted by Mead (1934): *signs*, whose meaning is not arbitrary but is learned by direct experience in the situation. In this way, we begin to delineate more clearly the connection of identities to the material world and the social structure that surrounds and sustains us. We also point to the role of resource flows including actual and potential resources in verifying people's identities and in maintaining the social structure.

IDENTITIES AND SOCIAL STRUCTURE

Identity theory grows out of the ideas and postulates of structural symbolic interaction as formulated by Stryker ([1980] 2002). These postulates frame our conception of both social structure and identities as well as the relation between them. To understand how identities create, recreate, maintain, and change the order of social structure, we begin with a review of Stryker's views on identity and social structure within the structural symbolic interaction framework. Stryker's ([1980] 2002: 33–34) first postulate is:

[People's] behavior is premised on a named or classified world. The names or class terms attached to aspects of the environment, both physical and social, carry meaning in the form of shared behavioral expectations that grow out of social interaction. From interaction with others, one learns how to classify objects one comes into contact with, and in that process also learns how one is expected to behave with reference to those objects.

This postulate makes clear both the symbolic character of the world as well as the physical existence of objects in the world to which we respond in the context of a shared culture. Our responses, which are learned and shared with others in the culture, give those objects meaning, and it is those meanings on which further behavior is based.

Stryker's ([1980] 2002: 54) second postulate makes clear the way in which social structure fits into the paradigm:

Among the class terms learned in interaction are the symbols that are used to designate 'positions,' which are the relatively stable, morphological components of social structure. These positions carry the shared behavioral expectations that are conventionally labeled 'roles'.

Thus roles like CEO, professor, or truck driver are not just constructed or created, but they exist as objects to be seen, reacted to, and labeled within society. Once created, these labels/categories are shared and understood by all in the culture.

Stryker's third and fourth postulates show how actors' identities fit into the scheme. The third postulate indicates that people in society are named or labeled in terms of the structural positions (roles) they occupy such as professor or truck driver. The fourth postulate indicates that people also name themselves with respect to these positional designations ("I am a professor" or "I am a truck driver"). Further, these labels and the expectations and meanings attached to them become internalized and form part of person's selves. These internalized labels are attached to positions, and the expectations and meanings attached to them are our identities. As individuals, we thus become a part of the social structure that is named in postulate two. In short, within the context of structural symbolic interaction, identity theory is really a theory about the relationship between the individual and society, identity and social structure.

Identities as Positions within Groups

Since this early statement by Stryker, the concept of an identity has developed and broadened in several ways, although the fundamental postulates remain intact. Identities are now understood as having two structural bases (Burke and Stets 2009). The first basis is the roles in the social structure that are mentioned above and about which we will have most to say. The second basis is the groups to which individuals belong and that are of two types: those based on category membership such as gender, social class or being in a particular racial or ethnic group, and those based on choice behavior such as being a member of a particular political party, company, professional organization, or local church. Thus, we have both role identities and social identities. Social categories and groups, like roles, are part of the "relatively stable, morphological components of social structure" mentioned in the second postulate.[1]

The meanings and expectations associated with the first basis – roles – are understood in relation to other roles, termed counter roles, in the social structure. For example, the meanings and expectations for the role of husband are understood in relationship to the meanings and expectations of the (counter) role of wife. The role of teacher is understood relative to the (counter) role of student. Further, roles are understood in the context of the social groups, organizations, or larger structures in which they are embedded. A teacher at the junior high school is different from a trained instructor at a yoga studio, or a leader of a church Bible class. The expectations and meanings of being a teacher in each of these different groups can vary around a central shared core of "teacher."

Figure 8.1 depicts several role identities that are connected to counter role identities embedded within each of two different groups or organizations: a UPS office and a bakery. Each of the small circles represents a specific role in each of the organizations. For example, at the UPS office, the different roles may include a manager, secretary, dispatcher, and delivery truck driver. One role in each organization also is connected with a counter role in the other organization that allows transactions between the two groups/organizations. The occupant of each role or position within and across organizations internalizes the meanings and expectations associated with the position. This internalized set of meanings (understandings, descriptions, or characterizations) and

---

[1] A third basis of identities, the person as a biosocial individual, that has come to be recognized in identity theory, is omitted in the present context of relating identities to elements of the social structure. We consider this basis later to understand the flows of persons through the social structure.

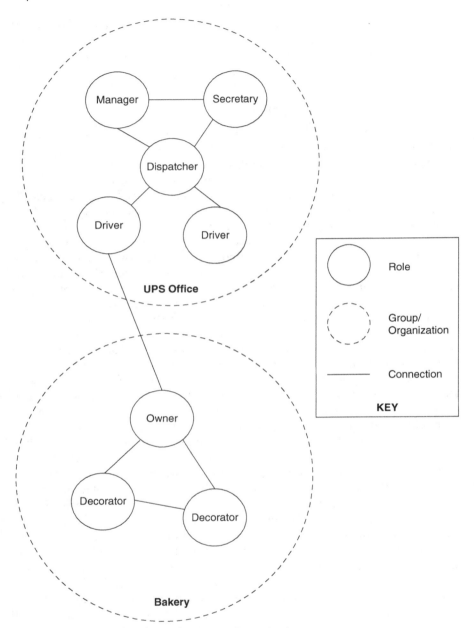

FIGURE 8.1. Example roles within groups/organizations.

expectations defines the identity of the occupant. Thus, each role has a role identity to which it is associated.

For example, in the role of a delivery truck driver, I have both the name (delivery truck driver) as well as the understanding and expectations (identity) of the things I should do and be as a delivery truck driver (loading packages for delivery, keeping gas in the truck, driving my route, delivering packages, getting receipts as necessary, as well as being prompt and courteous). The name (delivery truck driver) and expectations (with standards that must be met) are understood both by myself and others. As a delivery truck driver, I have relationships to other counter roles within the organization including the manager, secretary, dispatcher, and other delivery truck drivers as well as relationships to counter roles in other organizations such as the owner of the bakery when delivering office supplies or new equipment to the bakery. Thus, we begin to see positions and the connections between them within and across groups/ organizations. This first view of social structure, then, is the set of connected roles embedded within groups as illustrated in Figure 8.1.

Identities and Resource Transfers

A second view of the social structure focuses on what happens when the expectations associated with each of the roles are fulfilled and the organization both accomplishes its tasks and helps other organizations fulfill their tasks. For the UPS office, task accomplishment includes the pickup and delivery of packages, the creation of routes for efficient delivery, the maintenance of the trucks, the keeping of records, the transfer of information to the central office and the coordination of other offices, the payment of wages and salaries, the management of promotions, and many other things. All of these tasks are accomplished by persons whose identities tell them what to do in their specific roles.

As each role/identity plays itself out in relation to other role identities both within and between organizations, much is accomplished: the flow of packages, the flow of trucks, the flow of gasoline into the storage tanks and into the trucks, the flow of information within and between associated companies, the flow of people being hired, fired, or retiring and so on. These flows of resources (both material and nonmaterial) constitutes a second view of the social structure beyond the first view of roles being embedded within groups/ organizations. Identity theory combines these two views of social structure: the interconnections among the roles (role identities) and groups/organizations (social identities), as well as the accomplishments of identities in terms of the transfer and transformation of resources.

Identities as Controlling Meaning

Along with identifying additional bases of identities, another major development in identity theory is an understanding of the primary identity process, that is, identity verification. While role and social identities are based on named categories in the social structure, the identities themselves consist of culturally shared meanings that define who one is as an occupant of a role or a member of a social category or group. These meanings from the shared culture have been internalized by the identity holder, and perhaps modified some to fit with other identities that may be held, but they are understood to apply to the self. Thus, a professor may say to himself, "I am a professor, and that means I must do the things I understand professors do," "I must be the way I understand professors are," and "I must appear as I understand professors appear."

These ways of acting, being, and appearing are understood by the person as well as by other professors, students, deans, and administrative staff as indications of being a professor. To act and appear as a professor is to convey meanings in the situation so that both the self and others see and understand these accomplishments. Behavior controls the meanings so that "professor" is accomplished in the situation, and everyone in the situation shares this understanding because the meanings are shared. Thus, identities are attached to positions in the social structure and identities control meanings.

Meaning, as understood in identity theory, is a mediation response to a stimulus (Burke and Stets 2009; Osgood, Suci, and Tannenbaum 1957). Meanings or mediation responses are internal responses (in the form of ideas or feelings) to some stimulus. The internal responses (meaning) act as a stimulus for an outward behavioral response. In this way, the meaning or internal response mediates between the external stimulus and the behavioral response to it. Thus, meaning is the response to the stimulus and not in the stimulus itself.

For example, the word "professor" itself has no inherent meaning. It is an arbitrary word/label applied to certain individuals and what they do. The internal response to this stimulus, our images and thoughts about professors, is the meaning that mediates between the stimulus of the word "professor" and our response to such a person. Identity theory distinguishes two types of stimuli which Mead (1934) labeled conventional signs or symbols and natural signs or simply signs. Symbols are arbitrary in terms of what they represent, but their representation is agreed on by individuals in a culture, although the symbols may differ from culture to culture. Because the culture is shared, symbolic meanings of particular stimuli are shared. People have a similar response to a symbol (for example, the word "professor"), thus symbols can be used to communicate, reason, and plan.

Sign meanings, by contrast, are not shared. They are gained by direct experience with objects, patterns, and events in a situation. For example, people learn what their car sounds like when it is running well, and they can tell that it is making strange noises when it is not running well. The strange noise is the stimulus, and our response of anxiety and confusion is the meaning, which has been gained by prior experience with the noise. Because that knowledge and understanding is gained by direct experience, it is difficult to communicate it symbolically to the mechanic who must experience the sound

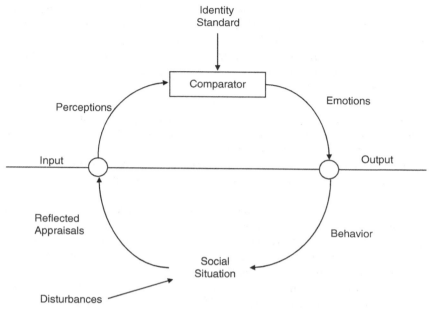

FIGURE 8.2. Identity model within identity theory.

to understand it. That sound is a sign of a potential problem to the car owner, and it may be a sign of a broken water-pump to the mechanic. Talking about the problem with the mechanic would be symbolic interaction with shared understanding of the meanings of the symbols (words) used. The mechanic and his assistant replacing the water-pump would be sign interaction, accomplished by direct experience and control of the objects in the situation.

By incorporating both symbols and signs into identity theory, we can understand identity processes as controlling both symbolic and sign meanings, the latter of which is directly tied to the experience of objects and resources in the situation. In this way, role identities can control the shared symbolic aspects of the role in communicating with others (our UPS driver can communicate with the dispatcher), but identities also can control the unshared, sign experiential meanings associated with managing resources and resource flows in the situation (driving the truck, getting caught in traffic, delivering packages and so on). The role identity of a UPS driver includes all of these aspects.

We turn now to see how the main identity processes accomplish this. Within identity theory, each identity, whether a role or social identity (and even a person identity) contains the same parts and functions. These are shown in Figure 8.2. First is the identity standard that contains all of the sign and symbol meanings that define the identity. Second is the input or perceptions of these same meanings in the situation based on one's own assessment (direct appraisals), and how one thinks others see oneself (reflected appraisals). Third is the comparator, which functions to compare the input meanings with the identity standard meanings and outputs the difference or error, sometimes called the discrepancy. If there is no difference, the error or discrepancy is zero. Fourth and fifth are the consequences of the error: emotion, and the output behavior. Negative emotion and distress generated by a nonzero error serve to motivate the behavior to restore the meanings in the situation to the levels indicated in the identity standard should there be any discrepancy. The output behavior, which influences the meanings in the situation that are perceived so that the perceptions match the meanings in the identity standard, reduces or eliminates any error or discrepancy, if it is present. Because it is the perceptions that are controlled to match the identity standard, this has been called a perceptual control system (Powers 1973).

When an identity is activated in a situation, it begins processing perceptions. What is the current state of the situation with respect to the self-relevant symbol and sign meanings that are being monitored and controlled? This is done by comparing the perceived meanings in the situation with the reference meanings in the identity standard. This is the role of the comparator. If there is no difference, no adjustment in output behavior is needed. The perceived meanings in the situation are what they should be according to the standard. For example, if my role identity standard meanings define me as being "reliable" and "supportive" to certain degrees in my parent role, and I think this is how my children see me (reflected appraisals), my perceptions match the standard and my identity is verified. If I think my daughters see me as less supportive than is given in my standard, the comparator registers a difference or error of a certain magnitude. For example, if my standard for being supportive is set at eight (on some scale from zero to ten), and because of a comment one of my daughters made, I think she has come to see me as a six, the comparator sends an error of six minus eight, or negative two. The comment, which led to this change of meanings in the situation, is a disturbance to the current meanings in the situation.

As mentioned above, an error or discrepancy has two immediate consequences. First, it modifies emotions. In identity theory, any discrepancy (other than zero) increases the level of distress and negative feelings. It will bother me if my daughter sees me as less supportive as a parent than I am. It also will bother me if she sees me as more reliable than I am, perhaps setting up expectations that I cannot meet. Thus, negative emotion in identity theory is a function of the square of the error or discrepancy between reflected appraisals and the identity standard with positive and negative discrepancies both increasing negative emotions.

The second effect of the error or discrepancy (combined with the negative emotion) is to induce me to adjust my behavior so that perceived situational meanings are the way they should be, according to my identity standard. In the example above, if I am perceived as less supportive than my identity standard meaning (the discrepancy is negative), I adjust my behavior in the opposite direction to increase the perceived level of support. Thus, I behave in a more "supportive" manner. If I am perceived as more supportive than my identity standard meaning, the error is positive, and I adjust my behavior to reduce the level of perceived support. This is a negative feedback process which counteracts the effects of the disturbance to the meanings in the situation. My behavior changes as a direct function of the discrepancy, but in the opposite direction in order to reduce and eliminate the discrepancy.

When the disturbance in the situation is counteracted and the meanings restored to reflect those in the identity standard, identity verification has occurred and my emotions change from being negative to being neutral or positive. Identity verification thus has the dual effect of making my feelings more positive and making the self-relevant meanings in the situation match those in the standard.[2]

When we combine the view of identities as structural positions with the view of identities as processes controlling meanings, we can begin to see how the multitude of identities across positions in the social structure operate to create, maintain, and repair that structure. Each identity, through the process of verification, is responsible to maintain both symbol and sign meanings, and through that, maintain the cultural meanings and the flow of resources that sustain individuals, roles, social categories, groups and organizations that define society. Most of the time, this verification process is automatic and habitual. It becomes more deliberate and thoughtful as the magnitude of the discrepancy between the situational meanings and the identity standard meanings increases.

RESOURCES

In identity theory, resources are defined functionally as anything that supports and sustains individuals, groups, or interactions (Freese and Burke 1994). Examples might be air, clothing, and interaction skills that support individuals; buildings, uniforms, and territorial markers that support groups; and conference tables and overhead projectors that support interactions. It does not matter whether the resources are valued, scarce, consumable, or negotiable. This is different than most conceptions of resources in sociology because they are not necessarily scarce or zero-sum. This view permits possessed entities of any sort, valuable or not, to be counted among the resources insofar as they function to sustain individuals and interaction. Also counted among resources are various conditions that are not entities at all – for example, conditions of sequencing,

---

[2] A third, less immediate, consequence of the discrepancy or error is to slowly begin to change the identity standard in the direction of the appraisals. This is a source of identity change (Burke 2004, 2006). Because it is slow, this source of identity change has consequences only if the discrepancy is persistent (Cast and Burke 2002). For a fuller discussion of the conditions under which identity change occurs see earlier work (Burke 2006).

or of structuring, or of sentiment, or of opportunity. This generalized conception of resources enables us to better link identities to the social structure.

We distinguish between two types of resources: *active* and *potential* resources (Freese and Burke 1994). Active resources are those resources that are currently functioning in the situation to sustain persons or the interaction, and in which individuals have direct experiential contact. These include, for example, the chair in which I am currently sitting, the water I am drinking, the glass that holds the water I am drinking, the computer I am using, the keyboard on which I am typing, the smiling look my spouse gives me, and so on. Potential resources are resources that are not currently functioning to sustain persons or an interaction, but that have some future use. These include, for example, the table in the other room on which I will have dinner; the food in the refrigerator for that dinner; the car parked in the garage that will transport me somewhere; the gasoline in the tank that will provide the fuel for my transportation; the answers to my, as yet unasked, questions of a colleague and so on.

Because signs are indicators of resources currently experienced in the situation, the control of sign meanings is the control of these resources in a situation, whether actual or potential. Symbols are indicators of potential resources that are not currently functioning to support an interaction, and in which individuals do not have direct experiential contact in the situation. Symbols allow people to manipulate potential resources including the transformations and transfers that are needed before they later will be used as active resources. However, we point out that symbols also can be used to control actual resources in a situation such as the information being verbally communicated to another or the emotional support given by words of encouragement to another.

Because identity standards contain the sign and symbolic meanings that define an identity, that is, the meanings that serve as a reference for the way the situation is supposed to be, making the situation meanings match the identity standard meanings is the same as making active and potential resources in the situation correspond to the identity meanings. Therefore, identity verification is the process of making sign and symbolic meanings (perceptions) or active and potential resources conform to the pattern of meanings in the identity standard.

To see this more concretely, let us imagine a steel mill and the kinds of resource flows in and through it that define it. We can imagine the flow of iron ore to the mill; the flow of coal and coke to the mill; the flow of water to the mill; the flow of electricity to the mill; the flow of heat, slag, and contaminated water out of the mill; the flow of steel out of the mill; the flow of people into the mill on a work day and home again in the evening; the flow of cranes, trucks, equipment, supplies, order forms, and computers through the mill; the flow of purchase orders, money, credit, and debt through the mill; the flow of information and skills through the mill; the flow of labor; the flow of organizational activities that enable the flows of physical resources and processes to be managed and utilized; and the flow of esteem, respect, and power to various managers and workers.

All of these objects, flows, and transformations in the steel mill are initiated and enabled by the actions of persons on the basis of their identities: railway engineers, crane operators, truck drivers, electricians, secretaries, accountants, managers, and workers. Further the resources themselves, material or intangible, have no function until they are in motion, that is, until they are flowing in a connected manner. What we suggest from this example is that the flows and organized transformations of resources at a very abstract level is the social system in the sense that they constitute it. It is the resource interactions of identities that guide, connect, and control those flows through the verification process, always making the perceived situation (meanings) be the way it is supposed to be. Identity verification produces, controls, and guides the social system.

It should be noted that resources can also be used to facilitate the verification process itself, which maintains identities and counteridentities. For example, Stets and Cast (2007) have shown how different resources such as personal resources (self-worth and self-efficacy), interpersonal resources (role-taking ability, being trusted, and being liked), and structural resources (level of education, occupational status, and income) all facilitate the verification of the spouse role identity and a sociable person identity. Looking at the effects over three time-points, each a year apart, higher levels of these resources at one time brought about higher levels of verification at a later time, thus helping to sustain these identities and counteridentities. They also found that higher levels of identity verification led to having higher levels of resources at a later time.

IDENTITY VERIFICATION AND CHANGE IN THE SOCIAL SYSTEM

The picture in the preceding section shows how the normal operation of the basic identity process of verification uses and produces the resource flows, transformations, and transfers that are associated with some position in the social structure. Because all of the positions or roles in the social structure are connected to and coordinated with other positions, or counterroles, the resource flows are also connected and coordinated, whether in dyads, groups, organizations, or larger structures. Our picture is one of existing roles and identities in a static structure and a constant flow of resources. However, in the identity model, there is room for change and development of both identities and the structures in which they are embedded.

We discuss two ways that a change in the social system could occur within the scope of identity theory. First, whereas the identity standard indicates the way that symbolic and sign meanings in the situation should be configured, and the perceptual control system indicates, through the comparator, when actions have the effect of bringing about the desired configuration of meanings, nothing in the identity indicates the exact way in which this is supposed to happen. People learn the behaviors that influence the situation through social-ization and direct and indirect learning processes. For every desired configura-tion of meanings in the situation, there are many ways to accomplish it. New ways may emerge in response to discrepancies between situational meanings and identity standard meanings when the identity is not being verified. If these new ways become incorporated into the identity standard, the identity changes and possibly the structural connections between roles and counter roles.

For example, my professor identity includes symbol and sign meanings in its reference/standard for accomplishing lectures to a class: expressing my ideas clearly and holding the attention of the class. This is part of the set of standards about how to be a professor held in my professor identity standard. I may over time perceive that some ideas are difficult to express in words, the attention of my class may be wavering, and student evaluations may be going down because they feel the class is boring. This would constitute a discrepancy with the meanings in my standard. By exploring the situation, I may discover, for example, that the use of PowerPoint slides allows me to express my ideas more clearly and hold the attention of the class better. By incorporating these into a slightly modified professor identity standard, I change my professor iden-tity. Being a professor now has new meanings (resources) and new perceptions (related to those actual and potential resources) to control. I no longer rely on my yellowing old lecture notes, but on computer files and programs as well as projectors and connectors and new levels of lighting in the lecture room. I may develop new relationships with the technology people to make sure everything is ready for my use of the PowerPoint projection system in the classroom. I may liaison with persons who know better all the features of the presentation software such as how to capture pictures, videos, and other media forms into my lecture. And, my student evaluations may return to levels suggested by my professor identity standard.

In this way, while the overall goals of being a professor have remained the same, how to accomplish being a professor has changed. New resource con-figuration and flows need to be maintained, and new connections to other roles and positions need to be made and maintained. Thus, both the identity and the structure of role and counter roles have changed. The identity standard has new meanings, the structure of connections among the positions in the organization has changed, and the resource flows have changed. The extent of such changes in the identity or in the organization may be rather small, as in the earlier example, or very large as in the following example.

For the professor role, a large change occurred with the introduction and adoption of desktop computers which had the effect of eliminating secretarial positions in the university, thus changing resource flows away from personnel to equipment. Initially resisted by many because of the identity discrepancy induced by the disturbance, slow changes in the standards of professors were made in the way in which research and writing were done and this raised the expected number of publications that professors should have, again changing resource flows. Not only did the introduction of desktop computer change the way in which things got done, they also found new things that could be done as new software was developed. With the introduction of the Internet, communication and collaboration possibilities changed the connections between role positions across universities as researchers began to work with more and different other researchers across the country. Identities changed to incorporate new resource manipulations (sign and symbolic meanings) involving ways in which research could be accomplished as the Internet facilitated the sharing of data and the learning of new data analytic techniques.

These examples are of change that is introduced as identities find new and better resources and connections (thus adding to the standards) to accomplish verification of existing standards. Finding new ways can also have the effect of creating new positions with new identity standards emerging as the positions are filled. For example, a CEO may verify his identity by creating West Coast and East Coast divisions of a company with new managerial positions. Each of these newly established managerial positions and corresponding identities will control vast flows of resources including buildings, information, and people through the verification process. In this way, identities may create other identities to be used as resources for identity verification.

In sum, identity change and structural change as well as changes in resource flows are built into the way in which identities operate to make the meanings in the situation be the same as those in the identity standard, that is, to achieve identity verification. This occurs because identities control perceptions by modifying behavior to find alternative ways in which those perceptions can best match the symbolic and sign meanings in the identity standard.

SYSTEM STABILITY THROUGH REPAIR

Returning to the identity model in Figure 8.2, there is a neglected process at the bottom of the figure, which plays a prominent role in identity verification: *disturbances*. As discussed earlier, when the perceived sign and symbolic meanings in the situation match those of the identity standard, the comparator emits an error signal of zero, which might be taken as the goal of the system. With an output of zero, emotions are neutral or positive and the behavioral output remains as it has been.[3] Because the value of the error signal indicates an increasing or decreasing amount by which to change existing output meanings, an error of zero indicates that no increase or decrease in any meanings needs to occur.

---

[3] We agree with Carver and Scheier (1998) who suggest that positive feelings arise during the process of reducing the error toward zero, but that at zero feelings are neutral. Thus, the process of verification produces positive feelings and the process of nonverification produces negative feelings.

The disturbances, however, consist of anything that changes the perceived situational meanings to be different than the meanings in the identity standard. Disturbances to the existing symbol and sign meanings may be the result of the actions of other people in the situation pursuing the verification of their own identities. In doing this, they may alter the level of resources, or change symbols that define the nature of the situation in competition with other identities. Disturbances may also occur as the result of various physical processes that occur as parts wear out or accidents happen such as floods, droughts, or other natural disasters. Any of these things can change meanings in the situation away from where they "should be" according to the identity standard. The verification process for the identity will result in the reestablishment of meanings in the situation to be in accord with the meanings in the identity standard once again. This may be accomplished through altering the levels and flows of resources, changing the interaction patterns, or even changing the structure of groups and organizations to reestablish meanings in accord with the identity standard.

Thus, the verification process can be thought of as a situational repair process, a process that repairs the situation from the damage or change that has occurred as a result of the disturbance. When a department in a company loses people who take jobs elsewhere, the director, whose director identity includes maintaining work flows at certain levels experiences identity nonverification. By hiring and training new employees, the director verifies his director identity and helps to maintain the department.

At the organizational level, revenues may fall below a level set in the CEO's corporate identity standard due to mismanagement on the part of an officer of the company. To bring her perceptions of revenue up to the standard set in the identity, the CEO may take some form of restorative action such as firing the officer, ordering the officer to receive extra training, or working more closely with the officer to ensure that such mismanagement does not continue. It may also involve bringing in a team to undo the bad decisions or find ways to counter the effects of those decisions. These repairs to the organization that result from identity verification on the part of the CEO thus returns the organization to the way it is supposed to be. Without this repair process in which identities normally engage, the resources that support any society would degenerate to the point they are no longer useful, that is, they can no longer sustain individuals, groups, or interaction.

Note that there really is no difference between identity verification and repair of the situational resources and meanings. Verification and repair are made necessary because the sign and symbol meanings, that is, active and potential resources and resource flows are disturbed, modified, or changed from what they "ought" to be. Verification and repair is what identities do. Social structure as organized resource flows is the result of the normal identity verification processes, but built into that process is the repair of the process when it is needed by simply making the situation be the way it is supposed to be. That means bringing all of the sign and symbol meanings in the situation into alignment with those of the identity standard.

SYSTEM STABILITY AND EMOTION

We mentioned the role of emotion in the identity verification process as helping to motivate the behavior that results in perceived situational meanings matching the identity standard meanings. In this process, it is the people who hold the identities that feel the emotion, not the identity itself. And, it is the behavior of the people who hold the identities that serves to modify situational meanings to bring them into congruence with the identity standard meanings. When an identity is not verified, when there is a discrepancy between the identity standard meanings and the perceived situational meanings, the discrepancy increases negative emotions.

Research has shown that the direction of the discrepancy does not matter with respect to the emotional consequences (Burke and Harrod 2005). Whether there is too much or too little of some meaning relative to the standard, negative emotions are increased. In the Burke and Harrod study, the identity standards were the way husbands and wives thought of themselves in terms of such characteristics as intelligence, friendliness, and likability. Each rated himself or herself on a scale from 0 to 100 reflecting degrees from "not at all" to "extremely." This represented their identity standard. If the perceived meanings in the situation given off by the spouse of the respondent differed from the identity standard ratings, the respondent felt more anger and more distress. It did not matter if the perceived meanings from the spouse were higher than the person's identity standard (for example, more intelligent than the self-rating), or if the perceived meanings from the spouse were lower (less intelligent than the self-rating). Either case increased distress and anger. These negative feelings helped motivate the person to reduce the discrepancy and increase the level of verification, thus making the situation be the way it is supposed to be.

Although negative emotions have the motivational effect of reducing identity discrepancy and increasing verification, positive emotions can help create a mutual verification context through role and counter role identities working together to verify each other as well as themselves. Burke and Stets (1999) examined the spousal identity of husbands and wives, and the degree to which mutual verification emerged in a marriage.

The emotions they investigated included positive emotions such as feelings of love for the spouse, trust in the spouse, commitment to the spouse, and the feeling of togetherness or "we-ness" as opposed to the separateness of a "you" or "I." These positive emotions were shown to be outcomes of spousal identity verification, and they motivated strong ties to the marriage partner. For example, the more one's spousal identity was verified, the stronger the love for the partner; the more the partner was trusted; the higher the commitment to the partner; and the more the spouses thought of themselves as a "we" rather than a "you" or "I." These increased positive emotions strengthened the bonds between the husband and wife and created a sense of "us" as a group. In such a context, love, commitment, and trust between the spouses were increased and a sense of the group or family as a social unit increased. Structurally, this has the effect of keeping the spousal identities connected to each other by keeping the individuals together with emotional bonds that also form part of the social structure. Thus, not only is the structure maintained in terms of the connection of roles with counter roles within the organization as well as the transformation and flows of resources, but the persons who hold the identities become attached to each other with trust, liking, and commitment, thus assuring that the identities stay together and are connected.

While most of the work done on the emotional consequences of identity verification and nonverification has considered generic positive and negative emotions, some theoretical work suggests that specific emotions including shame, embarrassment, fear, disappointment, and sadness, arise from the nonverification of identities in specific contexts (Stets and Burke 2005). For this, Stets and Burke considered the source of the nonverification, that is, whether it was due to something the individual had done through neglect or error, or whether it was due to something that another has done to bring about the nonverification. They also considered the relative status and power of the other in the situation who either caused the nonverification or witnessed it.

For example, if a higher status person such as an esteemed colleague changes meanings in the situation that results in an identity not to be verified, one may feel anxiety. But, if the status of the other is equal, one simply may feel annoyance. If the status of the other is lower than the person, the person may feel hostility. Each of these feelings may suggest different courses of action that might be taken to rectify the situation and counteract the discrepancy. By contrast, if the other differs in power rather than status, Stets and Burke hypothesized the self will feel fear toward a higher power other such as one's boss, anger at an equal power other, and rage at a lower power other.

The idea behind these hypotheses about specific emotions is that the source of the discrepancy and the relative status or power of the other within the group or organizational context provides additional meaning for the actor in the situation. These additional meanings must also be maintained. Stets and Burke suggest that these additional meanings arising from the source of the discrepancy and the relative status and power of the other yield particular emotions suggesting different courses of action that might be taken to reduce the present discrepancy and attempt to keep intact the self-other relationship. These specific emotions thus guide the kinds of repair work that gets done to maintain the person to person relationships as well as the role identity to role identity relationships. However, expressing rage at one's boss is not likely to do this, or alternatively, expressing annoyance to an underling, which may not assure proper behavior by the underling to maintain the role relationship.

Overall, then, emotion plays an important role in the relationship between identities and the social structure in which they are embedded. The distress and negative emotions that occur when identities are not verified motivates the person to increase his/her efforts and focus on counteracting the disturbance that is causing the nonverification. The positive feelings, attachments, trust, and group identity that arise when roles and counter roles are each verified in a mutual verification context establishes and maintains the person to person links between the persons occupying the structural positions. Finally, the varied and specific emotions that arise in the verification process, both positive and negative, bring about specific behaviors that are appropriate for the context in the sense of both counteracting the disturbance, but also of maintaining the person to person connection that is necessary for identities to operate to maintain the resource flows that both define and support the social structure in which the identities are embedded. It is not enough to repair the resource flows, it is also important to keep people in relationships that allow this.

PERSON IDENTITIES AND THE SOCIAL STRUCTURE

Thus far, we have talked mostly about identities based on roles, with some attention to identities based on social categories or groups, and the way in which the verification process creates, repairs, and maintains the social structure in terms of both the relationship among positions as well as the flows of resources that support those positions and relationships. In this section we examine the third basis of identities, the person as a biosocial entity, to understand the role of verification of these identities for the maintenance of structure.

Like role and social identities, person identities are defined by the meanings in the identity standard, and the verification process is the same. However, the meanings and expectations in the person identity standard are not attached to roles or groups. Rather, they are attached to the individual and define the person as a distinct and different from others. These meanings are based on culturally recognized characteristics that individuals internalize as their own and that serve to define and characterize them as unique. These meanings serve as identity standards guiding the identity verification process (Burke 2004). They may include such characteristics as how masterful, dominant and controlling is the person (Stets 1995a; Stets and Burke 1994), how moral is the person (Stets and Carter 2011; 2012), or what the person values (Hitlin 2003). Because the person identity meanings of being controlling or moral are culturally shared, others will draw upon these same meanings to identify the individual and thus facilitate the verification process.

Role identities are activated primarily when the person is in the appropriate role. Social identities are activated primarily when the person is in a situation relevant to the social category or group. Person identities are activated across roles, categories, groups, and situations because the person is always present. Because person identities are likely to be activated at any time, even when other identities, including role and social identities are activated, and because identities reside in individuals whose behavior must serve to verify all the identities that are activated in a situation, the standards of these multiple identities cannot be incompatible. A control system like the identity control system cannot have a standard that is set at two different levels.

A person cannot verify a "gentle" standard in his husband identity, and at the same time verify a "rough" standard in his gender (masculine) identity. If the person were to act in a gentle manner to verify the husband identity, he would have a discrepancy for the masculine identity that would generate distress. If a person were, in fact, caught in such a situation and could not easily leave, the meanings in the two standards would slowly shift to a compromise level between the two conflicting levels (Burke 2003; Stets 1995b). To avoid this stressful situation, people tend to take on identities that are compatible and to enter interactions that provide symbol and sign meanings that verify existing identities (Swann 1987; Swann, Pelham, and Krull 1989). This mechanism of (self-) selected interaction thus guides the movement and flow of persons into and through the social structure insofar as people have choices. It also assures that the identity verification process does not tear the social structure apart in conflicting actions.

As we indicated, the meanings and expectations in the identity standards of person identities come from the meanings available in the cultures and subcultures of society. These subcultures reflect the structural divisions of society that serve to allocate resources to positions, groups, and categories of individuals. We suggest that the meanings vary by subculture so that the person identities of individuals in those subcultures are conducive to the positions that such people may come to occupy. Because there is no hard line between the different cultures and subcultures, the meanings that are taken on in the person identities of individuals serve more to provide inclinations toward (or away from) various kinds of roles and group memberships where the role or group meanings will be more likely to be consistent (or inconsistent) with the person identity standard meanings. Thus, person identities may be thought to provide a mechanism for sorting people across roles and groups, bringing some persons together and keeping others apart, to limit the potential conflict and competition that may arise if everyone had the same values and inclinations.

CONCLUSION

Verifying role identities by controlling perceived signs and symbols maintains their connections to counter role identities and achieves the resource transformations and transfers in accordance with the meanings and expectations of the roles. Whether social structure is viewed as the set of interconnected roles or the transformation and flow of resources, both are the result of role identity verification. When those structures are disrupted by disturbances, identity verification repairs them. Verifying a social identity, based on a social category or group membership has similar consequences. Though not discussed extensively in this chapter, verification of social identities maintain the boundaries between groups, and the divisions among people in a complex society, thus facilitating the flow of various resources to some and not to others.

Verifying a person identity, based on the individual as a unique biosocial entity, moves people toward some situations, groups, and organizations where meanings are more consistent with their identity standard, and away from other parts of the social structure where meanings are less consistent with their identity standard. In this way, roles and groups or organizations tend to be filled by people who are more likely to be able to verify their identities. The consequence of this greater likelihood of verification is that such people will feel good and become attached to others in the situation, group or organization and work to maintain those connections and repair any disturbances. From all of this, it is easy to conclude that the process of identity verification is the process and structure of society.

REFERENCES

Burke, Peter J. 2003. "Relationships among Multiple Identities." Pp. 195–214 in *Advances in Identity Theory and Research*, edited by P. J. Burke, T. J. Owens, R. T. Serpe, and P. A. Thoits. New York: Kluwer Academic/Plenum.
  2004. "Identities and Social Structure: The 2003 Cooley-Mead Award Address." *Social Psychology Quarterly* 67: 5–15.
  2006. "Identity Change." *Social Psychology Quarterly* 69: 81–96.
Burke, Peter J. and Michael M. Harrod. 2005. "Too Much of a Good Thing?" *Social Psychology Quarterly* 68: 359–374.
Burke, Peter J., and Jan E. Stets. 1999. "Trust and Commitment through Self-Verification." *Social Psychology Quarterly* 62: 347–66.
  2009. *Identity Theory*. New York: Oxford University Press.
Carver, Charles S., and Michael F. Scheier. 1998. *On the Self-Regulation of Behavior*. New York: Cambridge University Press.
Cast, Alicia D., and Peter J. Burke. 2002. "A Theory of Self-Esteem." *Social Forces* 80: 1041–1068.
Freese, Lee, and Peter J. Burke. 1994. "Persons, Identities, and Social Interaction." *Advances in Group Processes* 11: 1–24.
Hitlin, Steven. 2003. "Values as the Core of Personal Identity: Drawing Links between Two Theories of Self." *Social Psychology Quarterly. Special Issue: Social identity: Sociological and social psychological perspectives* 66: 118–37.
Mead, George H. 1934. *Mind, Self, and Society*. Chicago: University of Chicago Press.
Osgood, Charles E., George J. Suci, and Percy H. Tannenbaum. 1957. *The Measurement of Meaning*. Urbana: University of Illinois Press.
Powers, William T. 1973. *Behavior: The Control of Perception*. Chicago: Aldine.
Stets, Jan E. 1995a. "Modelling Control in Relationships." *Journal of Marriage and the Family* 57: 489–501.
  1995b. "Role Identities and Person Identities: Gender Identity, Mastery Identity, and Controlling One's Partner." *Sociological Perspectives* 38: 129–50.

Stets, Jan E., and Peter J. Burke. 1994. "Inconsistent Self-Views in the Control Identity Model." *Social Science Research* 23: 236–262.

2005. "New Directions in Identity Control Theory." *Advances in Group Processes* 22: 43–64.

Stets, Jan E., and Michael J. Carter. 2011. "The Moral Self: Applying Identity Theory." *Social Psychology Quarterly* 74: 192–215.

2012. "A Theory of the Self for the Sociology of Morality." *American Sociological Review* 77: 120–140.

Stets, Jan E., and Alicia D. Cast. 2007. "Resources and Identity Verification from an Identity Theory Perspective." *Sociological Perspectives* 50: 517–43.

Stryker, Sheldon. [1980] 2002. *Symbolic Interactionism: A Social Structural Version.* Caldwell, NJ: Blackburn Press.

Swann, William B., Jr. 1987. "Identity Negotiation: Where Two Roads Meet." *Journal of Personality and Social Psychology* 53: 1038–51.

Swann, William B., Jr., Brett W. Pelham, and Douglas S. Krull. 1989. "Agreeable Fancy or Disagreeable Truth? Reconciling Self Enhancement and Self-Verification." *Journal of Personality and Social Psychology* 57: 782–91.

9

Identities, Roles, and Social Institutions

An Affect Control Account of Social Order

David R. Heise, Neil J. MacKinnon, and Wolfgang Scholl

Abstract

We locate the micro-foundations of social order in the cultural meanings of institutional identities and roles, the daily enactment of which ensures social order through the continual reproduction and legitimation of social institutions. Following discussion of a general conceptual model, we discuss two complementary, micro-level explanations of social order: a cognitive approach combining a classic micro-sociological theory of institutions with a recent method for analyzing the causal structures of social actions in institutional settings; and an affective approach based on affect control theory. We then present two analyses illustrating specific sectors of our conceptual model. The first deals with cognitive meanings, showing how social institutions are present as associative structures within individuals' minds, enabling them to define situations in institutional contexts. The second demonstrates how the evaluation, potency, and activity dimensions of affective meaning employed by affect control theory correspond to the structure of interdependence relations as represented in game matrices.

In the augmented symbolic interactionist perspective that we present here, human activities are stimulated and maintained by cognitive and affective meanings, and change emerges as new human activities evolve or are consciously designed in ways that instigate new meanings. This symbolic interactionism is "augmented" in that it incorporates affective meanings along with cognitive meanings, and it allows for multiple kinds of human activities, from various kinds of thought to individual behavior to coordinated group actions.

In this framework, cognitive experiences of successive generations accumulate as *practical knowledge* (Berger and Luckmann 1966), while emotional experiences accumulate as *cultural sentiments* (Heise 2007; MacKinnon and Heise 2010). Through socialization, individuals internalize both kinds of

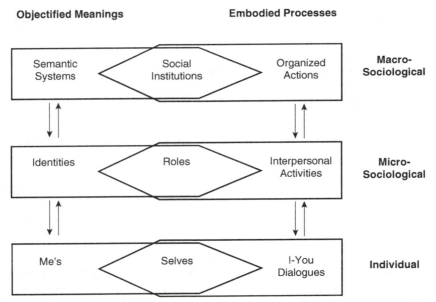

FIGURE 9.1. Schematic diagram of institutions, roles, and selves, interrelated through semiotic and behavioral functioning.
(Reproduced by permission from MacKinnon and Heise (2010:7)).

cultural meaning; and by employing practical knowledge and cultural sentiments to guide and motivate their interpersonal activities, they ensure the continual reproduction of the organized activities that embody society.

Social order is the outcome of complex, reciprocal relations among cultural and social processes at different levels of analysis, as portrayed in Figure 9.1, from MacKinnon and Heise's 2010 book. MacKinnon and Heise used this figure to explain the construction and interplay of selves and social institutions, but a lot of conceptual territory was left unanalyzed in their presentation. In this chapter, we employ Figure 9.1 as a theoretical scaffold for explaining selected aspects of social order.

Following a review and elaboration of the general conceptual model portrayed in Figure 9.1, we present two more detailed examinations of linkages represented in the model. The first deals with cognitive meanings, combining ideas from Berger and Luckmann's (1966) theory of social reality with event structure analysis (Heise 2014a, 1989; Heise and Durig 1997), and uses a form of meaning analysis introduced by MacKinnon and Heise (2010). This shows for the first time that major social institutions are present as structures of association within individuals' minds, so individuals are able to define situations in terms of the cultural templates for social institutions. The second examination deals with affective meanings as developed in affect control theory (Heise

1979, 2007; MacKinnon 1994; MacKinnon and Heise 2010; Smith-Lovin and Heise 1988; Hoey, Schröder, and Alhothali 2013). We show a linkage between affective meanings and material reward structures that bind individuals into interdependences. Thereby patterns of cooperation and conflict, of domination and servitude, are maintained by cultural sentiments about identities, while at the same time emergent patterns of cooperation, conflict, domination, and servitude re-form cultural sentiments.

In the conclusion to this chapter, we summarize our theoretical discussions and findings and discuss them in the context of other theories of social order based on consensus and consistency.

THEORETICAL FRAMEWORK

Elements of Society

Horizontally, Figure 9.1 distinguishes between a society's *objectified meanings* and *embodied processes*; vertically, among *macro-sociological, micro-sociological*, and *individual* levels of analysis. At the macro-sociological level, objectified meanings refer to *semantic systems* in which meanings of identities, settings, and behaviors are integrated into clusters that define the normative configurations of social institutions. At the micro-sociological level are the cognitive and affective meanings of *identities* that generate and control role-enactments. At the individual level, concepts' cognitive and affective meanings are constituted psychologically and involved in various kinds of thought. The diagram foregrounds identities that the individual has incorporated into the self-concept – the *me* – and thought processes that are involved in self-maintenance. However, as discussed later, the individual level involves other meanings and additional kinds of thought processes.

At the macro-sociological level embodied processes refer to *organized actions*, integrated action systems (Heise 2014a; Heise and Durig 1997) including functioning organizations. These action systems materially instantiate social institutions, and their natural evolution provides a path by which social institutions themselves evolve. At the micro-sociological level are *interpersonal activities*, including face-to-face conversations and social interaction between individuals who are electronically co-present. Material and symbolic rewards and punishments during interactions create patterns of role interdependence that provide a path for environmental changes in identity meanings. At the individual level are thought processes, perception, and corporal behavior. Thought processes include *I-you dialogues*, the internal dialogue of self where the pronominal *you* is addressed to self rather than to other people,[1] and other

---

[1] While we have drawn the pronominal terms from Wiley's (1994) I-you-me semiotic model of the self, we have separated me's from I-you dialogues to be consistent with the distinction in Figure 9.1 between meanings and processes.

forms of mental activity as well. Of particular importance in this chapter is the process of defining the situation on the basis of internalized conceptions about identities along with perceptions of the immediate environment.

Referring to the center of the model, *social institutions* are represented as the integration of a society's semantic systems and organized actions. This is consistent with the conventional definition of a social institution as the intersection of cultural structure (patterns or regularities in culturally shared beliefs and sentiments) and social structure (patterns or regularities in social interaction) (House 1981; Merton 1957; Parsons and Shils 1951; Wallace 1983). Moving down to the next level, *roles* are represented as the merging of the cultural meanings of identities and interpersonal activities – the intersection of culture and social structure at the micro-sociological level (Gross, Mason, and McEachern 1958; Sarbin 1968; Wallace 1983). This idea is captured by Sarbin's statement that a role "connotes not only overt actions and performances but also covert expectations held by an observer or by a group of observers" (1968: 546). Finally, at the individual level in the diagram, *selves* are represented as the intersection of me's (identities and other self-meanings) and I-you *dialogues*.

Turning to the relations among constructs in Figure 9.1, the *horizontal* block arrows represent the reciprocal effects of objectified meanings and embodied processes at each level of analysis. At the macro-sociological level, existing cultural meanings generally shape organizational structures and actions; but as organization activities evolve, they effect changes in the meanings of relevant identities, actions, and settings. At the micro-sociological level, identity meanings generally shape interpersonal activities, as elaborated in affect control theory, but creative performance of roles can change the meanings of identities. And, finally, at the individual level, the internal dialogue of self generally invokes familiar identities, but it can also modify existing self-conceptions or create new ones.

The *vertical* pairs of line arrows in Figure 9.1 represent the reciprocal effects of elements at different levels, with separate pairs for objectified meanings and embodied processes because connections of cultural meanings between-levels can be distinct from connections of embodied processes between-levels. Referring to the left side of Figure 9.1, cultural systems of meanings at the macro-sociological level are largely constructed from identity meanings at the micro-sociological level, and that is reflected in the upward arrow between the two levels of meanings. At the same time, changes in cultural systems of meaning may change the meanings of specific identities, and that is reflected in the downward arrow. Referring to the connections between self-meanings (me's) and identity meanings, the upward arrow represents the fact that every individual creates a unique, personal identity or persona; the downward arrow, that most of an individual's self-conceptions consist of preexisting cultural identities.

Referring to the right side of Figure 9.1, the upward arrow denotes that organized actions at the macro-sociological level are constituted from social interaction at the micro-sociological level and can change as interactions change; the downward arrow, that changes in the social structure and actions of organizations can affect routine social interaction. Finally, as indicated by an upward arrow, internal dialogues motivate social interaction; but, as indicated by a downward arrow, social interaction is incorporated into an individual's internal dialogue.

In summary, each set of arrows in Figure 9.1 represents an important socio-logical or social psychological process contributing to social order. While each process deserves in-depth analysis, we cannot accomplish this in a single chap-ter. Therefore, following a discussion of identities, roles, and social institutions, and the cognitive and affective basis of social order, we focus on two sectors of Figure 9.1: (a) the cognitive representation of macro-sociological phenom-ena in individual minds (Semantic Systems ←→ Identities ←→ conceptions in individual minds); and (b) the interplay between culturally-defined identities and embodied interpersonal activities (Identities ←→ Roles ←→ Interpersonal Activities). We present an empirical analysis related to each.

The first analysis connects the psychological conceptions of identities in indi-vidual minds to semantic systems at the macro-level – the cultural component of social institutions (left side of Figure 9.1). Specifically a network analysis of word associations shows that the full range of social institutions is avail-able psychologically, with activation of one institutional identity and role in an individual's mind evoking other identities and roles within the same institution.

The second analysis connects the affective-connotative meanings of identi-ties to roles and interpersonal activities at the micro-sociological level. This analysis shows how the evaluation, potency, and activity dimensions of affec-tive meaning employed in affect control reflect the structure of game matrices employed by interdependence, exchange, and rational choice theories, connect-ing affect control theory and its theory of social order to cognitive-rational theories in social psychology. Changes in the meanings of identities and roles at the level of interpersonal activities should produce gradual changes in orga-nized actions at the macro-sociological level – the social structural component of social institutions (right side of Figure 9.1).

Before presenting these two analyses, however, we must first discuss the foundational concepts of identities, roles and social institutions and the cognitive-affective processes at the base of all sectors of the model of social order represented in Figure 9.1.

Identities, Roles, and Social Institutions

Identities are social categories or positions with which people identify and that they may appropriate as self-conceptions. Every identity is related to a corresponding role, which is why identities are often called role-identities (McCall and Simmons 1978; Burke 1980).[2] People confirm identities by enacting corresponding roles (Heise 1979, 2007; MacKinnon 1994) – for example, the identity of doctor is confirmed by role-appropriate actions such as medicating and healing. The various data bases of affect control theory contain hundreds of institutional identities (e.g., mother, doctor, patient, evangelist, professor, salesman), and affect control simulations have provided many examples of predicting institutionally-scripted behavior corresponding to social roles.[3]

Identities connect to roles, and roles are the micro-sociological counterpart of social institutions (see discussion of Figure 9.1). These ideas accord with Berger and Luckmann's (1966) micro-sociological theory of social institutions. First, the theory proclaims that the evolution of social institutions is coextensive with the emergence of a typology of actors (institutional identities) and related actions (institutional roles) (1966);[4] second, that "the institutional order is real only insofar as it is realized in performed roles" (1966: 78–79), and is without "an ontological status apart from the human activity that produced it" (1966: 60–61). The institutional world becomes subjectively real to people as they internalize institutional roles as identities, so-called because "internalization entails identification with the role and its appropriate norms" (Berger and Luckmann 1966: 139).

Because institutional identities and roles are associated with counteridentities and roles (e.g., *husband* for wife; *patient* for doctor), they embody *relational* meanings[5] guiding and shaping social interaction (*interpersonal activities* in Figure 9.1). According to affect control simulations, for example, a judge might *remind* or *caution* an attorney but *convict* or *sentence* a thief (Heise 1979: 108). Because of their relational meanings, institutional roles have been described as "role integrates" (Parsons and Shils 1951) or as representing "an entire institutional nexus of conduct" (Berger and Luckmann 1966: 75), exemplified by a doctor's relationships with patients and other practitioners in the medical system. Because of such relational meanings, social institutions can be identified from semantic network analysis of the dictionary meanings of identities, as MacKinnon and Heise (2010) have shown. Later in this chapter, we show how social institutions can also be revealed by network analysis of word associations.

[2] To distinguish them from social or collective identities, which refer to identification with a group or collectivity rather than with an institutional role (see Thoits and Virshup 1997 and MacKinnon and Heise 2010 for discussions of this distinction).
[3] The affect control model also generates meaningful predictions for deviant identities and roles, as well as for improvised identities and roles in novel situations.
[4] "Institutionalization occurs whenever there is a reciprocal typification of habitualized actions *by types of actors*. Put differently, any such typification is an institution (Berger and Luckmann 1966: 54. Emphasis added)."
[5] The relational meaning of identities and roles is emphasized by Burke (1980). Just as roles in the external social structure are given meaning by their relation to counter-roles, he argues, identities in the internal structure of the self derive their meaning from their relation to counteridentities.

The Cognitive-Affective Foundation of Social Order

Although, by itself, the relational nature of institutional identities and roles makes an important contribution to our understanding of social institutions and social order, we must delve deeper into the underlying social psychological processes to attain a more profound understanding of social order. We begin with cognitive explanations, showing why they are not sufficient by themselves to explain social order.

Berger and Luckmann's (1966) micro-sociological theory of social institutions contains an implicit cognitive theory of social order based on the *practical knowledge* of social institutions acquired by adequately-socialized people. Like Mead (1934), they begin with the idea that language has enabled the human organism to objectify everyday experience as objects of consciousness and to attach meanings to these cognitions. Over time, meanings coalesce into "semantic fields or zones of meaning" that accumulate in a society as institutional knowledge.[6] Institutional knowledge is "learned as objective truth in the course of socialization and ... internalized as subjective reality" (1966: 67). Institutional knowledge is mostly taken-for-granted, practical, and unreflective – "the sum total of 'what everybody knows' about the social world" (1966: 65). At the level of particular institutions, "recipe knowledge" – "knowledge limited to pragmatic competence in routine performances" (1966: 42) – defines the available identities and roles, and provides guidelines for institutionally appropriate behavior. Finally, institutional knowledge is *socially distributed*, not only along institutional lines, but also by "degrees of familiarity" (1966: 43) and "relevance structures" (1966: 45) within a particular institution. For example, an individual's own identities and roles in an institutional setting are generally more familiar and relevant than those of other people in that setting.

Practical knowledge of the institutional world is the basis of social order – "the well-socialized individual simply 'knows' that his social world is a consistent whole" (Berger and Luckmann 1966: 64). This sense of cognitive coherence is arrived at in a "derivative fashion" as individuals reflect upon their everyday institutional actions and integrate them into a "subjectively meaningful universe" that is shared with other members of a society (1966: 65). And it is the transcendental and integrative power of language that enables people to *connect* and *integrate* different zones of meaning within particular institutions and within the overall institutional order itself.

Although quite compelling, there is a major problem with Berger and Luckmann's cognitive explanation of social order – its failure to address the problem of *motivation*. In terms of the two functions attributed to human motivation in the psychological literature: *mobilization* and *direction*, practical knowledge may *direct* individual action in institutional settings but it is

---

[6] "The objectivated meanings of institutional activity are conceived of as 'knowledge' and transmitted as such" (Berger and Luckmann 1966: 70).

not sufficient to *mobilize* it.[7] Cognitions must be imbued with affect in order to energize the mobilization of action (MacKinnon 1994). This leads into a discussion of another cognitive theory of social order based on practical institutional knowledge that addresses the problem of motivation.

Event Structure Analysis (ESA) (Heise 2014; Heise and Durig 1997) analyzes social actions in terms of causal linkages and outcomes. The theory focuses on *action schemes* – knowledge structures specifying actions that must take place along a causal linkage in order for outcome actions to occur. People employ action schemes for everyday activities such as going to work or making dinner, and action schemes structure routine activities in organizational and institutional settings. In general, action schemes operate at a preconscious level of cognition and unfold more or less automatically. Thus, the concept comes close to Berger and Luckmann's (1966) concept of practical or recipe knowledge discussed above.

Unlike Berger and Luckmann's explanation of social order, however, ESA recognizes the motivational problem in collaborative actions – that agents must be motivated to initiate and perform actions reliably along each step of a causal linkage in order for predictable outcomes to occur. Drawing from affect control theory, ESA proposes that people are motivated to initiate intrinsically fulfilling actions, especially actions that confirm organizational identities with which they personally identify and value (Heise 1979, 2007; MacKinnon 1994), creating a sense of self-actualization and authenticity (MacKinnon and Heise 2010).[8]

Affect control theory proposes that people are motivated to act in ways that confirm cultural sentiments for the identities of self and others in a situation. For example, a doctor is expected to assist, medicate, and cure a patient; a mother, to nurture and protect a child. What actually occurs in a situation, however, produces *transient feelings* that may or may not be consistent with the cultural sentiments for the identities of interactants. For example, a doctor who harms a patient or a mother who hits a child produces transient feelings that deviate dramatically from the cultural sentiments for the identities of doctor and mother, as well as for the recipients of their actions, patient and child. The discrepancy between cultural sentiments and transient feelings is called *deflection* in affect control theory, so

---

[7] Of course, practical knowledge in itself can be motivating in the limited sense that knowing what is expected (e.g., how to perform an institutional role) eliminates the impediment to action of cognitive uncertainty. From our position, however, practical knowledge contributes to the mobilization of action *indirectly* by evoking *feelings* of competence. Along with feelings of evaluation and activity, feelings of competence (potency) mobilize the required actions (e.g., role performances) to achieve an outcome (e.g., confirming an identity).

[8] In the absence of this kind of intrinsic motivation, ESA acknowledges that organizational actions that are unlikely to be intrinsically fulfilling for most people (e.g., assembly line work) must be made reliable by the application of *power schemes* – auxiliary action schemes that motivate people when the central action schemes of an organization prove unfulfilling.

confirming cultural sentiments for the identities of self and others is equivalent to minimizing deflection.

Cultural sentiments are measured by the EPA (evaluation, potency, activity) dimensions of affective meaning (Osgood 1962, 1969; Osgood, Suci, and Tannenbaum 1957; Osgood, May, and Miron 1975), where evaluation concerns goodness versus badness; potency concerns powerfulness versus powerlessness; and activity concerns liveliness versus quietness.[9] Transient feelings are also measured in EPA terms, enabling affect control theory to mathematically generate an ideal EPA profile for actions that would minimize deflection and optimally confirm the identities of interactants in a situation.

Because minimizing deflection is equivalent to maintaining consistency with cultural sentiments, the motivational principle of affect control also explains social order. People avoid deflection in institutional settings by enacting institutionally appropriate identities and roles; but in doing so, they simultaneously reproduce and legitimate the institutions in which these identities and roles are embedded.

The cognitive theory of social order implicit in Berger and Luckmann (1966) and the affective theory of social order contained in affect control theory are complementary explanations, each focusing on a different mode of meaning. At the same time, neither approach ignores the mode of meaning emphasized by the other. Berger and Luckmann, for example, acknowledge that successful learning and performance of an institutional role requires, not only the acquisition of cognitive knowledge and specialized skills, but also the "affective layers of the body of knowledge that is directly and indirectly appropriate to this role" (1966: 77). And although affect control theory emphasizes the affective basis of social order, it acknowledges the cognitive work involved in defining a situation and selecting among alternative actions that are affectively comparable (Heise 1979, 2007; MacKinnon 1994). In other words, role performances that are affectively motivated and bounded are also cognitively constrained by institutional limits. Under ordinary circumstance, for example, judges do not medicate and doctors do not sentence.

Cognitive and affective meanings are also connected intimately by the fact that each word in a language has both a cognitive-denotative meaning and an affective-connotative meaning. Affect control theory models the reciprocal process of translation between the two domains of meaning (see Heise 1979: 48–49). The advantage of working with affective meaning lies in its dimensional simplicity. Compared to the dimensional complexity and indeterminate content of cognitive meaning, affective meaning can be represented in three simple dimensions – evaluation, potency, and activity – enabling quantitative measurement and mathematical modeling of affective processes.

In conclusion, both cognitive and affective explanations are necessary for a comprehensive understanding of social order. Guided by practical

---

[9] EPA scales employed in electronic data collection range from –4.33 through 0 to +4.33.

institutional knowledge and energized by internalized cultural sentiments, adequately-socialized individuals ensure the continual reproduction and legitimation of social institutions through the daily enactment of institutional identities and roles. This is an extremely important idea. Social institutions are reproduced and continually legitimated – at even the most macro level of abstraction – through symbolic and situational action at the micro level of face-to-face interaction. Despite their emphasis on symbolic interaction and the causal priority of the immediate situation, symbolic interactionists embracing Blumer's (1969) views have missed this point, largely because of their aversion to macro-sociological concepts.

With these theoretical discussions in hand, we now turn to the two analyses representing specific sectors and pathways identified in our detailed discussion of Figure 9.1.

SOCIAL INSTITUTIONS IN THE MIND

MacKinnon and Heise (2010) showed that dictionary definitions link identities in the same institution to each other and to actions and objects relevant to the institution. For example, according to a dictionary definition, a nurse is someone who cares for patients under the supervision of a physician, and this definition relates the identity of nurse to the identity of patient by the action of caring for, while relating the identity of nurse to the identity of physician by the physician's action of supervising. Through analysis of hundreds of such dictionary definitions, MacKinnon and Heise showed interrelations among key identities in each social institution.

Dictionary definitions are cultural in that they are derived from interpersonal communications; that is, contemporary lexicologists compose definitions by examining word usages in multi-million-word corpuses of printed text. Thus, the MacKinnon–Heise analyses established that the cultural side of macro social structure is embedded in meanings of specific concepts, as expected in an augmented version of symbolic interactionism.

However, a richer understanding of social order must go beyond formal definitions of words and indicate how social structure is constituted within individuals' minds. Individuals do not memorize dictionary definitions of identities, yet they employ identity names in ways that imply the definitions. What goes on in people's heads that links institutional identities to one another, and that allows individuals to reproduce social structure while going about their practical affairs? We address this issue next by elaborating the individual layer in Figure 9.1 to incorporate additional psychological structures besides the "me" and additional psychological processes besides "I-you" dialogues. We show empirically for the first time that social institutions exist not merely as patterns of cultural meaning but also as networks of mental associations, with consciousness of one role-identity evoking consciousness of other role-identities within the same institutional cluster.

Thereby an individual's perceptual identification of another person fans out into consciousness of other identities in the same social institution, allowing the perceiver to choose an appropriate reciprocal role-identity. For example, encountering another fitted out with a white coat and stethoscope and identifying that person as a doctor primes other medicine-related identities like nurse and patient, thereby readying an appropriate self-identity for reciprocal interaction with the doctor.

Our data are norms of word associations provided by Nelson, McEvoy, and Schreiber (1998), based on 5,019 stimulus words and responses by more than 6,000 participants from the 1970s through the 1990s.[10] We focused on 409 stimuli designating role-identities.[11] All responses to a stimulus given by at least 2 out of 150 respondents were included in analyses, with no distinction between the most frequent and the least frequent responses.

Our analytic procedures paralleled those reported by MacKinnon and Heise (2010). In brief, we constructed a zero-one matrix with stimuli as columns and responses as rows. Ones in a column indicated role-identity responses to a stimulus, as well as responses that were not role-identities.[12] The matrix was used to compute correlations of the role-identity stimuli with each other, and the correlation matrix was analyzed into principal components, with varimax rotation of the top twenty components. Lists of identities defining each component were constructed by including all identities with loadings of 0.30 or more on that component. In sections below identities are listed in order of their loading sizes on a given component.

We organize results of our analyses in terms of the six social institutions that Turner (1997) used to examine the macro-sociological order of societies – economy, kinship, religion, polity, law, and education. In discussing results, we

[10] Respondents wrote the first word that came to mind in response to a printed stimulus word. Multiple associates were obtained for each stimulus because different participants often wrote different response words. Each participant responded to 100–120 English words, and an average of 149 participants responded to each stimulus. The researchers corrected obvious spelling errors in the responses, and pooled singular and plural forms of nouns and variations in tense and grammatical form in the case of verbs.

[11] A stimulus was included in our study if it was an obvious identity or if two or more responses were synonymous identities or reciprocal identities, when assuming that the stimulus was a role-identity. For example, "fool" might be interpreted as either a noun or a verb, and it was included because "idiot" and "clown" were among the responses. Three identities – "person," "woman," and "man" – were removed in order to eliminate excessively general clusters in the results.

[12] Our data matrix consisted of a square 406x406 matrix (R) showing role-identities' relations to one other, above a 1,925x406 matrix showing relations between role-identities and sundry other responses. Ones were inserted into the diagonal of the 406x406 matrix for computational reasons. The 1,925x406 matrix was reduced to a 1,061x406 matrix (S) by removing responses in the sundry category that had been given to just one role-identity stimulus. Following procedures introduced by MacKinnon and Heise (2010), matrix R was raised to Boolean powers to simulate spreading activation of associations from a stimulus word to other role-identities. Results are based on the Boolean square of R since higher powers generated no additional change.

make some comparisons with the MacKinnon and Heise (2010) analyses of three hundred role-identities, and with an unpublished analysis by Heise that expanded the MacKinnon and Heise analysis to 2,729 role-identities.

First we present our empirical evidence that social institutions are represented in individual minds as patterns of psychological excitation linking institutionally congruent identities. Then we discuss how the psychological structures shape definitions of situations, which in turn generate orderly role activities, which in turn instantiate institutional orders.

Economy

Turner (1997: 9) described economic institutions as concerned with gathering, conversion, and distribution of resources. About 16 percent of the identity stimuli in the word-association project loaded on components that were more or less related to Turner's characterization of the economic institution. One of the components clustered occupations largely related to extraction and conversion. A component clustering business and organizational identities and another component clustering food-service identities related mainly to the conversion and distribution of resources.

> **Occupations:** builder architect contractor technician mechanic mason engineer carpenter electrician manufacturer painter maker inventor plumber creator digger fireman designer employer miner operator farmer
>
> **Business Establishments:** worker employer employee manager owner secretary boss operator proprietor slave assistant clerk principal supervisor chairperson navigator executive director customer master co-pilot digger typist pilot farmer superior passenger cashier chauffeur captain chief receptionist
>
> **Food Services:** server waiter butler hostess waitress bartender chef host servant stewardess maid gourmet baker

According to MacKinnon and Heise (2010: 64), more than a third of all commonplace identities denote occupations. The under-representation of economic identities in our results reflected the small sample of role-identities in the word-association project as compared with the number that MacKinnon and Heise considered in their survey of identities – 406 compared to 9,199.

Kinship

Both descent and marriage were key aspects of Turner's (1997: 69–70) definition of the institution of kinship, and two corresponding clusters of roles emerged in MacKinnon and Heise's (2010) analyses of identity meanings. Turner (1997) mentioned regulation of sexuality as a key function of the kinship institution, and MacKinnon and Heise's analyses found a cluster of role-identities associated with sexuality.

Results from analyses of word associations reflected relations in the extended family, on one hand, and the world of children, on the other. No separate cluster represented a subinstitution of marriage.

Extended Family: uncle grandpa ancestor aunt grandparent nephew father niece relative relation dad elder brother parent cousin grandma kin nag guardian mom sister stranger son mother visitor guest adult mummy grown-up daughter keeper wife kid

Children: youth infant adolescent juvenile teenager minor junior doll adult kid snot baby delinquent child brat dependent son chick miner grown-up virgin daughter walker innocent sibling twin boy wimp beginner spouse mother parent snob kin independent rebel niece

A world of children is not typically mentioned in discussions of kinship such as Turner's, but it was evident in MacKinnon and Heise's analyses and is reproduced here on a smaller scale. No sexuality cluster emerged from the word association data, but sexuality identities like heterosexual, homosexual, and prostitute were not among the word association stimuli.

Religion

According to Turner (1997), the institution of religion encompasses socially constructed supernatural beings, emotional rituals, and ecclesiastic structures. MacKinnon and Heise's (2010) analyses of identity meanings found two groupings of religious identities, one involving divinities and the other dealing with ecclesiastic structures. Our analysis of word association data produced just one religious cluster.

Baptist Christian saint priest minister Methodist protestant Catholic preacher pope Christ nun angel cardinal savior monk bishop Satan Jesus idol devil rabbi Venus god friar almighty shepherd lord superior follower goddess prey hero maker creator

This cluster combines supernatural beings – Christ, angel, savior, Satan, Jesus, devil, Venus, god, almighty, lord, goddess, creator – with ecclesiastic role-identities.

Polity

According to Turner (1997), the institution of polity consists of power structures oriented toward decision making about the coordination and control of actors, and about the disbursing of resources. A political cluster did not emerge initially in MacKinnon and Heise's (2010) analysis of word meanings, but they were able to produce such a cluster by expanding the sample of words that they analyzed. Our analysis of word association data produced several clusters related to polity.

Rulers: king queen monarch prince emperor ruler princess president dictator governor knight friar communist leader bishop almighty mummy master guide democrat

Politics: mayor democrat senator candidate politician governor

Nationalism: brave American warrior patriot veteran knight soldier native fighter coward Indian sentry recruit citizen captive boxer sailor hero nomad cowboy guard champion idol

Military: colonel lieutenant corporal sergeant general commander officer captain major leader chief sheriff deputy marine policeman official sailor president supervisor agent guard cop mayor authority broad principal

The first two clusters have obvious relations to the polity. We believe the nationalism cluster also fits, given Turner's (1997) emphasis on emotionally charged symbols as a means of social control. Military control seems to be an aspect of the polity, though sometimes the military is treated as a separate institution, for example, by Reynolds and Herman-Kinney (2003).

Mingling of military roles with police and leadership roles occurs when clusters are based on word association data, but not when clusters are based on dictionary definitions. Perhaps the public is ahead of cultural reference books in apprehending emerging militarism of internal control forces.

Law

Turner (1997) characterized the institution of law as an offshoot of the polity oriented toward creating and administering laws about disputes over resources and about control of actors, and also oriented toward law enforcement. MacKinnon and Heise's (2010) analyses of identity meanings produced a cluster of role-identities consisting of legal professionals and criminals, and another cluster related to police and law enforcement. Our analysis of word associations produced only one cluster related to law.

crook thief burglar robber convict suspect killer criminal bandit murderer gangster victim cop outlaw prisoner villain fugitive inmate con witness salesman traitor delinquent hostage vagrant attorney hood guard detective lawyer liar beggar judge captive sheriff spy politician

Crime is the major emphasis in the word-association cluster, but police and courtroom identities (cop, witness, attorney, detective, lawyer, judge, sheriff) also appear.

Education

According to Turner (1997: 228), "the emergence of education as a distinctive institution revolves around formalized relations between teacher and student, explicit and delimited curricula, and ritualized passage through a curriculum." MacKinnon and Heise's (2010) analyses produced a cluster of identities naming kinds of students at all levels of education, along with various names for teachers. Our analysis of word association data produced one education-related cluster.

pupil instructor learner student professor teacher philosopher reader graduate speaker biologist tenor chemist rabbi scientist guide expert conductor coach assistant director superior preacher principal fellow supervisor professional parent

The word-association cluster focuses on students and teachers in schools, but includes some other kinds of teachers as well. The cluster includes some disciplinary specialists in the sciences. Reynolds and Herman-Kinney (2003) treated scientists in a scientific institution, and a science cluster of identities was found by Heise in his unpublished analysis of 2,729 word meanings. The implication is that education and science are somewhat merged in individual minds.

Medicine

Turner (1997) did not treat medicine as a major social institution, but Talcott Parsons (1951) devoted a chapter to discussing medical practice as an institutional pattern, and Reynolds and Herman–Kinney (2003) included a chapter on medicine as an institution in their handbook of symbolic interaction. MacKinnon and Heise's (2010) analyses of identity meanings produced a cluster consisting of medical practitioners and their patients. The word association data yielded a cluster focused on medical practitioners.

physician nurse patient dentist orthodontist orderly shrink quack doctor vet surgeon scientist witch professor lawyer biologist professional engineer sergeant expert

Although most of identities in the cluster are obviously medical, the final nine have weak or esoteric associations with the institution.

Leisure

Leisure activities in contemporary society are not often discussed as an institutional domain, but they do seem to fit the Parsonian perspective on institutions. Also, mass media was considered a distinct institution by Reynolds and Herman-Kinney (2003). Additionally, sports and entertainment emerged as distinct role-identity clusters in Heise's unpublished analysis of 2,729 identity meanings. Our analysis of word association data also found sports and entertainment clusters, as well as two other clusters that seem related to leisure activities.

> **Sports:** player athlete pitcher catcher pro opponent coach amateur character champion gymnast umpire referee acrobat jock swimmer professional beginner official expert

Entertainment: clown comedian talent juggler singer actor joker dancer
magician actress fool alto ballerina tenor producer character acrobat

Art Worlds: author publisher poet writer editor critic typist artist reader
singer producer ghost creator

Fantasy Worlds: monster ghoul goblin vampire demon ghost fairy elf
mummy freak giant midget predator dwarf

These results suggest that a leisure institution is emerging in contemporary society.

Quasi-Institutional Clusters

Three clusters from the word association analysis resembled no institution in
Parsons and Shils' (1951) sense of "a complex of institutionalized role integrates which is of strategic significance." However, they are institutionalized
areas in the weaker formulation provided by Berger and Luckmann (1966: 54).

Gender: gentleman guy lady gal male blonde brunette receptionist date miss
boy girl tramp model stud maiden cheerleader heroine hostess actress
chick maid mate stewardess goddess gossip nerd jock secretary partner
lord female mister

Intimates/Adversaries: buddy neighbor contact pal foe Hispanic girlfriend
intimate adversary enemy companion friend boyfriend partner roommate
sweetheart lover mate spouse member gossip bully associate boy female
mom girl stranger teacher fellow Jesus slob relation mother kin brother
guest cousin traitor visitor sibling sister relative husband helper valentine

Spurned Others: idiot moron drunk fool loser scapegoat freak hobo wimp
bum liar tourist beggar vagrant coward bully winner nerd

The gender cluster aggregates identities that foreground an individual's sex,
these perhaps being identities that frame a situation explicitly in sexual terms,
beyond the implicit background framing that ordinarily takes place (Ridgeway
2009). The intimates/adversaries cluster provides a polarized basis for emotionally orienting toward others, and perhaps such identifications are overlaid on others' institutional identities when strong feelings toward the others
emerge. The cluster of spurned others provides possible labels for individuals
who violate expectations in institutional settings.

Situation Definitions and Social Order

Psychological priming of institutional domains often is more specific than
sociological descriptions of institutions. In our analyses the economy split into
three sectors, kinship into two sectors, and polity into four clusters. Also, we
found two institutional areas – medicine and leisure – that are not always
mentioned in sociological descriptions. Additionally, clusters of non-kin relations and gender relations emerged in our analyses. These results indicate that

situations are more institutionally segmented in contemporary minds than sociologists propose. Psychologically, there are about twenty institutional arenas rather than a half dozen or so.

Our empirical results support the following conception of defining-the-situation as an individual psychological process. Those who are enacting specific roles provide perceivable cues about their identities via their countenance, attire, or their introductory comments. Others encountering them employ these cues as they define the situation: perceiving the cues,[13] recognizing the role-player's identity, experiencing consciousness of associated identities, and adopting a related identity as their self-identification for ensuing interaction. Because institutional identities evoke associations of related institutional identities, the presence of an institutional role-player causes others to define the situation in terms of that institution, and to take a reciprocal role with respect to the original role-player. Thus, initial presence of an institutional actor maintains appropriate institutional activity in the setting.[14]

SENTIMENTS AND INTERDEPENDENCE RELATIONS

In the middle of Figure 9.1 are reciprocal relations between identity meanings, roles, and interpersonal activities at the micro-sociological level. Next we elaborate a facet of this stratum arguing that affective meanings of identities relate to interdependence states among social interactants, such that the structure of game matrices used in exchange and rational choice theories corresponds to the *evaluation, potency,* and *activity* dimensions of affective meaning. The implication is that identity meanings generate interdependencies among interactants, and additionally emergent interdependence in social situations transforms the affective meanings of identities and the nature of corresponding roles.

Scholl (2013) argued that the evaluation, potency, and activity dimensions employed by affect control theory "reflect the inherent logic of any exchange between self-interested individuals" (2013: 19) in interdependence relations. The coordination and collaboration aspects of interdependence relations are generally depicted in game matrices (e.g., Cook and Rice 2006; Kelley 1979), and the structure of game matrices connects to the evaluation, potency, and activity dimensions of affective meaning in the following ways according to interdependence theory (Kelley 1979; Kelley et al. 2003; Scholl 2013).

Evaluation reflects the *correspondence of outcomes* for participants in interdependence relations. Correspondence of outcomes promotes coordination of individual efforts and affiliation, while the opposite of correspondence, zero-sum outcomes, promotes competition and hostility. Friends develop out of similar or compatible interests; enemies out of competing interests. Thus,

[13] Cues also are provided by features of the physical setting such as labelled buildings and settings containing emblems, icons, or totems.
[14] Schedules govern individuals' occupation of institutional identities without situational cues (Heise 2007).

people evaluate others with correspondent outcomes as positive, nice, and friendly; and others with competing interests, as negative, awful, and unfriendly.

Potency reflects possible *differences in dependence*, which establish (un) equal power among interactants (Emerson 1962), inducing impressions of powerfulness, strength, tenacity, or their opposites.

Activity arises from the magnitude of dependence in a game matrix: The larger the differences between alternative outcomes for each interactant, the more important it is to get the better outcome instead of the worse one. So, larger differences have a stronger motivational effect leading to more emotional arousal and behavioral activation.

In work outside interdependence theory, Fennell and Baddeley (2013) identified three dimensions of options in decision-making – *reward*, *risk*, and *uncertainty* – and connected them explicitly to the evaluation, potency, and activity dimensions of the semantic differential. They conducted an experiment in which subjects risked faux bank funds to bet on outcomes associated with six shapes. A win resulted in funds being added to the subject's bank account along with display of a smiley face; a loss caused funds to be removed from the subject's bank account with display of a sad face; and an indifferent outcome involved no change in the subject's bank account and display of a neutral face. Two shapes (randomly selected for each subject) had high probability of wins if they were selected, two shapes had high probability of losses, and two shapes had a high probability of indifferent outcomes. Subject *evaluation* of a shape changed in direct correspondence to that shape's association with wins relative to wins plus losses. *Potency* of a shape increased to the extent that losses predominated in win, loss, or indifferent events associated with that shape. And *activity* increased with the uncertainty or lack of control associated with a choice. Thus this study demonstrated that a person's history of rewards and punishments with an object of choice changes the affective meaning that the individual associates with that object.[15]

Of course, humans rarely consider dependencies and outcomes in abstract matrix terms and engage in the rational thought that such matrices require. Rather, they simply judge from both verbal and nonverbal communication,[16] and at a more or less preconscious level, whether the other seems nice and friendly or unkind and hostile (signaling the degree of correspondence and cooperation to be expected); whether the other is strong or weak, dominant or submissive (signaling differences in dependence); and whether the other is aroused or calm (signaling the magnitude of dependence in the situation).

[15] An even more direct test of affective meaning as a common basis of affect control theory and interdependence or exchange theory would be to ask experienced players to deliver ratings of different game structures on the three emotional dimensions and to register their following actions. A first example approaching such an investigation is provided by Wubben (2009).

[16] Sally (1995) has shown in his meta-analysis of dilemma experiments that face-to-face situations allowing verbal communication and nonverbal checks of trustworthiness are the best predictors of cooperation.

Thereby people substitute fast thinking based on affect for the slow thinking of rationality (Kahneman 2011) in order to estimate potential outcomes for self and other in interdependence relations.

The parallel between the evaluation, potency, and activity dimensions of affective meaning and the structure of dependencies represented in game matrices suggests that affect control theory could be applied to predict outcomes of interdependence relations represented in game matrices. Referring to Figure 9.1, the affective meanings of identities motivate individuals to engage in identity-confirming roles and social interaction. This can be recast in terms of interdependence relations and game matrices by translating evaluation, potency, and activity outcomes of social interaction into correspondence outcomes, difference in dependence, and magnitude of dependence, respectively.

Affect control theory has an added appeal over other micro-explanations. Because it is based on the motivation to avoid deflections from cultural sentiments embedded in the meanings of a common language, it is a truly sociological theory of social order. It is cultural consensus rather than individual opinion that determines what is good or bad, powerful or powerless, active or passive; and the motivational principle of avoiding deflections from cultural sentiments is based on a socioemotional view of consistency rather than an individual psychological one. This is not to deny, of course, that there are individual differences in cultural sentiments, resulting from socialization experiences, socioeconomic status, and membership in subcultures.

Affect Control and Rational Choice

It is well known from experimental game research that people usually do not behave according to a *homo economicus* logic and that they often apply different meanings to an abstract game description. We use an example from Kelley (1979: 24–29) to illustrate and discuss this finding in terms of the parallel between the evaluation, potency, and activity dimensions of affective meaning and the structure of game matrices.

Kelley conducted a survey of 100 young couples who estimated their preferences within a typical dilemma. On a scale of −10 to +10, the partners separately assessed how they feel about cleaning their joint apartment (a) together, (b) by the man only, (c) by the woman only, or (d) not at all. While the unpleasant task of cleaning must be done, each person has to perform other important tasks as well. So, a *homo economicus* would assign the highest value to the alternative where the other cleans, allowing self to address other important tasks, and would assign the lowest value to being exploited. Yet, as illustrated in Figure 9.2, the average valuations turn out to be quite different.

To begin with, the matrix does not represent a dilemma but largely a correspondence outcome. Obviously, a cooperative transformation of a potential

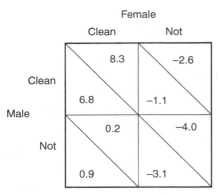

FIGURE 9.2. Rated outcomes for cleaning the joint apartment.
(from Kelley, 1979, p. 25).

dilemma has occurred, and the collaboration based on affiliation, sympathy, and love can proceed smoothly because both partners value joint cleaning most. Kelley (1979: chaps. 3, 5) discussed such transformations in detail. People who like each other and especially couples are expected to make cooperative transformations. Such transformations can be modeled in affect control theory just by changing the definition of the situation, from *roommates* (Evaluation 0.77, Potency 0.24, Activity 1.11) *working* (E: 0.07, P: 1.01, A: 0.51) to *trueloves* (E: 2.66, P: 1.74, A: 0.66) *helping each other* (E: 2.25, P: 1.64, A: 0.22),[17] thereby producing a cooperative transformation and little deflection in affect control predictions of affective outcomes.

One also has to consider gender stereotypes in interpreting the empirical pattern reported in Figure 9.2. (1) Cleaning is more positive for women than for men; in particular, women evaluate slightly negatively if their man cleans alone ("exploiting" him), but not if they themselves clean alone (being "exploited"). (2) Men are somewhat more dependent in their well-being on women who accept these role expectations.[18] (3) The activation is stronger in women than in men comparing the differences between the highest and the lowest valuation. Of course these are speculative reconstructions requiring detailed empirical investigations to substantiate them.

In any case, this example of interdependence analysis suggests that the rationality of human decisions and actions should not be judged from a *homo economicus* perspective alone. One must also take the cultural meanings of role-identities into account. When one does so, ostensibly non-rational

[17] Averaged male and female EPA profiles from University of North Carolina 1978 data on cultural sentiments. *Working* was substituted as a proxy for *cleaning*, which was not included in the data.
[18] Calculated as column differences in men's triangles versus row differences in women's triangles.

decisions might be reconsidered as socially reasonable within the culture of a particular society.[19]

SUMMARY AND CONCLUSION

We identified the cultural meanings of institutional identities and related roles as the micro-foundation of social order. Guided by cultural knowledge and energized by cultural sentiments, the enactment of institutional identities and roles in everyday social life ensures the continual reproduction and legitimation of social institutions. We advanced two complementary, micro-level explanations of social order: a cognitive approach combining a classic micro-sociological theory of institutions with a recent method for analyzing the causal structures of social actions in institutional settings; and an affective approach based on affect control theory. We then presented two analyses that illustrate some of these ideas. The first shows that the full range of social institutions can be revealed by a network analysis of cognitive-denotative associations among institutional identities and roles. The second shows how the evaluation, potency, and activity dimensions of affective-connotative meaning employed by affect control theory are inherent in the logic of interdependence underlying rational choice and exchange theories as represented in game matrices.

Parsons (1951) based his answer to the "Hobbesian problem of order" (Parsons 1937) on a consensus of *social values* (essentially, cognitions imbued with affect). Mead (1934) proposed that social integration is based on a consensus of cognitive meanings embodied in significant symbols or language (see MacKinnon 1994), a position that is mostly implicit in Berger and Luckmann (1966). Affect control theory explains social order in terms of culturally shared sentiments, and data supports this consensus theory of social order. Research has shown that there really is a substantial amount of consensus of cultural sentiments within a culture (Heise 2010; Ambrasat et al. 2014) as well as a surprising amount across cultures (Heise 2014b).

At the same time, none of the theorists cited earlier (with the possible and debateable exception of Parsons) views consensus as an absolute quantity, but rather as a working consensus ensuring a reasonable level of social order while allowing for deviance, conflict, and social change. In this regard, Berger and Luckmann have acknowledged that all symbolic universes of meaning legitimating the institutional world are "incipiently problematic" (1966: 106); and affect control research has always found individual differences in cultural sentiments, as indicated by modest standard deviations in EPA measurement.

Although based on maintaining consistency with cultural sentiments, affect control theory differs from psychological consistency theories such as Heider's

---

[19] For a new demonstration and extension of this line of theoretical and empirical analysis see Asghar and Hoey (2015).

(1946) balance theory and Festinger's (1957) dissonance theory, which focus on consistency or order in individual minds. In contrast, maintaining consistency with culturally-shared sentiments "binds together all well-socialized people within a given culture through their common language and ... collective meaning space" (Scholl 2013: 21). "The motivation to avoid larger deflections is a truly socio-emotional consistency because people thereby gain security in their worldview, harvest the experience of their culture and preserve their general cooperation opportunities through a common understanding of the emotional meaning of relevant social aspects." (Scholl 2013: 23).

REFERENCES

Ambrasat, Jens, Christian von Scheve, Markus Conrad, Gesche Schauenburg, and Tobias Schröder. 2014. "Consensus and Stratification in the Affective Meaning of Human Sociality." *Proceedings of the National Academy of Sciences.* http://dx.doi.org/10.1073/pnas.1313321111

Asghar, Nabiha, and Jesse Hoey. 2015. Intelligent Affect: Rational Decision Making for Socially Aligned Agents. *Proceedings of the 31st Conference on Uncertainty in Artificial Intelligence,* July 12–16, 2015, Amsterdam, Netherlands.

Berger, Peter L., and Thomas Luckmann. 1966. *The Social Construction of Reality: A Treatise in the Sociology of Knowledge.* New York: Doubleday.

Blumer, Herbert. 1969. *Symbolic Interactionism.* Berkeley: University of California Press.

Burke, Peter. 1980. "The Self: Measurement Requirements from an Interactionist Perspective." *Social Psychology Quarterly* 43: 18–30.

Cook, Karen S., and E. R. W. Rice. 2006. "Social Exchange Theory." Pp. 53–76 in *Handbook of Social Psychology,* edited by John DeLamater. New York: Springer.

Emerson, Richard M. 1962. "Power-Dependence Relations." *American Sociological Review* 27: 31–41.

Fennell, John G., and Roland J. Baddeley. 2013. "Reward Is Assessed in Three Dimensions That Correspond to the Semantic Differential." PLoS ONE 8:e55588.

Festinger, Leon (1957). *A Theory of Cognitive Dissonance.* Evanston, IL: Row, Peterson & Co.

Gross, Neal, Ward S. Mason, and A. W. McEachern. 1958. *Explorations in Role Analysis: Studies of the School Superintendency Role.* New York: Wiley.

Heider, Fritz. 1946. "Attitudes and Cognitive Organizations." *Journal of Psychology* 21: 107–12.

Heise, David R. 1979. *Understanding Events: Affect and the Construction of Social Action.* New York: Cambridge University Press.

   1989. "Modeling Event Structures." *Journal of Mathematical Sociology* 14: 139–69.

   2007. *Expressive Order: Confirming Sentiments in Social Actions.* New York: Springer.

   2010. *Surveying Cultures: Discovering Shared Conceptions and Sentiments.* Hoboken, NJ: Wiley Interscience.

   2014a. "Socially Constructed Causality: Action Schemes and Macroactions." Department of Sociology, Indiana University, Bloomington.

   2014b. "Cultural Variations in Sentiments." *SpringerPlus* 3: 170. doi: 1186/2193-1801-3-170.

Heise, David R., and Alex Durig. 1997. "A Frame for Organizational Actions and Macroactions." *Journal of Mathematical Sociology* 22: 95–123.

Hoey, Jesse, Tobias Schröder, and Areej Alhothali. 2013. "Bayesian Affect Control Theory." Pp. 166–172 in *Humaine Association Conference on Affective Computing and Intelligent Interaction*. Geneva, Switzerland: Institute of Electrical and Electronics Engineers, Computer Society.

House, James S. 1981. "Social Structure and Personality." Pp. 525–561 in *Social Psychology: Sociological Perspectives*, edited by M. Rosenberg and R. H. Turner. New York: Basic Books.

Kahneman, Daniel. 2011. *Thinking, Fast and Slow*. New York: Farrar, Straus, and Giroux.

Kelley, Harold H. (1979). *Personal Relationships: Their Structures and Processes*. Hillsdale, NJ: Erlbaum.

Kelley, Harold, John G. Holmes, Norbert L. Kerr, Harry T. Reis, Caryl E. Rusbult, and Paul A. M. Van Lange. 2003. *An Atlas of Interpersonal Situations*. New York: Cambridge University Press.

MacKinnon, Neil J. 1994. *Symbolic Interactionism as Affect Control*. Albany: State University of New York Press.

MacKinnon, Neil J., and David R. Heise. 2010. *Self, Identity, and Social Institutions*. New York: Palgrave Macmillan.

McCall, George J., and J. L. Simmons. 1978. *Identities and Interactions*. New York: The Free Press.

Mead, George Herbert. 1934. *Mind, Self, and Society*. Chicago: University of Chicago Press.

Merton, Robert K. 1957. *Social Theory and Social Structure*. New York: Free Press.

Nelson, Douglas L., Cathy L. McEvoy, and Thomas A. Schreiber. (1998). *The University of South Florida Word Association, Rhyme, and Word Fragment Norms*. 2013. http://w3.usf.edu/FreeAssociation/.

Osgood, Charles E. 1962. "Studies of the Generality of Affective Meaning Systems." *American Psychologist* 17: 10–28.

    1969. "On the Whys and Wherefores of EPA." *Journal of Personality and Social Psychology* 12: 194–99.

Osgood, Charles E., W.H. May, and M.S. Miron. 1975. *Cross-Cultural Universals of Affective Meaning*. Urbana: University of Illinois Press.

Osgood, Charles E., George C. Suci, and Percy H. Tannenbaum. 1957. *The Measurement of Meaning*. Urbana: University of Illinois Press.

Parsons, Talcott. 1937. *The Structure of Social Action: A Study in Social Theory with Special Reference to a Group of Recent European Writers*. New York: McGraw-Hill.

    1951. *The Social System*. New York: Free Press of Glencoe.

Parsons, Talcott R., and Edward A. Shils, eds. 1951. *Toward a General Theory of Action*. Cambridge, MA: Harvard University Press.

Reynolds, Larry T., and Nancy J. Herman-Kinney, eds. 2003. *Handbook of Symbolic Interactionism*. New York: Rowman & Littlefield.

Ridgeway, Cecilia L. (2009). "Framed Before We Know It: How Gender Shapes Social Relations." *Gender & Society* 23: 145–60.

Sally, David (1995). "Conversation and Cooperation in Social Dilemmas. A Meta-analysis of Experiments from 1958 to 1992." *Rationality and Society* 7 (1): 58–92.

Sarbin, Theodore R. 1968. "Role: Psychological Aspects." P. 546 in *International Encyclopedia of the Social Sciences*, edited by D. L. Sills. New York: Free Press.

Scholl, Wolfgang. 2013. "The Socio-Emotional Basis of Human Interaction and Communication: How We Construct our Social World." *Social Science Information* 52: 3–33.

Smith-Lovin, Lynn, and David R. Heise, eds. 1988. *Analyzing Social Interaction: Advances in Affect Control Theory*. New York: Gordon and Breach. Original ed., special issue of the *Journal of Mathematical Sociology* 13 (1987).

Thoits, Peggy A., and Lauren K. Virshup. 1997. "Me's and We's: Forms and Functions of Social Identities." Pp. 106–133 in *Self and Identity: Fundamental Issues*, edited by R. D. Ashmore and L. Jussim. New York: Oxford University Press.

Turner, Jonathan H. 1997. *The Institutional Order: Economy, Kinship, Religion, Polity, Law, and Education in Evolutionary and Comparative Perspective*. New York: Longman.

Wallace, Walter. 1983. *Principles of Scientific Sociology*. New York: Aldine.

Wiley, Norbert. 1994. *The Semiotic Self*. Chicago: University of Chicago Press.

Wubben, Maarten J. J. 2009. Social Functions of Emotions in Social Dilemmas. Doctoral thesis, Erasmus University, Rotterdam.

10

The Gender Frame and Social Order

Cecilia L. Ridgeway

Abstract

There is good evidence that gender acts as primary cultural framework that people rely on to initiate the process of making sense of one another in order to organize social relations. People's everyday use of gender as a cultural device for creating micro order has widespread consequences for the persistence of gender as social system of difference and inequality. This process continually exposes cultural beliefs about gender to another micro-ordering process, the development of status hierarchies, so that gender becomes a status difference. Acting in goal-oriented encounters in the workplace and home, gender status beliefs create biases in women's expected competence and authority compared to men that, in turn, contribute to the sex-segregation of jobs, the gender gap in wages and authority, and the unequal household division of labor. Acting in sites of innovation, these same processes also rewrite gender inequality into new social and economic arrangements as society changes, in effect reinventing gender inequality for the new era.

Gender, as a social system of difference among individuals based on sex categories of male and female, is a universal feature of human societies (Wood and Eagly 2002). Gender is typically also a basis for social hierarchy and inequality between men and women. At least in Western society, gender, as a system of inequality, also has had a perplexing feature. It has shown a remarkable ability to persist over major transformations in the material-economic and social arrangements on which the inequality between men and women is based in any given era. A social hierarchy based on gender in Western society survived the profound transformation from an agrarian to an industrialized society. In the more recent era, as women have flooded into the paid labor force and into many formally male jobs, gender inequality has nevertheless managed to persist in modified form (Cotter, Hermsen, and Vanneman 2004; England 2010).

I argue that these distinctive aspects of the broad social system of gender – that it is a powerful system of social difference among persons and a basis of social inequality that shows troubling powers of persistence – arise from the way people use gender as a *primary cultural framework* for organizing their social relations with others (Ridgeway 2011). The driving force behind the development and everyday use of a social system of gender within a society, I argue, is people's collective efforts to manage the fundamental problems of coordinating their behavior with others in order to organize social relations with them. As a consequence, gender is at root a cultural device for creating micro order, but people's continual use of gender as a micro-ordering mechanism has complex ramifications for the organization of society as a whole, contributing to the gendering of jobs and roles in the workplace, the sex-segregation of occupations, to the household division of labor, and to a variety of other social and economic features of contemporary society.

As we shall see, gender, as a cultural device for creating micro order, turns on social beliefs about differences between men and women. But social difference easily becomes social inequality between men and women. A key part of this process is the propensity for gender as a social difference to also become a basis for difference in social status (Ridgeway 2011). Social status is inequality based on differences in social esteem and presumed competence. Hierarchies among individuals based on social status also develop out of the problems people face in organizing their relations with others, but under the special, if very common, circumstances of pursuing a shared, collective goal. People's on-going use of both gender and status as micro-ordering processes in everyday interaction makes it highly likely that gender and status will become linked and that gender will become a basis not only for social difference, but also for social inequality. These same processes, I argue, also provide a means by which gender inequality is rewritten into new social and economic arrangements as society changes, in effect reinventing gender inequality for the new era. Thus, these processes also help explain gender inequality's powers of persistence in the face of changing material circumstances in society.

In this chapter, I develop these arguments and describe some of the evidence behind them. I start with the coordination problem in social relations which is basic to social order. I discuss how this encourages people to develop gender as a primary frame for social relations based on beliefs about gender difference. In this way, gender becomes a cultural device for micro order. Next, I turn to how links develop between gender and the parallel micro-ordering process of status. Then I describe the distinctive patterns of gender inequalities at the micro level that the link between gender and status creates. In the remaining part of the chapter I sketch the consequences of these distinctive patterns, which are, in effect, gender micro-orders, for larger structures of gender inequality in society, and in particular, for the persistence of gender inequality over social and economic changes in society.

THE COORDINATION PROBLEM IN SOCIAL RELATIONS

People are dependent on social relations with others to achieve most of what they want and need in life from the demands of basic survival to the pleasures of social engagement. But engaging in social relations with others poses a well-known organizational problem: finding a way to coordinate your behavior with the other(s). For the joint enterprise and shared meanings that constitute a social relation to emerge, actors must find a way coordinate their interaction (Mead 1934, Stryker and Vryan 2003). This is one of the simplest and most basic problems of micro order that actors face on an everyday basis. Coordination, in turn, requires that actors have a way to anticipate how the other will behave so that they can calibrate their own behavior accordingly. The interaction that leads to social relations, then, must be something like a dance, in which one actor can anticipate that the other will step back as he or she steps forward.

How do actors do this? Interestingly, interactional sociologists such as Goffman (1967) and economic game theorists (Chwe 2001) have come to the same conclusion about this question. To solve the coordination problem, actors need "common knowledge" that they can mutually draw upon to anticipate each other's behavior in the situation. Common knowledge is not just knowledge that the actors do share, but knowledge that they all can reasonably presume that they all share. In others words, it is consensual, "public" knowledge which, in effect, is widely shared cultural knowledge. By drawing on widely shared cultural beliefs and social scripts, actors can presume that the other is also acting on these same beliefs and scripts and coordinate behavior with the other effectively.

Coordination and Difference

To *initiate* the process of interacting with another to form a social relation, actors, I argue, need a very specific type of common knowledge. As symbolic interactionists have long argued, anticipating how another will behave in order to act in response requires that actors have some means of categorizing and defining "who" the other is in social terms (Stryker and Vryan 2003). And, in defining the other in the situation, actors by implication define who they are in relation to the other as well.

Systems for categorizing and defining things are based on contrast and, therefore, *difference*. Something can only be understood as this (a friend) because it is different from that (a foe). The fundamental micro-order problem of defining self and other in order to relate, then, focuses people on finding *shared principles of social difference* that they can use to categorize and make sense of one another. I argue, then, that the coordination problem that is inherent to organizing social relations drives populations of people who must regularly relate to one another to focus on differences among them, differences on which they can form broadly shared, "common knowledge" cultural category systems for making sense of one another. As we will see, sex, as a dimension of physical variation among people, provides just such a convenient difference upon which to create a shared category system for defining and coordinating with others.

To manage social relations in real time, some of these cultural category systems of difference must be so simplified that they can be quickly applied as framing devices to virtually anyone in order to start the process of defining self and other in the situation. These simplified *primary* category systems are cultural tools people use to "jumpstart" the process of defining another in order to relate to him or her. In fact, studies of social cognition suggest that a very small number of such cultural difference systems, about three or so, serve as the primary categories of person perception in a society (Brewer and Lui 1989; Fiske 1998). In the United States, sex, age, and race have been shown to be primary categories of person perception (Schneider 2004: 98). These primary categories define the things a person in that society must know about someone to render that someone sufficiently meaningful to relate to. I am arguing, then, that the problems that are inherent in organizing social encounters with others combine with the constraints of social cognition to encourage societies to develop a small number of primary cultural categories based on socially defined differences. People in that society rely on these primary categories as initial *frames* for making sense of one another.

Since people most often encounter others in an institutional context, say at work or in a grocery store, one might ask why primary categories are really necessary to solve the coordination problem. Institutional contexts have defined roles (e.g., employee-boss, or shopper-cashier) that indicate who actors are and how they should behave. But to use roles in a given context, actors need to already know the rules of that context, and there are many institutional contexts, each of which is slightly different. Primary categories are a more general kind of cultural tool that gets people out of the trap of needing complex institutional knowledge by applying to everyone rather than just those in a given institutional context. Because they transcend the limits of institutional contexts, they allow people to act quickly in the time constraints of interaction wherever they are. By offering all-purpose, initial frames for figuring out who the other is, primary categories allow people jump start the organization of social encounters whether in familiar institutional contexts or outside them.

SEX/GENDER AS A PRIMARY FRAME

Sex is a form a variation among people that is especially susceptible to being culturally amplified into a primary framing category for social relations (Ridgeway 2011: 38–39). Although physical sex is more complex than our cultural categories of male and female, it nevertheless is associated with a bimodal distribution of physical traits that encourages cultural simplification into a dichotomous, easily used category system. Furthermore, the resulting category system is of real interest to people because of its relevance to sexuality and reproduction and because it delineates between people who must regularly coordinate in social groups. When *sex* becomes culturally amplified into a common knowledge framing category for social relations it becomes *gender*. By gender, I mean a system of social practices that constitutes distinct, differentiated sex categories, sorts people into these categories, and organizes relations between people on the basis of presumed differences socially linked to their sex category (Ridgeway 2011).

A wide variety of evidence demonstrates that sex/gender is in fact a primary framing category for social relations in the United States, as it may be in all societies. On an anecdotal level, it is impressive to note how disturbing people find it when they cannot easily classify another person as male or female and how disruptive this is to their interaction with the person.[1] Going beyond anecdotes, research shows that when people have difficulty sex-categorizing another, it interferes with their cognitive ability to process other things in the relationship (Wisecup, McPherson, and Smith-Lovin 2005). And even in a world increasingly familiar with transgendered people, people still seek the social ease of relating to others as either men or women (Schilt 2010).

Social cognition research further confirms that sex category acts as a primary category of person perception (Brewer 1989; Prentice and Miller 2006; Schneider 2004: 98). Studies show that people automatically and nearly instantly sex categorize any specific person they attempt to relate to (Stangor, Lynch, Duan, and Glass 1992, Ito and Urland 2003; Zarate and Smith 1990). Subsequent categorizations of them as, say, bosses or co-workers, are nested in people's prior understandings of them as male or female and take on a slightly different meaning as a result (Brewer and Lui 1989; Fiske 1998). This happens not just in person but also over the internet and even imaginatively, as we examine a person's resume or think about the kind of person we would like to hire. This initial framing by sex never quite disappears from our understanding of them or ourselves in relation to them. While people may have a biological imperative to learn to sex categorize for reproductive reasons, we automatically sex categorize even those of no discernible reproductive relevance to us. The ubiquity with which we use sex/gender to categorize people reveals the social amplifications we have made of sex to transform it into a primary and general cultural frame for organizing social relations of any kind.

Primary categories of person perception, including sex category, work as cultural frames for coordinating behavior by associating category membership with widely shared, common knowledge cultural beliefs about how people in one category (e.g., men) are likely to behave compared to those in a contrasting

---

[1] Some may recall, for example, *Saturday Night Live's* skits about "Pat," an androgenous person who created interactional chaos in one setting after another by remaining sex unclassifiable to everyone present.

category (women). These common knowledge beliefs about social categories of people are, in effect, stereotypes. We all know common gender stereotypes as cultural knowledge even though many of us do not personally endorse them. But the point is, because we think "most people" hold these beliefs (because they are common knowledge), we expect others to act on them and to judge us according to them as well. As a result, we must take these beliefs into account in our own behavior even if we do not endorse them. In this way, these common knowledge cultural beliefs act as the "rules" for coordinating public behavior on the basis of gender. And, as we would expect from the "rules" for gender, widely shared gender stereotypes have been shown to have a prescriptive as well as descriptive quality (Eagly and Karau 2002, Prentice and Carranza 2002; Rudman et al. 2012). Thus, our use of sex/gender as a primary frame for making initial sense of others causes us to pull gendered cultural meanings in varying degrees into all activities that we carry out through social relations. As we shall see, this has major consequences for the gendering of social institutions and the persistence of gender inequality.

GENDER AND STATUS: FROM DIFFERENCE TO INEQUALITY

As a cultural device for coordinating behavior, sex/gender turns on cultural beliefs about gender differences in character and behavior. Beliefs about differences, however, are easily transformed into beliefs about inequality. The organizational problems of social relations that encourage a focus on difference also play a role in the transformation of difference to inequality. This transformation is not inevitable, but the conjunction of status inequality processes and gender framing in social relations make gender highly susceptible to this linkage.

People frequently find themselves dependent on one another to pursue a shared, collective goal or task. Such contexts are ubiquitous in the workplace but also in family or social contexts. When social relations take on this shared, goal-oriented focus, the coordination problems of interaction are intensified. Disagreements among actors must be resolved and the varying suggestions and efforts of the actors must somehow be weighted and combined into a collective line of action. These are the circumstances in which actors develop status hierarchies (Berger et al. 1977; Magee and Galinsky 2008). Status hierarchies grant greater esteem, deference, and influence over group activities to those perceived to offer more valuable contributions to the group goal effort. By providing a basis for deciding whose opinions should prevail in disagreements and whose opinions should count more in collective decisions, status hierarchies establish a micro order that addresses the special coordination problems of pursuing a shared task (Anderson and Kennedy 2012; Magee and Galinsky 2008).

While not all social relations are those that encourage the development of status hierarchies, many are. In these relations, like others, actors will have automatically sex categorized each other, evoking in the background cultural presumptions about gender difference. In a context in which participants are trying to decide to whom to defer and grant influence, what is the evaluative significance of this difference? A large body of evidence suggests that difference, in itself, causes people to presume that their own category is "better" than the other (Hogg 2003; Tajfel and Turner 1986). But in the context of an emerging status hierarchy, competing views of who is "better" are a problem. The collective efforts of the participants to create an agreed-on status hierarchy pressures people in one category or the other to give up their sense of being better and defer to those in the other category at least in this context.

If this happens one way in one context (men defer to women) and another in the next context (women defer to men), the participants need not make any long term, broad associations between beliefs about gender difference and presumptions about which sex category is generally "better." That is, participants need not form more general *status beliefs* about men and women as a group. Status beliefs are beliefs that people in one social category are presumed to be generally more competent and worthy of esteem than those in another category (Berger et al. 1977). But it is easy to see that anything that tips the string of associations people have between gender difference and presumed competence and status in task situations could indeed encourage them to form broader status beliefs about gender. This is the claim of status construction theory (Ridgeway 1991; Ridgeway et al. 2009).

Experimental studies have shown that after as few as two task-oriented encounters in which a salient social difference among the participants was consistently associated with higher (or lower) social influence and esteem, the participants formed status beliefs about the social difference (Ridgeway and Erickson 2000; Ridgeway et al. 2009). That is, they formed beliefs that "most people" would rate the typical member of the social category that was consistently more influential as generally higher status, more respected, and more competent, but not as considerate, as those from the other social category. Participants formed these beliefs even when the beliefs cast their own social category as lower status than the other category. In other words, the experience of participating in encounters in which people like them consistently became less influential and esteemed than the people different from them pressured people from the lower status group to give up their sense of being "better" and concede, as a matter of social reality, that most people would see the other group as "better."

These studies support status construction theory's claim that any factor that causes one sex category to be more consistently associated with influence and esteem in goal-oriented encounters between men and women will encourage the formation and spread of status beliefs favoring the more influential sex. One factor that has been shown to act as such a "tipping factor" is an advantage in material resources since greater resources frequently lead to social influence in encounters (Ridgeway 1991; Ridgeway et al. 1998). But a variety of other factors could also have such an effect. Any historical condition that caused men, on average, to have an advantage over women, on average, in some factor that gave them a consistent advantage in gaining influence over women in goal-oriented contexts would foster widely held gender status beliefs favoring men.

The actual historical origins of male dominance in Western societies are not known. But many current theories of these origins posit some factor, such as physical strength or the constraints faced by lactating mothers, which would have advantaged men in the control of resources and given them a systematic influence advantage in their relations with women (cf. Huber 2007; Wood and Eagly 2002). From the evidence about how status beliefs form, such a resource advantage on the part of men would have led to the development of widely shared status beliefs that men are more worthy of status and generally more competent than women.

Once such gender status beliefs develop, they have widespread consequences. Because they define men as diffusely "better" than women, especially in the things that "count most" in society, gender status beliefs advantage men just because they are men and not women (Ridgeway 2014). In that way, they give men an advantage even over women who are just as strong as they are or who have just as many resources as they do. Many societies have gender status beliefs like this, including the contemporary United States (Fiske et al. 2002; Glick et al. 2004).

When gender status beliefs develop, the primary frame of gender becomes a frame for organizing social relations on the basis of inequality as well as difference. We can see this in the content of contemporary American gender stereotypes. Studies of how high status and low status actors are perceived in North American show a consistent pattern. Conway, Pizzamiglio, and Mount (1996) showed that across status relations as diverse as gender, occupation, and hypothetical tribal status, high status actors are seen as more proactive and agentically competent while low status actors are viewed as more reactive and communal in nature. Fiske et al. (2002) have similarly shown that American groups perceived as high status are perceived as more competent, but not as warm, as those seen as lower status.

These characteristic patterns of status inequality are clearly embedded in our stereotypes of "who" men and women are. Studies of gender stereotypes show that men, as the higher status group, are perceived as more proactive and agentically competent ("from Mars"), while women are seen as more reactive, emotionally expressive, and warm ("from Venus") (Glick and Fiske 1999; Rudman et al. 2012; Wagner and Berger 1997). In this way, that which our cultural beliefs about gender define as essential differences between men and women are also differences that define status inequality. As a result, coordination of behavior on the basis of our shared gender beliefs produces social relations of inequality as well as difference.

HOW DOES THE GENDER FRAME SHAPE BEHAVIOR?

To see the joint implications of the status content of widely shared gender beliefs and people's use of gender as a primary frame for social relations, we need to examine more carefully how the gender frame shapes behavior and judgments in social relational contexts. Research shows that sex categorization, which we do automatically, unconsciously primes gender stereotypes in our minds and makes them cognitively available to shape behavior and judgments (Blair and Banaji 1996; Kunda and Spencer 2003). The extent to which gender stereotypes actually do shape our behavior, however, can vary from negligible to substantial depending on the nature of the particular situation and our own motives or interests in it. What matters is the extent to which the information in gender beliefs is diagnostic for us in that it helps us figure out how to behave in the situation in order to relate to the other and pursue our goals.

As part of the primary person frame, the instructions for behavior encoded in gender stereotypes are exceedingly abstract and diffuse (e.g., be agentic and strong, be responsive and warm). For this very reason, these stereotypic instructions can be applied to virtually any situation but by the same token, they do not take an actor very far in figuring out exactly how to behave. In contrast, the institutional frameworks that govern the contexts in which most everyday social relations take place (e.g., a workplace, a shopping mall) are much more specific. They contain defined roles (supervisor-employee; clerk-customer) that specify the expected relations among the actors. For individuals, then, it is these institutional identities and roles that are in the foreground of their sense of who they are and how they should behave in most settings.

Gender, in contrast, is almost always a *background identity* for individuals in social relations – that is, an identity that is less salient for the actor than a contextual, institutional identity. As a background identity, gender has a distinctive type of effect on behavior. Gender, as a situational identity triggered by sex categorization, typically acts to *bias* in gendered directions the performance of behaviors undertaken in the name of more concrete, foregrounded organizational roles or identities. Thus gender becomes a stereotypically masculine or feminine style with which one performs the duties of a doctor or project manager.

A wide variety of research shows that the extent and direction of the biases that the background gender frame, and the status beliefs embedded in it, introduce into our expectations and behavior fall into a distinctive pattern (see Ridgeway 2011: 73–87; Ridgeway and Correll 2004; Ridgeway and Smith-Lovin 1999 for reviews). In mixed sex settings in which the task or context is relatively gender neutral, cultural beliefs that men are more agentically competent and more worthy of status advantage them over otherwise similar women, but only modestly so. In settings that are culturally typed as masculine, gender beliefs bias judgments and behaviors more strongly in favor of men. In contexts culturally linked with women, biases weakly favor women except for positions of authority. Men are advantaged for authority in all settings.

In social relational contexts in the workplace, in educational settings, in the home, and elsewhere, these implicit biases shape a wide variety of behavioral and evaluative processes that have implications for gender inequality. By biasing self-other expectations for competence in the setting, they affect the confidence with which women, compared to similar men, speak up to offer their opinions. When women do speak up, they affect how others evaluate what they say. Not surprisingly, then, these biases also affect the influence women attain with others. They also affect others' and even women's own willingness to credit them with high ability based on a given good performance. And, together, these multiple evaluative biases affect the rewards given to women in these contexts compared to similar men (for reviews, see Correll 2001; Ridgeway and Correll 2004; Wagner and Berger 1997). In this way, through everyday social relations, systematic inequalities can emerge between initially similar men and women in the influence, prominence, resources, and positions of leadership and power that they attain in consequential contexts like the workplace.

We see, then, that people's everyday use of gender as a cultural device for managing a basic problem of social order at the micro-level, the framing of self and other to coordinate interaction, has cascading effects for gender as a social system of difference and inequality. Everyday gender framing facilitates the linking of gender and status. With the development of gender status beliefs, the background gender frame, evoked by automatic sex categorization, creates implicit biases in expectations, behaviors, and judgments in social relations. These biases in turn create micro-orders of status inequality between otherwise similar men and women.

GENDERED STRUCTURES OF INEQUALITY

The next task is to consider how these everyday micro-orders of gender inequality in social relations contribute to the emergence, enactment, and maintenance of larger social structures of gender inequality such as the sex segregation of jobs, the gender gap in wages and authority, and the unequal household division of labor (Ridgeway 2011). The role these processes at the social relational level play is complex because they interact with organizational structures and processes at the institutional level and with changing economic, technological and political circumstances. Although I cannot do justice to that complexity here, I sketch the general outline of the contributions micro-ordering gender processes make to gendered structures of inequality.

One of the most striking features of the organization of paid labor in the United States and many other places is the sex segregation of jobs and occupations (Charles and Grusky 2004; England 2010). That is, most people work in occupations in which the large majority of their co-workers are the same sex as they are. Many jobs are widely, if often implicitly considered "men's jobs" or "women's jobs." Equally striking, this pattern of sex-segregation in occupations is not just a dead relic of the past but is persistently re-created as old jobs disappear or change and new ones are created in an ever changing economy (Charles and Grusky 2004; Cotter et al. 2004).

Why do jobs become gender-labelled in the first place and how does this keep happening as new jobs emerge? People's routine sex-categorization of others to make sense of them and organize their behavior in relation to them plays a key role here, I argue, by gender framing the job-matching process. As employers imagine who their preferred worker would be for a job, they implicitly sex-categorize that ideal worker, further gendering their assumptions about that worker's traits (Acker 1990; Gorman 2005; Williams 2000). Job applicants also unconsciously or consciously consider the match between their gendered assumptions about themselves, the gendered traits the employer seems to be seeking, and the gender of others who hold such jobs. These employer-applicant gender framing processes do not act alone and are affected by a variety of organizational and economic factors, but they contribute in important ways to the job matching process out of which the sex-segregated occupational structure emerges.

Studies of the sex composition of occupations show an overall pattern that is consistent with the distinctive pattern of gender status biases that the gender frame introduces into social relations in the workplace. In a large scale study, Charles and Grusky (2004) find that men are more concentrated in occupations associated with stereotypic masculine skills, which include manual labor, and in top level jobs in any occupation. Women are more often in occupations associated with stereotypic feminine skills, which include service jobs, and in jobs of lesser authority. This is very much what we would expect if people in the workplace were repeatedly drawing on the gender frame to help organize their workplace relations.

The sex-segregation of occupations and jobs, in turn, is a major cause of the gender gaps in wages and authority since men's jobs tend to pay better and carry more authority (Petersen and Morgan 1995; Smith 2002). Also important for gender inequality in wages and authority, however, is the implicitly gendered nature of many organizational structures and procedures (Acker 1990). A classic example is the normative timing of promotion rituals in the professions that present greater challenges to promotion for women than men because they overlap with prime child-bearing years. But how do organizational structures and procedures become embedded with gendered assumptions about ideal workers and the authority and pay they deserve?

The root mechanism, I argue, is the way the gender frame brings gender status biases "into the room" at the social relational level as the new job definition, evaluation system, authority structure, or way of working is created (Ridgeway 2011: 119–22; Ridgeway 2014). Nelson and Bridges (1999), for instance, have shown that several widely used organizational pay-setting procedures were created in interpersonal decision-making contexts in which dominant actors, who were mostly men, denied women a significant voice in the process. As the result, the pay practices developed in these contexts were infused with gender status biases and systematically disadvantaged the pay levels created for female dominated jobs. Once created, implicitly gendered organizational structures spread through institutional processes and persist through bureaucratic inertia (Baron et al. 2007; Nelson and Bridges 1999).

Gender inequality at home, specifically inequality in the household division of labor, is also a powerful contributor to unequal life outcomes for men and women in society. The household division of labor is not only an important structure of gender inequality itself, but also a powerful contributor to gender inequality in the workplace since it affects people's availability for paid labor. The typical household division of labor in the contemporary United States is highly gendered. Women do more overall child care and housework and household tasks tend to be sex typed (i.e., cooking in the house vs. barbequing outside) (Bianchi, Robinson, and Milkie 2006; Hook 2010).

Homes and households, with their cultural associations with sex and child-rearing, are highly gendered contexts. They are also interpersonal, intimately relational contexts. Both factors bring the gender frame, and its implications for both gender difference and inequality, to the fore as people make sense of one another and organize their relations in the household, in that way shaping their division of labor. The power of the gender frame on people in the household likely plays a role in people's resistance to radical change in their division of household labor despite growing pressures on it created by women's increased involvement in the paid labor force (Ridgeway 2011: 127–55).

THE GENDER FRAME AND THE PERSISTENCE OF
GENDER INEQUALITY

I argued at the outset that people's on-going use of gender as a primary frame for social relations also acts as a powerful force for the persistence of gender inequality in the face of changing material circumstances in society. We have seen that the micro-ordering effects of the gender frame on interpersonal relations play a significant role in the everyday reproduction of gender inequality within established institutional structures in the workplace and the home. While such reproduction is an important part of the routine persistence of gender inequality, it does not tell us much about how gender inequality persists across significant changes in dominant institutional structures.

In fact, the future of gender as a principle of inequality lies with sites at the edge of social and technological change. These are sites where substantially new forms of work or new forms of heterosexual unions are innovated. Some of these innovations then become blueprints for new industries and ways of life. Can the gender frame, acting through social relations, infuse assumptions about gender inequality even into these innovative contexts that are explicitly devoted to doing things differently? If it did, it would reinvent gender inequality for the new era.

I argue that the gender frame can and does do this for reasons based on three sets of factors. First, "common knowledge" cultural beliefs about gender (i.e., gender stereotypes) change more slowly than do material arrangements between men and women, even though these beliefs do eventually respond to material changes. As a result of this cultural lag, at the edge of social change, people confront their new, uncertain circumstances with gender beliefs that are more traditional than those circumstances. Second, sites of innovation where people develop new forms of economic activity or new types of social organization tend to be small, interpersonal settings that are often outside established organizations. Think of the garages or college dorms that are often described as the origin sites of new information technology companies. Third, such sites are focused, goal-oriented settings that are likely to create status hierarchies.

The uncertain, goal-focused, and interpersonal nature of sites of innovation increase the likelihood that the participants will implicitly draw on the too convenient cultural frame of gender, with its implications for status, to help organize their new ways of doing things. As they do so, they reinscribe trailing cultural assumptions about gender difference and gender inequality into the new activities, procedures, and forms of organization that they create, in effect, reinventing gender inequality for a new era. In what follows, I briefly explain why the cultural beliefs about gender that make up the gender frame are likely to lag behind material changes in men's and women's circumstances and describe evidence that they do so. Then I outline some evidence that these beliefs infect sites of innovation, looking specifically at high-tech start-ups in the work world.

Lagging Gender Beliefs

When changing social circumstances such as women's growing commitment to the labor force cause men and women to have different experiences with one another, why would this not simply be reflected in changed gender stereotypes? Evidence suggests that such changes will eventually modify stereotypes (Diekman and Eagly 2000). But the impact of people's changing experiences is blunted by two processes that slow the change of stereotypes. At the individual level gender stereotypes are subject to powerful confirmation biases that cause people to not notice gender inconsistent information or to reinterpret it as consistent (Von Hippel et al. 1995; Dunning and Sherman 1997). At a more social level, people's assumption that gender stereotypes are "common knowledge" rules for gendered behavior that they can rely on to coordinate with others inhibits their public expression of explicitly gender disconfirming behavior or information (Clark and Kashima 2007). These two processes work together to encourage people to assume that "most people" still hold relatively traditional gender stereotypes (and, thus, such stereotypes are still "common knowledge") until people's gender atypical experiences become more extreme, causing widely held gender beliefs to lag behind social change.

In support of this conclusion, comparisons of gender stereotypes measured in the 1970s, when changes in American women's labor force involvement were just beginning to take off, and those measured more recently show surprising stability, given the enormity of the intervening changes in women's work roles (Spence and Buckner 2000). There has been a slight narrowing of the gender gap in instrumental, agentic traits, although men are still seen as substantially higher than women on the stronger aspects of agency like aggressive, forceful, leaderlike, or competitive (Prentice and Carranza 2002). There has been no change in the gender gap on communal, expressive traits associated with women (Diekman and Eagly 2000; Prentice and Carranza 2002; Rudman et al. 2012). Thus men are still from Mars and women are still mostly from Venus, but Venus is a little stronger than she used to be. This evidence suggests that "common knowledge" gender stereotypes have indeed lagged behind recent material changes in women's roles.

Sites of Innovation

What is the evidence that people's routine use of the gender frame causes them to infuse sites of innovation with these lagging cultural beliefs about gender, in that way rewriting gender inequality into newly emerging industries or ways of living? In the interests of brevity, I focus here on evidence from the work world but evidence can also be found for such effects in emerging forms of heterosexual unions (Ridgeway 2011: 181–4).

Whittington and Smith-Doer (2008; Whittington 2007) studied how women scientists fared in high-tech start-ups compared to traditional research firms. The start-ups shared a flexible organizational form based on project teams. Some were biotech firms based in the life sciences, a mixed sex, relatively gender neutral field of study in which women are now about half the PhDs (Ceci et al. 2011). Because of the mixed sex context with a gender neutral work task, the gender frame argument predicts that gender inequality will be recreated in these innovative biotech firms, but it will be moderate. Facing only modest challenges to their scientific competence, women scientists should be able to take advantage of the flexible organizational form and do rather well. Supporting this prediction, Whittington and Smith-Doer (2008) found that women did better in terms of patents and supervisory positions in these biotech start-ups than they did in traditional firms like pharmaceuticals. But, as predicted, a modest degree of gender inequality remained, with women still achieving fewer patents overall than did similar men scientists.

Other start-ups studied by Whittington had the same organizational form, but were information technology (IT) firms based in the physical sciences, fields still strongly sex-typed in favor of men in the United States. As a masculine typed setting, the gender frame argument predicts stronger implicit biases against women scientists' competence in the IT than the biotech setting. Facing strong challenges to their credibility, it will be harder for women in these IT start-ups to take advantage of the flexible structure and in the context of a masculine task, the informality may encourage a "boys club" atmosphere. Supporting these predictions, Whittington (2007) found women scientists were no better off in these innovative IT start-ups than in traditional firms like aerospace companies. In both, women were significantly disadvantaged compared to similar men, being less likely to patent at all and having fewer patents overall.

The fact that these IT and biotech start-ups shared the same organizational form adds support to the conclusion that the differing regimes of gender inequality that they developed were due to the effects of the background gender frame acting on social relations in the firms. The effects of the gender frame on the early workplace practices, routines, and procedures of start-ups potentially have long term consequences. Baron and colleagues (2007) have shown that these early practices act as organizational "blueprints" that have lasting implications for how men and women fare in the firm as it grows and develops (Baron et al. 2007). Furthermore, such organizational practices can spread to other similar firms, spreading their gender effects more widely (Phillips 2005). Thus, the way the background frame of gender infuses gender inequality into the organizational routines of small, pioneering firms potentially has long range consequences for the persistence of gender inequality as the economy changes and new industries emerge.

CONCLUSION

There is good evidence that gender acts as a primary cultural framework that people rely on to initiate the process of making sense of one another and organizing their social relations with each other. By the account I have given here, this everyday process of using gender as a cultural device for creating micro order has widespread social consequences that contribute to social order at the macro level. People's automatic sex categorization of one another in interaction, which is partially driven by the micro-ordering demands of coordinating behavior, evokes "common knowledge" cultural beliefs about gender difference. Interaction, in turn, repeatedly exposes these evoked gender meanings to another common micro-ordering process, the development of status hierarchies, facilitating their transformation into beliefs that imply status inequality as well as difference.

As a micro-ordering frame that creates status inequality, people's everyday use of the gender frame plays a significant role in the creation, enactment, and maintenance of larger structures of gender inequality. The gender frame implicitly sex-labels employers' images of preferred workers, evoking gender stereotype confirmation biases that further gender the traits employers look for. In a similar way, the gender frame shapes applicants' job searches. Together, these micro-ordering gender processes help create and maintain a larger occupational structure in which jobs are sex-segregated and men's jobs pay more and carry more authority on average than women's jobs. These same micro-ordering gender processes (automatic sex-categorization, the evocation of gender status beliefs, and resulting confirmation biases in judgments and behavior) also powerfully shape the unequal household division of labor that further contributes to macro-level patterns of inequality between men and women.

Perhaps the gender frame's most distinctive contribution to gender as a social system of inequality, however, is the way people's everyday use of the gender frame facilitates the persistence of gender inequality over major transformations in the social and economic organization of society that might otherwise undermine it. Acting "in the room" through social relations at sites where new types of work or new types of personal relations are pioneered, the micro-ordering processes of the gender frame implicitly shape the new practices, procedures, and structures that the participants develop, so that trailing cultural assumptions about gender status and difference are rewritten into the emerging new social order. This micro-level persistence dynamic is not all powerful and, thus, does not mean that gender inequality can never be overcome. In the contemporary American context, powerful legal, institutional, and economic forces work against traditional distinctions like gender and women's own interests in bettering their lives also continually push against gender inequality. But this persistence dynamic, which is rooted in people's use of gender as a micro-ordering device, does mean that the forces for change are not unopposed. As a result, progress toward equality may be both uneven and uncertain.

REFERENCES

Acker, Joan. 1990. "Hierarchies, Jobs, and Bodies: A Theory of Gendered Organizations." *Gender & Society* 4: 139–158.
Anderson, Cameron, and Jessica A. Kennedy. 2012. "Micropolitics: A New Model of Status Hierarchies in Teams." Pp. 49–80 in Looking Back, Moving Forward: A Review of Group and Team-Based Research. *Research on Managing Groups and Teams*, Vol. 15, edited by Margaret A. Neale and Elizabeth Mannix. Bingley, UK: Emerald Group Publishing.
Baron, James N., Michael T. Hannan, Greta Hsu, and Ozgecan Kocak. 2007. "In the Company of Women: Gender Inequality and the Logic of Bureaucracy in Start-Up Firms." *Work and Occupations* 34: 35–66.
Berger, Joseph, Hamit Fisek, Robert Norman, and Morris Zelditch. 1977. *Status Characteristics and Social Interaction*. New York: Elsevier.
Bianchi, Suzanne M., John P. Robinson, and Melissa Milkie. 2006. *Changing Rhythms of American Family Life*. New York: Russell Sage Foundation.
Blair, Irene V. and Mahzarin R. Banaji. 1996. "Automatic and Controlled Processes in Stereotype Priming." *Journal of Personality and Social Psychology* 70: 1142–63.

Brewer, Marilynn B., and Layton N. Lui. 1989. "The Primacy of Age and Sex in the Structure of Person Categories." *Social Cognition* 7: 262–74.

Ceci, Stephen J., and Wendy Williams. 2011. "Understanding Current Causes of Women's Underrepresentation in Science." *PNAS* 8: 3157–62.

Charles, Maria, and David Grusky. 2004. *Occupational Ghettos: The Worldwide Segregation of Women and Men.* Stanford, CA: Stanford University Press.

Chwe, Michael S. 2001. *Rational Ritual: Culture, Coordination, and Common Knowledge.* Princeton, NJ: Princeton University Press.

Clark, Anna E., and Yoshihisa Kashima. 2007. "Stereotypes Help People Connect with Others in the Community: A Situated Functional Analysis of the Stereotype Consistency Bias in Communication." *Journal of Personality and Social Psychology* 93: 1028–39.

Conway, Michael M., Teresa Pizzamiglio, and Lauren Mount. 1996. "Status, Communality, and Agency: Implications for Stereotypes of Gender and Other Groups." *Journal of Personality and Social Psychology* 71: 25–38.

Correll, Shelley J. 2001. "Gender and the Career Choice Process: The Role of Biased Self-Assessments." *American Journal of Sociology* 106: 1691–730.

Cotter, David A., Joan M. Hermsen, and Reeve Vanneman. 2004. "Gender Inequality at Work." *The American People Census 2000.* Russell Sage Foundation and Population Reference Bureau.

Diekman, Amanda B., and Alice H. Eagly. 2000. "Stereotypes as Dynamic Constructs: Women and Men of the Past, Present, and Future." *Personality and Social Psychology Bulletin* 26: 1171–88.

Dunning, David, and David A. Sherman. 1997. "Stereotypes and Trait Inference." *Journal of Personality and Social Psychology* 73: 459–71.

Eagly, Alice H., and Stephen J. Karau. 2002. "Role Congruity Theory of Prejudice Towards Female Leaders." *Psychological Review* 109: 573–79.

England, Paula. 2010. "The Gender Revolution: Uneven and Stalled." *Gender & Society* 24: 149–66.

Fiske, Susan T. 1998. "Stereotyping, Prejudice, and Discrimination." Pp. 357–411 in *The Handbook of Social Psychology*, edited by D.T. Gilbert, S.T. Fiske, and G. Lindzey. 4th ed. New York: McGraw-Hill.

Fiske, Susan T., Amy J. Cuddy, Peter Glick, and Jun Xu. 2002. "A Model of (Often Mixed) Stereotype Content: Competence and Warmth Respectively Follow from Perceived Status and Competition." *Journal of Personality and Social Psychology* 82: 878–902.

Glick, Peter and Susan T. Fiske. 1999. "Sexism and Other "Isms": Interdependence, Status, and the Ambivalent Content of Stereotypes." Pp. 193–221 in *Sexism and Stereotypes in Modern Society*, edited by W. B. Swan, J. H. Langlois, and L. A. Gilbert. Washington, DC: American Psychological Association.

Glick, Peter, Maria Lameiras, Susan T. Fiske, Thomas Eckes, Barbara Masser, Chiara Volpato, Anna Maria Manganelli, Jolynn C. X. Pek, Li-li Huang, Nuray Sakalli-Ugurlu, Yolanda Rodriguez Castro, Maria Luiza D'Avila Pereira, Tineke M. Willemsen, Annetje Brunner, Iris Six-Materna, and Robin Wells. 2004. "Bad but Bold: Ambivalent Attitudes toward Men Predict Gender Inequality in 16 Nations." *Journal of Personality and Social Psychology* 86: 713–28.

Goffman, Erving. 1967. *Interaction Ritual: Essays on Face-to-Face Behavior.* 1st ed. Garden City, NY: Anchor Books.

Gorman, Elizabeth H. 2005. "Gender Stereotypes, Same-Gender Preferences, and Organizational Variation in the Hiring of Women: Evidence from Law Firms." *American Sociological Review* 70: 702–28.

Hogg, Michael A. 2003. "Intergroup Relations." Pp. 479–502 in *Handbook of Social Psychology*, edited by J. D. Delamater. New York: Kluwer Academic/Plenum Publishers.

Hook, Jennifer. 2010. "Gender Inequality in the Welfare State: Sex Segregation in Housework, 1965–2003." *American Journal of Sociology* 115: 1480–523.

Huber, Joan. 2007. *On the Origins of Gender Inequality.* Boulder, CO: Paradigm Publishers.

Ito, Tiffany A. and Geoffrey R. Urland. 2003. "Race and Gender on the Brain: Electrocortical Measures of Attention to the Race and Gender of Multiply Categorizable Individuals." *Journal of Personality and Social Psychology* 85(4): 616–26.

Kunda, Ziva, and Steven J. Spencer. 2003. "When Do Stereotypes Come to Mind and When Do They Color Judgment? A Goal-Based Theoretical Framework for Stereotype Activation and Application." *Psychological Bulletin* 129(4): 522–54.

Magee, James C., and Adam D. Galinsky. 2008. "Social Hierarchy: The Self-reinforcing Nature of Power and Status." *Academy of Management Annals* 2: 351–98.

Mead, George H. 1934. *Mind, Self, and Society: From the Standpoint of a Social Behaviorist.* Chicago: University of Chicago Press.

Nelson, Robert, and William Bridges. 1999. *Legalizing Gender Inequality: Courts, Markets, and Unequal Pay for Women in America.* New York: Cambridge University Press.

Peterson, Trond, and Laurie A. Morgan. 1995. "Separate and Unequal: Occupation-Establishment Sex Segregation and the Gender Wage Gap." *American Journal of Sociology* 101: 329–65.

Phillips, Damon J. 2005. "Organizational Genealogies and the Persistence of Gender Inequality: The Case of Silicon Valley Law Firms." *Administrative Science Quarterly* 50: 440–72.

Prentice, Deborah A., and Erica Carranza. 2002. "What Women and Men Should Be, Shouldn't Be, Are Allowed to Be, and Don't Have to Be: The Contents of Prescriptive Gender Stereotypes." *Psychology of Women Quarterly* 26: 269–81.

Prentice, Deborah A., and Dale T. Miller. 2006. "Essentializing Differences between Women and Men." *Psychological Science* 17: 129–35.

Ridgeway, Cecilia L. 1991. "The Social Construction of Status Value: Gender and Other Nominal Characteristics." *Social Forces* 70: 367–86.

2011. *Framed by Gender: How Gender Inequality Persists in the Modern World.* New York: Oxford University Press.

2014. "Why Status Matters for Inequality." *American Sociological Review* 79: 1–16.

Ridgeway, Cecilia L., Kristen Backor, Yan E. Li, Justine E. Tinkler, and Kristan G. Erickson. 2009. "How Easily Does a Social Difference Become a Status Distinction? Gender Matters." *American Sociological Review* 74: 44–62.

Ridgeway, Cecilia L., Elizabeth Heger Boyle, Kathy Kuipers, and Dawn T. Robinson. 1998. "How Do Status Beliefs Develop? The Role of Resources and Interactional Experience." *American Sociological Review* 63: 331–50.

Ridgeway, Cecilia L., and Shelley J. Correll. 2004. "Unpacking the Gender System: A Theoretical Perspective on Cultural Beliefs and Social Relations." *Gender and Society* 18: 510–31.

Ridgeway, Cecilia L., and Kristan G. Erickson. 2000. "Creating and Spreading Status Beliefs." *American Journal of Sociology* 106: 579–615.

Ridgeway, Cecilia L., and Lynn Smith-Lovin. 1999. "The Gender System and Interaction." *Annual Review of Sociology* 25: 191–216.

Rudman, Laurie A., Corinne A. Moss-Racusin, Julie E. Phelan, and Sanne Nauts. 2012. "Status Incongruity and Backlash Effects: Defending the Gender Hierarchy Motivates Prejudice against Female Leaders." *Journal of Experimental Social Psychology* 48: 165–79.

Schilt, Kristen. 2010. *Just One of the Guys: Transgender Men and the Persistence of Gender Inequality*. Chicago: University of Chicago Press.

Schneider, Donald J. 2004. *The Psychology of Stereotyping*. New York: Guilford Press.

Smith, Ryan A. 2002. "Race, Gender, and Authority in the Workplace: Theory and Research." *Annual Review of Sociology* 28: 509–42.

Spence, Janet T. and Camille E. Buckner. 2000. "Instrumental and Expressive Traits, Trait Stereotypes, and Sexist Attitudes: What Do They Signify?" *Psychology of Women Quarterly* 24: 44–62.

Stangor, Charles, Laure Lynch, Changming Duan, and Beth Glass. 1992. "Categorization of Individuals on the Basis of Multiple Social Features." *Journal of Personality and Social Psychology* 62: 207–18.

Stryker, Sheldon, and Kevin D. Vryan. 2003. "The Symbolic Interactionist Frame." Pp. 3–28 in *The Handbook of Social Psychology*, edited by J. Delamater. New York: Kluwer Academic/Plenum Publishers.

Tajfel, Henri, and John C. Turner. 1986. "The Social Identity Theory of Intergroup Behavior." Pp. 7–24 in *Psychology of Intergroup Relations*, edited by S. Worchel and W. Austin. Chicago, IL: Nelson-Hall.

von Hippel, Willaim, Denise Sekaquaptewa, and Patrick T. Vargas. 1995. "On the Role of Encoding Processes in Stereotype Maintenance." *Advances in Experimental Social Psychology* 27: 177–254.

Wagner, David G., and Joseph Berger. 1997. "Gender and Interpersonal Task Behaviors: Status Expectation Accounts." *Sociological Perspectives* 40: 1–32.

Whittington, Kjersten Bunker. 2007. "Employment Sectors as Opportunity Structures: Male and Female: The Effects of Location on Male and Female Scientific Dissemination." PhD diss., Stanford, CA: Department of Sociology, Stanford University.

Whittington, Kjersten Bunker, and Laurel Smith-Doerr. 2008. "Women Inventors in Context: Disparities in Patenting Across Academia and Industry." *Gender and Society* 22: 194–218.

Williams, Joan E. 2000. *Unbending Gender: Why Family and Work Conflict and What to Do About It*. New York: Oxford University Press.

Wisecup, Allison K., Miller McPherson, and Lynn Smith-Lovin. 2005. "Recognition of Gender Identity and Task Performance." Pp. 177–202 in *Social Identification in Groups*, Vol. 22, edited by S. R. Thye and E. J. Lawler. San Diego, CA: Elsevier Ltd.

Wood, Wendy, and Alice H. Eagly. 2002. "A Cross-Cultural Analysis of the Behavior of Women and Men: Implications for the Origins of Sex Differences." *Psychological Bulletin* 128: 699–727.

Zárate, Michael A., and Eliot R. Smith. 1990. "Person Categorization and Stereotyping." *Social Cognition* 8: 161–85.

11

Status, Power, and Social Order

Theodore D. Kemper

Abstract

Thomas Hobbes and Talcott Parsons have set the terms of the debate over the question of social order in society, but their view of order/disorder, even though each differs from the other, is both incomplete and problematic. A different approach is to see order/disorder as resulting from patterns of technical activity, social relations and reference group influences. Central here is a theory of social relations, based on the behavioral dimensions of status and power. Derivations from status-power theory include a theory of emotions, some of which (pride, shame, guilt, fear, sadness and contempt) tend to favor social order while others (mainly anger and sadness/depression) tend toward disorder. Reference groups also mainly dispose to sustaining order but, when contravening the role-expectations of interaction partners, also instigate disorder. Ironically, the highest levels of social order, as defined in status-power relational terms, are found to have the seeds of disorder contained within them.

We must wonder whether Thomas Hobbes ([1651] 1968), when he was postulating his state of nature with its war of all against all, knew he was erecting a straw figure. How can there be a war of all-against-all when individuals are necessarily raised in families, where parents necessarily nurture their children and children not only fear their parents but also love them? If there is any possible reality to Hobbes's grim picture, it would be strain and conflict between families. Yet, even here the picture is awry, since families are ordinarily members of larger groups and, even if only out of utilitarian self-interest, form coalitions and recruit allies from them. Within such collectivities, there must be some coordination and cooperation (Hechter and Horne 2003; Collins 2004) – that is, order – otherwise, even though enlarged, such groups would be feckless. In sum, Hobbes's depiction of the state of nature is a sociological fiction. What is not a fiction is that all individuals are sometimes in conflict with and fail to cooperate with some other individuals. This is disorder. But it cannot be that as Hobbes supposed all individuals are in conflict with all other individuals at the same time.

We must wonder too whether Talcott Parsons (1937, 1951), when he was solving the "Hobbesian problem of order" by postulating collectivities in which members shared values, knew that he too was erecting a straw figure. Family harmony or coordination and cooperation do not inevitably depend on common values. The parents likely have values, and this is important in their devotion to the parenting role, but the children are nowhere near having values to guide their conduct. Yet the children are to varying degrees obedient and cooperative, not only fearing parental disapproval when they don't obey, but also wishing to obey out of motives of emulation and love.

Thus, while there is always the possibility of disorder, as will be explained below, the acting forces within existing groups dispose toward order. In large part, this is the result of relational dynamics that orient actors toward "playing well with others." Laying a groundwork for an understanding of the disposition toward social order, I will first present an understanding of the division of labor (technical activity) and its associated relational dynamics in terms of the status and power behavioral dimensions and their accompanying motives. In addition, I will consider the social environment of individuals as a grid of reference groups. These are groups (or individuals), including one's immediate interaction partner, but also others outside the immediate setting, that have an interest in the actor's behavior. Second, I will discuss three types of social order that follow from technical activity, status-power relations and reference groups. Third, I will discuss how the usual patterns of status-power relations and reference groups relate to different types of social order. Fourth, I will examine how emotions, derived from outcomes of status-power interaction, further or discourage social order. Fifth, I will take up some aspects of social *dis*order as implied by Hobbes and Parsons. Finally, I will consider how institutional structures such as bureaucracy and law (understood in status-power terms) affect the micro-to-macro linkages in the maintenance of social order.

STATUS-POWER AND REFERENCE GROUP THEORY

Status-power and reference group theory seeks to explain social life, both in its tendency toward cooperation and order as well as its not-infrequent occasions of actors at cross-purposes and disorder. It begins with the assumption that humans are born helpless and necessarily dependent on each other and would not survive were there a literal "state of nature" as Hobbes described it. Helpless dependency in the early years gives way later in time to cooperative interdependence or the division of labor. Of crucial and determinative importance, the sexual division of labor in reproduction enables the species to survive. I call the tasks of the division of labor *technical activity*. Technical activity is any mental or physical effort oriented to accomplishing what needs to be done writing.

done in the division of labor, from hunting and gathering to flying jet planes and writing computer code.

Humans, however, do not live by technical activity alone. This was well-demonstrated in the cases recorded by Spitz (1945; see also Hertenstein et al. 2009; Hertenstein 2010), where infants in orphan shelters were provided with what was thought to be adequate care in a technical sense, namely, nourishment and bedding, but not with holding and physical contact – deeper expressions of emotion and relationship – and who became sickly and perished (Spitz 1945) from lack of the latter attentions.

A model for the description of relational connections with others is thus needed. Status-power theory is a candidate for such a model and it has a long history. As early as twenty-five centuries ago, the pre-Socratic Greek philosopher Empedocles proposed the fundamental theorem that social life could be understood as the competition of two dynamic forces, namely, *love* and *strife* (Cleve 1969). Love brought people together and strife drove them apart. Freud ([1937] 1959) referred to Empedocles as "my great predecessor," since the philosopher had recognized the principles underlying Freud's own twin forces of *Eros* and *Thanatos* (life and death). But these premodern understandings had to wait for advances in mathematical statistics before their theoretical aperçus about social relations could stand up in the sphere of present-day empirical science.

Beginning during World War II and continuing into the 1950s, researchers working on questions of leadership for the U.S. War Department, undertook a series of observational studies of behavior in small groups by officers and enlisted men. The data from these studies were factor analyzed – that's the mathematical statistics part – and Launor F. Carter (1954) summarized the results and thereby imparted an up-to-date impetus to the understanding first proffered by Empedocles. Carter found that the factor analytic results could be understood in three dimensions, one dealing with tasks in the division of labor and two with social relations, but all relevant for the understanding of what social actors do, as will be developed later.

Carter's labeled the first factor, *Aiding Attainment by Group*.[1] It reflected engagement by actors in the technical activity required by the task or job at hand, and was indicated by such items and scales as "efficiency," "cooperation," "pointed toward group solution," "effective intelligence," "competent" and so on. This technical activity factor fits well into the theoretical understanding that human actors are ineluctably interdependent. (Empedocles had not mentioned technical activity; he was focused solely on social relations.)

Carter's second factor, named by him *Individual Prominence and Achievement*, was defined by items and scales such as "authoritarianism," "aggressiveness," "leadership," "boldness," "confidence," "forcefulness," and

---

[1] Factor analysts and those summarizing factor analytic findings are privileged to name factors however they wish.

the like. This is the first of the two relational factors and I will elaborate on it later.

Carter's third factor, labeled *Sociability*, was marked by such items and scales as "sociability," "adaptability," "behavior which is socially agreeable to group members," "sincere," "helpful," and the like. This is the second relational factor and will also be elaborated later.

Of singular importance for the study of social order is that *these three factors were the complete finding*. (We must consider that as an important guideline for theoretical purposes.) Inspired in part by Carter's interpretation of the factor-analytic results, many additional studies (see Kemper 1978, 2006) have found technical activity and/or the two relational factors. Kemper and Collins (1990) have reported on observations of interaction in non-military small-groups, the cognate findings of meanings in the Semantic Differential (Osgood, Suci, and Tannenbaum 1954; Heise 1979) and in cross-cultural studies of language and emotion (White 1980). In all these studies social actors were found to be engaged in, or to find meaning in, what can be understood as technical activity and/or relational activity as described earlier, both at the micro-level and up to and including the level of societies (see Kemper 1992 for a review of factor-analytic results defining interaction at the macro-level within and between societies).

Status and Power

I will now focus on the two relational factors. How may we understand them in a way relevant to social order? Both dimensions can be approached through the notion of compliance. In social interaction, actors often engage in *voluntary compliance* with the desires, interests and wishes of other actors (think of parents' efforts in behalf of their children; lovers' in behalf of their beloved; teachers in behalf of students; communicants in behalf of the object of their veneration). The behavior at stake consists of acts of deference, respect, attention, devotion, support, concern, praise, defense and the like. In all cases the action is uncoerced and freely undertaken. Carter's third-factor scales of sociability, agreeableness and helpfulness reflect this kind of voluntary compliance with the interests of others. I name this dimension *status*, since the actions entailed are what one would do for someone who has valorized standing in a social system, structure or relationship (see Kemper 2011). Weber ([1922] 1946) speaks of (high) status groups, which are collectivities that share some characteristic(s) that evoke attention and respect. The status dimension is widely noted in sociology. Durkheim ([1912] 1965) wrote of the "respect" manifested by actors toward a deity; Goffman ([1956] 1967) defined ritual in terms of "respect" for the human object of the ritual conduct; Collins (1975) has written of status as engaging a central life motive: "[E]veryone tries to arrange things so as to maximize his own status …" (p. 83). (See also Ridgeway, this volume.) Status relations represent social order in the highest degree, a point I discuss later.

The second relational dimension in Carter's analysis, reflects *involuntary compliance*. We can understand this as follows: when compliance in the form of status – which requires voluntary conferral – is not forthcoming, actors frequently threaten and coerce other actors to comply with their wishes, desires and interests. They shout, hit, scream, emotionally withdraw, deceive,[2] manipulate and otherwise behave in noxious ways that are intended to compel the other actor to comply when he or she does not wish to do so. Carter's scales of "aggressiveness," "authoritarianism" and "forcefulness" reflect this kind of conduct. I call this dimension *power*. This usage follows from Weber ([1922] 1946) who defined power as "action undertaken to overcome the resistance" of others (p. 180). Nor is power an alien concept in sociology (see, e.g., the review by Orum and Dale 2009; and see Alexander [2011] who also reads Weber's notion of power as the case of non-"voluntary compliance"). Power imposes social order, but at a price and of a different sort from the order obtained via status relations. In sum, the data tell us that technical activity and status and power behavior are what people do with, to, for, about and against other people and that that's all they do.

The status-power model of relationship implies that each actor (in a dyad, let us say) has some standing in both the status and power dimensions. Each actor is thus required to attend to four relational requirements that organize the actor's motivation. These motives are postulated to be universals and thus establish a framework for social order.

(1) **Own Status.** The actor must manifest the qualities that earn status from other actors. This requires acting so as to evoke the variety of forms of respect, regard, help, deference, and so on. This may entail attaining certain culturally approved goals, such as higher education, prestigious employment, marital status, parenthood, community contribution and so on. It may involve high level performance in technical activity (e.g., flying a plane, effective parenting, starting a business) which is then rewarded by respect, attention, praise and so on. Hamblin and Smith (1966) have shown how actors (in their case, university professors) who matched standards for status-accord did, in fact, receive status, that is, respect and regard, from graduate students. Along with Collins (1975), I regard the acquisition of status as a main motive of social life, determining the widest sweep of activities, interests and engagements with others.

(2) **Other's Status.** Not only does one try to gain status, but, in the normal course of events, one is inspired to accord it as well. Each actor faces the problem of having suitable cultural standards for status conferral

---

[2] Frequent among deceptions is feigned status behavior, that is, acting toward the other as if one authentically respected, deferred and cared for his or her welfare. This falls within the scope of power behavior as it is designed to evoke (involuntary) compliance, the target actor doing what he or she does not want to do, cozened by false appearances of status conferral.

and also the ability to confer status in the manner and to the degree warranted by the other person's qualities and performances, that is, what cultural definition and prescription deem appropriate. Crucially, once standards are in place, status-conferral is automatically evoked when the other actor displays the qualities or behaviors that the standards require for status conferral (Hamblin and Smith 1966). If I have a standard for intellectual achievement and you demonstrate that quality, I am impelled to confer status on you without thinking twice about it.

Emotional warmth, for example, smiles, touching, hugs, is frequently the way status is conferred. However, an actor may be psychically constricted by earlier experiences of hurt, withdrawal and abandonment and be unable to confer the status mandated by prevailing cultural standards. A failure to accord status when warranted by the match between qualities and standards is prima facie a step into social disorder, for example, in spousal or other intimate relationship or with coworkers or colleagues in the division of labor. Interactions vary in the degree to which one party is expected by cultural standards to accord status to another, from the bare minimum in the occasional transactions of commercial settings (e.g., with supermarket clerks) to full-blown emotional commitments that go by the name of love. A love relationship is defined for as one in which one actor accords or is prepared to accord an extreme amount of status to another actor (see Kemper 2006; 2011).

(3) **Own Power.** With rare exceptions – for example, the early stages of a love relationship (see Kemper 1978; 2011) – the normal pattern is for power to be present to some degree in the interaction between two parties. Having power differs from the motivation to use it, but having power often leads to using it when the other party is not conferring status in the amount and type one desires or feels one deserves. In general, 'best practices' suggest avoiding the use of power or moderate use of it in culturally-approved ways, for example, teasing reprovals instead of screaming one's frustration, mock pouting instead of the acid of real chagrin. Impulsiveness, however, overrides culturally-endorsed restraint on the use of power, as does low regard for the other party. In any case, a lesson is usually learned in respect to one's own power, namely, that, while it may get one what one wants, using power almost always evokes hatred – a combination of fear and anger (Kemper 1978, p. 124) – and very often retaliation, marking a decisive breakdown in social order.

(4) **Other's Power.** Just as one has power, so does the other party and the main issues here are two: first, is to avoid the other's power and, when one cannot avoid it, second, is having the ability to muster enough counter-power to cause the other to limit or cease using power. One way to avoid the other's power is through some degree of autonomy, so that

one is not dependent on the other party to a degree that makes one vulnerable. This understanding follows from Emerson's (1962) formulation of the relationship between power and dependence: $P_{AB} = D_{BA}$ and $P_{BA} = D_{AB}$, which reads: the power of A over B equals the dependence of B on A and the power of B over A equals the dependence of A on B.

In sum, a social relationship consists (in the dyad, for example) of two actors, each with some amount of status and some amount of power vis-à-vis each other. It is important to keep in mind that the status or standing of each actor in the relationship is the result of what the other actor accords. If I accord you no status in our relationship, you have no status in our relationship, regardless of how much status others may accord you in your relationship with them. Crucially, status-power relations may dispose either to social order or disorder, as will be seen below.

Reference Groups

The position of status-power theory with respect to the other party in the interaction setting is in the tradition of Weber ([1922] 1947): "Action is social in so far as, by virtue of the subjective meaning attached to it ... it takes account of the behavior of others and is thereby oriented in its course" (p. 88); and of Mead (1934), where symbolic interaction allows the actor to project in mind a probable response of the other actor and thereby to select his or her own action to elicit a desired response from the other. The question now is *which* other(s)? Whose reaction is being estimated, projected or being counted on? Parsons (1951) offered one kind of answer in his paradigmatic model of interaction in a role: "[T]here is a set of expectations relative to the contingently probable reactions of others. These will be called 'sanctions'.... The relation between role-expectations and sanctions is then clearly reciprocal. What are sanctions to ego are role-expectations to alter and vice versa" (p. 38). This focuses attention entirely on the dyad where the interaction takes place. Status-power theory introduces additional others who are also concerned with the individual's conduct. Taken together, the whole set of interested parties are the individual's *reference group*.[3]

Initially, reference groups were defined as those individuals or collectivities with whom an individual compared the favorability of his or her outcomes (Hyman 1942). Salary? How much were others in the same job earning? Politics? How were others in the community voting? Kemper (1968) extended the reference group concept to include "normative groups." These are groups that prescribe what to do in the interaction setting. This would ordinarily

---

[3] Merton (1957, pp. 368–84) proposed the concept of "role set," which included the institutionalized set of other actors with interests in the given role, for example, in the doctor-patient relationship, the role set would include the nurse, pharmacist, physical therapist, social worker, and so on. As used here, reference groups include any actors with interests bearing on the focal encounter, whether or not they are normally considered part of the Mertonian role-set.

include the interaction partner, but also include any parties interested in the outcome of the interaction. For example, a coworker might expect one to collude in a dubious transaction involving a customer; one's spouse, also a normative reference group, might support such an action, while a religious mentor might not. For the purposes of understanding motivation for acting to engender or to violate social order, reference groups must be taken into account. I turn now to a typology of social order based on the foregoing.

TYPES OF SOCIAL ORDER

From the status-power point of view, the highest level of social order is present when each actor's behavior is understandable as authentic status-conferral to the other actor. This is most likely to occur in love relations, which are by definition the ultimate in status-conferral (Kemper 2006, 2011) and which may include what can be called "faux disorder," as for example, when a parent spanks a child who consistently runs into the street despite many parental injunctions not to do so. The parent is clearly exercising power, but only in the highest interest of the child, conferring ultimate status – that is, preserving the child's life. However, love relations, especially of the romantic kind – the usual launching pad for marriage in Western societies – have a built-in incongruity. They feel so good that they engender dependence on the source of the good feeling. But dependence, as Emerson (1962) has strongly argued (see earlier) institutes power, not only by giving the non- or less-dependent party leverage over the interaction partner,[4] but also instigating the dependent party to use power to gain what he or she is dependent on (see Kemper 2006, 2011).

A second level of social order is where actors are at cross-purposes in regard to technical activity, but are committed to a status-power based agreement on procedures for resolving the difference. This may include an appeal to expert opinion ("What does the operating manual say?"), arbitration (a willingness to abide by the results dictated by impartial judges), selection via ballot ("Let's put it to a vote"). The important consideration here is that, despite disagreement and being on the verge of disorder, the parties mutually accept a formula for use of a mechanism to prevent disorder. This resolution is akin to the idea of the legitimacy that underlies authority, as defined in status-power terms. There, authority is understood as a status-grant to another, conferring on that other the right to use power, even against oneself, in defined circumstances. For example, citizenship in the United States generally entails the right of the Federal government to penalize tax-evaders (including oneself). This is approximately the Hobbesian type of social order, which Hobbes's out-of-control

---

[4] This has sometimes been referred to as the law of the least dependent lover. It was put in the following way by poet Charles Baudelaire ([1947] 2006): "[E]ven when two lovers love passionately and are full of mutual desire, one of the two will always be cooler or less self-abandoned than the other. He or she is the surgeon or executioner; the other, the patient or victim" (p. 33).

actors presumably arrive at after recognizing the deficits of the "nasty, brutish and short" state of nature. They give up the liberty to act as they please to a sovereign who has authority to keep them from depredations against others. This second level of social order allows for disagreement, but keeps disorder within bounds through institutionalized procedures to prevent deterioration into a pure power mode of order.

A third level of social order is when actors relate to each other exclusively through power. Such order as exists is entirely imposed by the power of each actor, as in the case where a stronger individual forces a weaker one into a regular pattern of compliance or where one country defeats another in a war and imposes a conqueror's administration on it. These cases differ from the Hobbesian solution of sovereign authority in that the dominant party has no authority and thereby legitimacy, operating only through open coercion or threat of coercion. Because there is order, though imposed through power, this is also not the equivalent of Hobbes's state of nature.

STATUS AND REFERENCE GROUP MECHANISMS
FOR SOCIAL ORDER

Axiomatically, actors seek compliance with their wishes from other actors. As detailed above, this can be done in two ways: The first is through evoking status-conferral via accomplishments of technical activity in the division of labor (bringing meat to the village, weaving a blanket, ministering to the sick). Although this requires effort and sometimes long preparation (through apprenticeship or formal education), it has the virtue of being relatively safe. One is ordinarily not putting oneself at risk. And when there is risk, there is frequently a bonus (in status) for doing so. On the principle that a loss is experienced as being more costly than an equivalent amount of gain (Kahneman 2011), individuals in general opt for this safe method of gaining their wishes, namely through earning status from others. The second method of gaining compliance is through coercion, with its unpredictabilities and dangers. Most of the time, most individuals prefer the safer method of obtaining compliance.

The advantages for social order of using safe methods are clear. By its nature, status-accord is a provenance of order. If order is a state of mutually acceptable accommodation to what is to be done, status relations inherently accomplish that. The one who confers status is interested in being beneficial to the object of his or her concern. If it becomes apparent that one's efforts at status conferral are misguided or are not accomplishing their intention to be of benefit to the other, there is a strong pull toward rectification and realignment so that the intended recipient of status is manifestly pleased or will soon be so. Because it is desirable to receive status, the recipient is likely to be aligned with the giver and read the conduct directed toward him or her as done with good intentions.

This is eventually true even in cases of what may called "faux disorder," as discussed above.

Reference Group Support for Social Order

In catering to the interests of their immediate interaction partners, actors give status and expect to receive it in return. The actual situation may involve technical activity, for example, handing a requested tool to a coworker, but the fact that the tool was handed over as requested, reflects compliance with the wishes of the actor who made the request, and since compliance is voluntary, is a fragment of status-conferral. The actors here may not think of what they are doing in relational terms, but analytically they are engaged in maintaining social order via the logic of status relations. Harmonious interaction, as just described, ramifies onward, as, armed with status derived from one sphere, actors are more likely to acquiesce to the interests of other interaction partners (Isen and Levin 1972), thus extending the domain in which cooperative relations prevail (see also Collins 2004). The obverse of this is that actors are also motivated to avoid negative sanctions from interaction partners, thus contributing to the same cooperative outcome.

Reference groups other than the immediate interaction partners play an important role here, whether to support social order or disrupt it. An actor may suppress a rebellious or otherwise deviant act not because he or she fears the negative sanctions of the immediate interaction partner, but to avoid the negative sanctions of a reference group that is not on the scene. For example, one resists telling the boss to "go to hell," not because one does not want to encounter the boss's outraged response, but because one does not want to incur the disappointment or wrath (both of these entail reduction in status) of one's spouse, who is anxious about the finances of the family. Or, one encounters a beggar and, while the first impulse is to hurry on without giving alms, one stops because of a reference group command implanted long ago to assist the needy. The approval of that reference group is likely to be far more important than any possible expression of gratitude from the beggar.

Reference groups may also foster disorder, as when they instigate behavior that challenges the traditional expectations of interaction partners. At times this can be a portal to civil war, as was the case in the battle over slavery and states' rights in the United States in the 1860s; but also can be the threshold of great social advances, as when reference groups support new ideas that overthrow conventional thinking, for example, in the case of the gender revolution in the United States beginning in the 1960s.

EMOTIONS AND SOCIAL ORDER

One of the most valuable derivations from the status-power model of social relations is a theory of emotions. The fundamental postulate here is that a large class of human emotions results from outcomes of social interaction as understood in status-power terms (Kemper 1978, 2006). Emotions may dispose either toward order or disorder in social life. Emotions provide the motivational push and the bodily disposition required for the "action readiness" (Frijda 2007) to cope with the ramifications of the interaction outcomes. In status-power theory, interaction outcomes include: (1) increase or expected maintenance of own status level; (2) loss of or unexpected failure to maintain or increase own status level; (3) increase or maintenance of other's status level; (4) loss of or unexpected failure by other to maintain or increase his or her status level; (5) increase or expected maintenance of own power level; (6) loss of or unexpected failure to maintain or increase own power level; (7) increase or maintenance of other's power level; (8) loss of or unexpected failure by other to maintain or increase his or her power level. Because each actor (in a dyad) has both a status and power standing, he or she will necessarily experience four of these outcomes, corresponding to own and other's status and power positions. For example, a possible set of outcomes for a given actor might include numbers 1, 3, 5, and 8 or numbers 2, 4, 5, and 7 and so on.

In general, gain or expected maintenance of status leads to satisfaction-happiness or, more specifically, pride (if the outcome was due to particular efforts of one's own, that is, one is the agent) and gratitude (if the outcome was due to the efforts of another party). Loss of status or unexpected failure to maintain status leads to anger (when the other is the agent of this outcome), shame (when one is oneself the agent) and/or sadness-depression (when the loss is irremediable). Gain or maintenance of status by other leads to own satisfaction-happiness (if one likes the other)[5] and the upset of equanimity we can call dissatisfaction-unhappiness and envy (if one dislikes the other). Loss or expected failure to maintain status by other leads to sympathy or dissatisfaction-unhappiness (if one likes the other) and to *Schadenfreude* or satisfaction-happiness (if one dislikes the other). In general, gain or expected maintenance of own power leads to satisfaction-happiness and a sense of security. Loss or unexpected failure to maintain own power level leads to fear-anxiety. Gain or unexpected maintenance of power by other leads to fear-anxiety (if one does not trust[6] the other) and to satisfaction-happiness (if one trusts the other). Loss or unexpected failure to maintain power by other leads to satisfaction-happiness and security (if one does not trust the other) and dissatisfaction-unhappiness (if one trusts the other). Several of these emotions affect the state of social order.

---

[5] Liking/disliking depends on whether the other party is according sufficient status and is low in power use against oneself (Kemper 1978).
[6] Trust is the feeling that, though one is making oneself vulnerable, for example, through disclosure of personal matters, the other party will not use power against oneself.

Emotions Favoring Social Order

Pride. Doing a "good job" ordinarily evokes status conferral from others, which in turn elicits the emotion of pride (satisfaction-happiness): "I *did* it!" If others are according status for the doing of the work, it is more or less certain that this is what they had expected and wanted, meaning that the effort upholds social order. Pride is an organismic confirmation of this.

Shame. When one fails to perform at a level for which one has claimed status, that is, one does not deserve the status one is being given, one is subject to feeling shame, a distinctly unpleasant emotion. In most cases, the sense that an action will evoke shame prevents the performance of the act. Thus, shame is a preemptive guardian of the social order and, if the shame-inducing action was committed, a motivation to engage in reparative conduct is frequently initiated (Goffman [1956] 1967; Kemper 1978).

Guilt. Guilt also protects the social order, but on different grounds from shame. Whereas shame is related to the failure to confirm one's status-deservingness, guilt emerges from the sense of having used an excess of power. Whether thoughtlessly or intentionally, whether by action or inaction, one has harmed another actor. Guilt is the distinctly unpleasant organismic response and bids for expiation of the fault through some kind of punishment (Kemper 1978). Because relationships are constituted by both status and power dimensions, one can feel both shame and guilt in respect to any interaction episode: shame for being unworthy and guilt for having harmed or hurt another. As with shame, guilt can operate prospectively and prevent action that would lead to disruption of social order.[7]

Fear-Anxiety. Hobbes believed that a sovereign with power exceeding the power of all members of society, was necessary to preserve social order. Disruption would be curtailed by fear of the punishment meted out by the supervening authority. And, indeed, such is widely the case. We often uphold social convention or order because we fear the consequences of deviation from the rule (which concretizes the order). We do not jaywalk, cheat on our taxes and murder someone who torments us, not necessarily because we believe that these acts are wrong in the given circumstances, but because we fear the punishment (power) that would likely follow.

But fear-anxiety, which upholds social order when we desist from disruptive action because we want to avoid punishment, also can uphold social order when the party experiencing the fear is prepared to make concessions to preserve social order, though in a revised status-power format. Barbalet (1998) argues that political elites who fear uprisings from lower orders sometimes acknowledge the growing status and power of the lower groups by accepting

---

[7] Although shame and guilt tend to preserve social order, they may also serve to upset order by reflecting a "higher" social order, as dictated by reference groups other than the immediate interaction partner. For example, conscientious objectors would likely suffer shame and/or guilt were they *not* to take a stand against performing violence.

their demands, in such manner pacifying them and maintaining social order, though changed in form.

Another type of fear felt by those with normally higher social standing and power is status anxiety. This is a fear of reduction of the status standing of one's own group through the rise in standing of lower groups. Hofstadter (1955) has traced the status-anxiety of traditional, local elites in post–Civil War America as new, national elites based on industry and commerce emerged to dominate the social landscape. The status-anxious lent their strength to the Progressive party, hoping thereby to retain a social order in which only their own traits would provide the basis for authentic status conferral. We may refer also to the status revolutions of more recent times, in which the status-anxieties of white males are reflected in electoral support for a conservative politics that supports a version of social order in which previous elites (of race and gender) regain their superior standing (New York Times 2014).

Optimism. Optimism, which can vary from high to low, is an emotion based on a "subjective estimate of probable success or failure" (Kemper 2011, p. 237) founded on past status-power experience. Those whose optimism is high are likely to be motivated to preserve the existing pattern of social order (or to keep changing it in ways favorable to themselves in status-power terms). Sometimes this is undertaken in circumstances that are not prima facie encouraging. Those who succeed in political forays against the odds are often pleased to announce that "the system worked," thus confirming the wisdom of a method of contestation that followed the rules of the existing social order, for example, the U.S. Senate hearings and their denouement of a presidential resignation in the matter of the Watergate break-in (see Alexander 1984).

Contempt. This emotion, linked to anger, is directed against status claimants who are thought not to have the credentials to make their claims, for example, the aristocracy responding to bourgeoisie claims for equal privileges or the bourgeoisie rejecting the status claims of the proletariat. Contempt accompanies the denial of such claims and, when expressed, informs the upstarts that their claims are viewed as factitious, impudent, and otherwise unworthy.

Emotions Favoring Disorder

Sadness/Depression. Sadness/depression, resulting from an irremediable loss of status (often the loss of an interaction partner, through death or abandonment; or through defeat in a status-power contest), leads frequently to a withdrawal from interaction and thus at least a temporary disorder. Such withdrawal may lead also to calming and pacification of an otherwise roiled social situation by leaving the field to the victor. When grieving is carried on excessively, according to the norms allowing such absence from responsibility, sadness/depression operates to breach social order (see Parsons 1951 on the "sick role").

Anger. Anger and its important cognate, envy, are prime emotional bases for disorder. Resulting from a sense of inadequate status conferral, anger often leads to coping behavior that is directly oppositional and contrary to existing structures of social relations, for example, by coups, revolutions, or other power grabs. Where the interaction partner is capable of strong retaliatory power, anger may operate covertly and proceed through sabotage, slander, and other devious means directed against the reigning order, but avoiding the consequences of open warfare.

When intense emotions have fostered social disorder, recovery may be achieved through two forms of social relations: (1) large amounts of status conferral to parties that were deprived of status in previous interactions; and (2) a minimum of power exercised against those who previously deprived others of status. The Truth and Reconciliation commission that has worked so well to recover social order in previously apartheid South Africa has achieved exactly this: It has assured status-conferral to the Black population through recognition of their earlier deprived state. At the same time, these commissions have not been punitive toward the White perpetrators of the deprivation. This rare, ideal state of social relations, overriding motives of vengeance, was made possible in part through accepting the directive, that is, conferring status, of charismatic Black leader Nelson Mandela.

SOCIAL DISORDER

Social disorder, as described by Hobbes, and social disorder as described by Parsons, are not the same. Hobbes's state of nature is strictly a case of unceasing predatory (power) relations. No rule or restraint governs actors in their efforts to satisfy their preferences and no one intentionally gives anything to anyone else voluntarily as status. Parsons's (1951) social disorder is not recognizably so extreme nor as violent. Parsons does entertain the idea of a "complete breakdown of normative order," which he labels "anomie" (p. 39), but in his view this is "never descriptive of a concrete social system" (p. 39). This seems to be true by definition, since a social system, qua system, would necessarily entail some degree of order. But more to the point, Parsons's disorder, a consequence of a failure to have values in common, resembles more the breakdown of communications and cooperation in the biblical story of the Tower of Babel. Indeed, in that tale, there was a common value, namely to build the tower to scale the heights of heaven, thus satisfying Parsons's main requirement for social order; but the workers shared no language in common, hence could not accomplish the technical activity together.

For Parsons (1951), social integration (i.e., order) via common values solved the "Hobbesian problem of order." But how common need the values be? Must all individuals agree on all values? This is not likely to be the case, nor is it even desirable, as Durkheim ([1895] 1982) argued, counterintuitively, about the normality of crime, which is a sure sign of disorder. If all agreed on what constituted crime and wished to extirpate it, the major crimes would be eliminated only to have lesser social deviances targeted in their wake, until, finally, not an iota of difference from any agreed-upon practice would be permissible. Disaster would follow, since contingencies always arise that require novel (ergo deviant) solutions. There is, thus, a built-in necessity for some social disorder by virtue of the need to preserve order. To his credit, Parsons (1951, pp. 16–17) recognized that perfect consensus cannot be obtained.

Thus, we may expect that even in ordered social settings there will be divergences and disagreement. One hyper-important social arena that is rife with contestation is science or the pursuit of knowledge, that is, how to think about technical activity at the highest level of abstraction. Collins (1998) argues that in the field of philosophy, a non-empirical cognate of science (Parsons 1951, p. 329), disagreement is the nourishing fire that tempers all arguments. The powers of reason and, in science, of empiricism, are the weapons with which thinkers contest the terrain. The frontiers of knowledge are perpetually a scene of disagreement and disorder. Order slowly emerges as thinkers come to adopt one or another strain of thought. Not that all thinkers are convinced by the new arguments, compelled by logic and/or empiricism. Rather, as mordantly proposed by Max Planck (see Kuhn 1962, p. 151), and with as much cynicism as truth, adherents of the older point of view die off and leave the field to younger thinkers who are not as committed to the conventional ideas of the day.

Although disagreement over the details of technical activity in philosophy and science has sometimes led to physical violence (Collins 1998), verbal turmoil is the usual mode of disputation in these domains. In other arenas, status-power conflicts are not so (relatively) irenic. Physical injury, murder and warfare are the frequent sequels to real or imagined disjunctions in status and power. The culture of honor, in which a status-slight leads to a duel, is a strongly-regulated social device intended to preserve order when the status injury could easily devolve into a family, clan or societal feud (see Wyatt-Brown 1982; Cohen et al. 1996).

On the border between how much status is claimed and how much status is conferred there is huge potential for disorder. The quotidian experience of many individuals is that others frequently don't confer enough status or reject or ignore the individuals' status claims entirely. Goffman (1959) proposed that status claims are customarily sanctioned as part of the "working consensus" (a version of social order) but he was likely being overly optimistic about this. In much of social life status availability is determined by those who have the power to enforce such determinations. This is especially true in occupational life, where the boss almost always has the final word. Bosses, with their attentions turned upward to their own superiors, are often indifferent or ignore opportunities to award status to their subordinates. A large part of people's daily "hassles" stem from the lack of status conferral both from those above and those below them (Kanner, Coyne, Schaeffer and Lazarus 1981). Except under conditions of authoritarian enforcement, the consequences of inadequate status-conferral almost always tend toward disorder: a slackness in following orders, implementing directives, and a search to avoid effort and responsibility. Though most social settings are to a large degree orderly on the surface, a steady hum of discontent, with the potential for disorder, may also be heard.

MICRO-MACRO LINKAGE TO MAINTAIN SOCIAL ORDER

Individuals relate directly to each other at a micro-level, but they are ordinarily encompassed by wider meso- and macro-orders. The labor force is almost entirely within the wraps of such arrangements via employment in organizations. As soon as there is hierarchy, meaning at least one level of authority, individuals in the context are connected with at least a meso-order, namely, the organization itself. The setting may be a simple local business, but that business is part of the economic structure of the community and anyone working in that business is likewise in connection with the community-at-large. The setting may be a national or multi-national corporation with thousands of employees spread over a wide geographic area. By its very existence and daily operations, it imposes its order over a wide swath of the society and any single employee participates in the enactment of that order. That the organization is a bureaucracy in the Weber ([1922] 1946) sense, a formalized edifice of technical activity and status-power relations, means that it is a frontline defense against social disorder. What needs to be done and how and whom to obey are in the house manual. This removes significant cognitive problems that might otherwise stand in the way of social order ("What shall I do? Whom shall I obey?") But bureaucracy has also been indicted for the blandness of modern life, its "mechanized petrifaction" (Weber [1904–1905] 1958, p. 182). This seems to be an intimation of a degree of regulation that restricts the free-play of reference groups external to the immediate interaction setting. Reference groups often bring to attention alternative solutions to problems of technical activity. And these creative moments can be immensely rewarding to individuals fortunate enough to have them. That is, the reference groups that promote novel solutions are lavish with status-accord when their urgings are adopted to create a new social order.

Correlatively, legal institutions are expressly designed to define and defend the social order. They follow specific technical procedures for the creation of law, via legislative bodies or through executive fiat. They include enforcement divisions that prosecute violators of what has been legitimately created as law. Most importantly, they serve in civil law as arbiters of status claims (as Durkheim [1893] 1964 argued) and as monitors of new power coalitions, so that it becomes costly for individuals or collectivities to oppose the existing order. Yet, usually under power stress from mobilized groups that threaten disorder, law changes to accommodate the demands of the groups with the ability to destroy order. What was legal one day is illegal the next or vice versa, the changes compelled by power to prevent major disorder.

Conclusion

Based on the status-power approach to social relations, status conferral is the ideal method for establishing social order. In this mode, individuals and coalitions of individuals voluntarily act to realize the wishes, interests and concerns of others and this leads to harmonious and cooperative relations with them, that is, social order. When authentic status relations prevail, misunderstandings or agreements that threaten social order are usually resolved via procedures either accepted beforehand by the parties concerned or arranged ad hoc in a spirit of trust. Democratic societies in general aim for such peaceful means to resolve disputes via constitutions or other declarations of status rights. When status conferral is at an extremely high level, we call it love and moments of mutual recognition of each other's love is one of the peaks of human experience (see Kemper 1978, 2006). Ironically, the very desirability of such moments leads to dependence for them on the other person. And as soon as there is dependence, there is as Emerson (1962) argued, power. The emergence of power is doubly sourced: first, the one who is dependent is subject to the power of the other. But the one who is dependent also exerts power, often passive-aggressively, to obtain what he or she is dependent for. Power, however, is coercion and coercion is neither status-conferral nor love. The reality thus seems to be that humans can attain moments of the highest community or social order, but these are only moments. Those who have experienced the full flush of love for another person – practically everyone has – know that the intoxicated feeling lasts only for a short while. (Skeptics have scoffed that twenty minutes is a lot.) The status-power approach to social relations thus allows for social order to the highest degree while also recognizing that social order is complicit in its own undoing. This argues for a level of social order that is only partial: good intentions toward others marbled with institutionalized mechanisms for resolving the unavoidable dependencies and social relational contretemps that are openings to social disorder.

REFERENCES

Alexander, Jeffrey. 1984. "Three Models of Culture and Society Relations: Toward an Analysis of Watergate." *Sociological Theory* 2: 290–314.
    2011. *Performance and Power*. Cambridge, UK: Polity Press.
Barbalet, Jack. 1998. *Emotion, Social Theory, and Social Structure: A Macrosociological Approach*. Cambridge: Cambridge University Press.
Baudelaire, Charles. [1947] 2006. *Intimate Journals*. Translated by Christopher Isherwood. New York: Dover.
Carter, Launor F. 1954. "Evaluating the Performance of Individual Members of Small Groups." *Personnel Psychology* 7: 477–84.
Cleve, Felix M. 1969. *The Giants of Pre-Socratic Greek Philosophy: An Attempt to Reconstruct their Thought, Vol. 2*. The Hague: Martinus Nijhoff.

Cohen, Dov, Richard E. Nisbett, Brian F. Bowdle, and Norbert Schwarz. 1996. "Insult, Aggression and the Southern Culture of Honor: An 'Experimental Ethnography'." *Journal of Personality and Social Psychology* 70: 945–60.

Collins, Randall. 1975. *Conflict Sociology: Toward and Explanatory Science.* New York: Academic Press.

1998. *The Sociology of Philosophies.* Cambridge, MA: Harvard University Press.

2004. *Interaction Ritual Chains.* Princeton, NJ: Princeton University Press.

Durkheim, Emile. [1893] 1964. *The Division of Labor in Society.* New York: Free Press.

[1895] 1982. *The Rules of Sociological Method.* New York: Simon and Schuster.

[1912] 1965. *The Elementary Forms of the Religious Life.* New York: Free Press.

Emerson, Richard. 1962. "Power-Dependence Relations." *American Sociological Review* 27: 31–40.

Frijda, Nico. 2007. *The Laws of Emotion.* Hillsdale, NJ: Erlbaum.

Freud, Sigmund. [1937] 1959. "Analysis Terminable and Interminable." Pp. 316–67 in *Collected* Papers, Vol. V, edited by Ernest Jones and translated by Joan Riviere. New York: Basic Books.

Goffman, Erving. [1956] 1967. *Interaction Ritual: Essays on Face-to-Face Behavior.* Garden City, NY: Doubleday and Company.

1959. *The Presentation of Self in Everyday Life.* Garden City, NY: Doubleday.

Hamblin, Robert, and Carol R. Smith. 1966. "Values, Status and Professors." *Sociometry* 29: 183–96.

Hechter, Michael, and Christine Horne. 2003. *Theories of Social Order: A Reader.* Stanford, CA: Stanford University Press.

Heise, David R. 1979. *Understanding Events: Affect and the Construction of Social Action.* New York: Cambridge University Press.

Hertenstein, Matthew. 2010. "Tactile Stimulation. Pp. 1469–1471 in Sam Goldstein and Jack A. Naglieri (Eds.), *Encyclopedia of Child Behavior and Development.* New York: Springer.

Hertenstein, Matthew, Rachel Holmes, Margaret McCullough, and Dacher Keltner. 2009. "The Communication of Emotion Via Touch." *Emotion* 9: 566–73.

Hobbes, Thomas. [1651] 1968. *Leviathan.* New York: Penguin.

Hofstadter, Richard. 1955. *The Age of Reform.* New York: Vintage Books.

Hyman, Herbert. 1942. "The Psychology of Status." *Archives of Psychology* 269: 1–94.

Isen, Alice M., and Paula F. Levin. 1972. "Effect of Feeling Good on Helping: Cookies and Kindness." *Journal of Personality and Social Psychology* 21: 384–8.

Kahneman, Daniel. 2011. *Thinking, Fast and Slow.* New York: Farrar, Giroux and Strauss.

Kanner, Allan D., James C. Coyne, Catherine Schaefer, and Richard S. Lazarus. 1981. "Correlation of Two Modes of Stress Measurement: Daily Hassles and Uplifts versus Major Life Events." *Journal of Behavioral Medicine,* 4: 1–39.

Kemper, Theodore D. 1968. "Reference Groups, Socialization and Achievement." *American Sociological Review* 33: 31–45.

1978. *A Social Interactional Theory of Emotions.* New York: Wiley.

1992. "Freedom and Justice: The Macro-Modes of Social Relations." *World Futures* 35: 141–62.

2006. "Power and Status and the Power-Status Theory of Emotions." Pp. 87–113 in *The Handbook of the Sociology of Emotions,* edited by Jan E. Stets and Jonathan H. Turner. New York: Springer.

2011. *Status, Power and Ritual Interaction: A Relational Reading of Durkheim, Goffman and Collins*. Farnam, UK: Ashgate.

Kemper, Theodore D. and Randall Collins. 1990. "Dimensions of Microinteraction." *American Journal of Sociology* 96: 32–68.

Kuhn, Thomas F. 1962. *The Structure of Scientific Revolutions*. Chicago: University of Chicago Press.

Mead, George H. 1934. *Mind, Self and Society*. Chicago: University of Chicago Press.

Merton, Robert K. 1957. *Social Theory and Social Structure, Revised and Enlarged Edition*. Glencoe, IL: Free Press.

New York Times. 2014. "Democrats Try Wooing One Who Got Away: White Men." March 3, p. A1.

Orum, Anthony, and John G. Dale. 2009. *Political Sociology: Power and Participation in the Modern World*. 5th ed. New York: Oxford University Press.

Osgood, Charles E., George J. Suci, and Percy H. Tannenbaum. 1957. *The Measurement of Meaning*. Urbana: University of Illinois Press.

Parsons, Talcott. 1937. *The Structure of Social Action*. Glencoe, IL: Free Press.

1951. *The Social System*. Glencoe, IL: Free Press.

Spitz, Rene A. 1945. "Hospitalism – An Inquiry into the Genesis of Psychiatric Conditions in Early Childhood." *Psychoanalytic Study of the Child* 1: 53–74.

Weber, Max. [1904–1905] 1958. *The Protestant Ethic and the Spirit of Capitalism*. New York: Charles Scribner.

[1922] 1946. "Class, Status and Party." Pp. 180–96 in Max Weber, *From Max Weber: Essays in Sociology*. Translated by H. Gerth and C. W. Mills. New York: Oxford University Press.

[1922] 1947. *The Theory of Social and Economic Organization*. Translated by A. M. Henderson and Talcott Parsons. New York: Oxford University Press.

White, Geoffrey M. 1980. "Conceptual Universals in Interpersonal Language." *American Anthropologist* 82: 759–81.

Wyatt-Brown, Bertram. 1982. *Southern Honor: Ethics and Behavior in the Old South*. New York: Oxford University Press.

12

Interaction Order

The Making of Social Facts

Anne Warfield Rawls

Abstract

The worry that a loss of tradition will lead to chaos in modernity has been a preoccupation since the 1800s. In 1893 Durkheim championed the idea that new forms of social practice were developing in modernity that could produce coherence, morality and solidarity in the absence of tradition. The Interaction Order approach developed by Garfinkel, Goffman and Sacks develops Durkheim's idea, treating social facts – like self, identity and social objects – as made through cooperative social actions that do not depend on tradition. The cooperation and reciprocity required for social fact making replace tradition as the foundation of social coherence in modernity. The result is a post individualist post utilitarian approach that challenges conventional assumptions about the coherence of modern life. The work of these three scholars taken together comprises a comprehensive contemporary approach that completes the challenge to individualism (naturalism) and utilitarianism launched by Durkheim, changes epistemological (how we know) and ontological (how things exist) questions and exposes worries about chaos in modernity as artifacts of the individualist approach.

INTRODUCTION

The contemporary Interaction Order approach, initiated by Garfinkel, Goffman, and Sacks, is an important advance in social theory that breaks down barriers to discovery through detailed observation of "social facts." It takes up Durkheim's proposal to replace individual centered approaches with a focus on the making of social facts. In doing so it overcomes epistemological limitations of individualist and naturalist approaches and reveals a strong cooperative and moral center to modern social life. Those hypothetical individuals, pictured as rational and utilitarian from birth, that populate other theories, are replaced by social selves that need to cooperate in interaction with others to create and sustain self, reason, sense, and value. The result is an innovative approach that locates coherence in the order properties of social practices in modern social contexts. The idea that chaos results when traditions and beliefs erode is replaced by studies of the coherence and stability created by mutual cooperation in situated interaction.

The discovery that interaction orders have performative criteria that are constitutive of the existence of social facts establishes that cooperative actions that meet these criteria can create social things. "Constitutive" order properties are those that make a thing recognizable as a particular thing (e.g., presentational properties that make "Agnes" a "woman"; Vehicle Identification Numbers (VIN) that make a vehicle a "car"; sequential preference orders that make an utterance a "greeting").[1] Sets of such order properties taken together comprise interaction orders (of a queue, a neighborhood, a classroom). The resulting view of society is dynamic rather than static, emergent rather than causal. Social order is moral (in a social contract sense) rather than utilitarian; Social change is no longer problematic, and the assumption that concepts frame the limits of understanding is overcome: Meaning is created through use, rather than limiting use. The observational character of the approach, which treats the order properties it discovers as actual building blocks of meaningful social action, without reducing meaning to "codes" or "concepts," enables the discovery of new forms of social order and new theoretical implications (Van Maanen et al 2007).[2]

The theme of this chapter is that the line of argument proposing social fact making processes as the order phenomenon on which social science should focus is consistent from Durkheim, through Parsons to Garfinkel, Goffman, and Sacks. Although much neglected, the epistemological innovation Durkheim introduced – treating social practices as creating human reason ("categories of the understanding") – is a transforming idea (Durkheim [1912] 1995; Rawls 1996, 2004). Created cooperatively, social facts are not like natural facts and cannot be accounted for by analyzing individual beliefs, perceptions, or actions. The actions that create social facts are defined by shared performative criteria and hence are inherently collective. Their study demands a new approach. Research on interaction order processes of social fact making examines the mutual collaboration that creates social facts in the situated interactions of modernity.

---

[1] See Rawls, Mann, and Jeffrey (2014) for discussion of constitutive properties of car, receipt and library book and Garfinkel 1967 for a discussion of Agnes. Early versions of this Interaction Order argument appeared in Rawls (1987, 1990).

[2] The prevalent idea that all data are conceptual and therefore that theory must come before method is an artifact of the individualist perspective inspired by Comte [1844] 2009, Spencer 1851 and Giddings [1894] 1912. If meaning is a collaborative production then it is not either conceptual or individual in the first instance. The empirical collaboration that produces meaning is data that can be inspected independently of theory to discover how mutually intelligible meaning is being cooperatively achieved.

The main difference between Durkheim's classical position and the Interaction Order approach lies in the degree of detail the cooperative making of social facts has been found to involve, the omnipresent character of the process, and the limits imposed on social interaction and social institutions by the need for reciprocity as a background condition. In Durkheim's view the viability of modernity rested on whether the constitutive practices of science and occupations are free from the constraints of belief and authority so that they can "self-organize." Because this requires reciprocity, participants need to be free and equal. Therefore, a need for justice becomes a force for change in modernity.

Garfinkel (referring to himself as "Working out Durkheim's Aphorism") expanded on the argument, setting out to demonstrate that all meaningful social objects have constitutive properties whether the situation is formal or informal, the reasoning ordinary or scientific. His research documented both the pervasiveness of constitutive practices and the "justice" requirement and underlying commitment to cooperation (which he called Trust conditions). Goffman (also drawing on Durkheim) elaborated the "ritual" and "sacred" character of performed and mutually constituted self, maintaining that the fragility of such a self requires constant performative work and mutual regard. Sacks, working with both Garfinkel and Goffman, extended the inquiry to the omnipresent and orderly character of constitutive aspects of communication. On the basis of their research it can be argued that constitutive practices and the cooperation and reciprocity that sustain them stand at the center of modern social life.

Durkheim's original intent had been twofold: first, to reorient social science toward processes of social fact making and away from individual reason – utilitarian and naturalist thinking; and, second to distinguish the order properties of modernity from those of traditional society. He proposed two sets of constitutive resources: a traditional set based on ritual and belief, and, another that "self-organizes" on the basis of order properties that vary by situation. He considered a scientific reorientation toward modern "self-organizing" practices of social fact making to be a practical necessity because the success of democracy and scientific progress will depend on supporting the role played by constitutive practices in a rapidly changing world.

Misinterpreted in various ways Durkheim's innovation was neutralized in the early Twentieth Century such that these important ideas did not resurface until Garfinkel and Goffman became popular in the 1960s. In the 1930s Parsons (1938) had attempted to revive Durkheim as an antidote to what he called the "proto-sociology" of his day; still based on individualism and still treating social objects as if they were natural. Although he succeeded in popularizing Durkheim, Parsons did not manage to reorient social science toward processes of social fact making. While studying at Harvard with Parsons in 1946 Garfinkel took up the challenge, arguing that a focus on empirical properties of the back and forth character of interactional exchange was required to bring social fact making into view. By 1949 Goffman had initiated his exploration of the "dramaturgical" properties of presentational self, focusing on reciprocities of exchange between self and other. In 1959 they were joined in this endeavor by Harvey Sacks who would focus on communication as an exchange system in which meaning is created through a mutual coordination of order properties that can be documented and specified.

Their approach challenges the naturalist (and positivist) assumption that objects and individuals just exist – overcoming the epistemological limits of naturalism (Rawls 1998). It challenges the popular idea that social facts consist of patterns of social action routinized over time (habits, mores, folkways), or institutionalized as constraints on social action (values, goals, beliefs). Popular concerns that erosion of social institutions and shared values in modernity will produce chaos are transformed. Since constitutive orders are the primary resource for achieving order in contemporary situations – chaos occurs immediately when constitutive requirements of interaction orders are violated (Rawls and David 2006) – rather than slowly as traditional institutions and values break down. Worry that constitutive practices are instrumental and lead to a loss of morality is shown to be misplaced.

Interaction orders are essentially cooperative and go hand in hand with moral commitment. Even instrumental action requires an underlying commitment to reciprocity. This finding reinforces Durkheim's claim that justice becomes increasingly necessary as societies modernize. Garfinkel referred to requirements for constitutive social fact making as "Trust" conditions. These are expectations about a practice and the commitment of participants to it that are necessary to achieve reciprocity and make meaningful objects together: Violating these conditions, he argued, results in "meaninglessness."[3] Goffman maintained that a tacit agreement between participants to a set of expectations – a "Working Consensus" involving mutual respect for one another's face and the situation – is required to achieve self as a performed social fact: In its absence the little universes of interaction in which we live out our lives can be shattered and selves destroyed. Sacks documented pervasive "listening and hearing obligations" enacted as orders of "preference" in conversation. In so doing he achieved an elaboration of social order and reciprocity obligations at an unprecedented level of empirical detail. His influence

---

[3] The reciprocity carditions underlying Garfinkel's Trust argument appear first in the 1946 paper discussed here in the formulation of necessary reciprocities (page 1). They become clearer in Garfinkel's discussion of "the Red" as a social object in 1947 – a research program which involved recorded materials. They are outlined again in the 1948 manuscript (2006). The first experiments were done in 1949 after Garfinkel purchased his own recording equipment. Those experiments are the primary data for his PhD dissertation (1952). The first presentation of the Trust argument was at sociological meetings in 1952. There was a version in 1956 that was also presented at sociology meetings. The argument was finally published as a paper in 1963. The final published version appeared in *Studies* in 1967.

on the idea that sequential resources for social fact making are pervasive has been profound.

Because, on the Interaction Order view, social facts – objects, social "things" – only exist when constitutive criteria for their existence have been adequately performed and confirmed by others, their order properties are witnessable and can be studied directly. This has enabled the approach to make its mark through observational research. Constitutive practices have been documented as "resources" used to make sense and social facts across many types of situation. For instance, the preference for treating a lack of response (silence) by the other as a request for clarification (or repair) is consistently used as a resource by people to make sense of machine responses. When machines are not programmed to observe (orient) this preference, however, it can lead to confusion (i.e., when a person treats a machine "pause" as a prompt for clarification). The role of such resources is increasingly impacting studies in many fields, including Science and Technology Studies (STS), Work, Social Psychology, Robotics, Computer Supported Cooperative Work (CSCW), Sociology and Communication. Lucy Suchman's ([1986] 2007) research on human machine interaction has been particularly important in popularizing the essential role such resources play in technical worksites (Orlikowski 2007, Rawls 2008, 2015).[4] Chuck Goodwin (1994), Christian Heath and Paul Luff (2000), Luff, Hindmarsh, and Heath (2000), Doug Maynard (2003), Mike Lynch (1997), Lorenza Mondada (2013), Stivers, Mondada, and Steensig (2011), Weick (1989), and others around the world are generating an increasingly extensive cumulative body of findings.

This chapter explores the early development of the Interaction Order approach. Garfinkel initiated a first iteration in 1946, proposing that Action Theory focus on those interactional processes through which mutually intelligible "Things" or "Objects" are cooperatively made in situations characterized by mutual regard (by 1962 Garfinkel's approach was known as Ethnomethodology); Goffman's elaboration of presentational aspects of "Self" and the obligations and limits the cooperation required by the process imposes on social institutions and interaction, comprises a second iteration; Sacks' findings with regard to constitutive orders of "Talk" and the research in Conversation Analysis (CA) it inspired comprise a third iteration documenting the detailed character and pervasiveness of constitutive orders. Although it is not well known, the three worked closely together for a number of years (1959–1964) and had important students and co-researchers in common. While the interactional "resources" documented by their combined research have become a research standard across many fields, their contribution to social theory has been obscured by the tendency to consider their work separately. It is important to recognize their contributions to a single coherent theoretical innovation.

---

[4] Suchman's (2007) chapter 7 presents a good summary discussion of these conversational resources.

FIRST ITERATION: GARFINKEL'S RESPECIFICATION OF
SOCIAL ACTION THEORY

While Garfinkel became famous in 1967 after the publication of *Studies in Ethnomethodology,* he initiated the contemporary interest in interaction orders of social fact making more than two decades earlier in the 1940s. At North Carolina, where he completed his MA in 1942, Garfinkel produced several empirical studies of accounting practices (1941, 1942). His war research (for the Army 1942–1946) involved detailed studies of social facts and practices (labeling sick-soldiers, relating leadership to constitutive practices, and pilot training, among them). But, it was when he arrived at Harvard just after WWII that he began to theoretically formulate the collaborative making of social objects. In a spring 1947 paper titled "The Red as an Ideal Object," Garfinkel ([1947] 2012) analyzed a social object – "The Red" (communist) – that was becoming important in American society after the war as fear of Stalinist Russia mounted. For most of the rest of his career Garfinkel would focus on interactional processes of making social objects in sciences, occupations and everyday life (pulsars, maps, queues).

The clearest statement of the relationship between his position and social theory appears in an unpublished paper on action theory written his first semester as a PhD student at Harvard in fall 1946. Titled "Some Reflections on Action Theory and the Theory of Social Systems," the paper succinctly outlined problems with approaches to social action characteristic of Florian Znaniecki and W. I. Thomas, on the one hand, and Talcott Parsons, on the other. Garfinkel proposed to respecify Parsons' Action Theory so that it was consistent with processes of social fact making.[5]

According to Garfinkel, interactionism and social action theory had both made two fundamental mistakes. First, they took the perspective of the actor when, as Garfinkel (1946: 1) says, "actual social action always involves the responses of the other, the actor's anticipation and evaluation of the other's response, and the actor's interpretation of what the other anticipates about what the actor anticipates about that response etc."[6] Focusing on the actor, instead of on what occurs between actors, has the result that approaches claiming to focus on interaction actually leave interaction out. The beliefs, attitudes and experiences of actors are allowed to stand in for what occurs between actors such that interactional processes are lost. The second mistake is that they lack a theory of the object. If objects are social facts and not natural objects then their created social character must be provided for. Garfinkel

[5] Garfinkel continued to work out this respecification of Parsons in seminars and manuscripts over the years titled "Parsons' Primer." These lectures explore Parsons for his relevance to the question of constitutive practices. The comments on interactionism are relevant to Znaniecki and Thomas whose work Garfinkel studied at North Carolina with Howard Odum. He considered Znaniecki's (1936) book *Social Actions* an important theoretical work.
[6] This is an early version of what Garfinkel would later elaborate as Trust conditions.

proposed that social objects stand in relation to the action frame in the same way as "identified actors" in social roles. Like the actor, the object has a role in the action frame; an identity that must be achieved ("library" book, "wedding" dress). Like the actor, objects and actions are situated in particular action frameworks – so the situation of an object in a particular action frame matters. But the tendency – then and now – is to treat social objects as if they are the same objects across action frames. Garfinkel argued that a theory of social objects that situates them in action frames and explains how they are achieved through interactional processes that involve mutual reciprocity, would correct these two mistakes.

In addition to these mistakes Garfinkel identified three foundational assumptions that had set research off in the wrong direction. The first assumption – involving the problem of meaning – posits the existence of invariant categories and assumes that language (communication) just works. The second treats social objects and action as existents instead of recognizing their status as meant objects that require being created. Most of the problems social theory has had, Garfinkel maintains, are artifacts of these two unexamined assumptions. The third assumption, that social change and motivation pose central theoretical problems, Garfinkel treats as an artifact of the first two assumptions. Change *is* a problem for a theory of action which assumes that meaning relies on invariant categories, consensus, or epistemic objects. Motivation is similarly problematic for a social theory that assumes order is merely a trend or pattern across many individual actions reflecting how they are influenced by social factors (beliefs, values, attitudes). By contrast, interaction orders are inherently orderly in each immediate instance, and within them configurations of objects and categories change constantly without problem. Furthermore, as Garfinkel notes, the need to use constitutive orders of practice to make sense together supplies everyone's primary motivation.

Garfinkel's (1946: 8) proposal was to fix action theory by "backing off a little so as to bring into view not only our original actor, but the fellow he was tangling with." This would put the focus on interaction itself; on the making of recognizable objects by persons for one another (and expose the constitutive rules involved). The action frame would also include the objects the actor treats in their "role" in the frame (i.e., "car" vs. "police car" while driving). Thus, the action frame indicates for "things" all that it indicates when applied to actors: identity, obligation, and so on. Garfinkel points out that it is characteristic of human actors that they hold others in mutual regard and persist in doing so. The experiences of a single actor are continually returned to them via the mutual regard of the others (and objects) with whom they stand in a relationship of mutual orientation. Social action theory as proposed by Garfinkel is a theory of the structures (or rules) of action that hold not only between people but also between people and objects in action frames. He (1946: 8) refers to the action frame as "an elementary social system."

Garfinkel's approach to these issues did not change essentially over the years – although his documentation of interaction orders became more detailed when his appreciation of the importance of the finely ordered details of interaction increased after he and Sacks began working together on telephone calls to the Suicide Prevention Center in the early 1960s. His later work can be seen as the adequate theory of social objects he argued for in 1946 – if we allow that "theory" includes the concrete specifications and contingencies that he understood are constitutive of social objects.

Garfinkel's approach to social objects as situated is a particularly important innovation. Objects for Garfinkel are always constituted as objects from a position of mutual regard within a situated social frame of reference. They do not just exist – they mean. Furthermore, an object "means" (not exists) along several different dimensions. According to Garfinkel (1946: 5) "What in effect the framework does for the actor is to define a finite province of meaning within which any given object acquires its particular significance for action." The object cannot be specified independently of, or disentangled from, the situated action/practice (Lynch 1997). This idea has become particularly important in understanding technical worksites (Orlikowski 2007).

Orders of interaction were initially introduced by Garfinkel as "logics" of action. "These transformations of object references," he (1946: 7) says, "proceed according to certain logics or rules." The plural is intentional here. Logics are situated like selves and objects. An early version of what he later called a "member's method" ("ethno-method"), a situated logic is shared by participants in ("members" of) a practice. They use it to make meaning together in that practice. There are many "logics of action." "Thus," according to Garfinkel (1946: 7) "we have the logic of rational discourse; the logic of expressional action; or the action of various pathological states; of free association; and so on." There are also logics of various orders of social relationship. Garfinkel (like Durkheim) is challenging the Kantian idea that logic is apriori and universal (Kant 1783). That idea is so prevalent, he says (1946: 7), that "once we get beyond the barriers that Kant set for us, we find a field that is practically unexplored." What member's logics as situated matters might be is uncharted territory that Garfinkel explores in developing his social theory of objects. It is a theory grounded in the empirical details of the constitutive logics of making those objects.

Overlooking the constitutive character of logics and objects and focusing instead on motivation has confounded the question of how change is possible, Garfinkel says, because in a motivation based schema "sameness" is achieved by orienting shared values. This requires conformity. In an interaction order, by contrast, what is required is that each object be constituted recognizably. If meant objects can be collaboratively constituted through constitutive practices there are no constraints on what motivations they can serve. The combinatorial possibilities are endless and the problem of change – innovation – is no longer an issue.

For Garfinkel we are each for the other a constituted object living our lives orienting others orienting us. Actors not only take each other into account, but persist in doing so, he (1946: 8) says, "until huge conglomerations of actors in an infinitude of permutations and combinations are busily occupied taking each other into account." There is a great deal of detail, cooperation and reciprocity going on: Glossing it as interaction in a general sense, while taking an observer's perspective on a single actor makes it look like chaos.

The apparent chaos is an artifact of the approach. The theorist who makes these problematic assumptions, he says, will seek out "regularities of interaction" and "invariant facts common to any situation of action" by going to the "people" involved in those actions. But, Garfinkel (1946: 9) maintains that what we need to know is "what the communicative process consists of." Therefore, to the extent that we make the assumption that communication works we solve the problem by fiat and fail to discover the social processes at the center of the issue.

Everything meaningful, from objects and words to society, Garfinkel (1946: 10) argues, is an accomplishment through cooperative action: "a society is defined not according to matters of fact, but matters of meaning; it is a creature of rules ..." His treatment of rules in terms of constitutive expectations grounds his entire position. It is how such expectations play out in constitutive orders of interaction and talk that creates meaning and stability in society.

SECOND ITERATION INTERACTION ORDERS OF SELF

Completing his MA and PhD degrees at the University of Chicago (1949 and 1953) Goffman (1956) wrote *The Presentation of Self in Everyday Life,* on the basis of his dissertation research in the Shetland Islands (between 1949 and1951). While Garfinkel had argued that the self should be treated as a social object – an "identified self" – in 1946 and again in 1948 ([1948] 2006), it was Goffman who developed and popularized the argument that the social self is presentational, depending on mutual collaboration in constitutive orders of interaction. Although he was at Chicago working with Everett Hughes and Lloyd Warner, Goffman also kept in touch with graduate students at Harvard and read copies of their seminar papers (including Garfinkel's) which were circulated in mimeograph. He maintained a working relationship with Garfinkel from at least 1953 (when Garfinkel went to Chicago to work on the Jury project).

In Goffman's view face-to-face interaction is organized around the presentation and protection of selves, and the protection of the interaction order on which that process depends. The fragile presentational character of the social self and the cooperative order it requires is a powerful constraint on the organization of social action – both formal and informal. A high degree of recognizable order is required. Through successive explorations of situated aspects of the process of creating self, Goffman further developed the ideas of "frames" and "identified self" that Garfinkel had outlined.

In *The Presentation of Self* Goffman introduced the idea that an *actual social agreement* – a "working consensus" – is necessary as the constitutive basis for the coherence of everyday social objects, like queues (lines) and selves. Goffman's argument that a working agreement is necessary as a constitutive prerequisite rests on his conception of the self as a constitutive achievement of and in interaction. Any changes to the conception of self and interaction that treat them as having more *resilience,* a built in *stability* over time, or as depending *less* on mutual reciprocity, would render the working agreement optional. The key is that both the self and its capacity to communicate through action are fragile matters. It is this *fragility* that explains *everything* and on which the Interaction Order argument hinges. Only if self and the meaning of action must be continually constituted and reconstituted in and through orders of interaction, will something be required to make this birthing, maintaining and dying of selves and meaning possible: some consistency in the way sounds and gestures are orchestrated that makes them recognizable as "moves" of a particular sort to other participants along with an underlying agreement that guarantees participants are extended "benefit of the doubt" when problems arise.

For Goffman ([1956] 1959: 253) the social self is the product of a scene, "a dramaturgical effect arising diffusely from a scene that is presented." Both in its capacity as performer and as performed, the self ultimately depends on interaction. While the character performed is a product of each interaction, the performer is a product of many interactions: "For a complete man to be expressed," he says (1967: 84–85), "individuals must hold hands in a chain of ceremony.... While it may be true that the individual has a unique self all his own, evidence of this possession is thoroughly a product of joint ceremonial labor." Goffman (1967: 19) maintained that face is "a sacred thing," and that "the expressive order required to sustain it is therefore a ritual one."

The mutual obligations Goffman ([1956] 1959: 10) referred to as a "working consensus" are generated by the requirements of reproducing self through its relations to other selves in interaction. These mutual obligations are a constitutive condition for both interaction and presentation of self. "Participation in any contact with others is a commitment," Goffman (1967: 6) says, "an involvement in the face of others that is as immediate and spontaneous as the involvement he has in his own face." An agreement or social contract is necessary because of the fragile nature of the interaction and the self. The constant threat of annihilation hangs over both: "When an incident occurs and spontaneous involvement is threatened, then reality is threatened" (1967: 135). It is spontaneous and cooperative involvement that creates social reality. Consequently for Goffman (1961: 81) "To be awkward or unkempt, to talk or move wrongly, is to be a dangerous giant, a destroyer of worlds." We live in many such worlds and possible identities and definitions of the situation can conflict. Thus, the individual can never be secure in an encounter. There is always the possibility that a discrepancy between their projected "front" and characteristics relevant to a conflicting identity, or situation, will be revealed. It is therefore, not only moral, but prudent to act in accordance with the working consensus.

On this view, persons ignorant of their future status in an interaction, enter into an agreement to accept at face value the "front" of all participants, thus protecting all positions they themselves might come to occupy. They must accept outward signs as evidence of mutual commitment. Persons who fulfill their interactional obligations are presumed to respect their moral obligations as well. Participants in interaction must therefore be constantly on the lookout for displays of commitment to and/or disregard for constitutive obligations. According to Goffman (1967: 11) "A state where everyone temporarily accepts everyone else's lines is established. This kind of mutual acceptance seems to be a basic structural feature of interaction, especially the interaction of face-to-face talk." The ability to take action depends on information about the character and intention of others; information that is acquired by attending to interactional displays of how each stands in relation to their respective moral/interactional obligations.

The dependence of self and interaction on mutual commitment to "involvement obligations" places constraints on formal social institutions as well. These constraints arise directly from the requirements of creating self and sustaining mutuality through constitutive orders of practice, not from social structure, class relations, or culture. Institutions that don't respect basic requirements for self and sensemaking destroy the "human materials" entrusted to them. Goffman explored the limits this imposes on total-institutions in *Asylums* (1961) (the research for which was done at St. Elizabeth's in Maryland 1954–1958). In that work he detailed exceptions to institutional rules he argued were necessary to sustain order and make possible the selves of inmates and attendants alike. Researchers have found similar dilemmas in prisons and other total-institutions (James Jacobs 1977, Larry Weider 1974, Gresham Sykes 1958).

It is because interaction involves contingency and risk that cooperation is necessary and the tacit agreement holds. What is at risk is of enormous consequence. The very existence of the social person and their ability to make sense with and of others is at stake. There is a risk that others will not ratify the self; a risk that one's actions and interpretations will be at fault and damage others, the situation, or oneself; a risk that the essential interaction order on which everything, including *individual self-interest,* depends could be damaged by actions that destroy mutual understanding of the particular constitutive order we happen to be involved in at the moment; and, so on ... The agreement manages and neutralizes these risks.

Research on conversation that documents the constitutive character of turn-taking preference orders, and their orientation toward an underlying working agreement, demonstrates Goffman's point. That Goffman criticized Sacks and Schegloff in *Forms of Talk* does not alter the essential compatibility between their positions on interaction orders. Sacks shared Garfinkel's commitment to a constitutive approach to meaning that Goffman did not accept. But, the difference is mainly that Goffman's position is partial; focused on self and action, while reserving a fundamental logic for concepts and symbols; while the other two treated all social facts, including logic and the meaning of concepts and symbols, as constituted in interaction.

THIRD ITERATION: SEQUENTIAL ORDERS OF MEANING AS SOCIAL FACT

Harvey Sacks, in pioneering what is known as Conversation Analysis, produced a third iteration of the interaction order position. After taking a Law degree at Yale in 1959 he spent the fall semester at Harvard on a law fellowship where he met Garfinkel and Goffman, both at Harvard that same year. While there the three discussed their ideas and collaborated with Parsons on his "Response to Dubin on Pattern Variables" (1960). Sacks subsequently went to Berkeley to study for his PhD in sociology with Goffman. He also traveled frequently to Los Angeles to work with Garfinkel who facilitated research at The Suicide Prevention Center (through Edwin Shneidman) that provided the telephone call data for Sacks' dissertation. Garfinkel and Sacks worked closely together on this project producing several co-authored papers. Sacks' lectures at UCLA from 1964 to 1975 were transcribed by Gail Jefferson and after earning international acclaim were published posthumously as *Lectures in Conversation* (1992).

Building on Garfinkel's approach to social objects and Goffman's presentational self, Sacks documented interaction order properties of talk. Although often treated as a purely empirical study of the sequential turn-taking orders involved in making mutually intelligible meaning in conversation, the body of research inspired by Sacks develops essentially the same theoretical perspective as Garfinkel and Goffman. Sacks pursued the problem Garfinkel had identified as the first problematic assumption – how communication works. The findings of Conversation Analysis detail constitutive interaction orders of language and communication. Conversational preference orders (rules) are not arbitrary – they orient Goffman's "benefit of the doubt preference" and Garfinkel's "Trust" conditions. Preferences for self-correction and agreement are face saving. The orientation toward saving face (and giving benefit of the doubt) results in a layering of preferences which can be very roughly summarized as follows: (1) Try to treat a problem as a mishearing; (2) In the face of a problem that is not fixable as a mishearing, first allow the other to self-correct, and only then initiate a correction; (3) Initiate a joke as a face saving move if the first two procedures don't work; and (4) Only after the first three procedures fail, or information suggests they will fail, treat the persistence of a problem as evidence of incompetence or failure to attend mutual obligations. The fourth and least preferred move abandons mutual reciprocity with immediate negative consequences for both the social self and the interaction order.

The preferences for self-correction, mitigated disagreement, and positive assessment elaborated in the "Turn-Taking Paper" by Sacks, Schegloff and Jefferson (1974), by Alene Terasaki in her work on "pre-announcements" ([1982] 2004) and by Anita Pomerantz in her work on "second assessments" (1975) involve issues like who has an obligation to tell whom about what, and when, and how these obligations should be displayed sequentially through turns. For instance, if good friends talked yesterday, there is a preference that if one of them had big news they would have told that news and good friends will not have to hear it secondhand from someone else later. If they do get the information secondhand later it is grounds not only for complaint but for reassessing the relationship. In recorded conversations speakers have been documented displaying their understanding of this obligation through management of sequential and turn-taking preference orders.

However, the idea of turn-taking did something more important than giving empirical detail to arguments made by Garfinkel and Goffman. It initiated a line of research documenting the use of communicational resources across many different situations that has given CA research an independent life. The properties of conversational resources are in some ways constant, while in other ways tied not only to particular types of situation, but to position within a situation or sequence. Who is obligated to speak and how they can decline the obligation, who can elect to speak and how they can indicate that, and an infinitude of other order issues are made evident through displays of orientation toward a turn-taking system (Sacks, Schegloff, and Jefferson 1974). Turn-by-turn, utterances achieve meaning through order properties of turn-taking and membership categorization (meaning achieved through indicating category membership rather than word definition: "gender" – *man*, woman; "family" – *man*, woman, child; "species" – *man*, beast). Through their use of these order properties participants make sense together, while at the same time demonstrating their commitment to the interaction order in play in any given situation, and the relationship between identified selves in that situation, move-by-move.

In speaking, participants tell stories, issue invitations and ask questions. They assess, confirm or indicate through silence, or repeat, that they do not understand. All of these "moves" indicate to a listener what kinds of attending they are being asked to do. Stories can project long turns and ask listeners to wait. Silences may ask listeners to do something right away (to clarify, or repair understanding). Each "turn-type" has characteristic markers that listeners are expected to attend to. Each imposes obligations on listeners that are different from obligations imposed by other turn types. Questions ask for answers, silences for corrections, "pre-invitations" (like "are you busy later?") for an "all clear" to go ahead and make an invitation, or an indication that an invitation should not be issued. Moves can be declined – but they must be declined recognizably. This mutual work is not only sensemaking, but also face saving. Problematic interactions can be avoided and competence and attention to working consensus and trust conditions preserved.

While there are characteristic sequential markers that can be associated with each turn type, criteria for their recognition cannot be pre-specified in the way approaches like John Searle's (1969) *Speech Act Theory* and Jurgen Habermas's (1984) *Theory of Communicative Action* have attempted. In building sequential meaning, position can override "type" criteria. As Schegloff (1980) argued, a "question" is only sometimes a question. Identity issues can override, as can object/identity/situation issues (i.e., If the police officer who stops me is my husband can he give me a ticket?). Each turn needs to be achieved in situ, built from one turn to the next, oriented to sequence sensitivities and identity issues, while maintaining and displaying mutual attention and reciprocity. These considerations are constitutive of what any particular act of speech (turn at talk) will be seen by other participants to have been doing. As with Garfinkel's theory of objects, the response of the other, the response to that response, and the response to that, and so on, are each in turn constitutive of the meaning that will turn out to have been achieved ("You were speeding I have to give you a ticket." To husband, "You wouldn't dare!).

The back and forth mutually confirming character of interaction that results is a solution to the problem of interpretation. Participants never need to achieve the adequacy of social objects on a first move. A response and a response to that response are always expected. It is through the back and forth exchange of turns that certainty is achieved and it can go on until it is achieved. Orienting a set of constitutive expectations on an initial move is only a first step. Jefferson's (1972) work on "side-sequences" documents the rarity of talk that needs to take a kind of "time out" for clarification before an initial turn or turns are completed.

In addition to turn-taking orders Sacks showed how membership categorization devices and pre-formatted utterances can carry institutionalized social relations into interaction. In some instances membership categories offer a device for sorting out word meaning as in Sacks famous illustration "the baby cried the mommy picked it up" for which he argued that the relevant membership category "mommy/baby" (in the absence of a contrary indication) would suggest that the mommy is the mommy of the baby and not some other mommy. In other cases the effect of membership categorization devices (e.g., "lowriders" – low-riding cars) can be to introduce inequalities into interaction that align speakers by enacting sets of persons who are not us: lowriders being strongly identified with Hispanic ethnicity in California at the time. In the case of formatted utterances like "May I help you?," by contrast, which appeared as a conversation opener by workers answering calls to the Suicide Prevention Center, the effect can be to normalize a conversation that is not in any way ordinary by invoking an ordinary service encounter, thus increasing the chances that participants remain calm and oriented toward their interactional obligations. In the case of callers expressing a wish to commit suicide this is an important achievement. The preference orders that continue to be documented by researchers add detail to the understanding of how these obligations are manifested in ordered features of talk.

As with the order properties of self and social objects elaborated by Goffman and Garfinkel, the constitutive practices of turn-taking and preference orders, elaborated by Sacks, work only insofar as a working agreement about such practices is actually maintained. Constant displays of that commitment must be performed. These displays must be adequate to the order properties participants will need to manage: giving everyone the information needed for next moves. Furthermore, the agreement provides for practices to be extended and amended. Participants have many conversational resources for remedying "troubles" and confusions as they come up in talk and order is typically maintained in spite of trouble. Garfinkel gave names to some of the ways people can carry interaction forward without destroying it. His elaborations of "etcetera clause," "ad hocing," "instruction" and "praxelogical validity" and research by Sacks and others on repair, side-sequences, jokes, the delivery of "bad news" and "troubles talk" demonstrate some of the order properties involved in handling ongoing contingencies.

RELEVANCE OF THE INTERACTION ORDER
APPROACH TO MODERNITY

The Interaction Order approach is essential to understanding modern life because it does not treat order and coherence as depending on traditional social relations (and beliefs and values) that break down in modernity. Instead, it treats the meaningful character of self and objects as a result of order properties of social action that are cooperatively enacted in specific situations. Meaning must be manifest in actual orders: If there is no recognizable order there is no meaning. To continue conceiving of order in traditional ways, Durkheim argued, not only courts the appearance of chaos – but creates actual chaos. Because social science plays an essential role in policy, education and planning, a social science that does not reflect the actual changes in forms of sociality that have occurred can itself be a source of chaos in modernity. Scientific progress, the development of modern occupations and democratic public life all suffer. By contrast, a social science that documents the order properties that are constitutive of meaning, and elaborates their underlying prerequisites, establishes the requirements for order and coherence in a diverse modern democratic public.

One result is a new appreciation for the importance of cooperation and tacit mutual commitment. The various iterations of the Interaction Order position all posit an underlying commitment to equality, mutual protection and reciprocity as a functional prerequisite for making social facts. Whereas most social thinkers since Hobbes (1642) have treated the social contract embodied in formal institutions and law as the source of social order and mutual protection, the Interaction Order perspective treats social contract as embedded in the constitutive prerequisites for meaningful social interaction.

The biggest threat of chaos in modernity on this view comes from conditions that prevent the required reciprocity and cooperation; the threat is not weakening beliefs and values, but rather beliefs and values that stand in the way of public reciprocity (e.g., beliefs about class, race, gender, or religious superiority). This constitutes a major transformation in perspective, suggesting that democratic society depends less on "top-down" imposition of democratic institutions and values and more on "bottom-up" development, of what Durkheim called "self-organizing" practices, through mutuality and reciprocity in work, science and public life. The new job of formal structures is to "translate" the constitutive practices that emerge from below, and support the justice and equality they require, not to "impose" order from above.

The theoretical innovation is important. The most prevalent approaches to social science, referred to by Parsons as "proto-sociology," posit an individual whose reason and self-awareness are givens – although influenced by social forces – and posit objects that exist independently of cooperative work. Morality is then reduced to beliefs and values layered on top of basic social processes. Conceived as such morality is relative to particular social institutions and/or cultures. Social order then consists of patterns to be searched for across large aggregates of individual action, not in actual ordered properties exhibited by each meaningful action. Research tends to be evaluated according to how generalizable it is and existing theory is treated as defining the research object: a problematic circularity (see footnote 2).

The Interaction Order approach advances social theory by freeing both theory and method from the constraints of these theoretical assumptions. Documenting the constitutive parameters (order properties) of social facts respecifies the social action question. The research results are actually more precise and more broadly applicable than conventional research that focuses on generalizable results. Morality is relocated to tacit commitments to reciprocity and cooperation that undergird everything. Taken together the Interaction Order line of argument from Garfinkel through Sacks proposes a conception of constitutive order in which cooperation is a basic necessity. The result looks something like a series of games with rules; but with unspecified and incomplete rules and incomplete information (completed through mutual feedback) and not one but many games which can change rapidly.

This social arena is inhabited by acting selves whose identities are embedded in the constitutive practices ("game"), and whose ability to make sense together is made possible by their mutual orientation to multiple layers of constitutive practice, background expectations, and a social agreement or contract. The job of participants is fundamentally cooperative: to constantly display the kind of move they are making, the practice they are in, and their commitment to it; to follow the displays of others as they make moves and/or change games (practices); and to display their own attention to and interpretation of the moves of others. To paraphrase Garfinkel, we get a conglomeration of people attending others attending them: a small social universe.

The approach reorients social science toward the fundamental character of collective social processes, cooperation and fair play and away from the particular values, attitudes and motives of individuals. One might even say that these collective practices are culture. In fact, the original title of the first chapter of Garfinkel's *Studies in Ethnomethodology* was "The Discovery of Culture." The relevant question, Garfinkel maintained, was "How" people manage to pursue shared goals in ways that make the meaning of their actions evident to others, not "Why." The resources used to make meaning and social facts cooperatively, comprise the culture of a place and its participants. The failure to take up this question of "How" meaning is made, and to do so with actual interaction in view, has obscured the Interaction Order resources that all of us use every day, while also obscuring its theoretical and moral implications.

CONCLUSION

While Durkheim's position on social facts and constitutive practices initiated a focus on social fact making it was Garfinkel, Goffman, and Sacks who demonstrated that Interaction Orders are involved in producing the meaningful things and selves of modern life. In modern public spaces when we face a city sidewalk, a queue in a coffee shop, or enter into a conversation with a stranger, we come face to face with "stuff" that we must make enough sense of to take an appropriate next move without recourse to abstract belief systems or institutionalized ritual. How we treat "it" transforms that stuff into meaningful social action and objects (or fails to do so). A "top-down" approach doesn't help much. Knowing that people queue up in coffee shops in New York City, or that one is in a deli, is information, but, it doesn't tell you just *How* this particular queue is organized, or *How* one makes an "order" in this deli. Furthermore, one can collaborate in the local order without knowing what kind of a deli or queue it is. What is needed is only the information necessary to make an appropriate next move. Discerning general "patterns" in behavior (as they might be related to attitudes or motivation – "that person is in a hurry") is not relevant to the task of making an appropriate next move. One needs to know what constitutive practices the person is using so as to effectively "get out of the way." The constitutive expectations of "this place" and how participants are committed to those expectations are what we need to orient. What are others doing move-by-move as those moves relate to the local order of service? "What do I need to do *exactly* to get coffee in this place?" As Goffman ([1956] 1959: 1) said in the opening lines of *The Presentation of Self*:

When an individual enters the presence of others, they commonly seek to acquire information about him.... Information about the individual helps define the situation, enabling others to know in advance what he will expect of them and what they may expect of him. Informed in these ways, the others will know how best to act in order to call forth a desired response from him.

To make enough sense to take an appropriate next move one needs to get information from the actions of others. Similarly, others need information from you. Social coherence requires information and information processing. Participants display their roles through their actions – who is serving vs waiting in line. One can listen and hear that others are ordering by number. Or having begun an order be redirected – "You want a number 3?" Participants display their commitment to the ongoing order through their actions. Others in the situation may adjust their actions to display order properties of the situation more obviously to someone who witnessably does not know what they are doing: A person in a queue might move subtly into a more explicit position to display that someone has misunderstood the properties of that particular queue. Such displays can be read as instructions. Try doing what others are doing. But if you miss a detail and get it wrong they will instruct you. The subtleties are face saving. When it works the cooperation and public display of mutual regard is a modern democratic public working on the ground.

Durkheim argued that such constitutive orders are necessary in modern societies. Their ability to cross group boundaries, to free thought from tradition, and the moral demands they exert on society are the foundation of modern Democratic social life. The Interaction Order approach to social facts, not as "instituted" but as "constituted" through mutual cooperation in local "Interaction Order" practices (Goffman 1983), against a background of constitutive "Trust" requirements (Garfinkel 1963) with constant attention paid to "listening and hearing obligations" of sequential orders (Sacks 1964) shows how social order in complex and diversified modern contexts is accomplished through constitutive practices. Misunderstanding the social fact position that explains this possibility has left social theory with the idea that modernity brings chaos, or the alternative that we are imprisoned in structure. In neither case is the potential for constitutive practices to free thought and action from traditional constraints appreciated.

Interaction Orders are liberating. We are not imprisoned in structure. Rather, we are bound together through our own actions in a huge cooperative undertaking to make social facts together that requires mutual attention, reciprocity, and equality. Morality in Interaction Order terms is tied to the enduring needs of sense and selves presenting to and with others, enacting sequences of practice in differentiated interactional publics, hoping and needing to achieve mutual understanding. Such orders are inherently moral and push society toward greater justice and equality. Social order conceived of in more conventional terms is not moral in this sense even though we typically refer to its expectations as "morals," "norms," and "values." Such values are relative and represent institutionalized inequalities.

The pivotal position of interaction orders in modern democratic publics demands attention to their requirements. Chaos in modernity will come not from the failure of traditional values, structures and beliefs – but, rather, from their failure to defer to constitutive practices and their prerequisites: the failure to promote the development of constitutive practices that are open to all, whose coherence can be achieved without recourse to traditional structures.

Most social theories today retain the problems Garfinkel outlined in 1946, exhibiting continued allegiance to what Parsons (1938) called "proto-sociology" (Comte [1844] 2009; Spencer (1851); Giddings [1894] 1912; and Sumner (1906)). In spite of its innovative character, and Parsons' effort to resurrect it, Durkheim's social fact challenge to the individualism, naturalism and utilitarianism of the earlier theoretical tradition has not been widely embraced. What most scholars mean by interaction still does not include actual interaction, because action and experience are still considered from the actor's point of view; the problem of meaning is still largely taken for granted; no adequate theory of the object or of social facts has been generally accepted; motivation (attitudes, beliefs, values) is still generally considered causal; and, change is still considered a problem. It is telling that while Goffman is widely acknowledged to have been one of the most important social thinkers of the twentieth century it is generally believed that he had few followers. Conversation analysis is typically considered atheoretical, while Garfinkel's approach (Ethnomethodology) is treated as a method with its own peculiar objectives. Recognizing the similarities between the three bodies of work, their grounding in the theoretical impetus to document social fact making (which traces back to Durkheim), and coming to terms with the original collaborative character of the research, restores coherence to the combined enterprise and clarifies the importance of the contribution.

REFERENCES

Comte, August. [1844] 2009. *A General View of Positivism.* Cambridge: Cambridge University Press.
Durkheim, Émile. [1893] 1933 *The Division of Labor in Society.* Chicago: Free Press.
    [1912] 1995. *The Elementary Forms of the Religious Life.* Chicago: Free Press.
Garfinkel, Harold. 1940. "Color Trouble." *Opportunity,* May, 144–51. Reprinted in Edward J. O'Brien (ed.), *The Best Short Stories of 1941: The Yearbook of the American Short Story.* Boston: Haughton Mifflin.
    1946. "Some Reflections on Action Theory and the Theory of Social Systems," Unpublished Graduate Essay, Harvard University.
    [1947] 2012. "The Red as an Ideal Object. Etnografia a Ricerca Qualitativa 1/2012.
    [1948] 2006. *Seeing Sociologically: The Routine Grounds of Social Action.* Boulder, CO: Paradigm Publishers.
    1963. "A Conception of and Experiments with "Trust" as a Condition of Stable Concerted Actions." In Harvey, O.J. (ed), *Motivation and Social Interaction,* 187–238. New York: Ronald Press.
    1967. *Studies in Ethnomethodology.* Boulder, CO: Prentice-Hall: New Jersey.

Giddings, Franklin. [1894] 2012. *The Theory of Sociology*. Forgotten Books Classic Reprints.

Goffman, Erving. [1956] 1959. *The Presentation of Self in Everyday Life*. Chicago: Free Press.

1961. *Asylums*. New York: Doubleday Anchor.

1967. *Interaction Ritual*. New York: Doubleday Anchor.

1981. *Forms of Talk*. Philadelphia: University of Pennsylvania Press.

1983. "The Interaction Order." *American Sociological Review* 48: 1–17.

Goodwin, Chuck. 1994. "Professional Vision." *American Anthropologist* 96(3): 606–33.

Habermas, Jurgen. [1981] 1984. *Theory of Communicative Action: Volume One*. Boston: Beacon Press.

Heath, Christian and P. Luff. 2000. *Technology in Action*. Cambridge: Cambridge University Press.

Hobbes, Thomas. 1642. *De Cive*. Originally published in Latin in Paris in 1642. First English translation London, Printed by J.C. for R. Royston, at the Angel in Ivie-Lane. 1651.

Jacobs, James. 1977. *Stateville: The Penitentiary in Mass Society*. University of Chicago Press.

Jefferson, Gail. 1972. "Side Sequences." In David Sudnow (Ed), *Studies in Social Interaction* (pp. 294–33). New York: Free Press.

Kant, Emmanuel. 1783. *Prolegomena to any Future Metaphysics*.

Luff, Paul, J. Hindmarsh, and C. Heath. 2000. *Workplace Studies: Recovering Work Practice and Informing System Design*. Cambridge: Cambridge University Press.

Lynch, Michael. 1997. *Scientific Practice and Ordinary Action: Ethnomethodology and Social Studies of Science*. Cambridge: Cambridge University Press.

Maynard, Doug. 2003. *Bad News Good News: Conversational Order in Everyday Talk and Clinical Settings*. Chicago: University of Chicago Press.

Mondada, Lorenza. 2013. "Displaying, Contesting, and Negotiating Epistemic Authorities in Social Interaction." *Discourse Studies* 15: 597–626.

Orlikowski, Wanda. 2007. "Sociomaterial Practices: Exploring Technology at Work." *Organization Studies* 28: 1435–48.

Pomerantz, Anita. 1975. "Second Assessments." Unpublished Ph.D. Dissertation, UCLA.

Parsons, Talcott. 1938. "The Role of Theory in Social Research." *American Sociological Review* 3(1): 13–20.

1960. "Response to Dubin on Pattern Variables." *American Sociological Review* 25(4): 467–83.

Rawls, Anne. 1987. "The Interaction Order Sui Generis: Goffman's Contribution to Social Theory." *Sociological Theory* 5(2): 136–49.

1990. "Emergent Sociality: A Dialectic of Commitment and Order." *Symbolic Interaction* 13(1): 63–82. (French Trans in *The Mauss Review* 2002 Number 19).

1996. "Durkheim's Epistemology: The Neglected Argument." *American Journal of Sociology* 102(2): 430–82.

1998. "Durkheim's Challenge to Philosophy: Human Reason as a Product of Enacted Social Practice." *American Journal of Sociology* 104(3): 887–901.

2004. *Epistemology and Practice: Durkheim's The Elementary Forms of Religious Life*. Cambridge: Cambridge University Press.

2008. "Harold Garfinkel, Ethnomethodology and Workplace Studies." *Organization Studies* 29(5): 701–32.

2012. "Durkheim's Theory of Modernity: Self-Regulating Practices as Constitutive Orders of Social & Moral Facts," *Journal of Classical Sociology* 12(3).

Rawls, Anne, and Gary David. 2006. "Accountably Other: Trust, Reciprocity and Exclusion in a Context of Situated Practice." *Human Studies* 28(4): 469–97.

Rawls, Anne, Dave Mann, and Adam Jeffrey. 2013. "Locating the Modern Sacred." *The Journal of Classical Sociology*, first published on November 18, 2013.

Rawls, Anne and David Mann. 2015. "Getting Information Systems to Interact: The Social Fact Character of "Object" Clarity as a Factor in Designing Information Systems". *The Information Society*. 31:2, 175–192.

Sacks, Harvey. 1992, 1995. *Lectures on Conversation* (Vols. 1–2), Oxford: Blackwell.

Sacks, H., E. Schegloff, and G. Jefferson. 1974. "A Simplest Systematics for the Organization of Turn-Taking in Conversation." *Language* 504: 696–735.

Schegloff, Emmanuel. 1980. "Preliminaries to Preliminaries: 'Can I ask you a Question?'" *Sociological Inquiry* 50(3–4): 104–52.

Searle, John. 1969. *Speech Acts: An Essay in the Philosophy of Language*. Cambridge: Cambridge University Press.

Spencer, Herbert. 1851. *Social Statics: Or, The Conditions Essential to Human Happiness Specified, and the First of Them Developed*. London: John Chapman.

Stivers, T., L. Mondada, and J. Steensig, eds. 2011. *Knowledge and Morality in Conversation. Rights, Responsibilities and Accountability*. Cambridge: Cambridge University Press.

Suchman, Lucy. [1986] 2007. *Human Machine Reconfigurations: Plans and Situated Actions*. Cambridge: Cambridge University Press.

Sumner, W. Graham. 1906. *Folkways: a Study of the Sociological Importance of Usages, Manners, Customs, Mores, and Morals*. Boston: Ginn and Co.

Sykes, Gresham. 1958. *The Society of Captives*. Princeton, NJ: Princeton University Press.

Terasaki, Alene. (2004 [1982]). "Pre-Announcement Sequences in Conversation." *Pragmatics and Beyond* (125): 171–223.

Van Maanen, John, J. B. Sorensen, and T. R. Mitchell. 2007. The interplay between theory and method. *Academy of Management Review* 32(4): 1145–54.

Weick, K. E. 1989. "Theory Construction as Disciplined Imagination." *Academy of Management Review* 14: 516–31.

Weider, Larry. 1974. *Telling the Convict Code*. The Hague: Mouton.

Znaniecki, Florian. 1936. *Social Actions*. New York: Russell and Russell.

13

The Arts of Together

Social Coordination as Dyadic Achievement

Hannah Wohl and Gary Alan Fine

Abstract

Coordination is the micro-foundation of social order. Smooth interaction requires individuals to attend and respond to one another within the flow of action, each individual continually calibrating actions to correspond to others. While this is taken for granted, the processes by which this occurs warrants examination. We apply philosophical theories of collective intentionality that specify the conditions necessary for two or more people to intend to act together to a sociological analysis of how individuals coordinate action. We treat the dyad as the most basic and prototypical group, examining dyadic encounters across three different social activities: walking together, engaging in sexual intercourse, and making music. We analyze the interplay of verbal and nonverbal communication, caution and risk, and scripted action and spontaneity, that underlies social coordination. Order implies a metaphor of rigidity and control, but social order, a product of interpersonal coordination, requires flexibility and adaptation, ranging from the minutest bodily movements to meta-understandings of local meaning.

> When people are acting together, doing whatever it is – crossing a street, running a factory, making dinner, playing a gig – they have to arrive at a way of doing that together, getting their specific activities to mesh in some way so that they can get something done, maybe not what they intended but something. How do they do that? Well, they can rely on things they already know (the canon or some version thereof) or they can make it all up from scratch (free jazz, maybe?), or who knows what in between.
>
> Howard Becker (Becker and Faulkner 2013)

We thank Michael Bratman, Robert Faulkner, David Gibson, Margaret Gilbert, and Edward Lawler for comments.

How do dyads coordinate action to achieve a goal? How is joint action possible? This is a problem of fitting together lines of action (Blumer 1969). We address Becker's discussion of social coordination, how people act together, illustrating the "who knows what" that lies between scripted routines and spontaneous reactions.

Social acts from the most basic, such as walking together, to the more complex, such as playing music, require collaboration that develops from social relations and shared histories. To understand this we treat the dyad as the most basic and most prototypical group (Bratman 1992:327), recognizing structural differences between dyads and larger groups (Simmel 1902–1903). Building on theories of collective intentionality in philosophy and group culture theory in sociology, we argue that smooth coordination is central to social order. We define social coordination as interaction in which individuals adapt their own actions in response to others for the purpose of carrying out a collective goal. In contrast to those analyses of coordination that focus on choices arising from potentially conflictual resource distribution (Schelling 1960), we focus on individuals who have cultural and interactional desires to smooth interaction. While coordination occurs at the macro, meso, and micro-level of social order, ranging from state-building to sexual intercourse, in this chapter we show how micro-level coordination underlies macro-level social organization. Coordination requires verbal and nonverbal signaling, commitments and intentions, and scripts and negotiation. While many conceptions of social order emphasize structure, norms, and control, we highlight the interactive flexibility that constitutes micro-mechanisms by which order is established.

That much collective action is performed routinely and without challenge reveals the tacit implications of the interaction order (Goffman 1983), even though shared action may not maximize outcomes for either party. To preserve the relationship, partners satisfice their desires, rather than maximizing them. Tacit conditions of social order build on a recognized group culture that structures actions, just as actions build a group culture (Fine 2012). While group culture serves as a basis for understanding, these collective meanings have an ethnomethodological penumbra: implicit et cetera rules (Garfinkel 1967) that permit those in co-presence (Campos-Castillo and Hitlin 2012) to adjust behaviors for smooth interaction. This becomes the desired default condition, whereas behavioral breakdown, even if mild and temporary, requires repair and accounts. Co-present participants make subtle adjustments to keep interaction flowing. Although collective meaning often aids coordination by providing a shared basis for action, it is not a necessary condition of coordination, as coordination only requires individuals to recognize that they have a shared goal and coordinate their actions toward this end; thus, coordination occurs within thick and thin group cultures.

When disciplines meet, translation is necessary; modes of analysis must be integrated. Sociologists focus on action and how structures channel choices, while philosophers examine the logical structure of relationships. In examining walking together, sociologists examine the practical structure of what Erving Goffman (1971:19) terms the "with" – a relationship that is recognizably joint, publically revealing that participants are "together," linked by interactional strategies (Fine, Stitt, and Finch 1984), whereas philosophers focus on commitment in principle to walk together (Gilbert 1990). However, positing philosophers as purely deductive theory-generators is an oversimplification, as philosophers rely on experience to shape their theories, drawing on these observations as illustrative examples. By viewing philosophical theories as fundamentally social, we establish foundations for interdisciplinary exchange.

Although interaction and group affiliation have long been topics of microsociological social theory, a branch of philosophy has addressed this same goal: establishing a theory of social action through a "micro-philosophical" approach. Operating from analytic philosophy, these scholars examine derivations of the logical conditions of social relations. Accounts of social action are based on theoretical propositions, rather than a discussion of how – in practice – people act in concert. The issue central to much philosophical analysis of collective action is whether and how intentions and actions can be jointly constituted. Theories of collective intentionality specify conditions necessary for two or more people to *intend* to do something together. These philosophical theories provide insight into the mental perspectives of individuals, including the qualities of their intentions, beliefs, and attitudes that allow them to coordinate action. By applying micro-philosophical theories to a micro-sociological perspective of coordination that reveals how intentions are enmeshed in interaction, we see how conditions underlying shared intentionality shape coordination. We build on writings of philosophers of group sociality, social action, and collective commitment, notably Michael Bratman, Margaret Gilbert, John Searle, and Raimo Tuomela, to develop a theory of coordination.

Philosophical theories of collective intentionality analyze how group affiliation constitutes more than a simple convergence of individual perspectives. Consistent with Olick (1999), this approach treats *collected* orientations in contrast to *collective* orientations to suggest that commitment to a group culture transforms individuals into a group (Gilbert 1989). Theories of collective intentionality distinguish between collected individuals and collectives. In his *Philosophy of Sociality*, Tuomela (2007) characterizes two distinct forms of commitment: "I-mode" relations and "we-mode" relations. I-mode cooperation occurs when participants, having a private commitment to the group ethos, try to satisfy personal goals by adjusting their goals and actions toward others with corresponding goals and actions. For example, two people may share a weekly walk, because, discovering that they shop at the same grocery, each may decide that it would be more pleasant to adjust their plans than walk alone. In contrast, the we-mode presupposes a collective acceptance of the group's ethos, operating from collective motivation. Even if individuals doubt the ethos, in we-mode thinking, they accept it as part of belonging. In this case, each person intends to walk with the other because the activity of walking together is part of what constitutes their relationship. Each relies on the other as a companion, and, if one did not need to shop, that person may accompany the other, because each recognizes that walking together enhances their relationship.

While either I-mode or we-mode can generate joint action, a group is only collectively committed *in the full sense* if members mutually accept the we-mode (although group members and the group as a whole may oscillate between modes). For Tuomela, the I-mode constitutes the weak sense of acting as a group member, while the we-mode, involving collective commitment and social sanctions, is a strong model of conceptualizing group action. More per-sistence and stability in task-fulfilment is expected in a we-mode group due to the presupposition that the others will perform their part, interact with flexibil-ity, and reveal respect-based trust (Tuomela 2007:167). The strength of collec-tive intentionality depends on the mental stance each person takes toward the other. Walking together may look identical to outsiders regardless of whether the individuals take an "I-mode" or "we-mode" stance; thus, acting together is not predicated on intersubjectivity. Moreover, one may take the I-mode while another may take the we-mode, constituting a joint action but not a collective commitment. The meaning that the activity holds for those involved rests on whether the individuals view their relation to the others as collected individu-als or as a collectivity; however, this meaning need not be shared to pursue the collective goal.

Individuals may not speak of the quality of their collective intentionality (or be able to speak of it); however, at times, individuals may make their com-mitment explicit. Margaret Gilbert's (1990) "plural subjects theory" entails a stronger form of collective intentionality than Tuomela's we-mode by stipu-lating an additional criterion of obligation in which participants *owe* each other future conforming actions relating to their joint commitment and have made this mutual obligation explicit (Gilbert 2009:175). While explicit mutual knowledge is not a condition of Tuomela's we-mode, he asserts that this thick, agreement-based joint intention strengthens the group (Tuomela 1992:309). For example, if walking together to the store is merely a tacit arrangement, then one partner might more easily decline when she does not need to shop; however, if one partner explicitly says, "Let's go grocery shopping together every week" and the other agrees, then an expectation is set, potentially los-ing the other's trust if it not fulfilled. However, people frequently complete activities without explicit agreements, both because compliance is assumed and because the activity may be difficult to describe. A tacit component exists in all interaction, not necessarily a point of weakness, but instead a point of risk. Risk, as well as stability, is necessary for coordination.

Theories of collective intentionality reveal conditions necessary for collec-tive intentions, as well as those that create the basis for strong collective action. Bratman (1993) posits that collective intention requires that more than one individual must intend to achieve the same goal, that they intend to achieve this goal by "meshing" their plans, and that they are aware of each other's intention to achieve the goal. Gilbert (2009:175) further stipulates that individuals must realize that they are entering an agreement collectively by communicating this intention explicitly, implying that each member is obligated to complete the goal. For Gilbert and Tuomela, shared intentions in the plural subjects' account and we-mode, respectively, are more connected to the independent power of groups than Bratman's notion of personal intentions in that they provide a more stable framework for bargaining, negotiation, and coordination, building on group history and local norms (Gilbert 1997; Tuomela and Tuomela 2005). In this view, collective intentions create expectations, and individuals must be mutually responsive to others' intentions and corresponding action. People need not share the same meaning, but instead strive for the same goal, be it an action, such as walking to the store together, or an attitude toward others, such a fostering a friendship, and they do so by meshing plans.

Nonsummative accounts of collective intentionality explain how collectives may hold intentions irreducible to individual intentions (Gilbert 1990; Searle 1990). A group might carry out an action that does not coincide with any member's preference, because each sees the action as furthering the group goal to which she is obligated, rather than personal desires that may diverge from group goals. For example, because of their we-mode relationship, individuals who are members of a political party may support the platform, while disagreeing with particular planks. In sum, the fundamental elements of collective intentionality are the presence, awareness, and obligation of joint goals. We treat these elements as the grounds on which collective intentions and actions unfold.

These theories stipulate the basis for coordination; however, while modeling the criteria for successful group action, they do not sufficiently show how these models operate in practice. By exploring how social coordination works in specific contexts, we expose the micro-mechanisms of coordination underlying social order. We show how collaboration is shaped by the form of action required, while revealing elements fundamental to all interaction. For this argument, we examine three paradigmatic cases of interpersonal coordination: walking together, engaging in sexual intercourse, and making music. These three activities have different characteristics, yet their comparison reveals underlying attributes of dyadic action.

We first address walking together, treating this example as a basic collaboration; despite its seeming simplicity, we highlight the complexity involved in shared activities by revealing that carrying out this task smoothly demands coordination. Walking together requires each partner to adapt to the other's bodily movements, the cultural context, and the physical environment. This reveals the micro-coordination underlying human interaction, showing how partners tacitly adjust movements temporally and directionally.

Next, we examine the more charged scenario of sexual intercourse. While walking together is a low-risk activity that occurs in public and is easily started and stopped, intercourse is higher risk, carried out in private, involving vulnerability and trust. Here the need for precise micro-coordination is heightened, as the partners' bodies move with and against one another, rather than merely being oriented toward a spatial destination. In contrast to walking, the pleasure in the activity depends on the actions of the partner, and this pleasure, leading to a climax, depends on subtle but consequential acts. While walking is *generous* in not shaping reputations and allowing for secondary engagements, sexual activity is *greedy*, demanding focus and causing negotiation to be potentially treated as condemnation. This case illustrates the dual role of risk and caution in coordination, as partners must discover each other's individual sexual preferences largely via trial-and-error, hoping to avoid actions that displease the other partner, while also taking enough risk for excitement.

Finally, we examine making music together. Like sexual intercourse, making music together involves risk and caution, simultaneously requiring musicians to harmonize and synchronize their tempo, while permitting improvisation. Making music together poses different problems as adjustments cannot be made after the fact, but only in the context of a do-over, as in rehearsals. A wrong or off-key note cannot easily be fixed, but only ignored. Unlike walking or sexual activity, music may either be rehearsed or performed for an evaluative public. Musical performance reveals practices of smooth coordination, as musicians must learn each other's styles and cues to achieve an ostensibly flawless performance, even as, to the players, coordination is rarely perfect. This epitomizes the delicate balance between structure and improvisation. Despite differences, each action domain requires shared understandings that are flexible in light of local adjustments, typically without extensive discourse. Success depends on reading signals. Each builds on bodies acting in concert. Given the absence of discussion of embodied satisfaction, participants might find adjustment problematic and confront what seems to be personal incompatibility.

The tacit ordering of groups and partnerships is highlighted in dyads, and dyads may constitute the ideal type of negotiated orders (Strauss 1978). Yet, as Goffman (1971) argues, we must avoid assuming that simply because two people have a relationship, they necessarily will create a group culture. The fact that two individuals stroll in tandem or engage in sexual acts, does not make them, by that criterion alone, a group with the affective, cultural, and identity characteristics that a group culture model suggests.

Walking Together

In its seeming simplicity, walking together elucidates the structure of coordination. Two people share a goal: walking *together*, not just side-by-side. Following Gilbert's (1990) plural subject theory, individuals are obligated to remain together for the duration of the walk, impelling each to keep in stride. This shared goal has a plural subject in that each participant must express readiness to commit to the joint goal. While the intent to walk together is evident in a request and responding agreement, the mechanics remains largely tacit.

Walking together as an act of mutual commitment is common, as in the Bible's Book of Amos (3:3): "Can two walk together, except they be agreed?" Many people walk in dyads, although the precise proportion is a function of the context (Moussaïd et al. 2010; McPhail 1991). Observers suggest that public dyads are more common than other groups (Goffman 1971:20). People do not only use these occasions for transit from one location to another, but for social purposes, such as to talk or demonstrate affiliation.

Strolling is integral to the micro-romance of relationships. If walks are a notable or recurrent activity, how (and where and when) to walk belongs to the culture of couples. These traditions give the relationship tensile strength. The strong form of walking together is the romantic stroll in which walking together is not merely synchronous, but the couple is roped together through such "ritual idioms" (Goffman 1971:225) as hand-holding, waist-hugging, intertwined arms, a shoulder-squeeze, or back-guiding. Walking together also sustains platonic intimacy. As one friendship card states, "Best friends walk always together through a single path with hand in hand forever." While female friends may walk hand-in-hand, many males avoid touching, as prevailing gender norms prevent such intimacies (Goffman 1971:226).

These public displays of mundane intimacy, what Goffman (1971) calls "tie-signs," signal not only to the couple, but also to others, the status of the relationship. Due to the potential romantic connotations of walking together, rules of etiquette surround the activity, although these have loosened over time. A letter to Miss Manners, an advice columnist, written in 1992, asks, "When a lady takes the arm of a gentleman while walking, how should the gentleman respond?" Miss Manners replies tartly, "A lady does not initiate taking a gentleman's arm, unless she is otherwise going to slide off and break her hip. The gentleman offers his arm, the right one to be specific, with the elbow bent. She then delicately puts her hand under his arm and curls the hand back over it. They are not drawn close by this joining, but promenade in a stately fashion, whether they are usher and guest at a wedding, or a friend and friend out for an airing" (Martin 1992:2D). The most minute movements and positions of each individual's body in relation to the other are carefully considered so as to give the impression of warm civility without excessive intimacy.

By displaying tie-signs, individuals create "change signals" that may, if accepted, transform the nature of the relationship. Goffman (1971) recalls Sartre's (1966 [1956]: 55–56) example of a man who attempts to establish a romantic relationship with his date by grasping her hand: "But then, suppose he takes her hand. This act of her companion risks changing the situation by calling for an immediate decision. To leave the hand there is a consent to flirt, to engage herself. To withdraw it is to break the troubled and unstable harmony which gives the hour its charm." When walking together, physical intimacies can be graciously received, maintaining or heightening the partner's romantic relationship, whether or not both partners are comfortable with this status, or rebuffed, creating awkwardness as the platonic relationship is restored. In this case, individuals reveal a collective intention to walk together; however, alternative goals, such as making a sexual advance, may emerge in the course of interaction, in light of the other's goals. With incongruent goals, collective action cannot be sustained unless individuals compromise their personal intentions. One partner realizing the other had no romantic desires may withdraw his own advances while the other tactfully overlooks the original advance.

While heterosexual couples may scarcely think about this public performance, it is a more fraught decision for same-sex couples. The couple may wish to protect themselves, as physical displays might provoke unwanted attention or even aggression (Bruni 2013; Klayman 2013); in contrast, the couple may want to display their affection, enjoying the same freedom as heterosexual couples. While walking together goes unquestioned among heterosexuals, these considerations may prompt explicit discussion elsewhere, depending on local conditions. Although less true today, the same applies to couples of different races or ethnicities. Further, certain cultures frown on public hand-holding, indicating greater sexual openness than the parties might desire, as Suttles (1968:113) reports of Italian neighborhoods in Chicago.

To walk together, each party must monitor movement in light of their partner and adjust speed to remain in stride. Partners may adjust their movements tacitly, and even unconsciously. Given their intimacy, the individuals may signal their movements tactilely or visually as well as verbally, regulating pace. Additionally, they match their strides, as their arms swing synchronously while linked. Given different ideal velocities (a choice that varies with terrain, mood, and traffic), the walkers must determine – often implicitly – who sets the pace. This can create discomfort for one (or both) walkers, and occasionally produces explicit negotiation or the expression of power. An extreme case is the children's game, "The Three-Legged Race," wherein pairs race with the middle leg of each partner tied to the other. The challenge and the entertainment lie in moments of rupture, when one partner moves the tied leg too quickly or slowly causing the other to be jerked along and both to fall. In Cormac McCarthy's (2006:79) *The Road,* the boy struggles to keep pace with his father in their postapocalyptic journey: "The boy kept falling behind and he stopped and waited for him. Stay with me, he said. / You walk too fast. / I'll go slower. / They went on." By complaining, the walkers reveal they have failed in their shared journey.

Walking together requires regulating both direction and speed. If only one person is aware of the directions to the destination, she becomes the *de facto* leader. She might announce where to turn or turn, expecting the other to follow. In the latter case, the other person might fall a half-step behind in anticipation of following, slowing at a potential turn and then accelerating. Each choice depends on local considerations, consistent with the relationship (Fine 2012). At other times, when they do not have a set destination, the shared goal is the walk itself, and so individuals negotiate where and how far to travel.

Walking in tandem involves awareness of the context, including the presence of others. When walking on a narrow or crowded sidewalk, one partner may slow to let others pass. This often involves a quick slowing by one; if both do so simultaneously further adjustment is needed. Individuals must also respond to the built and natural environment from potholes to trees. The unit can split in such tight or organized places, only to form again without much explanation. Walking together involves both somatic-limit tacit knowledge and collective tacit knowledge (Collins 2007). With somatic-limit tacit knowledge, knowledge is indescribable because it is learned through embodiment, while with collective tacit knowledge, knowledge is unstipulated because it is local, responding to dynamic environments. Individuals cannot tell each other how to walk together because the knowledge is *embodied*, as unconscious bodily adjustments are made to walk in tandem, and *local*, as walking together requires adaptation to specific environments and partners.

Explicit authority in mutual walking is observed between parents and children, revealing affection, protection, and discipline. Parents often hold children by the hand, not only to show affection, as with romantic relationships and friendships, but to control the child's speed and direction, preventing running ahead or into traffic without verbal reminders. In crowded public places, such as amusement parks or airports, parents may even leash children as a more secure form of bodily control. While children race ahead, the elderly often lag behind. Slowing to match the stride of an elderly partner reveals thoughtfulness, as it is more difficult for the elderly person to hurry than for the other to slow down. Disabled people using a cane or wheelchair require additional coordination, as their partner must anticipate accessibility difficulties, such as stairs or uneven paths, and navigate accordingly. In the case of pushing a wheelchair, the mobile partner completely controls the pace and direction.

The most salient characteristics of walking together are the instantaneous micro-adjustments; however, special cases of walking together require that these micro-adjustments are made explicit. When a patient learns to walk again after a stroke (Latham et al. 2005), a blind person navigates an unfamiliar environment, or a parent leads a toddler, individuals coordinate their movements using verbal instructions or explicit tactile guidance. The difficulty in making these mechanics explicit underlines the centrality of tacit awareness.

If walking is unsatisfying and if the relationship does not demand its continuation, bonds of action are loosened. However, in most cases, micro-adjustments are made in the name of cooperation. As Tuomela and Tuomela (2005:57) note, cooperation has two central dimensions: a teleological end, the purpose that participants intentionally strive to achieve, and the social content, how the participants plan to carry out the joint intention, continually recalibrated in the flux of social interaction. While philosophical theories of collective intentionality stress that collective action relies on explicit and mutual plans, the empirical case of walking together shows that although plans and subplans are made, coordination becomes increasingly tacit at micro-levels of action. Ultimately, through the prism of walking together, we recognize how small moments of correction formulate the social order.

"Loving" Together[1]

Close friends are joined at the hip, but lovers are joined at the pelvis. Depending on the couple's preferences, sometimes they are joined elsewhere. Engaging in sexual *intercourse* raises different problems from walking or making music, in part a function of privacy and, on occasion, that the actions are performed in the dark, privileging the tactile. Unlike walking together, sexual relations require framing a reality that is apart from the mundane: an erotic reality (Davis 1983) or an altered state (Carrillo 2002:183). Mutually sustaining this reality requires partitioning time and space for the sexual encounter. Davis speaks of a "sensual slide" from everyday reality to erotic reality and back again, often involving a dimming of the lights to signify the private and a move into the bedroom to signify intimacy. Due to the privacy of the intimate encounter, sexual practices are notoriously difficult to examine. With some notable exceptions, including Armstrong's studies of collegiate sexual experiences and Newmahr's (2011) ethnographic research in a BDSM community, research focuses on self-reports of sexual practices, rather than how these practices are negotiated face-to-face. While scenes in erotica and romantic novels and films may, like porn, portray an idealized vision of sexual compatibility, comic sex scenes often portray coordination difficulties with exaggerated humor.

In walking together partners perform the same act: they travel the same route. However, in sexual coordination, acts may be parallel (as in kissing) or dissimilar (evident in heterosexual intercourse, a function of different bodily contours). When partners perform the same act, such as with walking together, they can communicate about necessary adjustments; however, when partners play different roles, collaboration is more challenging. A female may know that she likes a particular feeling or that she achieved orgasm with a specific partner, but she might not know exactly what act made intercourse successful. Even if she desires to give explicit directives to a new partner, she might not know what to say. In sexual acts, explicit negotiation can be read as a claim of incompatibility, threatening the basis of the relationship that may depend on the hope of physical and psychic union, a strong problem of coordination, given unspoken sexual preferences.

Each partner must recognize sexual cues of the other. This involves an intersection among personal scripts, imagined expectations and desires in which

---

[1] Expressions for sexual intercourse abound, tending toward vulgar colloquialisms, romanticized idioms, or quasi-scientific terminology. Using the sentimental aphorism, "Loving Together," we place "loving" in quotation marks to recognize that intercourse need not involve love but, nevertheless, demands coordination.

the two communicate and apply cultural scenarios (Simon and Gagnon 1986). Through these scripts, individuals enjoy sexual fantasies; however, when engaging in the sexual encounter, personal scripts must be coordinated with the scripts of the other, producing interpersonal scripts. When scripts are congruent, sexual desires are satisfied, whereas failure places a strain on the couple, requiring realignment. While cultural scripts are important, perfect congruence is impossible as everyone has desires, expectations, and fantasies that cannot fully be communicated. In a literal as well as figurative sense each partner may be in the dark. In this setting, the risk of interpersonal blindness is high.

Furthermore, there is no rehearsal before intercourse. Masturbation provides poor training, because there is no need for coordination. Pornography, with its posturing for the camera, is also inadequate, as those who emulate pornographic scenes inevitably find. As Terry Real, a relationship counselor, stated (Gottlieb 2014): "What will you never see in a porn video? 'Honey, I don't like that, could you stop doing that, could you take a shower first?' … What you don't see in porn is anything that needs to be negotiated, the woman having needs of her own or the roles being reversed." In real life, intercourse may be awkward, especially at first. If only one partner is a virgin, the sexually experienced partner may guide the others' body and provide verbal cues, while if both are virgins, they must rely on cultural scripts. Regardless of experience, preferences and contexts evolve. Sexual interaction is always, to some extent, uncertain, and therefore, risky. Before intercourse, partners indicate sexual interest through flirtation (Henningsen 2004). Often a firm definition of the situation is desired; however, flirtation trades on ambiguity, permitting cost-free exits and different avenues of action (Tavory 2009). In its open-endedness, flirtation provides a safe way of testing whether sexual interest is mutual as the sexual definition of the situation can be withdrawn if not reciprocated, allowing actors to save face (Goffman 1959).

Although individuals apply experiences from past partners to their current sexual encounter, no guarantee exists that successful techniques will work again. As each individual has unique preferences (and unique bodies), satisfying encounters require communicating these preferences in uncertain encounters. As Anais Nin (1977:88) illustrates in *Delta of Venus*: "Was she pleased? When he bent over her, was she more responsive? He could not tell." Uncertainty may produce both anxiety and excitement.

As with flirtation, analysis is problematic, as spontaneity is central to sexual scripts. Moreover, individuals rarely embarrass their partner by criticism, as evaluation douses the fire. Thus, coordination requires considerable delicacy. Some preferences are explicitly stated; however, much is conveyed through bodily guidance (Carrillo 2002:200). If feelings are too divergent, intercourse will not be pleasurable. In the film, *Bridesmaids* (Feig 2011), Annie tries to alter her partner's gyrations, saying "Let's slow it down, let's slow it down. Good, there we go. See, isn't that nice?" Oblivious to her dissatisfaction, her partner responds with repeated quick thrusts, stating excitedly, "I want to go fast. I want to go fast." She gingerly notes, "I think maybe we have different rhythms here." For sexual intercourse to continue, partners must respond to one another's signals in the same tenor.

New partners require a *sexual culture*, as they lack shared memories that can create a sexual repertoire and erotic history. Thus, attentiveness to verbal and nonverbal cues is necessary. Repeated sexual partners rely on established practices, while perhaps introducing novelty to prevent routine. Either novelty or routine can be rejected, a complicated negotiation in that both partners are making choices in the same amatory encounter.

Another threat to coordination is breaches, either internal or external. Internal breaches include bodily and technical failures (Goffman 1959:34), such as erectile dysfunction, flatus, and condom breakage. External breaches include environmental interruptions, such as the intrusion of a third person or a ringing phone. Both external and internal breaches unceremoniously shift the situation from erotic to mundane reality. To maintain erotic reality, the dyad must realign their coordination, perhaps by ignoring or joking about the breach, allowing the encounter to continue.

The hallmark of successful intercourse is taken to be the orgasm. While one cannot be sure that one's partner is having a pleasurable experience, the orgasm becomes proof of satisfaction (Armstrong, England, and Fogarty 2012). In the absence of orgasm, intercourse may be judged a failure; repeated inability to climax may be seen as sexual dysfunction, if attributed to one partner, or a relationship failure, if deemed a problem of compatibility. Good partners respect the other's needs. With heterosexual couples, this may mean ensuring that the female has an orgasm first, since the male orgasm marks the culmination of intercourse, as one woman in Armstrong, England, and Fogarty's (2012:455) study reveals: "I didn't come during sex but I did come from oral sex.... So he made sure I came before he came. And he was like okay with having sex and then going down on me, so I came, and then going back to having sex and then he came.... It was great." Unlike men, women have the liberty of faking orgasms, if an actual orgasm is clearly not imminent (Roberts et al. 1995). The faked orgasm is a courtesy gesture, saving the male from feelings of sexual inadequacy and preserving the relationship. In absence of the orgasm, assurances of pleasure may salve identity threats.

In sexual activity, as in all human interaction, coordination is difficult because people assign different meanings to the same situation. As Bratman (1992:329) notes, each person may be committed to the joint activity for different reasons. These differences may create unpleasant surprises when participants realize that a meaning assumed to be shared was, in fact, only held by one. While one partner may see the relationship as a "one-night stand," the other may see the beginning of a relationship, unhappily aware of the disjuncture when the other quickly departs after intercourse. Conflict may also arise because of varied gender norms. While these gender norms have been called into question by feminists, in most Western cultures, men are expected to be more dominant, initiating intercourse and directing changes of position; in contrast, women are expected to need coaxing and follow the male's cues. Furthermore, during heterosexual intercourse, especially in "one-night stands," partners often prioritize male pleasure, achieving the male's orgasm. College women often negotiate oral sex, if they are to receive it (Backstrom, Armstrong, and Puentes 2012:6). One woman explains, "So I'm pretty vocal and I will, if I'm about to go down on a guy, I'll say, 'By the way, if this isn't gonna get reciprocated, then just leave;' " another states, "I hate it when a guy is like take your head and try and push it down, because I then just switch it around to make them go down first usually." Women bartered for pleasure through verbal claims and physical adjustments. Divergences in expectations occur both on the micro-level of sexual movements and on the meso-level of ascribing meaning to the dyad.

Negotiating safe-sex is famously unsexy, as it requires breaking the spontaneous and playful nature of the erotic encounter with explicit communication about contraception as well as the hiatus of sexual activity (but see Adelman 1991). Moreover, in negotiating safe-sex, an individual risks offending a lover in requiring condom use by implying that the partner is untrustworthy or promiscuous. However, in avoiding this discussion, one may be imperiled if the other does not disclose sexual health issues. Individuals might either hold protective or trusting frames of the sexual situation: the former requiring explicit negotiation of contraceptive use and the latter assuming appropriate disclosure. Believing that the partner does not hold the same frame, an individual might switch frames, moving from a protective to trusting frame or vice versa (Fontdevila 2009). Coordination of safe-sex depends on assumptions about the other, and these assumptions change as partners reveal themselves.

However, individuals would not risk embarrassment, awkwardness, and displeasure without the potential for satisfaction. While romantic comedies highlight the pratfalls of intercourse, romantic and erotic novels illustrate its magic. These texts portray partners as attentive to verbal and nonverbal cues: "She moved quicker to bring the climax, and when he saw this, he hastened his motions inside of her and incited her to come with him, with words, with his hands caressing her, and finally with his mouth soldered to hers, so that the tongues moved in the same rhythm as the womb and penis" (Nin 1977:99). At least in fiction partners may feel as though their bodies have literally merged. The promise of flawless coordination and the pleasure individuals experience during "great sex" thrusts individuals together in spite of hazards. The case of sexual intercourse illustrates the riskiness underlying all coordination. Risk is a manifestation of the tacit and emergent elements of social coordination. Smooth coordination does not require an avoidance or minimization of all risk; instead, it hinges upon a delicate give-and-take between cautious and spontaneous action, where the ability to attend to others' actions and respond accordingly is vital.

Playing Together

Creating music as a duet presents special challenges. Unlike walking together, which is forgiving if the participants do not walk perfectly in alignment, music depends on ongoing harmony. Establishing harmony is tricky in that participants cannot make adjustments after the fact; ideally any adjustment must be immediate. One cannot take back an inharmonious note. While one or both musicians may be "out-of-tune," the key challenge is not only to play on-tune and within a key, but to play so that the notes blend into a single performance rather than two performances temporally and spatially stapled. This requires what Bratman (1992:331–2) refers to as "meshing subplans," so that musicians play not only simultaneously, but *together*.

Like sexual activity, playing music together requires partitioning time and space. In their "working repertoire," the duet selects what, when, and where to play (Becker 2006). To prepare for playing, musicians listen to recordings of other musicians interpreting the same piece, sometimes borrowing a phrase as a nod to collective history. A shared repertoire eases musical coordination by sharing background knowledge and providing rules that limits the uncertainty of playing together. However, although repertoires overlap significantly, each musician's repertoire is distinct. The repertoire is a "living, breathing thing," binding a community that is constantly "in process" as musicians continually exchange repertoires, creating an open and evolving culture (Becker and Faulkner 2013).

Once playing commences, the musicians must avoid cacophony by "keeping time" with one another. Music depends on both inner and outer time, the former referring to the perceived rhythm felt by the players and the latter to the tempo as it is managed (Schutz 1976:175). Similar to sexual intercourse, where intrapersonal and interpersonal scripts must be compatible, in musical interaction, inner and outer time must be congruent. Each player must make a personal rhythmic sense consistent with the joint performance, requiring a "mutual tuning-in" in which inner time is synchronous with outer time (Schutz 1951). Players must know when to "step up" or "fall back" in a give-and-take pattern, since if both step up or fall back simultaneously, there will either be an awkward gap or cacophony. Errors may occur when someone plays with the wrong rhythm or at the wrong time, with the wrong note or out of tune, or in an inappropriate style. The source of these errors may be more or less obvious. Errors, while temporarily problematic, can generate innovation as they prompt a collective search for a solution.

Like sexual activity and walking together, musical collaboration requires both verbal and nonverbal communication. Musicians gesture to one another, nodding or signaling the other to play a certain way (Malhotra 1981:106). While some cues are conventional, those who play together consistently develop a nonverbal musical culture. Conventions of communication vary according to the specific repertoire (Dempsey 2008:59). For example, Sun Ra's experimental jazz band communicated through nods and gestures. Trombonist Julian Priester explained, "Sun Ra gave us very little concrete information or music that we were performing, and we had to depend on our ears to ... make sense out of the sounds that the band created, that Sun Ra dictated. He would point to individuals and indicate to just start playing, without any guidelines" (Gluck 2012:10). Musical constructions occur during rehearsals, a pre-performance mode that is absent in walking or in sexual activity. These rehearsals create a frame distinguished from that of public performances in which errors have different meanings (Goffman 1974). During rehearsals, interrupting the musical flow is accepted, while performances rely on "unseen" communication to maintain the perception of effortless collaboration. The illusion is that harmony emerged spontaneously, while in fact harmonious playing relies on complex coordination, continually recalibrated.

Public performances vary in the amount of permissible error. At Carnegie Hall, performances are to be flawless and gaffes can ruin careers. In a bar, errors may be met with sympathetic amusement or the performers might treat the set as "practice." Still, mistakes during performance are potentially serious, as they cannot be corrected, only ignored, playing over the error to minimize it. Rehearsal provides a simulation of the performance in which the margin of error is reduced by increasing coordinated precision (Hoffman 2006). As flubs impact the perceived competency of the duet, the partners must work together to save face (Goffman 1959). In Tuomela's (2007:167) "we-mode cooperation," there is a presupposition that each will perform so as to help one another. This kind of cooperation involves respect-based trust. Members of a musical group expect each another to gloss over blunders. The shared attempt to save face is not only an empathetic act of social tact, but also a collective strategy to preserve the group's reputation.

Correctness is a matter of interpretation, such as when deciding the length of a pause or how briskly to play a note (Dempsey 2008). Yet, errors can become happy accidents, as jazz pianist Herbie Hancock describes playing with trumpeter Miles Davis: "I hit a wrong chord. It was amazing. And – Miles is playing his solo, getting to the peak of his solo and then, I played this chord that was so wrong ... I thought I had just, like ... a house of cards and I just destroyed them all, you know? And Miles just took a breath and he played some notes that made my chord right" (CBS News 2013). In Hancock's Mwandishi Sextet, mistakes led to innovation, as bassist Buster Williams explains: "These rhythms, these lines, these motifs would morph into something else. And sometimes it would happen because I mistakenly played it wrong. You know, I always remembered what Monk and Art Blakey told me: 'If you make a mistake, play it again and it ain't a mistake.' What's important is whether or not it worked" (Gluck 2012:158). Continued coordination requires musicians to strike out in new directions as well as to respond to one another's leads.

Disagreements over how to play a sequence may require compromise. In this way, the final product of the performed piece may not be identical to either player's imagined or desired interpretation. As Gilbert (1987:196) claims, joint acceptance does not require that one *personally* accepts what one accepts *jointly*; instead, one must believe that acting on the joint premise is one's obligation. Searle (1990) states that collective intentional behavior is not merely a summation of individual intentions, but is its own primitive form of intentionality.

In analyzing "improvisation as work," Faulkner (2006:92) describes the delicate interplay between imagination and control inherent in making music together: "Improvising together is a collective action.... The musical activity is simultaneously deliberative *and* spontaneous, imitative *and* experimental, routinized *and* innovation." For Faulkner (2006:99), improvisation rests on a firm foundation of routines, rules, and rituals requiring both monastic daily practice as well as a willingness to "break out." Making music together is inherently risky, because this imaginative element should never be brought under complete control. Instead, "the uncertainty that exists because reactions to a product (the solo, the tune, the chord changes), let alone the reactions of fellow musician, or the audience for that matter, are known neither beforehand nor easily understood afterward. Thus 'nobody knows' what would happen" (Berliner 1994:221–2; Faulkner 2006:114). Even in play, structure must never devolve into chaos.

While walking together and intercourse require bodily coordination, playing music demands the coordination of sound. Performing can create deep bonds of intimacy, as musicians who play over a long period of time feel that they speak a personal musical language. Evolutionary anthropologist Steve Mithen (2005:215) explains, "Those who make music together will mold their own minds and bodies into a shared emotional state, and with that will come a loss of self-identity and a concomitant increase in the ability to cooperate with others. In fact, 'cooperate' is not quite correct, because as identities merge there is no 'other' with whom to cooperate, just one group making decisions about how to behave." The experience of successful coordination can be deeply pleasurable, sustaining ongoing relationships. Playing together well – with spontaneity, yet in sync – is a rare and transcendental experience.

Being Together

Coordination constitutes the micro-foundation of social order. In order to carry out shared activities smoothly, individuals must not only plan to do something together, but must also adapt to one another throughout interaction so as to maintain corresponding and complementary actions. To explore the micro-level processes by which this occurs, we applied philosophical theories of collective intentionality to a sociological analysis of coordination. While the former considers explicit mutual plans as conditional for coordination, the latter emphasizes the tacit and emergent quality of coordination. Using the dyad as the most basic and prototypical unit constituting a group, we analyzed three cases: walking together, engaging in sexual intercourse, and making music. Across these cases, we find that social coordination involves a delicate interplay between verbal and nonverbal communication, caution and risk, scripted action and spontaneity. While coordination ranges from the minutest bodily movements to meta-understandings of local meaning, coordination, and by extension, social order, is increasingly tacit and emergent at the micro-level of moment-to-moment coordination.

Coordination includes both verbal and nonverbal communication. While Tuomela (2005) proposes that explicit agreements improve coordination, the literature on tacit knowledge (Collins 1974; Polanyi 1958) emphasizes nonverbal communication. We argue that in some situations, coordination depends on nonverbal communication, with verbal communication playing a supportive role by confirming or clarifying the other's understanding. Verbal communication predominates before and after the coordinated activity, used to facilitate coordination through rehearsal and review. Nonverbal communication transmits that which would be inappropriate to discuss explicitly or that which cannot be well articulated. Coordination, especially when embodied, may be too subtle to be captured verbally, tied to sensory perceptions.

Partners must recognize established social scripts and negotiate these scripts to fit an occasion. Knowledge "in theory" must apply knowledge "in context." Individuals may simulate activities or recall relevant experiences; however, joint action requires local improvisation. Coordination involves a risk of failure through misinterpretation or performed error. When errors are evident, the failed actor must save face to align with the group's culture. Others aid in restoring the interaction, perhaps by covering over, ignoring, or adapting to the rupture. Although coordination is fundamental to social order, social order does not require complete stability. Instead, "ideal stability," as Bratman (1987:73) calls it, involves reconsidering joint intentions to benefit the group. However, redirecting joint intentions is constrained because excessive capriciousness is inimical to stability. To sustain order, individuals must both respond with caution and take risks, delicately balancing routine and novelty.

Maintaining social order occurs on the micro-level. Coordination ranges from the minutest bodily movements to meta-understandings of local meaning. Achieving social order raises the challenge of intersubjectivity (Schutz 1953). Each participant has a personal perspective, yet these perspectives must intersect for smooth interaction. Just as when playing music, one must know both parts to play competently in a world of role-taking. Shared action requires an awareness of how multiple roles operate in concert so that the individual fits into the situation seamlessly, bolstering the interaction order.

As perfect intersubjectivity is impossible, negotiation is inevitable. While order implies a metaphor of rigidity and control, social order, a product of interpersonal coordination, requires openness to adaptation. With this in mind, dyadic relations serve as a model of a flexible social order in which "who knows what" becomes the basis for community.

REFERENCES

Adelman, Mara. 1991. "Play and Incongruity: Framing Safe-Sex Talk." *Health Communication* 3(3): 139–55.

Armstrong, Elizabeth, Paula England, and Alison Fogarty. 2012. "Accounting for Women's Orgasm and Sexual Enjoyment in College Hookups and Relationships." *American Sociological Review* 77(3): 435–62.

Backstrom, Laura, Elizabeth Armstrong, and Jennifer Puentes. 2012. "Women's Negotiation of Cunnilingus in College Hookups and Relationships." *Journal of Sex Research* 49(1): 1–12.

Becker, Howard. 2006. "The Jazz Repertoire." Pp. 243–51 in *Enonciation Artistique et Socialité*, edited by J. Uzel. Paris: Harmattan.

Becker, Howard, and Robert Faulkner. 2013. *Thinking Together: An E-Mail Exchange and All That Jazz*, edited by Diane Hagaman. Los Angeles: USC Annenberg Press.

Berliner, Paul. 1994. *Thinking in Jazz*. Chicago: University of Chicago Press.

Blumer, Herbert. 1969. *Symbolic Interactionism*. Englewood Cliffs, NJ: Prentice Hall.

Bratman, Michael. 1987. *Intention, Plans, and Practical Reason*. Cambridge, MA: Harvard University Press.

   1992. "Shared Cooperative Activity." *Philosophical Review* 101(2): 327–341.

   1993. "Shared Intention." *Ethics* 104(1): 97–113.

Bruni, Frank. 2013. "Gay and Fearful." *New York Times* (August 15). http://bruni .blogs.nytimes.com/2013/08/15/gay-and-fearful (accessed January 12, 2014).

Campos-Castillo, Celeste, and Steven Hitlin. 2012. "Revisiting Copresence: A Building Block for Models of Social Interaction." *Sociological Theory* 31: 168–92.

Carrillo, Héctor. 2002. *The Night Is Young: Sexuality in Mexico in the Time of AIDS*. Chicago: University of Chicago Press.

CBS News. 2013. "Jazz Legend Herbie Hancock on his Career and Future" (December 25). http://www.cbsnews.com/news/jazz-legend-herbie-hancock-on -his-career-and-future/ (accessed February 12, 2014).

Collins, Harry. 1974. "The TEA Set: Tacit Knowledge and Scientific Networks." *Science Studies*, 4: 165–85.

   2007. "Bicycling on the Moon: Collective Tacit Knowledge and Somatic-limit Tacit Knowledge." *Organization Studies*, 28(2): 257–62.

Davis, Murray. 1983. *Erotic Reality/Obscene Ideology*. Chicago: University of Chicago Press.

Dempsey, Nicholas. 2008. "Hook-Ups and Train Wrecks: Contextual Parameters and the Coordination of Jazz Interactions." *Symbolic Interaction* 31(1): 57–75.

Faulkner, Robert. 2006. "Shedding Culture." Pp. 91–117 in *Art from Start to Finish*, edited by Howard Becker, Robert Faulkner, and Barbara Kirshenblatt-Gimblett. Chicago: University of Chicago Press.

Feig, Paul. 2011. *Bridesmaids*. DVD. Culver City, CA: Universal Studios Home Entertainment.

Fine, Gary Alan. 2012. *Tiny Publics: A Theory of Group Action and Culture*. New York: Russell Sage Foundation.

Fine, Gary Alan, Stitt, Jeffrey, and Finch, Michael. 1984. Couple Tie-signs and Inter-personal Threat: A Field Experiment. *Social Psychology Quarterly* 47(3): 282–86.

Fontdevila, Jorge. 2009. "Framing Dilemmas during Sex: A Micro-Sociological Approach to HIV Risk." *Social Theory & Health* 7(3): 241–63.

Garfinkel, Harold. 1967. *Studies in Ethnomethodology*. Cambridge, UK: Polity.

Gilbert, Margaret. 1987. "Modelling Collective Belief." *Synthese* 73(1): 185–204.

  1989. *On Social Facts*. London and New York: Routledge.

  1990. "Walking Together: A Paradigmatic Social Phenomenon." *Midwest Studies in Philosophy* 15: 1–14.

  1997. "What Is it for Us to Intend?" *Synthese Library* 65–86.

  2009. "Shared Intentions and Personal Intentions." *Philosophical Studies* 144: 167–87.

Gluck, Bob. 2012. *You'll Know When You Get There: Herbie Hancock and the Mwandishi Band*. Chicago: University of Chicago Press.

Goffman, Erving. 1959. *The Presentation of Self in Everyday Life*. New York: Doubleday.

  1971. *Relations in Public*. New York: Basic Books.

  1974. *Frame Analysis: An Essay on the Organization of Experience*. Cambridge: Harvard University Press.

  1983. "The Interaction Order." *American Sociological Review* 48: 1–17.

Gottlieb, Lori. 2014. "Does a More Equal Marriage Mean less Sex?" *New York Times Magazine* (January 6). http://www.nytimes.com/2014/02/09/magazine/does-a-more -equal-marriage-mean-less-sex.html?src=dayp&_r=2 (accessed February 12, 2014).

Henningsen, David. 2004. "Flirting with Meaning: An Examination of Miscommunication in Flirting Interactions." *Sex Roles* 50(7–8): 481–89.

Hoffman, Steve. 2006. "How to Punch Someone and Stay Friends: An Inductive Theory of Simulation." *Sociological Theory* 24(2): 170–93.

Klayman, Alison. 2013. "An Attack on Equality." *New York Times* (August 6). http:// www.nytimes.com/2013/08/07/opinion/opinion/an-attack-on-equality.html (accessed January 12, 2014).

Latham, Nancy, Diane Jette, Mary Slavin, Lorie Richards, Adam Procino, Randall Smout, Susan Horn. 2005. "Physical Therapy during Stroke Rehabilitation for People with Different Walking Abilities," *Archives of Physical Medicine and Rehabilitation* 85(12): 41–50.

Malhotra, Valerie. 1981. "The Social Accomplishment of Music in a Symphony Orchestra: A Phenomenological Analysis." *Qualitative Sociology* 4(2): 102–25.

Martin, Judith. 1992. "Intent Dictates How to Walk Arm-in-Arm." *Star-News* (December 31): 2D.

McCarthy, Cormac. 2006. *The Road*. New York: Vintage.

McPhail, Clark. 1991. *The Myth of the Madding Crowd*. Piscataway, NJ: Transaction.

Mithen, Steven. 2005. *The Singing Neanderthals: The Origins of Music, Language, Mind, and Body*. Cambridge, MA: Harvard University Press.

Moussaïd, Mehdi, Niriaska Perozo, Simon Garnier, Dirk Helbing, and Guy Theraulaz. 2010. "The Walking Behaviour of Pedestrian Social Groups and Its Impact on Crowd Dynamics." *PloS one* 5(4):e10047.

Newmahr, Staci. 2011. *Playing on the Edge: Sadomasochism, Risk, and Intimacy*. Bloomington: Indiana University Press.

Nin, Anais. 1977. *Delta of Venus: Erotica*. New York: Harcourt Brace Jovanovich.

Olick, Jeffrey. 1999. "Collective Memory: The Two Cultures." *Sociological Theory* 17(3): 333–48.

Polanyi, Michael. 1958. *Personal Knowledge: Towards a Post-Critical Philosophy*. Chicago: University of Chicago Press.

Roberts, Celia, Susan Kippax, Catherine Waldby, and June Crawford. 1995. "Faking It: The Story of 'Ohh!'" *Women's Studies International Forum* 18(5): 523–32.

Sartre, Jean-Paul. [1956] 1966. *Being and Nothingness*. London: Methuen.

Schelling, Thomas. 1960. *The Strategy of Conflict*. Cambridge, MA: Harvard University Press.

Schutz, Alfred. 1951. "Making Music Together: A Study in Social Relationships." *Social Research* 18: 76–97.

   1953. "Common-Sense and Scientific Interpretation in Human Action." *Philosophy and Phenomenological Research* 14: 1–38.

   1976. *Collected Papers II: Studies in Social Theory*. The Hague: Nijhoff.

Searle, John. 1990. "Collective Intentions and Actions." In *Intentions in Communication*, edited by Cohen, P. R., J. L. Morgan, and M. E. Pollack. Cambridge, MA: MIT Press.

Simmel, Georg. 1902–3. "The Number of Members as Determining the Sociological Form of the Group." *American Journal of Sociology* 8: 1–46.

Simon, William, and John H. Gagnon. 1986. "Sexual Scripts: Permanence and Change." *Archives of Sexual Behavior* 15(2): 97–120.

Strauss, Anselm L. 1978. *Negotiations: Varieties, Contexts, Processes, and Social Order*. San Francisco: Jossey-Bass.

Suttles, Gerald. 1968. *The Social Order of the Slum*. Chicago: University of Chicago Press.

Tavory, Iddo. 2009. "The Structure of Flirtation: On the Construction of Interactional Ambiguity." *Studies in Symbolic Interaction* 33: 59–74.

Tuomela, Raimo. 1992. "Group Beliefs." *Synthese* 91(3): 285–318.

   2005. "We-Intentions Revisited." *Philosophical Studies* 125: 327–69.

   2007. *The Philosophy of Sociality: The Shared Point of View*. Oxford: Oxford University Press.

Tuomela Raimo, and Maj Tuomela. 2005. "Cooperation and Trust in Group Context." *Mind and Society* 4: 49–84.

14

Dignity as Moral Motivation
The Problem of Social Order Writ Small

Steven Hitlin and Matthew A. Andersson

Abstract

How can we account for order while also recognizing agency and individuality? We propose dignity as a moral motivation for social personhood that represents a parsimonious theoretical – and ideally empirical – pivot for relating the agentic individual with social evaluations underlying the study of social order. A desire for dignity compels individuals to assert themselves socially while also contributing to the maintenance of social order. Because the bases of dignity are socially determined, an individual-level desire for dignity effectively serves to uphold social order. We draw on scholarship by Lamont, Goffman, Habermas, and others to identify a number of components, paradoxes and measurement issues relevant to the study of dignity as the locus of moralized individual selfhood. In closing, we cast the resurgent field of the sociology of morality as an ideal venue for advancing scholarship on human dignity.

INTRODUCTION

The study of morality is undergoing something of a resurgence in sociology (Abend 2014; Hitlin and Vaisey 2013), reinvigorating phenomena that were core to the founding of the discipline (Hodgkiss 2013; Powell 2010), instilling a focus on values, normative culture, and fundamental evaluative frameworks for understanding interaction and the social order.[1] Morality ranges from the most personal inner experience up to the most macro-oriented forces that hold a cultural group or society together. It comprises intuitions, emotions, and

---

[1] The study of morality was central to the work of many of the most prominent scholars in the history of sociology (Durkheim 1961 [1925]; Parsons 1935; Weber 1930 [1905]), though interest in such topics waned over the second half of the twentieth century (Joas and Knobl 2009; Spates 1983). In recent years, sociology has begun to reinvigorate the study of morality (Hitlin and Vaisey 2010), by linking morality to a variety of structural precursors (Sayer 2005), interactional processes (Stets and Carter 2012), and important social outcomes (Fourcade and Healy 2007).

thoughts that people share in defining proper, laudatory, and taboo thoughts, behaviors, and relationships (Haidt 2008). An actor's moral sense implicates the "socially defined systems of rules and roles" that give meaning to situations and actions (Kurtines 1984).

A modern sociological approach to morality, rather than attempting to establish or explain some single basis for morality across human societies, is anchored more firmly in groups, social position, and culture (Hitlin and Vaisey 2013). Within and across societal groups, subjective interpretations of 'right' and 'good' are experienced as externally binding, *a priori* axiomatic social forces (Joas 2000). Subjective moral experience derives from structural and cultural forces and maintains social order. Just as important variation exists regarding what is moral, so too does variation regarding what constitutes dignity in given situations, groups and societies (Hitlin and Piliavin 2004; Schwartz 2011). Similar to the idea of 'thin' versus 'thick' morality (Abend 2011), we believe dignity can be understood within particular situations as well as on a larger scale dealing with institutions, life courses, and ultimate ends.

We suggest that dignity (Hitlin and Andersson 2013) should be located at the forefront of microsociological theorizing, as it speaks to the problem of order while incorporating culture's evaluative element, a core aspect of morality (Parish 2014). As Sayer (2011) points out, dignity is a concept that is self-evidently important to human beings, even as it remains an elusive construct, more often asserted than defined or specified. In thinking about dignity as a basis of human individuality, social order, and motivation, we have diverse intellectual company (e.g., Crowley 2013; Goffman 1967; Habermas 2010; Hodson 2001; Kateb 2011; Lamont 2000; Misztal 2013; Rosen 2012; Schwalbe 1991; Smith 2010).

We propose that dignity is a continual balancing act: one that, like the problem of order, interweaves the social and the personal. Foreshadowing our treatment, Lamont (2000:270) cites Hodson (1996) to define dignity as "having autonomy for defining one's identity and protecting oneself from abuse" (see also Rosen 2012:21). A formal definition of autonomy is difficult to find in the sociological literature. Deci and Ryan (2012) draw upon decades of social-psychological research to argue that, in a routine or daily sense, "to be autonomous means to behave with a sense of volition, willingness, and congruence; it means to fully endorse and concur with the behavior one is engaged in."

Taken together, this gets to the essence of dignity: autonomy mixed particularly with social structure. Through society, autonomy takes on beliefs, associations, identities, and ultimately personhood, and also may be challenged by coercion, destruction or violence. A desire to exert autonomy also means an insistence on individuality, on what one agentically brings to the interpretation of social structure. When autonomy is compromised, so is well-being, and autonomy is then experienced as a desire to oppose or retreat from society.

Dignity, or the achievement of social personhood, is the problem of social order writ small. Dignity is achieved by balancing social integration and personal autonomy, by being neither oversocialized nor undersocialized. As Wrong (1994:70) puts it, the quest for dignity embodies the fact that humans are at once "social, asocial, and antisocial."

BACKGROUND: DIGNITY AND EMBEDDED ACTION

As Wrong (1961:187) argued, norms do not *dictate* behavior – rather, they prescribe and proscribe it. Those individuals who seem most extremely social also seem the least real or mentally healthy (Durkheim [1865] 1952). The issue becomes one of conceptualizing an interaction order that explains the overwhelming patterning of society while allowing for the equally overwhelming fact that many actors deviate from patterns. Pursuant to Wrong's perspective, if we are to understand human behavior rather than an idealized conception of human behavior, how can we explain order at the same time as we allow for expected instances of disorder? Disorder is more, he points out, than simple error and is not simply due to "special circumstances" (ibid.), a curiously passive view of the actor that seems to keep something "safe from sociology" (Goffman 1961).

Modern discussions of agency (Emirbayer and Mische 1998; Hitlin and Elder 2007) make moves toward addressing the possibility that social actors actively orient themselves toward the interaction order without being passive instantiations of it, but sociologists still struggle to balance this sort of regulated action with what we might term 'individuality'. Even those models best-suited for balancing situational demands with individual subjectivity (Burke and Stets 2009), tend to downplay the multifaceted, agentic person who exists in multiple situations across a constructed life course (Archer 2006; Elder 1994). The question remains, can sociology grasp social personhood in a parsimonious way that still reflects lived experience?

Modern sociological theorizing largely has moved beyond extreme conceptions of the actor, focusing not on how individuals are over- or undersocialized, but rather are embedded (Granovetter 1985) or relational (Emirbayer 1997). Still, these conceptions tend to leave unanswered what might be a useful approach to human motivation. A motivated actor would need to be routinized, yet also volitional and agentic: an actor is "social though never a fully socialized creature" (Wrong 1961:183). Many scholars offer implicit or truncated notions of what motivates the human actor, such as a need for approval, utility or ontological security (Coleman 1998; Giddens 1984; Wrong 1961, 1994).[2] These particular motivations, however, may be part of an overarching social personality. Following Wrong (1961, 1994), social individuality is an ideal-typical balancing act, one that takes place between self-interested, destructive or erratic impulses and habits on the one hand (akin to the Freudian id) and the norm-abiding, self-denying impulses and habits on the other (akin to the Freudian superego). While Freudian psychology should not be viewed as incontrovertible or *de rigueur*, the important basic point regarding social action

---

[2] These are just two general examples. Needs for efficiency or other ultimate ends may obtain within specific cultural contexts (Boltanski and Thévenot 2006).

that Freud makes – and that action theory has since reiterated (Granovetter 1985) – is that individuality and society coexist in a difficultly intertwined balance. This suggests not only that society is, as Lawler and colleagues mention at the front of this volume, perennially "on the edge of chaos," but it also suggests that integration cannot sustain itself whenever it threatens autonomy – unless coercion is continual and powerful, as in the case of dependence or slavery.

Autonomy in many respects is socially endowed and constructed, making self-interest far more consistent with collective interests than would be predicted by strict rationality (e.g., D'Andrade 1995; Deci and Ryan 2012). Thus, "chaos" is largely restrained, as society often is experienced as self, and the human desire to make meaning overlaps with the symbolic material society offers as tools for constructing that meaning. Yet, the potentially dire consequences of squelching autonomy are represented in Durkheim's case of the overintegrated individual, and perhaps even more famously in Marx's study of labor relations and worker alienation (Crowley 2013). Maintaining dignity can be difficult because this involves fulfilling certain duties as dictated by allegiance to social memberships even despite conflicting personal wishes (Rosen 2012:36).

People develop senses of self through interaction, perhaps the core insight within sociological social psychology. This self (or selves, depending on one's theoretical commitments; see Owens, Robinson, and Smith-Lovin 2010) reflects commonly held meanings while allowing for creativity and interpretation within a world of social forces. Less often discussed is the moral, evaluative dimension of selfhood. Indeed, sociologists stand to benefit from putting the fact that people 'matter' to themselves more to the center of theorizing about the self (e.g., Sayer 2011; Smith 2003; Taylor 1988; 1989).

Moral concerns form the core of selfhood (Hitlin 2008; Smith 2003; Taylor 1992). To be a person, in this line of thinking, is to possess a self that fundamentally evaluates self and others with reference to values or commitments.[3] Actors tend to legitimize their actions in light of some sort of code, not 'moral' in the prosocial sense, necessarily, but as justifiable according to moral or cultural logics.[4] Dignity implicates subjective and third-person (Lukes 2008) evaluative feelings of moral worthiness, capturing how individuals feel their enacted performances live up to their own personal standards (Erickson 1995) as well as those of the wider community. Dignity thus is both a moral motivation and a moral judgment.

The self, in core social-psychological theorizing, both influences action and is subject to the reflective appraisals of others; dignity, we suggest, captures the nature of the reflexive, morally embedded social actor. To the extent that we

---

[3] This goes deeper than work on the moral self (see Stets, this volume) focused on conventionally outlined internalization of prosocial norms.

[4] Thanks to such justification, rarely does a person see themselves as a villain (Baumeister, Stillwell, and Wotman 1990).

interpret our own actions as fulfilling important personal codes and ideals, we develop a subjective sense of dignity. Dignity thus becomes a locus for getting a theoretical – and potentially empirical – handle on Wrong's problem of order, as people consciously and unconsciously strive to become adequate, possibly exemplary, carriers of the interaction order (Goffman 1983; see Rawls 1987).

Dignity

Dignity, across definitions and usages, denotes a locally recognized humanity marked by autonomy, lack of humiliation, and the realization of social purpose, however constructed (Misztal 2013; Habermas 2010; Hodson 2001; Lamont 2000). Rather than being trivial, this is nothing short of crucial: the motivation and practice of dignity seems the very basis of social stability, especially in pluralistic and heterogeneous societies marked by conflicting actions and beliefs (Dworkin 2006; Hodgkiss 2013; Misztal 2013).[5] Members of social communities reciprocally recognize and transmit understandings of what it is to be a valued, or minimally competent, member of that community. To achieve this takes self-control and an understanding of those standards; to feel good about oneself is to successfully enact these standards and have them recognized by significant others.

In practice, society and individuality represent a false duality. As Mead's (1934) outline of the social self-concept makes clear, the social and the personal are at times in harmony and other times at odds. To the extent that individuals meet evaluative standards, they experience more or less of a sense of dignity. The "me," the self-concept that is precipitated through interaction, is a particularized product of one's structural position, embeddedness, and interaction history. The "me" balances the social and the personal in a way that embodies social individuality. Human dignity may be understood as a deeply felt motivation to regulate and assert "me": to 'do' social personhood, to be a person who is socially embedded.

Dignity has several supporting motivations, which (Sayer 2007) outlines as (a) being competently autonomous, (b) exercising the capacity to flourish, (c) earning others' respect, and (d) displaying composure or face, however locally defined. Dignity hinges on a capacity to exert self-control, a core

---

[5] Elsewhere (Andersson and Hitlin 2013), we provide an extensive overview of previous definitions of dignity, and a discussion of how dignity compares to other related concepts such as respect or self-esteem. Given our interest here in microsociology and the problem of social order inherent to scaling up from micro foundations, such critical exposition lies outside our current aims. However, as a general takeaway from that overview and the discussion that accompanies it, we simply note here that dignity refers to a status of social personhood as well as the enacted construction of that social personhood (see Waldron 2007 for a similar treatment). Social personhood begins with the notion of humans as having "inherent value" or a Kantian irreplaceability (Rosen 2012; Sensen 2011). It then implicates positive reflected appraisals (Anderson and Snow 2001; Hodson 2001).

sociological aspect of agency (e.g., Emirbayer and Mische 1998; Hitlin and Elder 2007), and dignity implicates notions of self-presentation (Goffman 1959), goal-oriented achievement (Carver and Scheier 1998), personal mastery (Pearlin et al. 1981), trust (Uslaner 2002), planful competence and perseverance (Clausen 1991; 1993), and participation in basic social commitments such as work or marriage. Dignity moves beyond the popular concept of self-esteem (Cast and Burke 2002; Rosenberg et al. 1995), as the latter is largely an asituational measure of self-regard, while dignity captures a more situated individual. In fact, the original conception of self-esteem was more anchored in 'self-worth' (Rosenberg 1965), an aspect of self-esteem closer to a notion of dignity that has largely been overshadowed by self-esteem as an indicator of how much one likes oneself, or feel others like them (Leary et al. 1995).

While dignity indeed has sparked interest among social theorists and scientists, the concept has attracted criticism. Bases of dignity can vary radically between groups and societies (Smith 2010). This has led Steven Pinker and Arthur Schopenhauer, among other scholars, to question the very intellectual value of the concept (Misztal 2013; Rosen 2012) as a global representation of the human condition. We suggest that understanding dignity as a product of social relations allows for vast variation in the content of dignity evaluations across societies, addressing this core criticism. As Goffman (1967) illustrates with vivid examples, personhood, even if it is not "real," is reified and continually constructed through daily acts, making it real and important in a very practical sense despite local variations. Similar to societies and people, what dignity means in practice can differ greatly between situations, across a single person's life course, or between groups and cultures. Yet, like societies and people, dignity also has core characteristics.

This leads to a complication in assigning a single definition of the concept, as dignity does not have an invariant essence. Dignity is more like a social instrument that measures and characterizes participation in social order, with at least six measurable characteristics or "senses" we discuss, later. Habermas (2010:469) instructively notes that "'human dignity' performs the function of a seismograph that registers what is constitutive for a demographic legal order." Carrying on with this metaphor, while earthquakes vary in terms of implicated tectonic faults, epicenters, severity, and aftershocks, for example – while each earthquake is a unique event – this does not obviate the need for talking about earthquakes objectively and devising common metrics for them. We hold similar aspirations for dignity despite the irreducibility and, rigorously speaking, unprecedented nature of each social order. Within each order, the realization of dignity is correspondingly measurable and falls along some predictable axes.

In what follows, we discuss six potential senses that may serve as a backdrop for conceptualizing and measuring dignity across cultures. We array these six senses to forge three paradoxes, since treatments of dignity sometimes highlight apparently irreconcilable properties. Just as water may be liquid or gaseous depending on its kinetic energy and upon local atmospheric conditions, or just as light may treated by physicists as being a wave or particle, we believe dignity may have diverse states that, at first blush, seem paradoxical.

Sense of Dignity	Description
1. Ascribed Dignity	Dignity as given by agency, social membership, socialization
2. Achieved Dignity	Dignity as continually realized through social interaction
3. Situational Dignity	Dignity as it exists within particular social situations
4. Life-Course Dignity	Dignity as an emergent phenomenon of agency and time
5. Reflexive Dignity	Dignity as apprehended from a first-person perspective
6. Third-Person Dignity	Dignity as apprehended by a(n) (generalized) other

First, dignity is both ascribed and achieved. Ascription comes in the form of "initial dignity" (Sensen 2011:73), or what is given by the social order to particular individuals. This initial endowment is both general (as in the case of human rights) as well as particularistic (as in ascription to a social position on birth). Achievement of dignity refers to variation or lapses in dignity despite – or sometimes even due to – such endowments. Achieved dignity is dignity in a classic Goffmanian sense: as unfolding moment-by-moment and depending on the concerted and careful routines and habits of interacting persons. Emblematic of this sense, Goffman (1967:43) notes that "societies everywhere … must mobilize their members as self-regulating participants in social encounters." Of course, these two senses are not independent, as the achievement of dignity relies on structural ascriptions of dignity for normative guidance: think of doctor-patient relationships, or any situation in which status differences are salient and guide patterns of attention, waiting, othering and deference (Anderson and Snow 2001; Gould 2002; Schwalbe et al. 2000). This precisely is why scholars of dignity never tire of noting that dignity refers to a universalistic or egalitarian endowment at the same time that it marks and reifies status distinctions (Sensen 2011; Waldron 2007).

Next, dignity is both situational and inherent to the life course. Thus, what makes for dignity within a particular situation may eventually be at odds with dignity over the span of a lifetime. For instance, a criminal episode may ultimately forge the basis of new social roles after prison release (Sampson and Laub 1993), or the loss of a significant other to untimely death may spur new, deep involvements in work or community roles. As a third apparent paradox, dignity is apprehended from first- and third-person perspectives. This means that a given person may view their own life as dignified at the same time that an observer does not. Arguably, such tension is the basis of interactional studies of social oppression; oppressed persons in many cases enlist a variety of interactional strategies in an attempt to bring third-person apprehensions of themselves in line with self-views (Anderson and Snow 2001). Also, such tension may well raise the question of whose perspective is (more) "correct." For matters of social or civic participation, third-person accounts are bound to carry primacy, whereas for personal matters or private deliberations first-person accounts may be privileged. While reflected appraisals form the basis of the self-concept, Gecas and Burke (1995) raise the basic but valuable point that individuals may reject certain appraisals of themselves.

Examples: Illuminating Senses of Dignity

In the next section, we offer a variety of applied and specific recommendations for how dignity might be indicated or measured. First, though, we take stock of the conceptualization of dignity we offered in the previous section. These examples capture our proposed senses of dignity.

Economics. The Nobel Prize–winning economist Paul Krugman recently suggested that stark inequality of pay between managers and their workers subverts the idea of "equal dignity of work" (Krugman 2014). Specifically, he suggested that talk of dignity "rings hollow" when "essentials" such as healthcare and a living income are absent. At the same time, sociologists of labor and class, such as Michèle Lamont and Randy Hodson (see also Anderson and Snow 2001), view dignity of work not as an issue of wage inequality per se but more as an issue of social classes and their particularized strategies for achieving dignity in light of material circumstances and adversities. Social practices serve in part to reinterpret the meanings of economic indignities, and in fact they seem to be spurred into existence by material conditions (Lamont 2000; Silva 2013). In terms of our senses of dignity, the distinction between Krugman's view and a sociological treatment amounts roughly to the distinction between ascription and achievement of dignity. That is, whereas Krugman's emphasis is on material conditions that circumscribe possibilities for dignity, Lamont and Hodson, and Marx before them, focus on subjective existence within and through material conditions, and how dignity therefore also is an ongoing achievement that takes place within structural constraints.

Pursuant to economic and material conditions, volatile economic times with brittle social safety nets arguably have succeeded in "privatizing" the achievement of emotional well-being and rendering the inner life and perceived personal growth more central to dignity regardless of one's class standing (Silva 2013; Stevenson 2014). Especially for the working class, dignity may take the shape of a tenacious, basic commitment to "emotional growth" as one vies to negotiate a stark landscape of inequality, inhospitable institutions and betrayed interpersonal trust (Silva 2013:12).

Death. A dignified death might be one in which one dies without excess pain and in the company of loved ones, rather than alone or without physical composure (Smith 2010). In fact, talk of "dying with dignity" raises a larger point relevant to life-course dignity: the end of a life seems to carry disproportionate weight for how that life is interpreted as a whole. Individuals with Alzheimer's disease become increasingly forgetful, often losing the sense of selfhood and self-presentation that defined their life, to where their quality of life and ability to work productively are compromised. Dignifying an individual with Alzheimer's might involve regarding that person for who they once were and how they see themselves – focusing on their years of "intactness" – rather than remembering them only in terms of their late-stage disease (Kolata 1997). McAdams (2006) has suggested that a life narrative may be contaminated by sudden loss.

One's past may also be disproportionately weighted in the determination of life-course dignity. One's biography is fundamentally shaped by material and historical conditions (Elder 1994). In this vein, Silva (2013) posits that volatile economies may manifest at the individual level during the process of biographical narration as "hypersymbolization" – in this case, as a romanticization of when economic times were better, and an emphasis on one's past prior to an economic downturn as a basis for interpreting one's personal integrity and achievements. Or, in the case of childhood neglect, abuse or trauma, which also is socially distributed, the past may be construed in one's biography as a dark cloud from which one had to "break free" in order to achieve dignity (Silva 2013:118).

Crime. Being authentic or "true to oneself" (Turner 1976) seems a touchstone of human dignity. Feelings of inauthenticity are disheartening and alienating and they likely run contrary to the achievement of social personhood (Erickson 1995; Taylor 1992). In June 2014, a gunman reportedly quit taking mental-health medications so he could "feel the hate," or gains a truer, more authentic sense of his convictions and desires (Clarridge and Sullivan 2014). This raises a basic point about how autonomy may express itself in ways that undercut or threaten social order.[6] Moreover, this case highlights the sometimes contentious distinction between reflexive and third-person dignity. From the shooter's perspective, opening fire on a college campus may have been a meaningful, dignified act. It may have validated his sense of personhood within a reference group of other campus shooters (Clarridge and Sullivan 2014), while also validating his autonomy due to employing particular technical or interpersonal strategies. From the perspective of the wider community, however, this act was criminal and destructive of life.

Dignity: Conceptual Elements and Measurement Strategies

If dignity is to have empirical utility for social psychology, it needs to be situated alongside related constructs. At present, sociological treatments of dignity refer to deeply subjective as well as convincing (third-person) achievements of

[6] One might argue that autonomy in the case of mental pathology is qualitatively distinct from autonomy in the case of healthy mental functioning. For instance, autonomy in the case of mental illness may be experienced differently or contribute to dignity differently than in the healthy case. The cleaving of autonomy into distinct or privileged types then becomes a question of labeling and deviance. Due to space constraints, we do not pursue this here.

social personhood in given cultural, social or role contexts. Likely symptomatic of the budding nature of research, dignity tends to be inferred on behalf of subjects rather than determined and measured directly. Unfortunately, this creates a formidable threat to gaining cumulative and empirical knowledge about what dignity is and how it is shaped. Moving forward, then, it would be useful to begin erecting common ground for the conceptualization and measurement of dignity. Toward that end, we offer some preliminary direction. For each of the six senses, listed previously, we discuss micro and macro forms of measurement, offering ways that we might capture dignity's subjective sense and its place in signifying wider social recognition.

First, dignity often is construed in terms of autonomy and volition, whether in routine actions or in the workplace (Anderson and Snow 2001; Crowley 2013). To demonstrate dignity also involves self-control, however, as losing dignity is often associated with a loss of control, such as aging and declining bodily functioning, or being in an impaired state (such as by intoxication). Self-control is most often studied behaviorally (but see Antonaccio and Tittle 2008 for one self-report measure), but items that might implicate self-control would inquire as to one's perceived capacity to rein in one's behavior in the face of temptation.

In labor and occupational contexts, structural allowance for personal autonomy may be measured, in terms of, for example, direct supervision, the presence of task segmentation, automation, and worker participation (Crowley 2013). Of course, dignity of labor is proactive as well as reactive (Hodson 2001:17). As such, it encompasses citizenship and the pursuit of meaning among workers as well as worker resistance (ibid). Labor-based treatments of dignity should take care to identify the relevant categories and sources of dignity within particular cultures and occupational contexts. At the same time, it seems fairly clear that certain labor conditions such as participation and organizational citizenship are relevant to dignity regardless of the labor situation being considered.

In addition to autonomy, dignity also implicates notions of self-worth and respect (Hodson 2001; Silva 2013). Hodson (2001:i) indeed defines dignity as "the ability to establish a sense of self-worth and self-respect and to enjoy the respect of others." Several of the items typically used to measure self-esteem (Rosenberg 1965) invoke the idea of being "at least on an equal plane with others," and having respect for oneself, both of which are common refrains in theoretical discussions of dignity.[7] In addition to this generic assessment

---

[7] For a period, self-esteem was perhaps the most-researched topic in social psychology, standing in as a proxy for measuring motivation and subjective senses of self resulting from the feedback of others (Cast, Alicia D., and Peter. Burke. 2002. "A Theory of Self-Esteem." *Social Forces* 80(3):1041–68). There are a variety of approaches to studying self-esteem, including debates over its positive vs. negative aspects (Owens, Timothy J. 1993. "Accentuate the Positive – and the Negative: Rethinking Self-Esteem, Self-Deprecation, and Self-Confidence." *Social Psychology Quarterly* 56:288–99), its global versus specific instantiations (Rosenberg,

of self-worth, it makes sense to query structural bases of this achievement of worth. For instance, Lamont (2000) and Silva (2013) outline several bases of self-worth as structured by social class. Lamont (2000) shows that members of the American working class do not identify as strongly as the middle-class with principles such as self-actualization, conflict avoidance, and skillful self-presentation. The psychologist Crocker argues that one can measure different bases of self-esteem, a potential avenue for bridging disciplines around the concept of dignity (Crocker 2002; Crocker and Wolfe 2001). Treating dignity as equivalent to self-esteem or self-worth, however, obscures one of its central advantages as a constructed aimed at illuminating social order; dignity standards change across time and space (Stevenson 2014), and reflect societal and in-group priorities. Certain political structures intersect with class membership and cultural heritage to determine how important self, personhood and time are to dignity.

Finally, dignity invokes social attachment and integration. Silva (2013:24) calls this "longing for a witness" to legitimate and validate one's life story. To a large extent, dignity flows forth from how one is recognized and how one treats others, which makes it a profoundly interpersonal matter (Sayer 2011:200–1). This returns us to Goffman's interactional scenes in which, moment by moment, interactants follow a "particular set of rules which transforms [a fellow individual] into a human being" (Goffman 1967:45). These rules, in their intricate, habitualized structure, make allowances for innumerable social buffers, those "blindnesses, half-truths, illusions, and rationalizations" that are the very basis of making society and social interactions work (p. 43). Schwalbe et al. (2000) incorporate status into these interactional principles, noting how othering and deference are the outcomes of role-based expectations (see also Gould 2002).

While interactions are made dignifying by an arsenal of rules, habits and behaviors, life stories also are rendered successful by Goffmanian tact. Narratives of one's marriage or one's life course may pivot on certain vague cultural ideas such as devotion, passion, or growth, which act to filter and streamline socially ambiguous experience – and alter memory – in the service of developing an effective narrative for conveying one's commitments to oneself and significant others (Swidler 2001). Measuring narratives typically involves qualitative work, though Vaisey (2009) might offer a parsimonious way to capture moral-cultural dispositions that shape the sorts of logics, metaphors and themes people value and thus recruit for their life stories.

Morris, Carmi Schooler, Carrie Schoenbach, and Florence Rosenberg. 1995. "Global Self-Esteem and Specific Self-Esteem: Different Concepts, Different Outcomes." *American Sociological Review* 60(1):141–56), its potential role in explaining violence and aggression (Baumeister, Roy F., Laura Smart, and Joseph M. Boden. 1996. "The Relation of Threatened Egotism to Violence and Aggression: The Dark Side of Self-Esteem." *Psychological Review* 103(1):5–33), and its place as simply a measure of social belonging or integration (Leary, Mark R., Ellen S. Tambor, Sonja K. Terdal, and Deborah L. Downs. 1995. "Self-Esteem and Interpersonal Monitor: The Sociometer Hypothesis." *Journal of Personality and Social Psychology* 68:518–30).

Oddly enough, quantitative measurement of dignity might be more advanced drawing from literatures that demonstrate the negative consequences of failing to live up to self- and societal notions of a morally decent person. A failure to achieve dignity is linked to feelings of shame, a more global self-assessment that involves an embodied sense of failure and shortcoming based on social standards (Scheff 1988; Tangney, Stuewig, and Mashek 2007). Low self-esteem, as currently conceptualized, is not equivalent to feeling shame (although they are likely correlated). Rather, shame involves a deeper, ongoing sense of deep moral violation, and represents a potential indicator of dignity. Future work should engage the extent that popular models of the self and emotions in social psychology intersect with the richer construct of dignity, to better understand how local order, cultural expectations, and subjective selfhood intersect.

In practice, these aspects of dignity may undermine and complicate each other. Consider, for instance, how an exaggerated emphasis on self-reliance may undermine social integration, as among Silva's working-class informants. Or, a rewarding job – marked by high emotional rewards and autonomous working conditions – may limit one's time for family and thus may hamper self-esteem by making devoted parenting difficult. As a final example, social currents of neoliberalism and class-based inequality may clash with notions of dignity as egalitarian or as based in some intrinsic goodness given all citizens (Stevenson 2014). Elsewhere, we more deeply engage dignity's paradoxical elements, and estimate a single-factor measurement model of dignity using a nationally representative dataset (Andersson and Hitlin under review).[8]

At this stage of inquiry, we see these intellectual obstacles surrounding dignity as both reasonable and necessary – as welcome challenges, in other words – as they invite the dialogue necessary to distill the essence of dignity for social scientists. However, given the way that dignity embeds both individual and cultural standards, what (Abend 2014) refers to as the 'moral background', and touches on established literatures on self-esteem and autonomy (or self-efficacy), there is good face validity for the potential of a concrete measure to serve as a useful, concise, repeatable proxy for studying the development and maintenance of social order.

SUMMARY AND CONCLUSION

Dignity as an essential human potential exists, we suggest, in any intersubjectively oriented group or society that creates evaluative standards through which members can assess and achieve a sense of identity. The sort of dignity

---

[8] Our measurement model of dignity includes one latent factor that is indicated by autonomy, mastery, social contribution, social integration, respect, pride, self-respect, life integration, trust and warm relationships, hard work and responsibility. Each of these eleven indicators relate to one or more of the six senses of dignity we discussed earlier. The excellent fit of a single-factor measurement model across all six senses suggests that dignity may be a unitary social-psychological construct even despite the at times paradoxical relationships among the six senses.

that is discussed in many of the sociological works of the last quarter-century typically appeals to what Sayer (2007, 2011) refers to as a 'modern, universal, egalitarian one', a notion that all humans have intrinsic worth based in their capacities for reflexivity and self-control. Even at this level of abstraction, dignity can be seen as a dependent variable in the sense that its contents are shaped by particular cultural histories and structural realities, but we reiterate, even the oppressed, maligned, and powerless have local opportunities to achieve at least a modicum of dignity.

As we stated earlier, we do not believe that the contextual basis of dignity by any means undermines its value for sociology or for understanding social order. In fact, this is what makes dignity quintessentially sociological, just as societies and persons markedly differ in their scope or nature. The raw individual force behind dignity is autonomy, but autonomy is enabled through social forces and structure. Individualism, so understood, can only develop and exist within a social framework that defines the rules, boundaries, and moral meaning of the individual and her character (Katz 1975). Recognition may be a raw social force underlying dignity, which may be provided by positive identity feedback.[9]

Creating an empirical measure of dignity has its challenges for at least two reasons, based on our read of the literature. First, senses and indicators of dignity may at times be paradoxically related. Secondly, given the myriad ways individuals might achieve a sense of dignity – something we suggest humans are strongly motivated to achieve – most individuals would likely end up with a moderate to high reported sense of dignity even despite great adversity (Andersson and Hitlin under review), creating a negatively skewed distribution also seen in representative research on optimism or self-esteem. This may limit meaningful variation in the dignity measure, or make it less clear what observed variation in dignity actually represents. In modern society, 'typically' functioning individuals would likely be grouped to one (high) end of such an index, suggesting that there are thresholds under which other mental health issues might emerge, but that at some point 'more' dignity may or may not lead to greater advantages in well-being. However, a model that specifies different routes to dignity, whereby some people achieve it through solidly integrated social roles, while others achieve it through superior achievement, might tell us a lot about the evaluative standards that individuals utilize to achieve a sense of competent personhood. Those standards, we are suggesting, with their moral components, tell us as much about the social group as they do about the individual, and allow us to potentially be more refined than the classic notion of reflected appraisals in understanding how individuals conceive of themselves.

While an overarching motivation for dignity provides a *why* (or telic impulse, "first mover") at the individual level, social structure provides the starting and continuing materials for *how*. By proposing dignity as an overarching motivation, we admit that we are subsuming other deep treatments of action, such

---

[9] We thank the editors for pointing out this possibility.

as those focused on practical consciousness, habitus, moral-cultural dispositions, habitual action, preconscious awareness or personal moral orientations
(Bourdieu 1990; Haidt 2001; Joas 2000; Simpson and Willer 2008; Vaisey
2009; Wilson 2002). Certain dispositions or habits may enable the continual
achievement of dignity: they are, quite possibly, practical solutions to balancing the social and the personal that are learned through the trials of accumulated human experience and then are transmitted intersubjectively. These
dispositions or habits, often lying outside established tools for measuring the
self, are micro-interactional substrates for achieving dignity.

REFERENCES

Abend, Gabriel. 2011. "Thick Concepts and the Moral Brain." *European Journal of Sociology* 52(1): 143–72.
    2012. "What the Science of Morality Doesn't Say about Morality." *Philosophy of the Social Sciences* 1–42.
    2014. *The Moral Background: An Inquiry into the History of Business Ethics.* Princeton, NJ: Princeton University Press.
Anderson, Leon and David A. Snow. 2001. "Inequality and the Self: Exploring Connections from an Interactionist Perspective." *Symbolic Interaction* 24: 395–406.
Andersson, Matthew A. and Steven Hitlin. under review. "Six Senses of Dignity: An Integrative Review and Empirical Assessment."
Antonaccio, Olena, and Charles R. Tittle. 2008. "Morality, Self-Control, and Crime." *Criminology* 46(2): 479–510.
Archer, Margaret. 2006. *Making our Way through the World: Human Reflexivity and Social Mobility.* Cambridge: Cambridge University Press.
Baumeister, Roy F., Laura Smart, and Joseph M. Boden. 1996. "The Relation of Threatened Egotism to Violence and Aggression: The Dark Side of Self-Esteem." *Psychological Review* 103(1): 5–33.
Baumeister, Roy F., Arlene Stillwell, and Sara R. Wotman. 1990. "Victim and Perpetrator Accounts of Interpersonal Conflict: Autobiographical Narratives about Anger." *Journal of Personality and Social Psychology* 59(5): 994–1005.
Boltanski, Luc, and Laurent Thévenot. 2006. *On Justification: Economies of Worth.* Princeton, NJ: Princeton University Press.
Bourdieu, Pierre. 1990. *The Logic of Practice.* Stanford University Press.
Burke, Peter and Jan Stets. 2009. *Identity Theory.* New York: Oxford University Press.
Carver, Charles S., and Michael Scheier. 1998. *On the Self-Regulation of Behavior.* Cambridge: Cambridge University Press.
Cast, Alicia D., and Peter. Burke. 2002. "A Theory of Self-Esteem." *Social Forces* 80(3): 1041–68.
Clarridge, Christine and Jennifers Ullivan. 2014. "Prosecutor: Gunman 'wanted to feel the hate,' scouted SPU." *Seattle Times* June 11.
Clausen, John A. 1991. "Adolescent Competence and the Shaping of the Life Course." *American Journal of Sociology* 96: 805–42.
    1993. *American Lives: Looking Back at Children of the Great Depression.* New York: Free Press.

Coleman, James. 1998. *Foundations of Social Theory*. Cambridge, MA: Harvard University Press.

Crocker, Jennifer. 2002. "Contingencies of Self-Worth: Implications for Self-Regulation and Psychological Vulnerability." *Self and Identity* 1: 143–49.

Crocker, Jennifer, and Connie T. Wolfe. 2001. "Contingencies of Self-Worth." *Psychological review* 108(3): 593–623.

Crowley, Martha. 2013. "Gender, the Labor Process and Dignity at Work." *Social Forces* 91: 1209–38.

D'Andrade, Roy. 1995. *The Development of Cognitive Anthropology*. Cambridge: Cambridge University Press.

Deci, Edward L., and Richard M. Ryan. 2012. "Motivation, Personality, and Development within Embedded Social Contexts: An Overview of Self-Determination Theory." Pp. 85–110 in *Oxford Handbook of Human Motivation*, edited by Richard M. Ryan. Oxford: Oxford University Press.

Durkheim, Emile. [1865] 1952. *Suicide: A Study in Sociology*. Translated by George Simpson. New York: Psychology Press.

———. 1961 [1925]. *Moral Education*. Glencoe, IL: Free Press.

Dworkin, Richard. 2006. *Is Democracy Possible Here?* Princeton, NJ: Princeton University Press.

Elder Jr., Glen H. 1994. "Time, Human Agency, and Social Change: Perspectives on the Life Course." *Social Psychology Quarterly* 57(1): 4–15.

Emirbayer, Mustafa. 1997. "Manifesto for a Relational Sociology." *American Journal of Sociology* 103(2): 281–317.

Emirbayer, Mustafa, and Ann Mische. 1998. "What Is Agency?" *American Journal of Sociology* 103(4): 962–1023.

Erickson, Rebecca J. 1995. "The Importance of Authenticity for Self and Society." *Symbolic Interaction* 18: 121–44.

Fourcade, Marion, and Kieran Healy. 2007. "Moral Views of Market Society." *Annual Review of Sociology* 33: 285–31.

Gecas, Viktor and Peter Burke. 1995. "Self and Identity." Pp. 156–73 in *Sociological Perspectives on Social Psychology*, edited by Karen S. Cook, Gary Alan Fine, and James T. House. Boston: Allyn and Bacon.

Giddens, Anthony. 1984. *The Constitution of Society: Outline of the Theory of Structuration*. Berkeley: University of California Press.

Goffman, Erving. 1959. *The Presentation of Self in Everyday Life*. New York: Anchor Books.

——— (Ed.). 1961. *Asylums: Essays on the Social Situation of Mental Patients and Other Inmates*. Garden City, NY: Anchor Books.

———. 1967. *The Interaction Ritual*. New York: Doubleday Anchor.

———. 1983. "The Interaction Order: American Sociological Association, 1982 Presidential Address." *American Sociological Review* 48(1): 1–17.

Gould, Roger. 2002. "The Origins of Status Hierarchies: A Formal Theory and Empirical Test." *American Journal of Sociology* 107: 1143–1178.

Granovetter, Mark. 1985. "Economic Action and Social Structure: The Problem of Embeddedness." *American Journal of Sociology* 91: 481–510.

Habermas, Jürgen. 2010. "The Concept of Human Dignity and the Realistic Utopia of Human Rights." *Metaphilosophy* 41: 464–480.

Haidt, Jonathan. 2001. "The Emotional Dog and Its Rational Tail: A Social Intuitionist Approach to Moral Judgement." *Psychological Review* 108(4): 814–34.

2008. "Morality." *Perspectives on Psychological Science* 3(1): 65–72.

Hitlin, Steven. 2008. *Moral Selves, Evil Selves: The Social Psychology of Conscience.* New York: Palgrave Macmillan.

Hitlin, Steven, and Matthew A. Andersson. 2013. "Social Psychology." Pp. 384–93 in *Handbook of Sociology and Human Rights*, edited by David L Brunsma, Keri E. Iyall Smith, and Brian K. Bran. Boulder, CO: Paradigm.

Hitlin, Steven, and Glen H. Elder Jr. 2007. "Understanding 'Agency': Clarifying a Curiously Abstract Concept." *Sociological Theory* 25(2): 170–91.

Hitlin, Steven and Jane A. Piliavin. 2004. "Values: A Review of Recent Research and Theory." *Annual Review of Sociology* 30: 359–93.

Hitlin, Steven, and Stephen Vaisey (Eds.). 2010. *Handbook of the Sociology of Morality*. New York: Springer.

2013. "The New Sociology of Morality." *Annual Review of Sociology* 39: 51–68.

Hodgkiss, Philip. 2013. "A Moral Vision: Human Dignity in the Eyes of the Founders of Sociology." *The Sociological Review* 61(3): 417–39.

Hodson, Randy. 1996. "Dignity in the Workplace under Participative Management: Alienation and Freedom Revisited." *American Sociological Review* 61: 719–38.

2001. *Dignity at Work*. Cambridge: Cambridge University Press.

Joas, Hans (Ed.). 2000. *The Genesis of Values*. Cambridge, UK: Polity Press.

Joas, Hans, and Wolfgang Knobl. 2009. *Social Theory: Twenty Introductory Lectures.* Cambridge: Cambridge University Press.

Kateb, George. 2011. *Human Dignity*. Cambridge, MA: Belknap Press.

Katz, Jack. 1975. "Essences as Moral Identities: Verifiability and Responsibility in Imputations of Deviance and Charisma." *American Journal of Sociology* 80(6): 1369–90.

Kolata, Gina. 1997. "Alzheimer's Patients Present a Lesson on Human Dignity." *New York Times* January 1.

Krugman, Paul. 2014. "Inequality, Dignity, and Freedom." *New York Times* February 14, p. A31.

Kurtines, William M. 1984. "Moral Behavior as Rule-Governed Behavior: A Psychosocial Role-Theoretical Approach to Moral Behavior and Development." Pp. 303–24 in *Morality, Moral Behavior, and Moral Development*, edited by William M. Kurtines and Jacob L. Gewirtz. New York: Wiley.

Lamont, Michèle. 2000. *The Dignity of Working Men*. New York: Russell Sage Foundation.

Leary, Mark R., Ellen S. Tambor, Sonja K. Terdal, and Deborah L. Downs. 1995. "Self-Esteem and Interpersonal Monitor: The Sociometer Hypothesis." *Journal of Personality and Social Psychology* 68: 518–30.

Lukes, Steven. 2008. *Moral Relativism*. New York: Picador.

McAdams, Dan P. 2006. *The Redemptive Self: Stories Americans Live by.* New York: Oxford University Press.

Mead, George H. 1934. *Mind, Self, and Society*. Chicago: University of Chicago.

Misztal, Barbara A. 2013. "The Idea of Dignity: Its Modern Significance." *European Journal of Social Theory* 16: 101–21.

Owens, Timothy J. 1993. "Accentuate the Positive – and the Negative: Rethinking Self-Esteem, Self-Deprecation, and Self-Confidence." *Social Psychology Quarterly* 56: 288–99.

Owens, Timothy, Dawn Robinson, and Lynn Smith-Lovin. 2010. "Three Faces of Identity." *Annual Review of Sociology* 36: 477–99.

Parish, Steven M. 2014. "Between Persons: How Concepts of the Person Make Moral Experience Possible." *Ethos* 42(1): 31–50.

Parsons, Talcott. 1935. "The Place of Ultimate Values in Sociological Theory." *International Journal of Ethics* 45(3): 282–316.

Pearlin, Leonard I., Elizabeth G. Menaghan, A. Lieberman Morton, and Joseph T. Mullan. 1981. "The Stress Process." *Journal of Health and Social Behavior* 22(4): 337–56.

Powell, Christopher. 2010. "Four Concepts of Morality." Pp. 35–56 in *Handbook of the Sociology of Morality*, edited by Steven Hitlin and Stephen Vaisey. New York: Springer.

Rawls, Anne Warfield. 1987. "The Interaction Order Sui Generis: Goffman's Contribution to Social Theory." *Sociological Theory* 5(2): 136–49.

Rosen, Michael. 2012. *Dignity*. Cambridge, MA: Harvard University Press.

Rosenberg, Morris. 1965. *Society and the Adolescent Self-Image*. Princeton, NJ: Princeton University Press.

Rosenberg, Morris, Carmi Schooler, Carrie Schoenbach, and Florence Rosenberg. 1995. "Global Self-Esteem and Specific Self-Esteem: Different Concepts, Different Outcomes." *American Sociological Review* 60(1): 141–56.

Sampson, Robert J. and John H. Laub. 1993. *Crime in the Making: Pathways and Turning Points through Life*. Cambridge, MA: Harvard University Press.

Sayer, Andrew. 2005. *The Moral Significance of Class*. New York: Cambridge University Press.

2007. "Dignity at Work: Broadening the Agenda." *Organization* 14(4): 565–81.

2011. *Why Things Matter to People: Social Science, Values, and Ethical Life*. Cambridge: Cambridge University Press.

Scheff, Thomas J. 1988. "Shame and Conformity: The Deference-Emotion System." *American Sociological Review* 53(3): 395–406.

Schwalbe, Michael L. 1991. "Social Structure and the Moral Self." Pp. 281–303 in *The Self-Society Dynamic: Cognition, Emotion, and Action*. New York: Cambridge University Press.

Schwalbe, Michael, Sandra Godwin, Daphne Holden, Douglas Schrock, Shealy Thompson et al. 2000. "Generic Processes in the Reproduction of Inequality: An Interactionist Analysis." *Social Forces* 79: 419–52.

Schwartz, Shalom H. 2011. "Studying Values: Personal Adventure, Future Directions." *Journal of Cross-Cultural Psychology* 42: 307–19.

Sensen, Oliver. 2011. "Human Dignity in Historical Perspective: The Contemporary and Traditional Paradigms." *European Journal of Political Theory* 10: 71–91.

Silva, Jennifer. 2013. *Coming Up Short: Working-Class Adulthood in an Age of Uncertainty*. Oxford: Oxford University Press.

Simpson, B. and R. Willer (2008). "Altruism and Indirect Reciprocity: The Interaction of Person and Situation in Prosocial Behavior." *Social Psychology Quarterly* 71(1): 37–52.

Smith, Christian. 2003. *Moral, Believing Animals: Human Personhood and Culture*. New York: Oxford University Press.

2010. *What is a Person?* Chicago: University of Chicago Press.

Spates, James L. 1983. "The Sociology of Values." *Annual Review of Sociology* 9: 27–49.

Stets, Jan E., and Michael J. Carter. 2012. "A Theory of the Self for the Sociology of Morality." *American Sociological Review* 77(1): 120–40.

Stevenson, Nick. 2014. "Human (e) Rights and the Cosmopolitan Imagination: Questions of Human Dignity and Cultural Identity." *Cultural Sociology* 8(2): 180–96.

Swidler, Ann. 2011. *Talk of Love*. Chicago: University of Chicago Press.

Tangney, June Price, Jeff Stuewig, and Debra J. Mashek. 2007. "Moral Emotions and Moral Behavior." *Annual Review of Psychology* 58: 345–72.

Taylor, Charles. 1988. "The Moral Topography of the Self." Pp. 298–320 in *Hermeneutics and Psychological Theory*, edited by S. B. Messer, L. A. Saas, and R. L. Woolfolk. New Brunswick, NJ: Rutgers.

   1989. *Sources of the Self: The Making of the Modern Identity*. Cambridge: Harvard University Press.

   1992. *The Ethics of Authenticity*. Cambridge: Harvard University Press.

Turner, Ralph H. 1976. "The Real Self: From Institution to Impulse." *American Journal of Sociology* 84: 1–23.

Uslaner, Eric. 2002. *The Moral Foundations of Trust*. Cambridge: Cambridge University Press.

Vaisey, Stephen. 2009. "Motivation and Justification: A Dual-Process Model of Culture in Action." *American Journal of Sociology* 114(6): 1675–715.

Waldron, Jeremy. 2007. "Dignity and Rank." *European Journal of Sociology* 48: 201–37.

Weber, Max. 1930 [1905]. *The Protestant Ethic and the Spirit of Capitalism*. New York: Scribner's.

Wrong, Dennis H. 1961. "The Oversocialized Conception of Man in Modern Sociology." *American Sociological Review* 26: 183–93.

   1994. *The Problem of Order: What Unites and Divides Society*. New York: Free Press.

15

The Legitimacy of Groups and the Mobilization of Resources

Morris Zelditch

Abstract

The legitimacy of a group has important consequences for social order: It is a condition under which the collective interest over-rides self interest. The present chapter is a theory that describes how and under what conditions groups that depend for their survival on mobilizing the resources of their own members acquire legitimacy and its consequences for the organizational capacity of the group. Legitimacy is not only a condition of collective rationality, it is also a mechanism of achieving it. Previous research finds that cooperation is conditional on the cooperation of others. Legitimacy at the collective level assures the cooperation of others. The structure of the mechanism itself has an important implication for the problem of order: Much theory of legitimacy thinks of legitimacy as consent. Coercion is its antonym. But legitimacy at the collective level creates both consent and coercion. It depends on both to achieve collective rationality. It is based on principal, but principal backed by sanctions. But coercion absent legitimacy is resisted, costly, depends on capricious, unstable, resources. A stable social order therefore depends not only on principal backed by coercion but also on coercion backed by principal.

INTRODUCTION

In most theories of legitimacy, its importance derives from the impotence of pure power. Classic theories of legitimacy were mostly concerned with the stability of systems of power (Zelditch 2001). Compliance induced by the

I would like to acknowledge the support of NSF grants SOC 7817434 for research on "Group Determinants of Agenda Setting," SES 8712097 for research on "Agenda Gatekeeping," 9022774 for research on "Status, Power, and Accounts," and SES 8420238 for research on "Legitimacy and the Stability of Authority."

naked exercise of power is involuntary. Involuntary compliance induces resistance (Lovaglia 1995). Resistance escalates the transaction costs of exercising power– the costs of monitoring and punishing noncompliance, the costs of police forces, armies, and prisons (Hechter 1984). Furthermore, absent legitimacy, the incentives motivating police forces, armies, and prisons are purely instrumental, often unreliable in bad times (Gellner 1983:22). A stable system of power therefore depends, at least in part, on consent. Its legitimacy, its acceptance as "right" even by those disadvantaged by it (Anderson et al. 2005; Connel 1992; Linz 1978), is important because it gives rise to consent.

The power these theories are talking about is the power of one actor *over* another, inter-personal or "micro" power (the sort of power analyzed by Emerson (1962) or Willer and Anderson (1981)). But there are two sorts of power: There is not only "power over" but also "the power *to*" (Russell 1938). "The power to" at the group level, "macro" power (the sort of power analyzed by Hawley (1963) or Parsons (1963)), defines the organizational capacity of a group, the capacity, for example, of states to provide collective goods (Bates 2008; Migdal 1988) or movement organizations collective action (Gamson 1975; McCarthy and Zald 1977; Tilly 1978).

In the case of "the power to" of a group, the impotence of pure power lies in its absence rather than its nakedness. In sufficiently small groups, one or perhaps a few individuals may, by themselves, possess sufficient resources to compel others to comply with claims made on them by the group. But no general is sufficiently well armed to personally force the unwilling compliance of a whole army. As groups increase in size, they increasingly depend for their power on the mobilization of the resources of others. It is the organizational capacity of a group that empowers both its capacity to accomplish its purposes and its power over its members. It is the mobilization of the resources of others that creates the organizational capacity of a group.

But the organizational capacity of a group is a variable. The key to the organizational capacity of the group is the mobilization of the resources of others. But mobilization of the resources of others depends on the legitimacy of the group's claim to them. No matter how rich in land, labor, or capital the environment or membership of a group, resources that are not mobilized are not power. Absent legitimacy, a group is powerless to either accomplish its purposes or exercise power over its members.

Like regimes (Weber [1918] 1968), groups therefore try to cultivate a belief in their legitimacy –of who they are, what they do, and why they exist. But the legitimacy of groups is as problematic as the legitimacy of regimes. What is being legitimated is itself problematic. New nations are common examples. Boundaries, for example, are often arbitrary. Iraq was an ancient civilization. But the "Iraq" founded by the mandate of the League of Nations in 1920 was a fiction, joining to it regions not previously part of its history (Dodge 2010). Who is a "member" is also often arbitrary: Claims are sometimes made on members who are not in fact treated by the state as members; the combination of nationalism as a legitimating myth with the exclusion of some nations from the benefits of the polity is a common source of internal disorder (Wimmer 2013b). And they frequently fail to mobilize their resources. Somalia, for example, was in 2013 at the top of a list of 126 states so weak or ineffective that they had little or no practical control over law or order in much of their territory and provided little or no public services, infra-structure or welfare (Fund for Peace 2013).[1]

Groups try to cultivate a belief in their legitimacy whether they mobilize resources external to their boundaries (e.g., Meyer and Rowan 1977) or internal to them (e.g., Zelditch 2011). But groups that mobilize some or all of their resources from their own members, like states, clubs, or social movement organizations, also cultivate a belief not only in the legitimacy of the group but also in the legitimacy of their mobilization regimes, the policies, practices, and procedures of their claims, whether formal or informal, to the resources of their members – to their services, for example, conscription (Levi 1997), their participation in rallies, riots, or demonstrations (Gamson 1975; McCarthy and Zald 1977; Tilly 1978), their donations, dues, tithes, or taxes (Levi 1988). There is in fact a good deal to legitimate: The agent who makes the claim for the group may have no right to act for the group, the group no right to plea for or demand any resource, or no right to plea for or demand the particular resource it claims, or no right to the amount of the resource it claims, or no right to the resources of the particular person of whom they are claimed.

Objectives

The present paper has three objectives: First, a theory of the causes and conditions of the legitimacy of groups; second, a theory of its effect, and the mechanisms of its effect, on the mobilization of the resources of its members; third, a theory of its effect, and the mechanism of its effect, on compliance with the authority to tax.[2]

Its method extends to each of its objectives a previous theory of legitimacy and the stability of authority.[3] Extending its scope to groups, in part I, is straightforward. But extending its domain to the mobilization of resources, in part II, presents problems of additivity of both theory and measurement not previously encountered by the theory (Zelditch 2011). Part II models the

[1] The Fund for Peace's Index of Failed States lists 178 states but the last 52 are either stable or sustainable.
[2] In its original usage, a tax was any claim to any resource, monetized or not (*The American Heritage Dictionary* 1992).
[3] Originating in Weber (Weber [1918] 1968, especially pp. 31–33), the theory took much its present form in Dornbusch and Scott (1975). Elaborated some by Zelditch and Walker (1984), it has been progressively extended to acts, persons, and positions by Walker, Rogers, and Zelditch (2002), to regimes by Zelditch and Walker (2003), and to organizational fields by Zelditch (2004). A review of the theory and the evidence in support of it can be found in Zelditch (2006).

nonlinearity of the effect of legitimacy on the mobilization of resources and the nonadditivity of nonmonetized resources. Extending its domain to tax compliance, in Part III, also has problems the theory has not previously encountered. Groups that mobilize the resources of their own members have problems of both agency and collective action not previously encountered by the theory. Agency tempts moral hazard (Ross 1973), collective action tempts free-riding (Olson 1965), fear of the opportunism of others tempts noncompliance with a group's authority to tax by even those who are willing to comply (Pruitt and Kimmel 1977). Part III models the conditions of actual compliance.

THE LEGITIMACY OF GROUPS

Scope of the Theory

Not all groups fall within the scope of the theory. It applies only to corporate actors oriented to one or more collective goals, at least one of which is a public good (such as collective action), and that depend either in whole or in part on their own members for the resources they require to attain their goals. It assumes nothing about the structure of ties, interaction, or communication between members of the group. But it does presuppose that a pregiven normative order exists either in the group or its environment that observably governs the conduct of the group. Finally, it also presupposes that the resources claimed by the group are of a kind that can either be freely given (e.g., participation, effort) or transferred to it (e.g., gifts, donations, dues, tithes, or taxes).

Examples include states, political parties, interest groups, churches, professional, occupational, and trade associations and unions, social movement organizations that are membership groups, fraternal orders, and clubs (such as country clubs). Examples that do not satisfy the scope of the theory include aggregates, such as "the middle class" (in its non-Marxist sense), nonmembership advocacy groups, such as lobbies, networks, such as patron-client systems, and everyday encounters, gatherings, or social interaction.

Many things called "groups" are in fact not groups in the sense required by the present theory. A nation-state or an ethnic association is but a "nation" or an "ethnic group" may or may not be a group. It may well be collective but is often neither corporate nor an actor (Wimmer 2013a). Furthermore, some groups that satisfy all its other scope conditions do not depend on their own members for their resources. Market-oriented firms, government agencies (as distinct from the states they serve), hospitals, universities, and foundations consist, except for their clients, largely, often wholly, of paid employees even if they provide public goods and services.

But the theory is easily stretched to groups in the process of formation if they at least have corporate identities. Furthermore, its scope is analytic, not concrete, hence its reasoning will apply to parts of, rather than the whole of, some concrete cases (such as unions within firms (McAdam and Scott 2005)).

Basic Concepts and Assumptions

There are two sources of the legitimacy of a group (say G) that satisfies these conditions. One is the ends and conditions of its situation of action (say S). Both the goals of the group, such as security, order, or welfare, and its conditions of action, such as the threat of inter-group conflict, play a central role in its legitimation. The other is a pre given framework (say F) of norms, values, beliefs, practices, and procedures recognized by any member (say m) of G as observably governing the conduct of other members of G.[4] F may be either internal or external to G but is more typically both, A legitimating relation (say λ) is a relation between any defined, uncontested element of S or F and any undefined or contested element of G such that S or F either implies or is implied by the undefined or contested element(s) of λ. For example, wars have frequently justified taxation (Levi 1988) and conscription (Levi 1997). If a defined or uncontested element implies an undefined or contested element, the legitimacy of the defined, uncontested element can be said to *spread* to the undefined or contested element of λ.

There are, however, four very important conditions that have to be satisfied if λ is to legitimate G, its mobilization regime, or its claims on the resources of its members. The legitimacy of F and S can be said to spread to them if and only if, first, m believes that the defined, uncontested elements of λ are consensually accepted in G (Zelditch and Walker 2003:225–28). For example, the legitimacy of war as a justification of taxation or conscription is not a given: There may have been little resistance in the United States to participation in World War II after Pearl Harbor but there was substantial resistance to its participation in the war in Viet Nam.

Second, m must believe that any benefits promised by λ or any burdens imposed by it must be either in the group interest or, if not, must apply equally to everyone. For example, if the burdens of individuals who are similar in their ability to pay differ, the burdens are inequitable. The legitimacy of claims by a group on the resources of its members is directly proportional to the equity of the incidence of their burdens (Zelditch et al. 1983).

Third, m must believe that any belief to which λ appeals is a matter of objective fact (Zelditch and Walker 2003:232–3). For example, decline in the belief in Iraq's weapons of mass destruction, supposedly justifying the invasion of Iraq by the United States, was a substantial factor in the declining legitimacy of the war.

Fourth, m must believe that any condition to which λ appeals to justify the legitimacy of G is applicable to the situation to which λ is actually applied. For example, nations that are not nations do not justify nation-states (Wimmer 2013b).

[4] There is no need to assume anything at all about how homogeneous or heterogeneous or how tightly or loosely integrated F is. Many cultures are made up of heterogeneous mixes of disparate, sometimes even contradictory, very loosely integrated elements.

However, it is important to understand that the defined, uncontested elements of λ may be valenced. Some are disvalued, some disbelieved, some prohibited. If an act, person, position, regime, or group implies or is implied by negatively valenced elements of S or F it is delegitimated rather than legitimated by λ. After all, the whole point of *Das Capital* was to delegitimate capitalism.

It also involves a complex process of multiple sources and objects. Any object of λ may have more than one source legitimating or delegitimating it. Any source of λ may have more than one object it legitimates. Any object of legitimacy may be inter-related with one or more other objects affected by the object legitimated by λ. Furthermore, λ is a transitive relation: If an undefined or contested element of G is legitimated or de-legitimated by λ, its legitimacy or illegitimacy spreads to any other object with which it is, in turn, related.

For example, a claim made by G on a resource of m is a quite complex social object. It typically involves not only G, a resource, and m, but also an agent either formally or informally acting for G and a rate that the agent claims of the resource. It also typically involves the administrative policies, practices, and procedures of its agents, their methods of assessing the resources of their members, collecting them, monitoring compliance with their claims on them, and enforcing their claims.

Claims can therefore be legitimate or illegitimate in a number of different ways: The agent may not have a right to act for G, the resource may not be one that G has a right to claim, the rate not an amount it has a right to claim, its target not someone of whom it has a right to make a claim, its administrative practices corrupt or inequitable.

Furthermore, because each of the elements of a claim may have exogenous sources of legitimacy that differ from the others, the valences of its elements may be different. Hence, legitimate agents of legitimate groups may make illegitimate claims, illegitimate agents may make legitimate claims, and they may make claims to the right resources of the wrong people or the wrong resources of the right people.

All this would be a serious complication were it not for the fact that empirical investigation of multiple sources and objects of legitimation (Walker, Rogers, and Zelditch 2002) allows the assumption that the legitimacy of a complex object simply aggregates the legitimacy of each of its components, each of which has an independent, additive effect.

Thus, in addition to the fact that elements of S or F that are consensually understood to be contested neither legitimate nor delegitimate undefined, contested elements of λ, the additivity of the sources and objects of legitimacy implies that equal and opposite uncontested sources of legitimacy cancel each other's effects (Zelditch and Walker 2003:235–6) and, more generally, that inconsistency of the legitimating sources of any object weakens its legitimacy (Zelditch 2006:330–4).

Four Corollaries

These basic concepts and assumptions imply four corollaries frequently mentioned in the literature on the legitimacy of groups and the mobilization of resources.

The Categorical Imperative

The "form" of a group is a category of the kind of a group it is together with a set of features associated with that kind of group (Hannan, Polos, and Carroll 2007). There may or may not be a form such as G's in F. Among the beliefs and values of F are pregiven conceptions of the forms taken by different kinds of groups, that is, groups with different kinds of purposes or functions. If the form of G is a recognizable form in F, it will fit a category in F and possesses the features that that kind of category possesses in F. Its purposes will be ends valued in F, its features beliefs in F. The forms in F create expectations among both members and nonmembers of G for features that actually observed groups ought to possess in S. The better the fit between the form of G and one and only one form in F, the greater the legitimacy of G.

The expectations that forms in F create are normative. If the form of G is classifiable by a category in F but not in accord with its features, the form of G is illegitimate. By contrast, if it is unclassifiable, if there is no category in F at all resembling the form of G, F confers no legitimacy on G. From the point of view of F it is a nonentity (Zuckerman 1999). Its legitimacy depends entirely on (potentially less stable) situational factors.

If the form of G crosses the boundaries of two or more forms in F, it is classifiable but more ambiguously than a form that fits one and only one category. Ambiguously classifiable groups are less legitimate than unambiguously classifiable groups (Rao, Monin, and Durand 2005). The legitimacy of G depends on how unambiguously G is classifiable in terms of the cognitive schema of F. The more features possessed by a category in F that are not possessed by G or the more features possessed by G that are not possessed by a category in F, the poorer the fit of G with F. The poorer the fit of G with F, the less the legitimacy of G (Hsu, Hannan, and Kocak 2009).

Effectiveness. Much of the literature on the legitimation of regimes is dominated by the idea that if g is an accepted goal of G, any element of a regime that is instrumental to accomplishment of g is legitimate in G (Linz 1978; Lipset 1959; for more recent examples, see Hechter, 2013; Levi 1988; Levi 1997; Zelditch and Walker 2003). The same can be said for groups. Much of the literature on the evolution of cooperation is dominated by their evolutionary advantages (Zaggl 2014). Some goals cannot be accomplished by any one actor acting alone. Others could be but can be better accomplished by cooperation with others. Either argument is sufficient: A group is legitimate if it is either a necessary or sufficient condition of attaining some collectively valued end.

A considerable literature exists on the consequences of ineffectiveness. Ineffectiveness is failure to provide a good or service the provision of which justifies the claims of G to the resources of m. Its consequences have been studied for the legitimacy of taxation, regimes, and states. Much of the literature on taxation views it as a contract, a tax in return for a benefit. Failure to provide the benefit is a breach of contract. Breach of contract undermines the legitimacy of the tax (Levi 1988). Even where the approach is not contractarian, as in much of the literature on the stability of regimes, ineffectiveness undermines the legitimacy, hence stability, of regimes. Legitimacy in this literature creates diffuse support for a regime. Its destabilization lags behind its ineffectiveness, but only in the short-run. In the long run it leads to regime change (Linz 1978; Lipset 1959). In the literature on state failure this extends to the survival of the state as a state (Bates 2008).

Justice. The literature on the mobilization of resources, especially the literature on taxation, is much concerned with the fairness of the claims made by a group on the resources of its members (e.g., Levi 1988; Levi and Sacks 2009; Levi, Sacks, and Tyler 2009; Smith 1992).

A claim to a resource is just if and only if it is proportional to m's ability to pay. But the justice of a burden, like that of a reward, depends on a comparison process. The absolute amount of a burden is relative. If actors who are similar have burdens that are different or actors who are different have burdens that are similar, the burden is unfair. But, by itself, interpersonal comparison is indeterminate: if m_i is giving or paying more than m_j, either m_i is giving or paying too much, m_j is giving or paying too little, or both. The meaning of the interpersonal comparison is determinate only if compared to a consensually accepted referential structure that typifies the burdens of typical members of G (Berger et al. 1972). A burden is just if and only if m's actual burden is similar to the burden of a typical actor similar to m. A mobilization regime is just only if the incidence of its claims, the distribution of its actual burdens, is just.

That the legitimacy of a claim depends on its justice has four implications for processes of resource mobilization that are often noted especially in the literature on taxation (e.g., Musgrave 1959). One is that a claim is legitimate only if it exempts those unable to pay. "Need" may be a relative concept and difficult to define, but justice implies an exemption for need, in the case of taxation often measured by subsistence level.

A second is that the rate r of a claim is legitimate only if it is equal for every member of G. If two m differ in ability to pay, inequality makes a difference in the amount it is legitimate for G to claim but the difference in the amounts the two should pay should be equal to the same ratio of their burden to their ability to pay.

A third is that the scope of a group's claims is just only if its resource base is comprehensive. For example, if a claim is to a particular resource R_i, unless the resource base is comprehensive, one way of evading a claim is to transfer assets to an untaxed resource, which in effect induces an injustice in the incidence of a tax on R_i.

Finally, a fourth is that G's claims are just only if the domain of the claims is universalistic. Neither directly nor indirectly should a claim apply either to a particular person or to a particular status, such as age, gender, race, or ethnicity. The claims of the group should not arbitrarily discriminate by any characteristic other than ability to pay.

Moral Hazard. Mobilization regimes are classic examples of the problem of agency: The interests of agents acting for a group may or may not be aligned with the interests of the group (Ross 1973). "Moral hazard" is the probability of misalignment of the interests of agent and principal, in this case G. The probability of it, hence much of agency theory, has no bearing on legitimacy. But actual misalignment does. For the present purpose, "moral hazard" refers to the actual conduct of agents of G, i.e. the actual alignment or misalignment of the interests of agents of a group with the interests of the group.

"Rent-seeking" is the chief example of moral hazard in the literature on the mobilization of resources by a group (Tullock 1967, concisely updated by Tullock 1987). A "rent" in principal/agent theory is a payment by some third party, that is, some party other than either principal or agent, to an agent a for the private use of goods, services, or resources of G, access to which is controlled by a. "Rent-seeking" is the exploitation of that access by a for the private gain of a. Its effect is the unproductive use of the public fisc, that is, its use for the private benefit of either a or some third party at the expense of the provision of some public good.

The examples that dominate the literature are political – rent seeking by policy makers, agents, or members of a polity. For example, "predation" by policy makers uses the power of their position to extract more of a resource from members of a group than is required to produce a desired public good. "Clientelism" diverts public assets to patrons of private networks who distribute them as favors to their clients in return for their political support as opposed to use of the assets to produce a public good (Schmidt et al. 1977). "Expropriation" uses the powers of a to misappropriate the resources of the group for their own private use. "Bribery" colludes with third parties to avoid or evade a tax in return for money, a gift, or favors. All "corrupt" public office for private gain (Rose-Ackerman 1978). But members of the polity also seek rents: "Lobbying" purchases scarce access to public policy that favors special treatment of special interests (Tullock 1967).[5]

---

[5] Zelditch and Walker (2003) deduce four corollaries from the basic legitimation assumption for regimes. Only one is repeated here (because it plays such a prominent role in some of the more important theory and research on the subject, e.g., Levi 1988; Levi 1997; Hechter 2013). But the three others apply to groups as well.

THE MOBILIZATION OF RESOURCES

Domain of the Theory

The mobilization of resources is the key to the organizational capacity of the group. The organizational capacity of the group is its capacity to undertake and implement its purposes, whether the order and security of a state or the riots and demonstrations of a social movement organization. But the organizational capacity of the group is important at both of the levels of the power of a group. The micro-power of the group, for example its authority to tax, presupposes the macro-power of the group. It is the organizational capacity of the group that empowers its authority. The mobilization of resources is therefore the key to both levels of the power of a group. As the size of the group increases, the organizational capacity of a group increasingly depends on mobilizing the resources of others. In groups that depend for their survival on pooling the resources of their own members, legitimacy is the key to the organizational capacity of the group because it is the key to mobilization of the resources of others.

The Nature of the Process

A resource is any object or characteristic instrumental to accomplishing some purpose. Its mobilization by G presupposes the kind of resource that can either be freely given to G by its members, such as participation in a rally, or transferred to G by its members, for example by a donation. One can think of the *yield* of any particular claim by G to any particular resource of any particular member as the actual return[6] to G of the resource it claims. Examples include man-hours volunteered by a member, anything from office work, to recruiting new members, to participation in rallies, marches, riots, or demonstrations; or dollars donated, for example to pleas like that of the March of Dimes, or dues paid to clubs, or tithes to churches, or taxes to states. Any particular yield of any particular claim, y_{ii}, is some fraction r of the ith resource contributed by the ith member.

Legitimacy plays the role of catalytic agent in the mobilization of resources. It does not matter how much legitimacy a group has if it has no land, labor, human, social, or financial capital, technology, or organization. Legitimacy cannot create the organizational capacity of a group out of nothing. By contrast, it does not matter how much land, labor, human, social or financial capital, technology or organization it has if it has no legitimacy. It is the interaction of legitimacy with resources that yields the organizational capacity

---

[6] Many factors besides legitimacy affect actual returns, such as the efficiency and effectiveness of G's mobilization regime and the many reasons besides legitimacy that affect evasion and avoidance of taxation. Here, "actual returns" refers only to the magnitude of the returns due to the effects of legitimacy.

of the group. The basic principle of resource mobilization is that the yield of a claim by G to a fraction r of the ith resource of the ith member of G is directly proportional to the product of the amount of the resource possessed by m_i multiplied by the legitimacy of G and its mobilization regime in the eyes of m_i (Zelditch 2011). Pooling yields across members and resources measures the organizational capacity of G. But formulating the basic principle is complicated by the fact that legitimacy has multiple levels, resources multiple objects.

In characterizing the extent to which the ith m of G accepts the legitimacy of its claim to the ith resource of m, the "legitimacy" of the claim refers to two distinct levels of legitimacy (Dornbusch and Scott 1975). It refers, first, to its *propriety*, an individual-level, personal, belief in it that varies across m. For example, individual variation in the propriety of a war is likely to affect the incidence of draft resistance, as it did during the Viet Nam war. Second, it refers to its *validity*, a group-level variable referring to the extent to which legitimacy observably governs the conduct of a group. Because it is a group property, validity, unlike propriety, is constant for any particular G. But because propriety varies across members, the total effect of legitimacy is specific to m.

Nonmonetized resources complicate the resources-side of the interaction between legitimacy and resources. For example, some states both tax revenues and conscript soldiers. Some social movements not only appeal for donations but also mobilize labor directly for marches, rallies, demonstrations, sit-ins and riots and networks are often the social capital used in organizing them. Absent full monetization, measures of different resources are incommensurable. Hence yields are not only m-specific, they are also resource-specific.

Multiple Levels of Legitimacy and the Mobilization of Resources

At the individual level, propriety moderates the actual yield of a claim by G. More exactly, the actual fraction returned of a claim by G to a rate r of a resource R of a member m is directly proportional to its propriety. Propriety asymmetrically amplifies the fraction of r that is actually returned. But the actual amount returned, y, also depends on the actual amount of R possessed by m.

At the collective level, whether or not m personally believes in the legitimacy of G's authority to tax, validity, independently of propriety, also asymmetrically amplifies the fraction of R actually returned by m. Validity is the belief that others in G believe in some element of S, such as the aims of the group, or of F, such as its authority to tax, inferred from the fact that, as an object of orientation, F observably governs the conduct of others in G.

What "observably governs the conduct of others" means is that some element of F is in fact observably enacted, the conduct of others in G is in fact observably in accord with it, either explicitly validating it, for example by positive sanctions, or implicitly validating it, for example, by doing nothing that observably contradicts or challenges it. If others respond negatively to its enactment or at least do something that observably contradicts it, any actor in G has reason to question that F is consensually accepted in the group. From the fact that F observably governs the conduct of others in the group, any actor observing others in G presupposes that others in the group consensually accept F. Whether m personally believes in any particular norm, value, belief, practice, or procedure, they may nevertheless motivate m to comply with them, either because they are so taken for granted that any alternative is unthinkable; out of sheer habituation; because the perceived belief in them by others implies an obligation on m's part to comply; or simply because that they observably govern the conduct of others implies that it is expedient to comply. In addition, owing to the social influence of others on m, the propriety of a claim by G to a resource of m is also very probably proportional to its validity.

Finally, compliance is likely to be even greater if it is both proper and valid. That is, the effect of propriety is accentuated by the fact that it is backed by validity. The effect of validity is accentuated by the fact that m personally believes in the right of the group to a claim on m's resources. By contrast, if a claim is proper but invalid, invalidity diminishes the effect of its propriety. If it is improper but valid, impropriety diminishes the effect of its validity.

Because they are independent of each other, and therefore additive, propriety, validity, and their interaction combine to yield the total legitimacy of the group and its mobilization regime for any given m with respect to any given R. Pooling R across m is simply a matter of adding the product of the propriety, validity, and their interaction by R across m. But unless G fully monetizes all R, pooling across R is problematic. The metrics quantifying different kinds of resources, such as conscripts and revenues, are incommensurable. Because they are nonadditive, unless all its R is fully monetized, quantifying the organizational capacity of G remains R-specific.

LEGITIMACY AND COMPLIANCE WITH THE AUTHORITY TO TAX

Why Compliance Is a Problem

Legitimation of a claim by G to the resources of its members may be thought of as conferring on its agents the right, hence the authority, to tax its members. The basic idea of virtually any theory of legitimacy is that it induces acceptance of such a right *because* it is right. Furthermore, if it is accepted because it is right, the compliance it induces is typically understood to be voluntary and, if it is authority that is right, the compliance it induces does not depend on the personal preferences of the members. Hence, if it is authority that is legitimate, members are typically understood to voluntarily comply whether or not they are personally advantaged or disadvantaged by the claims the group makes on them (Connell 1992; Linz 1978).

But the compliance of groups that mobilize the resources of their own members is famously a problem: Groups that mobilize the resources of their members for the purpose of providing a public good have problems of both collective action and agency. Groups themselves are a public good. Public goods tempt the greed of free riders (Olson 1965). Predation, corruption, and shirking tempt the greed of agents (Ross 1973). Fear of the opportunism of others deters the compliance even of those willing to comply (Bonacich 1972; Pruitt and Kimmel 1977; Yamagishi and Sato 1986). Being willing to comply is therefore not a sufficient condition of actual compliance. But legitimacy plays an important role not only in willingness to comply but also in the conditions under which actors actually comply.

Willingness to Comply

Propriety, validity, and their interaction all have direct effects on at least being willing to comply. At the individual level, being willing to comply with a claim by G to a resource R of m is directly proportional to propriety. At the collective level, whether or not m personally believes in G's authority to tax, the collective level of legitimacy may nevertheless motivate a willingness to comply with it, either because m takes its authority so much for granted that no alternative is thinkable or because the fact that it observably governs the conduct of others presupposes a consensus among others in the group that any member of the group is obligated to comply. Finally, willingness to comply is likely to be even greater if it is both proper and valid.

Conditions of Actual Compliance

A review of the literature by Pruitt and Kimmel (1977) found many people who would be willing to comply were it not for fear of opportunism by others. Actual compliance therefore depends on expectations of compliance by others. This inference is strongly supported by evidence that individuals do in fact cooperate as long as they are assured that others will also cooperate: Assurance[7] has played a central role in both experimental (e.g. Simpson 2003; Yamagishi 1986; 1988) and nonexperimental studies of the evolution of cooperation (e.g., Levi 1997; 1988; Ostrom 1990; Ostrom, Walker, and Gardner 1992).

Legitimacy is not only a condition of mobilization, it is also a mechanism of compliance with the claims it makes on the resources of its members. The

---

[7] The term is borrowed from game theory but "assurance games" are pure coordination games, not public goods games. In some uses of them a public goods game is said to be transformed into an assurance game (e.g., Simpson 2003). But I do not assume any transformation of the game. I merely use the idea that cooperation depends on assurance of the cooperation of others.

collective level of legitimacy is a mechanism that assures the members of the group of the compliance and cooperation of others, whether the others are agents or other members of G. That validity observably governs the conduct of others is evidence of their compliance. Explicit and implicit validation by third parties in support of that compliance or observable sanctions for non-compliance is evidence of the cooperation of others, whether agents or other members, in support of it.

While observation of behavior in accord with the authority to tax is suf-ficient to create expectations assuring the compliance of others, the effect of legitimacy is probabilistic: Not every a resists the temptations of moral hazard, not every m resists the temptation to free ride. But validity not only reflects, it is also a determinant of a G's support for compliance. Observation of support by others for compliance assures those otherwise willing to comply that compli-ance is in the interest of even those who are not. But the fact that an authority structure, such as the authority to tax, is a system, not merely a dyad, requires some further analysis of the concept of "support."

Support by Others of the Authority to Tax

That authority is a system, not merely a dyad, means that the execution of a claim by an agent of a group on the resources of its members requires the cooperation of a whole system of others, both other agents and other members.

The basic unit of any structure of authority is an ordered pair, for example $[a, m]$. But the actual exercise of authority is systemic, not dyadic: A claim by a, acting for G, to a resource R of a member m of G will be meaningless if other agents of G and other members of G do not back the authority of a by cooperating in the execution of a claim's many tasks – assessing the resources of the members of G, making claims to them, collecting them, and monitoring, enforcing, and endorsing compliance with claims on them.

Because $[a, m]$ is ranked as well as ordered, a theory of the legitimacy of $[a>m]$ multiplies not only levels of legitimacy but also levels of authority. Even in informally organized groups, if they are groups that depend for their sur-vival on the mobilization of the resources of their members, differences in levels of authority can evolve between the agents acting for G, whether or not they are formally delegated the authority to tax, and the members whose resources they claim. Backing of the authority of a by other a can be said to *authorize* it. Backing of it by other m can be said to *endorse* it (Dornbusch and Scott 1975). Both can be said to *support* the authority of a to tax m.

That a claim by a_i on the resources of m – and any subsequent use of them by any other agent, a_j, of G – is *supported* by another agent, say a_k, of G, means that a_k (1) executes any directives by a_i required to make a valid claim on the resources of m and provides a_i with any resources required to execute them, (2) executes any directives by a_i required to sanction noncompliance by m or any challenge by m to a_i's authority to tax m and provides a_i with any resources required by a_i to execute them and (3) withholds cooperation or resources from any a_i who does not comply with valid norms, values, beliefs, practices and procedures of the mobilization regime of G.

If the authority of $a>m$ is legitimate, "backing of it by others" depends as much on support of it by other members as it does on support of it by other agents. That a claim by a on the resources of m_i is supported by other m, say m_j, means that m_j (1) does nothing to contradict conduct by m_i that is in accord with a claim by a, (2) negatively sanctions m_i for noncompliance with or challenge of a's authority to tax m_i, and/or (3) withholds cooperation with or resources from any m who challenges the authority of a to tax m_i.

Others back the exercise of authority if and only if it is legitimate (Zelditch and Walker 2000). At the individual level, if some actor, say p, (whether a or m) personally believes in the legitimacy of a's claim to the resource R of m, p is more likely to support it. But whether or not p personally believes in the legitimacy of either the authority of G to tax its members or the legitimacy of any particular claim it makes, the probability of support of it by p (whether a or m) is directly proportional to its validity.

Validity is particularly important because of the role it plays in normatively regulating power (Zelditch and Walker 2000). The normative regulation of power is the price power pays for its legitimacy. Legitimacy defines the scope and domain of G's authority to tax, the proper conditions of its use, and the scope and domain of the powers of its agents. Hence, some uses of its powers are "abuses" of it. "Abuses" of it are less likely to be backed by the support of others (whether a or m). Propriety, which may be idiosyncratic, is a frail reed on which to rest the normative regulation of power. But idiosyncratic conduct is less likely to be sustainable in a system of multiple actors observably governed by the validity of the administrative practices and procedures of the mobilization regime of G. If the code of the regime is valid, others, whether a or m, are more likely to withhold support of invalid directives by a.

Thus, whether or not p personally believes in it, if p (whether a or m) believes that others believe that the authority of a to tax members of G is valid, then p accepts that a has the right and duty to make a claim on the resources of m; that m has a duty to comply; and that other a and other m have the right and duty to support a valid claim by a to the resources of m. And again, its effect is even more likely if its validity is backed by the conscience of p (whether a or m) and the conscience of p by its validity.

Support by others is recursive: That is, not only is p likely to support a claim that is legitimate, but if another supports it, p is also likely to support another's support of it (Fehr and Fischbacher 2004; Horne 2004). This is not a trivial assumption. Many groups, whether or not legitimate, institute formal penalties for noncompliance. That they are formal is no guarantee of legitimacy. Whether they are legitimate or not is indicated by whether or not they in fact observably govern the conduct of others in G.[8] If a observably sanctions m for noncompliance, whether the sanction is legitimate or not should be observable in whether or not it is observably supported by others.

Expectations of Cooperation and Compliance by Others

Validation, as a process, presupposes the observable enactment of a practice such as the authority to tax. It is validated or invalidated by the reactions of others. It may be validated by others behaving in accord with it or overtly confirming it, for example by positive sanctions for behavior in accord with it or negative sanctions for behavior not in accord with it. Even if it is not explicitly validated, others may implicitly validate it by doing nothing that either contradicts or challenges a's claim or m's compliance. It may be invalidated either by negative sanctions for behavior in accord with or in support of it, positive sanctions for behavior not in accord with or not in support of it, or simply by behavior that contradicts it or challenges it (Berger et al. 2002).

But validation not only constructs validity, it also signals it: One of its unintended consequences is that conduct observably governing others signals to those observing it, whether or not they personally believe in it, either the acceptance or rejection by others in G of its authority to tax, its mobilization regime, and the claims it makes on the resources of its members. Groups vary in the probability that they have a future, but to the extent that the future casts a shadow on them (Axelrod and Hamilton 1981), the effect of signaling is the emergence of expectations. Observing the support of others, whether implicit or explicit, of the claims made by the group on the resources of its members, p, whether a or m, comes to expect its support by others with whom p actually interacts.

Unlike the effect of propriety and validity, the effect of observed practice is not necessarily recursive. Observed support of support is nevertheless important, especially if a group has formally instituted penalties for noncompliance. Their validity is observable in support of them by others. Observing it, p also comes to expect support of support by others with whom p actually interacts.

Independently of observed compliance, observed support by others and support of that support by others makes p, whether a or m, more likely to expect compliance by others, again whether a or m. An important consequence of the idea that legitimacy normatively regulates power is that it applies to the expectations of support and compliance of both a and m. The effect of the normative regulation of power is as much about deterring abuses of a's power as free riding by m (Zelditch and Walker 2000). Both a and m expect support of their conduct if and only if it is legitimate. The support they expect is by both other a and other m. Finally, both expect the compliance of both other a and other m.

---

[8] For example, it is evident in the erosion of the tax base of developing countries. For a case study, see Fjelstad and Semboja (2001), a study of tax resistance in Tanzania. For a review, see Alm, Bahl, and Murray (1991).

Taken together, the effect of validity on support and of observed support on expectations of support and compliance imply that validity is an assurance structure in G. That is, they imply that it is a sufficient condition of expectations of the cooperation and compliance of others. In part, this is because it is a control structure in G. Observation of practices that observably govern the conduct of others is, in part, observation of sanctions, support of sanctions, and support of support of them. Sanctions are a sufficient condition of expectations of compliance by others, willing or not (Yamagishi 1986; 1988). Validity therefore assures those willing to comply of the cooperation of others, whether willing or not. But, although sanctions are sufficient, they are not necessary. Validation is sometimes implicit, it merely does nothing that contradicts or challenges a practice (Berger et al. 2002). Going along to get along does not imply consent (Weber [1918] 1968), but it is sufficient to assure those willing to cooperate of the cooperation of others. Support of it, its authorization or endorsement, is also as often implicit as explicit. In Ostrom's words, validity assures the cooperation and compliance of others with or without the sword (Ostrom, Walker, and Gardner 1992).

The Probability of Actual Compliance

Nevertheless the sword is sometimes what matters. Not everyone is willing to comply. Compliance by those unwilling to comply is as conditional as the compliance of those willing to comply. But its condition is expected sanctions by others. It is therefore important that validity is in part a control structure. Its effect as a control structure is that if a were unwilling to comply with a mobilization practice of G or m with a claim made by a to a resource R of m, their actual compliance would be directly proportional to expected sanctions in support of the practices and claims of G and support of them by other a or m. Its effect on those willing to comply, by contrast, does not necessarily depend on the sword. Even without it, if a were willing to comply with a mobilization practice of G or m with a claim made by a to a resource R of m were it not for fear of the opportunism of others, their actual compliance is directly proportional to the expected compliance of other a and other m.

The conditions of actual compliance imply that, as Levi put it, actual compliance is "quasi-voluntary." Levi's *Of Rule and Revenue* found that compliance "is voluntary because actors choose to pay" but it is "quasi-voluntary because the noncompliant are subject to coercion." It is a matter of principle, "but not only a matter of principle ... Taxpayers make a calculated decision based on the behavior of others." But it is not purely self-interested behavior. "It cannot be accounted for solely by coercion and only rarely by positive selective incentives (Levi 1988:52)." Quasi-voluntary compliance was the major empirical finding not only of her study of taxation but also her study of conscription (Levi 1997). Although she was thinking largely of members, the conditions of actual compliance imply that it is equally true of agents.

CONCLUSION

The Legitimacy of Groups and the Problem of Order

Legitimacy, in itself, does not create any particular structure. It does not create ties, it does not create groups, it does not create status, power, or rewards, it does not create systems of social control. It is nevertheless fundamental to the problem of order because, auxiliary to other processes, it is a process that determines the stability of the structures that emerge from them (Zelditch 2001).

But its importance in the case of groups is that legitimacy is a condition under which the collective interest overrides individual self-interest. It is also a mechanism that mediates the process of cooperation with others. Contributions towards provision of a public good, such as collective action, are conditional on the cooperation of others. They are conditional, for example, on agents not tempted by greed to predation, corruption, or shirking and other members not tempted by greed to ride free. At the collective level, legitimacy is a mechanism that assures any particular agent or member of the group of the cooperation of others.

The structure of the mechanism itself has an important implication for the problem of order. Many theories of legitimacy think of consent and coercion as antonyms, founding the theory of consent on pure principal and coercion on pure rational choice (Zelditch 2001). But what legitimacy actually creates is both consent and coercion. The two are complementary. Absent sanctions for noncompliance, the compliance of even those who would be willing to comply were it not for fear of the opportunism of others would be in doubt. But it makes a difference that the coercion depends as much as consent on legitimacy. Absent legitimacy, coercion is often resisted, costly, the resources backing it capricious, often unstable. There is no evidence, at least to date, that might, in itself, makes either itself or anything else right. Conquest does sometimes legitimate itself, but what studies of alien rule show is that its legitimacy depends on satisfying the same conditions as any other sort of legitimacy (Hechter 2013). If not made right, if its coercion is not backed by principle, its rule is unstable, as coup-prone as post-colonial Africa (McGowan 2006). The stability of a social order depends on both, on principle if it is backed by coercion, on coercion if it is backed by principal.

REFERENCES

Alm, J., R. Bahl, and M. N. Murray. 1991. "Tax Base Erosion in Developing Countries." *Economic Development and Cultural Change* 39: 849–72.

Anderson, Christopher, Andre Blais, Shaun Bowler, Todd Donovan, and Ola Listhaug. 2005. *Losers' Consent: Elections and Democratic Legitimacy.* New York: Oxford University Press.

Axelrod, Robert and William D. Hamilton. 1981. "The Evolution of Cooperation." *Science* 211: 1390–96.

Bates, Robert H. (2008). "State Failure." *Annual Review of Political Science* 11: 1–12.

Berger, Joseph, Cecilia L. Ridgeway, and Morris Zelditch. 2002. "Construction of Status and Referential Structures." *Sociological Theory* 20: 150–79.

Berger, Joseph, Morris Zelditch, Bo Anderson, and Bernard P. Cohen. 1972. "Structural Aspects of Distributive Justice: A Status Value Formulation." Pp 119–46 in *Sociological Theories in Progress*. Vol 2, edited by Joseph Berger, Morris Zelditch, and Bo Anderson. Boston: Houghton Mifflin.

Bonacich, Phillip. 1972. "Norms and Cohesion as Adaptive Responses to Potential Conflict: An Experimental Study." *Sociometry* 35: 357–75.

Connel, Carrol. 1992. "Legitimacy." Pp 1095–99 in *Encyclopedia of Sociology*. Vol. 3, edited by E. Borgatta and M. L. Borgatta. New York: Macmillan.

Dodge, Toby. 2010. *Inventing Iraq: The Failure of Nation-building and a History Denied*, updated edition. New York: Columbia University Press.

Dornbusch, Sanford M. and W. Richard Scott. 1975. *Evaluations and the Exercise of Authority*. San Francisco: Jossey-Bass.

Emerson, Richard M. 1962. "Power-Dependence Relations." *American Sociological Review* 27: 31–41.

Fehr, Ernst and Urs Fischbacher. 2004. "Third-party Punishment and Social Norms." *Evolution of Human Behavior* 25: 63–87.

Fjelstadt, Odd-Helge and Joseph Semboja. 2001. "Why People Pay Taxes: The Case of the Development Levy in Tanzania." *World Development* 29: 2059–74.

Fund for Peace. 2013. "Failed States Index." ffp.statesindex.org/rankings 2013.

Gamson, William A. 1975. *The Strategy of Social Protest*. Belmont, CA: Wadsworth.

Gellner, Ernest. 1983. *Nations and Nationalism*. Ithaca, NY: Cornell University Press.

Hannan, Michael T., Laszlo Polos, and Glenn R. Carroll. 2007. *Logics of Organization Theory: Audiences, Codes, and Ecologies*. Princeton, NJ: Princeton University Press.

Hawley, Amos H. 1963. "Community Power and Urban Renewal Success." *American Journal of Sociology* 68, 422–31.

Hechter, Michael. 2013. *Alien Rule*. New York: Cambridge University Press.

1984. "When Actors Comply: Monitoring Costs and the Production of Social Order." *Acta Sociologica* 27: 161–83.

Horne, Cristine. 2004. "Collective Benefits, Exchange Interests, and Norm Enforcement." *Social Forces* 82: 1037–62.

Hsu, Greta, Michael T. Hannan and Ozgecan Kocak. 2009. "Multiple Category Memberships and Markets: An Integrative Theory and Two Empirical Tests." *American Sociological Review* 74: 150–69.

Levi, Margaret. 1997. *Consent, Dissent, and Patriotism*. Cambridge: Cambridge University Press.

1988. *Of Rule and Revenue*. Berkeley: University of California Press.

Levi, Margaret, and Audrey Sacks. 2009. "Legitimating Beliefs: Sources and Indicators." *Regulation and Governance* 3: 311–33.

Levi, Margaret, Audrey Sacks, and Tom Tyler. 2009. "Conceptualizing Legitimacy, Measuring Legitimating Beliefs." *American Behavioral Scientist* 53: 354–75.

Linz, Juan J. 1978. *Crisis, Breakdown, and Re-equilibration*. Baltimore: Johns Hopkins University Press.

Lipset, Seymour M. 1959. "Some Social Requisites of Democracy: Economic Development and Political Legitimacy." *American Political Science Review* 53: 69–105.

Lovaglia, Michael J. 1995. "Status and Power: Exchange, Attribution and Expectation States." *Small Group Research* 26: 400–26.

McAdam, Douglas, and W. Richard Scott. 2005. "Organizations and Movements." Pp. 4–40 in *Social Movements and Organization Theory*, edited by Gerald F. Davis, Douglas McAdam, W. Richard Scott, and Mayer N. Zald. Cambridge: Cambridge University Press.

McCarthy, John D. and Mayer N. Zald. 1977. "Resource Mobilization and Social Movements." *American Journal of Sociology* 82, 1212–41.

McGowan, Patrick. 2006. "Coups and Conflict in West Africa, 1955–2004. Part II, Empirical Findings." *Armed Forces & Society* 32: 234–53.

Meyer, John W. and Brian Rowan. 1977. "Institutionalized Organizations: Formal Structure as Myth and Ceremony." *American Journal of Sociology* 83: 340–63.

Migdal, Joel S. 1988. *Strong Societies and Weak States: State-Society Relations and State Capabilities in the Third World*. Princeton, NJ: Princeton University Press.

Musgrave, Richard A. 1959. *The Theory of Public Finance*. New York: McGraw-Hill.

Olson, Mancur. 1965. *The Logic of Collective Action: Public Goods and the Theory of Groups*. Cambridge, MA: Harvard University Press.

Ostrom, Elinor. 1990. *Governing the Commons: The Evolution of Institutions for Collective Action*. New York: Cambridge University Press.

Ostrom, Elinor, James A. Walker, and Roy Gardner. 1992. "Covenants with and without the Sword: Self-governance Is Possible." *American Political Science Review* 86: 404–17.

Parsons, Talcott. 1963. "On the Concept of Political Power." *Proceedings of the American Philosophical Society* 107: 232–62.

Pruitt, D. G. and M. J. Kimmel. 1977. "Twenty Years of Experimental Gaming: Critique, Synthesis, and Suggestions for the Future." *Annual Review of Psychology* 28: 363–92.

Rao, Hayagreeva, Philippe Monin, and Rodolphe Durand, R. 2005. "Border-Crossing: Bricolage, and the Erosion of Categorical Boundaries in French Gastronomy." *American Journal of Sociology* 108: 795–843.

Rose-Ackerman, Susan. 1978. *Corruption: A Study in Political Economy*. New York: Academic Press.

Ross, Stephen A. 1973. "The Economic Theory of Agency: The Principal's Problem." *American Economic Review* 63: 134–9.

Russell, Bertrand. 1938. *Power: A New Social Analysis*. New York: W.W. Norton.

Schmidt, Steffen W., James C. Scott, Carl Lande, and Laura Guasti (Eds.). 1977. *Friends, Followers, and Factions: A Reader in Political Clientelism*. Berkeley: University of California Press.

Simpson, Brent. 2003. "Sex, Fear, and Greed: A Social Dilemma Analysis of Gender and Cooperation." *Social Forces* 82: 35–52.

Smith, K. W. 1992a. "Reciprocity and Fairness: Positive Incentives." Pp. 223–250 in *Why People Pay Taxes. Tax Compliance and Tax Enforcement*, edited by Joel Slemrod. Ann Arbor: University of Michigan Press.

1992b. *The American Heritage Dictionary of the English Language*. 3rd ed. Boston: Houghton Mifflin.

Tilly, Charles. 1978. *From Mobilization to Revolution*. Menlo Park, CA: Addison-Wesley.

Tullock, Gordon. 1987. "Rent-seeking." Pp. 147–9 in *The New Palgrave: A Dictionary of Economics*, 2nd ed, Volume 4, edited by John Eatwell, Murray Milgate, and Peter Newman. New York: Stockton Press.

1967. "The Welfare Costs of Tariffs, Monopolies, and Theft." *Western Economic Journal* 5: 224–32.

Walker, Henry A., Larry Rogers, and Morris Zelditch. 2002. "Acts, Persons, Positions, and Institutions: Legitimating Multiple Objects and Compliance with Authority." Pp. 232–339 in *Structure, Culture, and History: Recent Issues in Social Theory*, edited by Sing C. Chew and J. David Knottnerus. New York: Rowman & Littlefield.

Weber, Max. [1918] 1968. *Economy and Society*. Edited by G. Roth and C. Wittich. Berkeley: University of California Press.

Willer, David, and Bo Anderson, eds. 1981. *Networks, Exchange, and Coercion: The Elementary Theory and its Applications*. New York: Elsevier.

Wimmer, Andreas. 2013a. *Ethnic Boundary Making: Institutions, Power, Networks*. New York: Oxford University Press.

2013b. *Waves of War: Nationalism, State Formation, Ethnic Exclusion, and the Modern World*. New York: Cambridge University Press.

Yamagishi, Toshio. 1988. "Seriousness of Social Dilemmas and the Provision of a Sanctioning System." *Social Psychology Quarterly* 51: 32–42.

1986. "The Provision of a Sanctioning System as a Public Good." *Journal of Personality and Social Psychology* 51: 110–16.

Yamagishi, Toshio, and Kaori Sato. 1986. "Motivational Bases of the Public Goods Problem." *Journal of Personality and Social Psychology* 50: 67–73.

Zaggl, Michael A. 2014. "Eleven Mechanisms for the Evolution of Cooperation." *Journal of Institutional Economics* 10: 197–230.

Zelditch, Morris. 2011. "Three Questions about the Legitimacy of Groups and the Mobilization of Resources." *Advances in Group Processes* 28: 255–83. Emerald Group Publishing Ltd.

2006. "Legitimacy Theory." Pp. 324–356 in *Contemporary Social Psychological Theories*, edited by Peter Burke. Stanford, CA: Stanford University Press.

2004. "Institutional Effects on the Stability of Organizational Authority." *Research in the Sociology of Organizations* 22: 25–48.

2001. "Theories of Legitimacy." Pp. 33–53 in *The Psychology of Legitimacy*, edited by John J. Jost and Brenda Major. New York: Cambridge University Press.

Zelditch, Morris, William A. Harris, George W. Thomas, and Henry A. Walker. 1983. "Decisions, NonDecisions, and Meta-Decisions." Pp. 1–32 in *Research on Social Movements, Conflict, and Change* Vol 5, edited by Louis Kriesberg. Greenwich, CT: JAI Press.

Zelditch, Morris, and Henry A. Walker. 2003. "The Legitimacy of Regimes." *Advances in Group Processes* 20: 217–49.

2000. The Normative Regulation of Power. *Advances in Group Processes* 17: 155–78.

1984. "Legitimacy and the Stability of Authority." *Advances in Group Processes* 1: 1–25.

Zuckerman, Ezra W. 1999. "The Categorical Imperative: Securities Analysts and the Legitimacy Discount." *American Journal of Sociology* 104: 1398–438.

COMMENTARY: CONTRASTS AND COMPLEMENTARITIES

16

Social Order from the Bottom Up?

Peter V. Marsden

In the chapters collected here, distinguished representatives of major research traditions in sociological social psychology highlight its bearing on understanding social order – that is, in general, predictability, regularity, and stability in social relations. Some focus more specifically on coordination problems in which mutual rewards result when two or more participants select compatible actions, others on cooperation in partial conflict/collective action situations in which self-interested actions are at cross-purposes with group-oriented ones. All examine processes – omnipresent though often informal and taken-for-granted – that undergird social organization, noticed more in their absence than presence. Most facilitate mutual adjustment, the most basic and ubiquitous approach to aligning the activities of multiple and possibly heterogeneous actors (Mintzberg 1992).

It was a compliment to be invited to identify commonalities and contrasts in these essays. I do so from the standpoint of a sociologist with most experience in studying networks and organizations; I specialize in neither social psychology nor the problem of social order. The arguments set out in this book do offer insights into network and organizational phenomena, and my remarks allude to some of those connections. In what follows, I first depict the intellectual setting for these statements on sources of micro-order. Next I consider microfoundations for the work, emphasizing the affective capacities that many (although not all) authors stress. Following that is a survey of the major ordering mechanisms and the meso- and macro-level features that shape them, and then the corresponding sources of disorder and fragility. After a brief discussion of scaling up from the micro-level, I conclude with conjectures about the bearing of this primarily theoretical work on organizational practice.

THE SHARED INTELLECTUAL BACKGROUND

I began by examining the common intellectual roots of the chapters, as reflected by similarities and differences in their citations. Figure 16.1 depicts a chapter-to-first author citation network for this book;[1] only authors cited by more than one chapter appear in the display. The diagram locates chapters near the authors they cite, and vice versa.

Consider first the chapters, labeled in UPPERCASE and identified by first author. The horizontal dimension distinguishes between chapters that stress ordering mechanisms involving emotions (at the left) and those that reflect a greater influence of social exchange and rational choice-oriented theories (toward the right). Lawler, Thye, and Yoon's chapter, near the middle, involves both types of mechanisms. Clustered in the lower left and center are chapters drawing on major branches of sociological social psychology – including symbolic interaction, interaction order, identity theory, affect control, and expectation states approaches.

The positions of the cited authors (labeled in lowercase) reveal both a sociological core and the multidisciplinary influences that shape this work. The most often-cited authors whose works provide the most widely shared intellectual stimuli lie in the center-left region. Some of these (Hobbes,[2] Parsons) wrote significant earlier treatments of the problem of social order that serve as anchoring points. Others – including Durkheim (cited by seven chapters), Goffman (seven), Mead (six), Osgood (four), and Garfinkel (four) – are major theorists whose works offer inspiration for several chapters here.[3] In the lower portion are authors responsible for classic contributions to social psychology, such as Blumer, Festinger, and Stryker. The edges of Figure 16.1 show that approaches from several social science disciplines shape the study of micro-social order. Toward the middle and right are economists (e.g., Frey), political scientists (e.g., Levi, Ostrom), and sociologists with exchange and/or rational choice orientations (e.g., Coleman, Emerson, Hechter, Yamagishi). Among the heterogeneous authors at the left are some evolutionary anthropologists (Dunbar and Tomasello).

---

[1] Using the reference list in the final draft of each chapter, I constructed a two-mode network linking chapters to first authors of cited works, recording the number of times a chapter cited a work by a given first author. I then removed the 440 first authors cited by one chapter only, since they generate no links between chapters and add considerable clutter. I used nonmetric multidimensional scaling (stress coefficient=0.061) to establish locations for the 14 chapters and the remaining 66 first authors whose works were cited by more than one chapter, weighting chapter-to-first author links by the number of citations. To improve readability, I slightly adjusted the locations of some chapters and authors.
[2] Only two chapters cite Hobbes as a reference, but four others mention his framing of the order problem.
[3] Five chapters cite works by Weber, but he appears in the upper middle region.

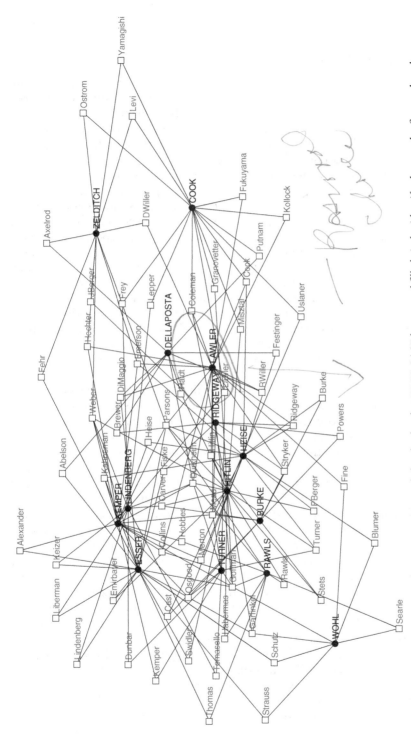

FIGURE 16.1. Chapter-to-author citation network for this book. UPPERCASE letters and filled circles identify chapters by first author; lowercase letters and open squares identify first authors cited by more than one chapter. First authors cited by one chapter only omitted from diagram. *Note:* Graph constructed using NETDRAW software (Borgatti, 2002).

MICROFOUNDATIONS

Many influential analyses of social order problems assume actors who are rational, gain-seeking, and selfish. Since self- and group-serving actions need not be consistent, this point of departure effectively problematizes challenges of achieving cooperation and coordination. The perspectives taken here, though, adopt much richer images of individuals that – at least under some conditions – can be more conducive to social order.

Turner's discussion of the human evolutionary past takes the longest-term view. With others including Kemper and Lindenberg, he observes that a flexible capacity to cooperate in groups conveyed advantages on humans (see also Greene 2013). He emphasizes the comparatively *low* sociality of the closest primate human ancestors; this is also, however, a *different* sociality involving a capacity for weaker relationships and an orientation to comparatively large groups and territories. When later augmented with an elaborate emotional capacity that supports the maintenance of strong ties as well, such foundations leveraged propensities for nonverbal coordination via reading of gestures and emotions, synchronization, role-taking, and the like. In turn, these enable the instantaneous adjustments required for coordination within dyadic interactions (Wohl and Fine) or interaction orders (Rawls). They also support the formation of multiple groups – primary, secondary and even tertiary – in complex societies.

Affective and emotional capacities underlie many of the ordering mechanisms outlined here, often in combination with cognitive factors. For Lawler et al., emotional byproducts are key to transforming instrumental exchange relations into social commitments, and in generating attachments to meso- or macro-level units. Emotions serve to motivate behavior change within several frameworks: people adjust their behavior to match an identity standard (Burke and Stets), and to minimize affective deflections from the cultural sentiments associated with a role (Heise, MacKinnon, and Scholl). Kemper asserts that different status and power configurations prompt characteristic emotional responses that can either strengthen (e.g., pride, optimism, shame) or detract from (anger, sadness) the extent of order. Affect and feelings are primary within Lindenberg's hedonistic goal frame, which tends to be a default orientation.

In many of these models, much action is based on implicit, unconscious cognition as well as emotional foundations – that is, on "fast thinking" in an automatic or intuitive mode (Kahneman 2011) rather than on conscious deliberation. This may reflect, for example, implicit rules for interaction (Wohl and Fine), or deeply ingrained primary frames for social identities that channel categorization (Ridgeway). The fact that such actions are taken without reflection can make them especially resistant to change.

Several authors allow for individuals who can operate in both automatic and consciously reasoned modes. Burke and Stets, for example, posit that identity verification is generally an automatic process, but that it can become conscious if the discrepancy between a perceived identity and its realization in a situation grows large. Most elaborated is Esser and Kroneberg's dual-process model of frame selection that permits both "automatic-spontaneous" and "rational-calculating" orientations to norms. In the automatic frame, norms are followed unconditionally; in the rational one, compliance is conditional on incentives. Such models beg the question of what guides mode selection. For Esser and Kroneberg, this is an automatic process responsive to opportunities, motivation, effort, and the availability of routines;[4] use of the rational-calculating frame becomes more likely when a situation is unfamiliar and uncertain. Related are Lindenberg's three "overarching goals" or mind-sets: hedonic, gain, and normative goals. Environing social circumstances can shape the relative salience of these, but the hedonic one tends to predominate in the absence of supports for the others.

With dual-process models, the more automatic mode serves as a default, so its content matters a great deal for social order. A hedonic mind-set focused on an individual's feelings would seem to prompt selfish action, but Lindenberg – invoking Lawler et al.'s relational cohesion theory – observes that interpersonal dependencies can lead people to take others' feelings into account. Indeed, Greene (2013: 62) contends that such empathy is typical, an element of "psychological machinery ... perfectly designed to promote cooperation among otherwise selfish individuals." It may contribute more to solving within-group than between-group cooperation problems, however.

It seems undeniable that advantage-seeking and selfishness are an important part of social life. Taken together, though, these chapters suggest that positing stylized rational actors as those populating a counterfactual "state of nature" to be anticipated in the absence of social order is to oversimplify. It may exaggerate the extent of conscious, calculative action and downplay cooperative predispositions and emotional factors. It might even overstate the difficulty of the problem of achieving some degree of social order.

SOCIAL CONTEXTS AND ORDER-ENHANCING MECHANISMS

Focusing on micro-level processes that support (or undermine) social order is an especially apt problem for social psychology. Its sociological branch gives special attention to the reciprocal influences of individuals and their context on one another (Kaplan 2000). The presentations here emphasize the individual-to-group flow, focusing on micro-level actions that contribute to either sustaining or weakening social order. These are not strictly bottom-up

---

[4] In some respects, this account of toggling between modes is reminiscent of organization-level processes for alternating between routines and active search (March and Simon 1958). An important distinction is the contrast between the automaticity of mode choice in the Esser/ Kroneberg model and its deliberateness in March and Simon.

processes, however, because they operate within meso- and macro-social conditions. Here, I recount the principal micro-ordering mechanisms these chapters set out, taking account of the larger-scale environments – both institutional and interpersonal – in which they arise.

Several authors assume task-oriented groups that presumably draw on resources in the material environment. Lawler et al. begin with an exchange framework in which social order rests on instrumentally useful transactions that develop into ongoing exchange relations for several reasons, notably uncertain conditions that engender trust (see Cook). On their own, such relations would endure only as long as the exchanges remain rewarding. Layered onto this foundation is their central dynamic: repeated exchanges generate emotional rewards in the form of positive sentiments (Homans 1950), emotional energy (Collins 1981) and thereby affective attachments to relationships that transcend their strictly instrumental value. Lawler et al.'s theory of social commitments asserts that dyadic attachments can transform into person-to-group attachments when tasks are joint ones involving shared responsibility, and participants attribute rewarding outcomes to the group. Turner sets out a very similar account, underlining the importance of a multivalent emotional capacity.

Large-scale institutional formations, social and cultural alike, are important elements of the environment for micro-level processes (see Figure 9.1 in Heise et al. and Figure 2.1 in Turner). The formal organizations and other action systems that undertake instrumental tasks consist of interlocking roles and their characteristic packages of obligations and expectations; these serve to define role-identity ideals on the cultural side. Identity verification – aligning one's behavior with that deemed role-suitable in a given situation – is the central ordering process for Burke and Stets; mutual identity verification by occupants of a role and its counterpart roles heightens solidarity. In Heise et al., affective rewards motivate people to enact role identities, thereby affirming and legitimating wider institutional patterns.

Roles associated with positions in institutionalized systems can have both lateral and hierarchical relationships with one another. Kemper focuses on the status/power dynamics arising out of these, and the emotions associated with them. These support orders of varying strength – the strongest and arguably most resilient involving voluntary cooperation resting on mutual status conferral and recognition, the weakest and perhaps most fragile based on involuntary compliance enforced by power use.

Each of the fourteen chapters uses the term "norm" (or "normative") at least once, often together with other concepts (e.g., a norm as the complex of expectations associated with a role). Norms serve as an especially central ordering principle for several authors. Those stressing them seek to avoid depicting people as unreflective rule-followers. Esser and Kroneberg refer to a norm as a "combination of particular (social) preferences and expectations" or as a "complex of knowledge, affects and associated behaviors." Their model of frame selection allows for both automatic/unconditional and more calculating conditional compliance with norms, depending on circumstances.

Lindenberg's normative goal mind-set includes a set of general solidary norms that promote collective action – sharing, helping, cooperation, role-taking, and consideration among them. When conditions make it cognitively prominent, the normative mind-set can generate strong ingroup solidarity but make between-group cooperation challenging. If both the normative and the individual-interest-oriented gain mind-set are salient, a weak solidarity resembling Esser and Kroneberg's conditional compliance emerges, facilitating a social order that can ramify across multiple groups. Weak solidarity would seem compatible with certain structural arrangements commonly found in complex societies, for example, small-world social network configurations that mix local density and bridging ties (Watts 2003), or loosely coupled organizational designs (Weick 1976).

Hitlin and Andersson focus on the individual's quest for dignity, a condition achieved by "balancing social integration and personal autonomy." Dignity is achieved via meeting group-level standards for social personhood; an individual enacts "understandings of what it is to be a valued ... member" of a community or group, while retaining the discretion to introduce variations as she or he interprets roles or norms, and to otherwise act freely. A vital component of dignity is social recognition as someone who behaves in accord with shared standards; receiving such recognition generates positive affect and thereby promotes order.

For Zelditch, a key larger-scale order condition is the degree of structural-cultural consistency between group goals, norms for attaining them, and organizational forms. Displaying a form consistent with normative expectations furthers a group's legitimacy in the eyes of stakeholders – as do other conditions including effective performance and internal equity. Legitimacy enhances the willingness of members to make their resources available to a collectivity for use toward group goals, and thereby the group's collective efficacy or capacity to act. It also can generate consent to the use of coercion within a delimited scope, in pursuit of shared goals.

Diffuse cultural understandings about social identities, gender in particular, are Ridgeway's central concern. These associate visible categorical distinctions with expectations about competence in task-oriented situations, giving rise to status beliefs. As a practical matter, such stereotypes facilitate micro-social order by providing default identities that simplify real-time sense-making, thereby promoting coordination. Acting in accord with them, though, has a downside: it reinforces presumptions about the competence and value of individuals with different social identities. Unlike the role identities discussed earlier, actors may or may not espouse these. Since others in counter-roles ascribe them based on visible features (e.g., age, gender, race) alone, though, the associated expectations often pose strong constraints. Such widely shared understandings can have especially insidious effects; in institutionalized settings, social identities like gender are usually less salient than role identities, and hence their effects often go unnoticed.

Scripts – shared conceptions of typical behaviors and their sequencing – serve as important ordering devices for several authors. For Esser and Kroneberg, the accessibility and applicability of scripted routines helps to shape selection of either an automatic-spontaneous or a rational-calculating action frame, and subsequently guides action within a frame. While Wohl and Fine give closest attention to the negotiations and adjustments that underlie coordination within dyads, this relies importantly on more or less abstract scripts. Each participant must envision the joint performance in order to role-take the other's perspective and successfully enact their own part. Even coordinated walking abides by rules of etiquette and considers the meanings that third parties may attribute to particular enactments – meanings that may be either general or specific to a local idioculture (Fine 1979). Partners in sexual encounters may act out scripts depicted in media images or other cultural lore, or privatized interpersonal ones resting on experience with one another. Musical duets often begin with an explicit script (in the form of a score), which is subject to local stylistic and interpretive modifications.

Related but conceivably even more local are the "enabling conventions" (Goffman 1983) that support an interaction order. As Rawls describes them, such orders are "something like a series of games with rules; but with unspecified and incomplete rules and incomplete information (completed through mutual feedback) and not one but many games which can change rapidly." Some of these rules, such as implicit understandings of typical conversation sequences and the meaning attributed to pauses, may be trans-situational. Complying with them may represent a pragmatic accommodation rather than an endorsement. The approach holds that everything about a social fact – including "identities" of participants and understandings of transactions between them – is negotiable, created and sustained by mutual consent and collaboration, and thus in principle changeable. Tacit mutual agreements among participants to accept others' self-presentations offer some short-term stability.

Interpersonal social network configurations and issue opinion distributions are the primary contextual factors of interest to DellaPosta and Macy. They ask about a group's capacity to generate collective decisions, contrasting consensus, polarized, and pluralist models. Pluralist settings – where preferences on different issues are weakly aligned with one another and cross-cutting social networks link people holding differing viewpoints – offer good prospects for negotiation and compromise. There, social influence processes may bring disparate views closer together, and interested parties can bargain with one another by giving ground in one area in order to realize preferences in others. DellaPosta and Macy argue, however, that order within a pluralist regime is fragile for two reasons. First, cross-issue preference consistency may rise as actors align their views across multiple domains with those of their strong ties. Second, homophily biases in forming new relationships and dissolving old ones reduce the number of cross-cutting ties. Absent other countervailing factors, such network evolution dynamics yield polarized, homogeneous opinion clusters with little basis for locating common ground.

For others, the pertinent interpersonal setting involves the density of beliefs among others in the group. Zelditch contends that group-interested behavior is contingent not only on an individual's own assessment of the group's legitimacy (termed propriety) but also on its perceived legitimacy among others (validity); either overt approval by others or the absence of dissent may signal validity. Validity rises to the extent that ordinary members endorse the authority of agents, or that agents authorize one another, and offers contributors assurance against exploitation. Similarly, for Lindenberg, the relative salience of hedonic, gain, and normative goals can be shaped by the emphasis placed on each of them by others in a setting. Kemper highlights the importance of reference groups whose interests bear on an interaction; these groups may or may not be in direct contact with participants in a situation. Depending on the content of their beliefs, reference group influence can either support or undermine an existing social order.

Cook defines trust relationally as a condition in which one party believes that his or her interests are encapsulated in another's interest, and that the other will act to advance his/her well-being; it can promote cooperation, effort, commitment and citizenship behaviors, while limiting conflict. Her discussion asserts that some knowledge is prerequisite to a judgment that another is trustworthy, identifying several features of interpersonal environments that heighten trust. Among these are direct observation, a history of repeated exchange, or third-party information about reputation. A contextual factor, generalized trust – the density of beliefs regarding trustworthiness of people in general – also can shape judgments about relational trust.

Together, the authors describe a range of micro mechanisms that operate at levels ranging from the encounter to the person-to-group tie. While some are clearly related (e.g., the affect-commitment connections in Lawler et al. and in Turner), most appear complementary, and few if any are clearly incompatible.[5] It would seem, then, that they can operate simultaneously, sometimes bearing on different facets of order. Importantly, most operate implicitly, often in the shadow of more explicit structural coordination devices. Several are "control" mechanisms that prompt corrective actions to adjust behavior toward consistency with a desired identity or other condition. These, like social commitments that extend beyond the immediate instrumental utility of a relationship or group, serve to promote stability in social relations. This in turn is one source of the inertia that simultaneously makes social organization predictable and reliable, and renders it resistant to (rapid) change (Hannan and Freeman, 1984).

---

[5] A possible exception may be Rawls's interaction order approach, under which concepts fundamental to other models – such as identities and roles – are ever open to negotiation.

SOURCES OF FRAGILITY

The word "order" appears frequently in these pages, over seven hundred times by my count.[6] That it does should not be misunderstood as a preference for any particular level of order, or as an endorsement of any given empirical social order, the status quo in particular (Hechter and Horne 2009: p. xii). Disorder is the back side of order, always a prospect. And while at least some of these ordering processes exhibit resilience, these essays also point to ways in which social order can be partial or tenuous.

Disorder can take various forms, something noted most clearly by Kemper. One is a state of mutual hostility and conflict, the Hobbesian "war of all against all." Another, perhaps more common, form involves a lack of articulation among participants in a group or situation, and a consequent incapacity to communicate and coordinate. A mild form of this arises in awkward encounters or meetings that do not "work," essentially for lack of a common understanding of a script or other protocol for interacting.

The challenges of maintaining an existing order, even a small-scale one, should not be understated. Wohl and Fine illustrate this most vividly, noting the dexterity and careful attention involved in dyadic cooperation, and the caution with which gambits toward transformation or improvisation are ventured. The same precarity is evident in Rawls's account of the ubiquitous processes of negotiation and reciprocity that underlie an outwardly stable interaction order.

In complex settings involving multiple potential bases of commitment, excessive order at one level can constitute a form of disorder at another, as strong subgroup solidarities compromise a more inclusive group's capacity to act. DellaPosta and Macy's polarization scenario exemplifies this; an order resting on pluralism can be undermined, endogenously, via network evolution dynamics. For Lindenberg, nearly exclusive salience of a normative mind-set can create a strong solidarity bordering on tribalism that problematizes intergroup relations. Such processes manifest themselves, for instance, as centrifugal forces that create strong subunit identifications in decentralized organizational settings (Ahrne 1994). Social commitments to the wider collectivity generated via Lawler et al.'s theory could be a counterweight, but as both Lawler et al. and Turner indicate, developing these must contend with a proximal bias toward local units.

Corresponding to each order-generating process are risks of deterioration, incomplete realization, or failure. A participant may not fully embrace a role identity, thereby limiting the degree to which lack of verification or affective deflection motivates corrective actions toward conforming with it. Incumbents of roles and their counter-roles may hold partially incompatible expectations of one another, prompting either an uneasy interaction or some localized identity

---

[6] In final drafts, the range is from 12 (in Turner) to 138 (Kemper). Counts include any occurrence (e.g., "disorder") of the string "order."

adjustment. Resources available to role incumbents may not be sufficient to support high-fidelity enactment of a role or achieve dignity. Participants may fail to recognize status-worthy qualities and performances on each other's part, or use power assets in ways that compromise legitimacy and trust – perhaps promoting reluctant cooperation, a work-to-the-rule orientation. External reference groups may advocate alternative conceptions of order.

As noted, many order-producing processes outlined here rest on their capacity to produce emotional rewards. Numerous conditions – such as inequality, lack of legitimacy, blocked opportunities, and distributive injustice – can generate negative emotions, however, which in turn can prompt noncompliance, minimal compliance, or withdrawal. Such emotions can have an especially pernicious effect on social order.

In dual-process frameworks, the ever-present prospect of shifting from an order-oriented mind-set to a selfish one presents an additional risk of fragility. Lindenberg stresses the importance of education as a support for at least modest salience of his normative goal; one might conjecture that attention to the content as well as the amount of education is warranted. The density of prosocial public opinion is another important support, one that may be subject to performance swings or shocks induced by external events.

SCALING UP

Though the authors stress micro-processes that operate in small group settings, many aspire to contribute to understanding social order at a larger scale. The Lawler et al. social commitments theory is expressly intended to account for how person-to-person exchanges can develop into person-to-group attachments. Ridgeway contends that the pervasiveness and subtlety of the gender frame in small group interactions allows it to infuse into broader institutional settings – for example, as organizations design jobs and envision ideal incumbents for them. This in turn supports the persistence of structured gender inequality at a societal level.

Cook's discussion of trust engages the question of scaling at greatest length. She asserts that trust is not, in and of itself, sufficient as a basis for order in meso- or macro-social settings. These latter require other devices that provide incentives for cooperation or guarantees against loss. Among them are a range of alternative modes including informal contracting and sanctioning practices embedded in networks or communities, theoretically self-regulating institutional formations such as markets, and regimes of both private (organizational) and public (governmental) power/authority (see also Hechter and Horne 2009).

It is difficult to contest Cook's position that trust alone cannot sustain order in large-scale settings. It is worth underlining, though, her further claims that trust can enhance cooperation within systems organized via other devices, via promoting effort and citizenship behaviors that heighten both solidarity and performance. Formal coordination devices are not the least blunt tools, and resorting to formal controls has mixed long-term consequences for order. An atmosphere of trust can offer psychological safety (Edmondson 1999) that supports risk-taking and avoids formal social sanctioning. Indeed, Cook remarks on a paradox of sanctioning (produced, perhaps, via negative emotions associated with power use) in which reliance on formal controls reduces trust.

One can wonder whether Cook's argument about scaling might not apply to any of the micro-level mechanisms set out here. Most of them, in fact, presume and operate within some more or less institutionalized setting; few if any serve as a sufficient condition for order. Most also, however, can enhance order in combination with other mechanisms.

CONCLUDING THOUGHTS

These theoretical essays collectively highlight insights from contemporary sociological social psychology into understanding important group processes. In closing, I speculate briefly on what they have to say to organizational practitioners who seek to strengthen – or to alter – social orders.

Perhaps most obvious is the importance of emotional processes in sustaining or disrupting social organization. The long-standing emphasis on "human relations" (e.g., McGregor, 1960) in management recognizes this, of course, and I doubt that the essays here will lead to the next management fad. They do offer appreciable intellectual insight, however, into how affective processes shape group resiliency and performance. By prompting and supporting salient role identities, recognizing achievement when warranted, minimizing power use, and leaving room for self-direction and autonomy, formal and informal leaders can allow participants to realize emotional rewards that build commitment and solidarity. Some of this surely involves symbolic management, ceremonies, and the like. It also entails creation of suitable conditions – to include necessary resources – for successful performances (Hackman 2002), thereby allowing participants to enact valued identities and achieve a dignified condition.

Other sensible steps to consider would sustain legitimacy and trust, for example, by promoting the alignment of structural forms and goals, and maintaining the commensurability of contributions and compensation. In the multi-unit and multi-layered settings of much contemporary social organization, the comparative salience of local and proximal units may be of concern. Promoting more cosmopolitan outlooks by highlighting the resources and rewards offered by more encompassing units may help to counter the typical proximal biases toward the locality.

The social orders we have may not be the ones we want, and both internal reformers and external reference groups seek to introduce change. One thing for them to take away from this book is an appreciation for the difficulty of the enterprise. Automatic, habitual, and implicit processes confer a default status on existing patterns of social organization, whether deliberately designed or not. "Surfacing" these by making them explicit, thereby prompting more conscious, deliberate processing, can probably help. To be effective, though, such attention likely must be sustained rather than episodic.

External shifts in material conditions may also support change in social orders, perhaps with lags due to the inertia-inducing processes described here. Heise et al., for example, point to new activities or innovative technologies for accomplishing existing activities that can create new roles, or new meanings for existing roles; for Kemper, these are resources and opportunities that may rejigger status and power relations. Ridgeway observes that changing patterns of participation in collaborative activities by women and men will eventually – if slowly – undermine the associations between gender and competence on which the gender frame rests, thereby dampening its influence in interaction settings. And notwithstanding the forces that reinforce their stability, change agents may also take heart in the many fragilities of micro-social orders, and be alert to openings for intervention.

REFERENCES

Ahrne, Göran. 1994. *Social Organizations: Interaction Inside, Outside, and Between Organizations.* London: Sage Publications.

Borgatti, Stephen P. 2002. *NetDraw: Graph Visualization Software.* Harvard, MA: Analytic Technologies.

Collins, Randall. 1981. "On the Microfoundations of Macrosociology." *American Journal of Sociology* 86(5): 984–1014.

Edmondson, Amy. 1999. "Psychological Safety and Learning Behavior in Work Teams." *Administrative Science Quarterly* 44(2): 350–83.

Fine, Gary Alan. 1979. "Groups and Culture Creation: The Idioculture of Little League Baseball Teams." *American Sociological Review* 44(5): 733–45.

Goffman, Erving. 1983. "The Interaction Order." *American Sociological Review* 48(1): 1–17.

Greene, Joshua. 2013. *Moral Tribes: Emotion, Reason and the Gap between Us and Them.* New York: The Penguin Press.

Hackman, J. Richard. 2002. *Leading Teams: Setting the Stage for Great Performances.* Boston, MA: Harvard Business School Press.

Hannan, Michael T., and John Freeman. 1984. "Structural Inertia and Organizational Change." *American Sociological Review* 49(2): 149–64.

Hechter, Michael, and Christine Horne. 2009. *Theories of Social Order: A Reader.* 2nd ed. Stanford, CA: Stanford University Press.

Homans, George Caspar. 1950. *The Human Group.* New York: Harcourt Brace.

Kahneman, Daniel. 2011. *Thinking, Fast and Slow.* New York: Farrar, Strauss and Giroux.

Kaplan, Howard. 2000. "Social Psychology." Pp. 2766–80 in *Encyclopedia of Sociology,* 2nd ed., edited by Edgar F. Borgatta and Rhonda J. V. Montgomery. New York: Macmillan Reference USA.

March, James G., and Herbert A. Simon. 1958. *Organizations.* New York: Wiley.

McGregor, Douglas. 1960. *The Human Side of Enterprise*. New York: McGraw-Hill.

Mintzberg, Henry. 1992. *Structure in Fives: Designing Effective Organizations.* Englewood Cliffs, NJ: Prentice Hall.

Watts, Duncan J. 2003. *Small Worlds: The Dynamics of Networks between Order and Randomness*. Princeton, NJ: Princeton University Press.

Weick, Karl E. 1976. "Educational Organizations as Loosely Coupled Systems." *Administrative Science Quarterly* 21(1): 1–19.

Index

Abelson, R. P., 94–95
Affect control theory
  activity dimension, affective
    meanings, 181–83
  affective meanings, 166–67, 169, 173,
    181–83, 182n15, 185–86
  affect mechanism, 111–14, 113n3
  cognitive coherence, 171
  component clustering, 176
  correspondence of outcomes, 181–82
  cultural sentiments, meaning, 165–66
  decision-making, 182
  deflection, 172–73, 183
  embodied processes, 166f9.1, 167, 168
  emotions, 107, 112, 114, 115n5, 116–17,
    117n9, 118, 121
  evaluation dimension, affective
    meanings, 181–83
  Event Structure Analysis (ESA), 172, 172n8,
    173, 185
  group identity, 116n8, 118–20
  identities, 166f9.1, 167, 169–70
  institutional identity, 9, 166f9.1, 167–68,
    170, 173–74, 180–81, 185–86
  institutional knowledge, 171
  institutional roles, 170
  institutional structures, 106, 109–10, 118
  instrumental ties, 106–7, 107n2, 113n3
  integrated action systems, 166f9.1, 167–68
  interaction ritual chains, 111
  interdependence relations, 166f9.1, 181–83
  interpersonal activities, 166f9.1, 167–68,
    169, 170
  I-you dialogues, 166f9.1, 167–68, 167n1

material reward structures, 166–67
mental representations, 166–67, 174–76,
  175n10, 175n11, 175n12
objectified meanings, 166f9.1, 167, 168
organized actions, 166f9.1, 167–68, 169
potency dimension, affective
  meanings, 181–83
power relationships, 172n8, 182
practical knowledge, 165–66, 171, 171n6,
  172n7
potency dimension, affective
  meanings, 181–83
roles, 166f9.1, 168, 169–70, 170n2, 170n3,
  170n4, 173, 185–86
self-concept, 166f9.1, 167, 167n1, 169–70
selves, 166f9.1, 168
semantic systems, 166f9.1, 167
sentiments, 166f9.1, 181–83
transient feelings, 172–73
Agency, 294
Anderson, B., 13, 315
Armstrong, E., 257
Arunta aborigines, 27
Asylums (Goffman), 237
Autonomy
  dignity, 269–70, 276, 276n6, 277, 280
  power and status theory, 213–14
Axelrod, R., 94–95, 96

Bacharach, M., 131
Baddeley, R. J., 182
Balance theory, 185–86
Baldassarri, D., 92–93, 99, 100
Barbalet, J., 219–20